China's Carbon-Energy Policy and Asia's Energy Transition

This book seeks to examine the impacts associated with China's carbon-energy policy in Asia and how, coupled with the Belt and Road Initiative, these effects prompt foreign direct investments in coal power and exports of renewable energy technologies.

China shows a co-evolution of carbon-energy policy and energy transitions from coal to renewables. Assessing how the policy intensifies pressures and motivations to Chinese companies, chapters in this edited volume analyse how the policy has changed energy and CO_2 emissions in Asia through the lens of carbon leakage, relocation, and halos. Contributors present in-depth studies on China's investments and exports, and also its impacts on Indonesia, India, Vietnam, and Japan. Using applied computable general equilibrium and scenario input-output analyses, chapters investigate if regional electricity connectivity reduces new coal power investments through efficiency gain. Arguing that China is shifting from the world's factory to the leading innovator and Asia's demand centre, it is ultimately demonstrated that China is likely to achieve climate targets whereas Asia to increase CO_2 emissions and economic reliance on China.

China's Carbon-Energy Policy and Asia's Energy Transition will be of significant interest to students and scholars of energy, environment, and sustainability studies, as well as Chinese studies and economics.

Akihisa Mori is an Associate Professor at Kyoto University and a vice president of the Asian Association of Environmental and Resource Economics. His research focus is on sustainability transitions and China's Belt and Road Initiative. His other publications with Routledge include *China's Climate-Energy Policy: Domestic and International Impacts*.

Routledge Contemporary China Series

Homeownership in Hong Kong
House Buying as Hope Mechanism
Chung-kin Tsang

Local Clan Communities in Rural China
Revolution and Urbanisation since the Late Qing Dynasty
Zongli Tang

China's Energy Security and Relations With Petrostates
Oil as an Idea
Anna Kuteleva

Ethnic Identity of the Kam People in Contemporary China
Government versus Local Perspectives
Wei Wang and Lisong Jiang

China's Globalization from Below
Chinese Entrepreneurial Migrants and the Belt and Road Initiative
Theodor Tudoroiu

Civil Society in China
How Society Speaks to the State
Runya Qiaoan

China's Foreign Policy since 1949
Kevin G Cai

China's Carbon-Energy Policy and Asia's Energy Transition
Carbon Leakage, Relocation and Halos
Edited by Akihisa Mori

For more information about this series, please visit: https://www.routledge.com/Routledge-Contemporary-China-Series/book-series/SE0768

China's Carbon-Energy Policy and Asia's Energy Transition

Carbon Leakage, Relocation and Halos

Edited by
Akihisa Mori

Routledge
Taylor & Francis Group
LONDON AND NEW YORK

First published 2022
by Routledge
2 Park Square, Milton Park, Abingdon, Oxon OX14 4RN

and by Routledge
605 Third Avenue, New York, NY 10158

Routledge is an imprint of the Taylor & Francis Group, an informa business

British Library Cataloguing-in-Publication Data
A catalogue record for this book is available from the British Library

Library of Congress Cataloging-in-Publication Data
Names: Mori, Akihisa, 1970- editor.
Title: China's carbon-energy policy and Asia's energy transition : carbon leakage, relocation and halos / edited by Akihisa Mori.
Subjects: LCSH: Energy policy—China. | Carbon dioxide mitigation—China. | Emissions trading—China. | Investments, Foreign—China. | Renewable energy sources—Government policy—China. | China—Foreign economic relations—Asia. | Asia—Foreign economic relations—China.
Classification: LCC HD9502.C6 C4838 2022 | DDC 333.790951—dc23/eng/20211027
LC record available at https://lccn.loc.gov/2021037465

ISBN: 978-1-032-04180-3 (hbk)
ISBN: 978-1-032-04189-6 (pbk)
ISBN: 978-1-003-19090-5 (ebk)

DOI: 10.4324/9781003190905

Typeset in Times New Roman
by codeMantra

Contents

Figures

Tables

Acronyms and abbreviations

ASEAN	Association for South East Asian Nations
ATE	average treatment effect
ATT	average treatment effect for treated
AVR(s)	automatic voltage regulator(s)
BAU	Business as Usual
BRI	Belt and Road Initiative
CCEF	California's Clean Energy Future
CDB	China Development Bank
CDIAC	Carbon Dioxide Information Analysis Center
CEC	China Electricity Council
CES	Constant Elasticity of Substitution
CGE	Computable General Equilibrium
CHEXIM	Export-Import Bank of China
CHN	China
CL	carbon leakage
CM1	Counter Measure 1 scenario (unconditional) in Indonesia
CM2	Counter Measure 2 scenario (conditional) in Indonesia
CO_2	carbon dioxide
COVID	coronavirus disease
EDGAR	Emission Database for Global Atmospheric Research
EFTA	European Free Trade Association
EGs	Environmental Goods
EMI	Energy Market Integration
EPC	Engineering, Procurement, and Construction
ERIA	Economic Research Institute for ASEAN and East Asia
ESDM	Ministry of Energy and Mineral Resources in Indonesia
ESG	Environmental, Social, and Governance
EU	European Union
EU ETS	EU emissions trading system
EV	equivalent variation
FDI	foreign direct investment
FIES	Family Income and Expenditure Survey in the Philippines
FiT	feed-in tariff

FTA	Free Trade Agreement
GDP	Gross Domestic Product
GHG	greenhouse gas
GTAP	Global Trade Analysis Project
GTAP-E	Energy-Environmental Version of the Global Trade Analysis Project
GW	Giga Watt
IDN	Indonesia
IEA	International Energy Agency
IND	India
IPCC	Intergovernmental Panel on Climate Change
IPP(s)	Independent Power Producer(s)
IR-CFPM	Inter-Regional Constrained Fixed Price Multiplier
IRENA	International Renewable Energy Agency
IRSAM	Inter-Regional Social Accounting Matrix
JPEA	Japan Photovoltaic Energy Association
JPN	Japan
KOR	Republic of Korea
LCOE	levelized cost of electricity
LFS	Labour Force Survey in the Philippines
METI	Japanese Ministry of Economy, Trade and Industry
Million t-CO_2	million tonnes carbon dioxide
MRIO	multi-region input output
Mtoe	million tons of oil equivalent
MW	Mega Watt
NAFTA	North American Free Trade Agreement
NBSC	National Bureau of Statistics of China
NDC(s)	Nationally Determined Contribution(s)
NEA	Nuclear Energy Agency
NOx	nitrogen oxides
OECD	Organisation for Economic Co-operation and Development
OFDI	Outward Foreign Direct Investment
OITDA	Optoelectronics Industry and Technology Development Association
PERC	passivated emitter and rear cell
PHH	pollution haven hypothesis
PLN	Perusahaan Listrik Negara (State Electricity Company) in Indonesia
PPA(s)	power purchase agreement(s)
PPP	public-private partnership
PRIMAP	Postdam Real-time Integrated Model for the probabilistic Assessment of emission Paths
PV	photovoltaic
R&D	Research and Development
RCOT	Rectangular Choice of Technology

RE	renewable energy
RES-E	renewable energy-sourced electricity
ROW	rest of the world
RPS	Renewable Portfolio Standard
RUEN	Rencana Umum Energi Nasional (National Energy Plan) in Indonesia
RUKN	Rencana Umum Ketenagalistrikan Nasional (National Electricity General Plan) in Indonesia
RUPTL	Rencana Usaha Penyediaan Tenaga Listrik (Electricity Power Supply Business Plan) in Indonesia
SEHEN	super extra energy saving
SES	socio-economic survey
SHS	solar home system
SO_2	sulfur dioxide
solar PV	solar photovoltaic
SRIO	single-region input output
SUSENAS	*Survei Sosial Ekonomi Nasional* (National Socio-Economic Survey) in Indonesia
UNFCCC	United Nations Framework Convention on Climate Change
USA	United States of America
VHLSS	Vietnam Household Living Standards Survey
VNM	Vietnam
WEC	World Energy Council
WIOD	World Input-Output Database

Contributors

Hikari Ban is a Professor of Economics at Kobe Gakuin University.

Yi-chun Chen is a Project Researcher of Institute for Future Initiatives at the University of Tokyo.

Yuventus Effendi is a Researcher of Fiscal Policy at the Indonesian Ministry of Finance and a PhD candidate at Australian National University.

Kiyoshi Fujikawa is a Professor Emeritus of International Development at Nagoya University.

Takashi Hattori is a Professor of Economics at Kyoto University and a researcher at Japanese Ministry of Economy, Trade and Industry.

Nobuhiro Horii is an Associate Professor of Economics at Kyushu University.

Nandakumar Janardhanan is a Research Manager at Institute for Global Environmental Strategies (IGES).

Yiyi Ju is a Researcher at Waseda Institute for Advanced Study, Waseda University, Japan.

Akihisa Mori is an Associate Professor of Global Environmental Economics at Kyoto University and an ex-vice president of the Asian Association of Environmental and Resource Economics.

Yasuhiro Ogura is a Research Fellow at Osaka Prefecture University.

Budy P. Resosudarmo is a Professor of Public Policy at Australian National University and the president of the Asian Association of Environmental and Resource Economics.

Maxensius Tri Sambodo is a Senior Researcher at Indonesian Institute of Sciences (LIPI).

Le Tuyet Vo is a PhD candidate at Nagoya University.

Jiayang Wang is a Researcher at the Renewable Energy Institute.

Preface

In August 2017, three of us got together one very hot afternoon in Osaka to discuss the future of China's climate-energy policy. At that time, it became apparent that China shifted the gear from massive resource imports for economic growth toward high-tech, clean, and green industrial development. With this recognition, we framed China's climate-energy policy as an underlying cause of resource boom and bust for resource-exporting countries and analysed the impacts of China's gear shift on these countries in the previous research. Then, the discussion turned toward possible carbon leakage associated with the country's stringent climate policy. Chinese researchers had criticized the current production-based CO_2 emissions accounting for overestimating CO_2 emissions in exporting countries of industrial goods such as China, which exports them for the consumption of final destination such as United States, EU member states, and Japan. However, China's stringent climate-energy policy, coupled with its outward foreign direct investments (FDI) under the Belt and Road Initiative, would turn it into an importer of CO_2 emissions.

Subsequently, our thoughts became more focused on electricity sector. China began outward FDI in coal power projects in the late 2000s, and has increased the number of host countries since then. The country also began exports of components of wind and solar power at the same period, and has expanded exports to an increasing number of countries. Empirical analyses covering all the host countries are ambitious agenda, thus narrowing the scope to Asian countries with special focus on India, Indonesia, Japan, and Vietnam. We invited prominent researchers in these countries as co-investigators, who agreed to contribute chapters that developed one or more of the themes—carbon relocation, carbon halos, and carbon leakage. Since the project launch in July 2018, the team has held workshops and seminars at Kyoto, Nagoya, Fukuoka, Bali, and online after the outbreak of the COVID-19 pandemic.

The book is the outcome of this research project. Each contributor capitalizes on their capabilities to employ a variety of academic disciplines, analytical frameworks, methodologies, and scopes and coverages. This results in both optimistic and pessimistic findings in each chapter, and nuanced implications throughout the book. Nonetheless, we believe critical thinking, more rigorous analysis with stronger evidence, and mutual learning must have enhanced social value of our work, and we hope you enjoy sharing it.

Akihisa Mori
Kyoto, June 2021

Acknowledgements

The editor would like to thank the Japan Society for the Promotion of Science (JSPS) for funding the research project (grant number 20KK0034). The editor also would like to thank Mamiko Sunago for managing the research project, and Eri Miyazawa and Nur Firdous for their help in the editing work. We have had a very constructive relationship with Emily Pickthall, Stephanie Rogers, and other colleagues at Routledge, and their support in publishing a high-quality book is highly appreciated. Finally, the editor and authors would like to thank Kyoto University for funding the open access conversion.

Part I

Energy transition and carbon leakage, relocation, and halos

Concepts and framework

1 Carbon leakage, relocation, and halo

A framework to understand impacts of China's carbon-energy policy on Asia's energy transitions

Akihisa Mori

1 The Paris Agreement and Asia

In 2015, 195 countries and the European Union (EU) signed the Paris Agreement under the United Nations Framework for Climate Change Convention (UNFCC). The agreement aims to strengthen the global response to the threat of climate change by limiting the global temperature rise in this century to below 2°C, above pre-industrial levels, and endeavoring to limit the temperature increase even further to 1.5°C (UNFCCC, 2015). This goal requires all Parties to submit nationally determined contributions (NDCs), report their emission and efforts regularly, and update them every five years.

In response, 186 countries submitted their first NDCs by September 2020 (UNFCCC, 2020), but only some submitted their updates. Except for Brunei and the Philippines, all the countries in Northeast, Southeast, and South Asia submitted their NDCs (Table 1.1). Although full implementation of unconditional NDCs is estimated to result in a 15 gigaton gap in CO_2 emissions ($GtCO_2e$) by 2030 compared with the 2°C scenario, and a global mean temperature rise of 3.2°C by 2100 (UNEP, 2019), the step is an advancement toward reducing greenhouse gas (GHG) emissions.

In its NDC, China committed to achieving peak carbon dioxide (CO_2) in approximately 2030 and to an endeavor to peak early and reduce CO_2 per unit of GDP or carbon intensity by 60%–65% from the 2005 level. To achieve the targets, the government committed to an increase of approximately 20% in the share of non-fossil fuels in primary energy consumption, and an increase of approximately 4.5 billion cubic meters in the forest stock volume compared with the 2005 level (NDRC, 2015). However, these commitments can raise the long-standing concerns of energy security and the cost of climate change measures decreasing economic growth.

To prevent climate policy from restricting economic growth, the government reframed climate change prevention as part of development (NDRC, 2007) and clean energies as new growth points (Chen, 2013). It fostered renewable and nuclear power industries and energy efficiency as a means of

DOI: 10.4324/9781003190905-2

Table 1.1 Nationally determined contributions (NDCs) in selected Asian countries

	Unconditional contribution target	*Conditional contribution target (international support)*	*Year of achievement*	*Metrics*	*Base year*	*Year of submission*
Northeast Asia						
China	60%–65%	-	2030	Intensity	2005	2016
Japan	25%	-	2030	Absolute	2005	2016/2020
South Korea	37%	-	2030	BAU scenario	2020	2016
Taiwan		-	2030	BAU scenario		-
Mongolia	14%	-	2030	BAU scenario	2030	2016
Southeast Asia						
Cambodia	27%		2030	BAU scenario		2017
Indonesia	29%	41%	2030	BAU scenario	2010	2016
Malaysia	35%	45%	2030	Intensity	2005	2016
Singapore	36%	-	2030	Intensity	2005	2016/2020
Thailand	20%	25%	2030	BAU scenario	2005	2016
Vietnam	9%	27%	2030	BAU scenario	2014	2016/2020
South Asia						
Bangladesh	5%	15%	2030	BAU scenario		2016
India	33%–35%		2030	Intensity	2005	2016
Pakistan	-	20%	2030	BAU scenario		2016
Sri Lanka	3%	7%	2030	BAU scenario	2010	2016

Note: As of September 2020.
Source: The author's compilation based on UNFCCC (2020) and Industrial Energy Saving and Carbon Reduction Information Web, Taiwan (n.a).

safeguarding energy security. The government mandated large power generators to supply renewable energy-sourced electrcity (RES=E), and annually increased its ratio to the total power supply. Additionally, it implemented various preferential measures to foster renewable-energy manufacturers (de la Tour et al., 2011; Horii, 2014) and expanded the scope of the feed-in tariff (FiT) to solar photovoltaic (PV) to rescue their manufacturers from the adverse impacts of the anti-dumping measures by the EU and the United States. The government also initiated local carbon emission trading pilots in four provinces and five cities to advance the nationwide emission trading scheme, and low-carbon development pilots in 42 provinces and cities. After the government implemented these measures, in the 13th Five-Year Plan for Energy (2016–2020), it set mandatory targets, for example, to reduce carbon intensity by 18% of the 2015 level and increase the installation capacity of wind and solar power by 210–250 and 110–150 GW, respectively.

The sudden increase in wind and solar power in the domestic market intensified the contestation with incumbent coal power generators, resulting in substantial wind and solar curtailment in the first half of the 2010s (Mori, 2018). In addition, rising health concerns over China's worsening air pollution, represented by Chai Jing's 104-minute documentary *Under the Dome* (2015), provided opportunities to transform consumer behavior and government policy (Koehn, 2016). The government responded to the pressures to implement administrative order and regulations on coal power and heating plants, including consolidation of small and obsolete plants, mandates to employ technologies that are more efficient, and installation of fuel-gas desulfurization. It also prompted State Grid to invest in long-distance ultra-voltage transmission lines to mitigate the renewable curtailment and increased consumption of wind and solar power.

These stringent regulations on coal power and complementary measures to increase RES-E have increased the installed capacity of wind and solar PV and their power generation (Figures 1.1a and 1.1b) and decreased the potential new coal power opportunities within China.

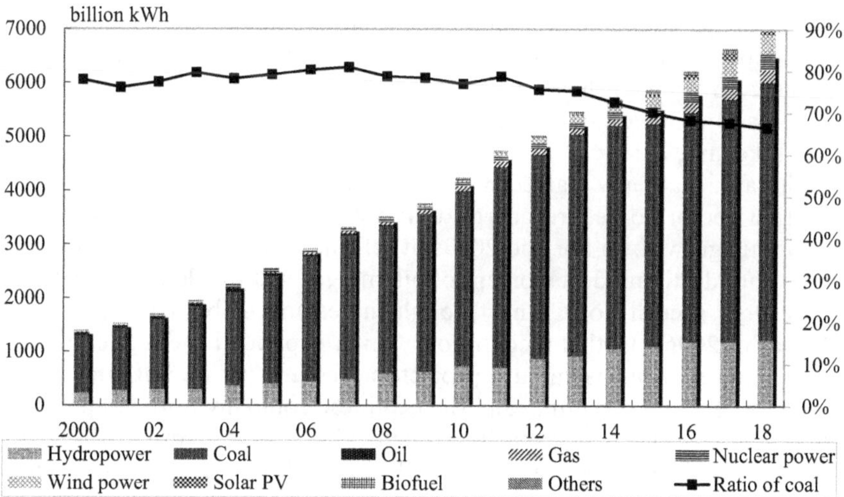

Figure 1.1a Energy mix in power generation in China in 2000–2018.
Source: The author's compilation based on IEA (2020).

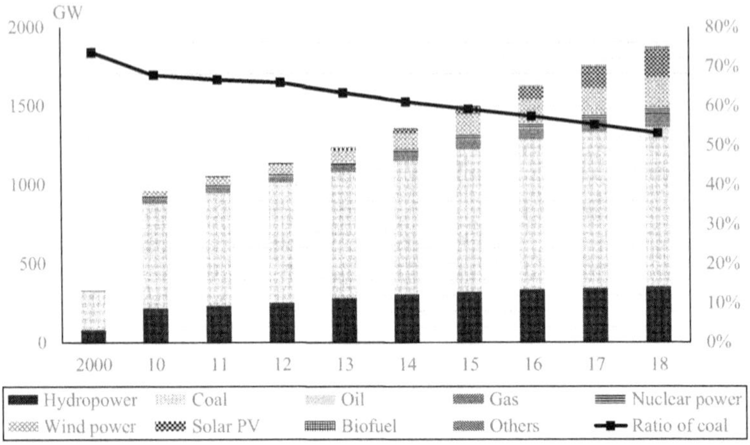

Figure 1.1b Energy mix in installed power generation capacity in China in 2000–2018.

Note: Data for the years 2001–2009 is available only for thermal power as a whole.

Source: The author's compilation based on *China Electricity Power Statistical Yearbook*, each year.

2 Implications to China–Asia energy relation

The decreased opportunity for new coal power projects and fierce competition over RES-E have motivated the Chinese power industry—including existing power companies, emerging RES-E producers, manufacturers, and developers (engineering and construction companies)—to seek business opportunities in foreign countries.[1] On this temporal occasion, the Chinese government has accelerated its "going global" strategy and Belt and Road Initiative (BRI), which direct them toward foreign projects (Mori and Takehara, 2018).

China had already started overseas official finance in the resource extraction sector to secure energy that was indispensable for sustaining economic growth. In the mid-2000s, it reframed energy security to recognize that additional development of oil and gas worldwide would enhance the energy security of China through increasing global energy security (Hayashi, 2006). In this recognition, China expanded the scope of overseas finance to infrastructure projects necessary for mining and transporting resources to China, and then Chinese company-initiated projects, including new installed capacity (greenfield investment) in the electricity sector (Hervé-Mignucci and Wang, 2015). To reduce country and commercial risks, the country employed the resource-financed infrastructure in which host country governments pledge their interest in some or all of the revenue flows it will receive from the resource production project to a lender (Beardsworth and Schmidt, 2014). In addition, the Chinese government set up bilateral and regional development funds to finance investments in connectivity infrastructure as a part of the BRI. These funds amounted to US$164.4 billion, of which the Silk Road Fund accounted for the largest contributors (Gallagher et al., 2018). Fossil fuel investments accounted for 91% of energy-sector syndicated loans by the six major Chinese banks and 61% of energy-sector loans financed entirely by state-backed China Development Bank or Export-Import Bank of China between 2014 and 2017 (Lechner et al., 2020).

Finance and investments can satisfy increasing electricity demand in developing countries, helping them increase access to affordable, reliable modern energy, overcome power shortages, and sustain economic growth at a lower cost. In particular, developing countries with power shortages that could easily access cheap coal accepted China's finance and investments in the 2000s. Indonesia's ratio of coal power increased from 24% in 1995 to 36% in 2000, and to 56% in 2015. Vietnam's ratio also increased from 12% in 2000 to 30% in 2015, despite a temporal decline in 2006–2009 due to the completion of large-scale hydropower (Figure 1.2). This finance and investments go beyond coal-rich countries to arrive at coal-poor small countries, such as Cambodia, Laos, and Uzbekistan, after the global financial crisis in 2008–2009; the crisis sharply reduced the appetite of commercial banks for

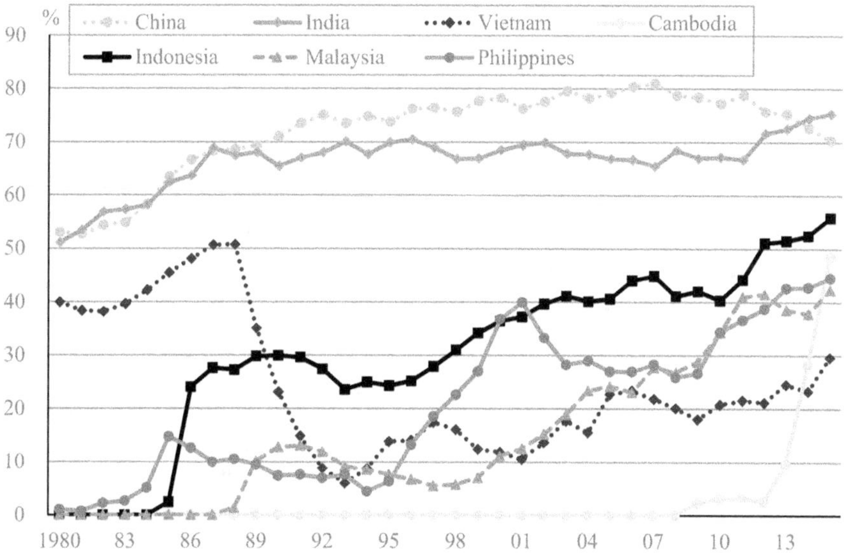

Figure 1.2 Ratio of coal power in power generation in selective Asian countries in 1980–2015.

Source: The author's compilation based on World Bank (2020).

long-term financing, and Chinese financing institutions became a valuable source for power projects (Vagliasindi, 2013). As a result, these countries have sharply increased coal and lignite imports (Figure 1.3), deteriorating the trade balance.

Foreign finance and investments result in the suspicion that they might generate cross-border carbon relocation or relocation of CO_2 emissions to countries with lax commitments in GHG emissions reduction in their NDCs, in addition to ecological and social concerns that have triggered local protests and the suspension or abandonment of coal power projects (Vidal, 2016; Boulle, 2019), as well as hydropower (Fawthrop, 2019). The increase in coal power can intensify a tradeoff with NDCs in host countries, especially those who entrench dependency on China and the institutional lock-in for coal-centered energy systems. It makes these countries incapable of moving the system toward a more sustainable pathway (Mori, 2020).

In response, Ma et al. (2019) argue that decarbonizing the Belt and Road is a means to mitigate adverse environmental impacts of finance and investments. Such de-carbonization requires a mandatory environmental assessment of Chinese investments, applying the green investment principle, transparency regarding the carbon footprint of infrastructure investments for the international society, and building capabilities for green finance in host countries.

Whether such a mitigation measure is sufficient to prevent carbon haven and generate halo effects remain unknown. This investigation became a critical focal point of the argument when President Xi Jinping, at the United

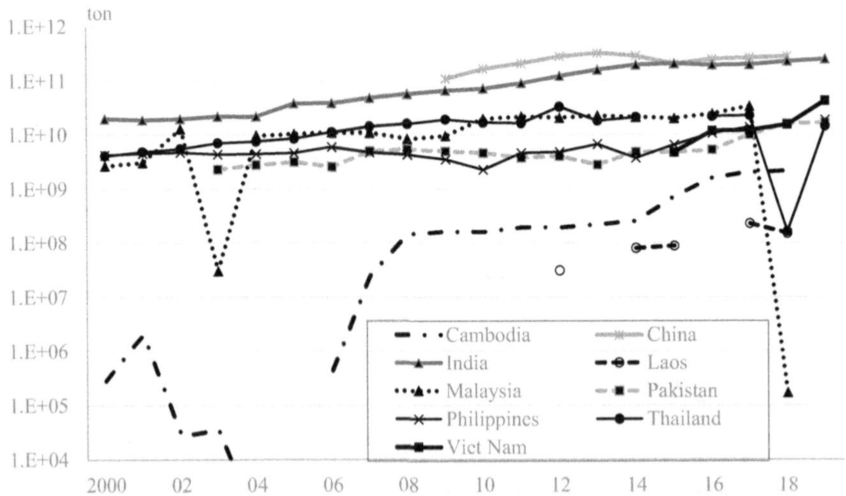

Figure 1.3 Net coal and lignite imports in the selected Asian countries in 2000–2018.
Source: The author's compilation based on United Nations Statistics Division (n.a).

Nations assembly in 2020, pledged carbon neutrality before 2060, without providing details. This ambitious target would result in substantial carbon relocation and creation of carbon havens without a deeper understanding of push and pull factors; mechanisms of and institutions for carbon leakage, relocation, and halos; and evidence-based countermeasures in China and host countries.

3 Pollution haven and halos

Increasing the foreign direct investment (FDI) flows accompanied by globalization has raised concerns about their side effects, including those on the environment. On the one hand, a country with lax environmental policies tends to specialize in more pollution- or resource-intensive sectors, becoming a pollution haven of "dirty" industries. To attract foreign investment, developing countries compete to relax or not strictly enforce environmental regulations, resulting in a "race to the bottom" phenomenon in environmental protection called the pollution haven hypothesis. When there are strict environmental regulations, footloose investors of pollution-intensive industries relocate their plants to regions or countries with lax environmental regulation to decrease the costs of protecting the environment, called the industrial flight hypothesis.

On the other hand, the economic structural transformation from manufacturing to services and stringent environmental regulations in investing countries could lead to the relocation of manufacturing industries (Araya, 2005). Alternatively, this transformation provides opportunities for other countries to increase the international competitive edge of their manufacturing sectors. This industrial relocation and the change in comparative advantage might cause negative consequences for the environment.

Theoretically, whether environmental regulations propel pollution-intensive industries to relocate depends on pollutant generation intensity, pollution abatement cost, and relocation cost. Corruption in host countries loosens enforcement of environmental regulations, thus inviting relocation (Candau and Dienesch, 2017). The total amount and intensity of pollutant emissions increase after relocation, and the extent of the increase is positively correlated with the regulation in the home country and negatively correlated with that in the host country (Li and Wang, 2020). This implies that industrial relocation reduces pollution in the home country while increasing it in the host countries.

Empirical studies have supported the pollution haven hypothesis partially at best. Many researchers have pointed out the international relocation of production to countries with weaker environmental regulations in specific periods and regions (Mani and Wheeler, 1998; Zarsky, 1999; Brunnermeier and Levinson, 2004, Ogura and Mori, 2015), and in industries such as resource extraction (Boocock, 2002; Dam and Scholtens, 2012). However, the evidence is weak. Higher pollution abatement costs induced by stringent environmental regulations have not substantially affected international trade and FDI flow compared with other factors such as income, trade openness, and the manufacturing share of host countries (Copeland and Taylor, 2003; Cole, 2004). "Dirty" industries do not always invest in dirty technologies and practices (Auer, 2000).

Instead, many empirical studies have found that FDI significantly reduces environmental emissions (Demena and Afesorgbor, 2020). Foreign investors provide more energy-efficient technologies and better management practices, and use cleaner types of energy (Eskeland and Harriso, 2003). Some researchers have further supported pollution halo effects or pollution reduction by demonstrating positive externalities of cleaner technologies and practices (Zarsky, 1999) in countries with higher emissions (Zhu et al., 2016) and in countries with strong governance and quality institutions (Wang and Chen, 2014; Bokpin, 2017; Liu et al., 2017).

However, the halo effect does not always reduce emissions in a host country as a whole. FDI inflow tends to be a tiny portion of domestic capital stock. As long as domestic capital stock is pollution intensive, its net increases lead to increases in production activities and emissions that outweigh the halo effects (Sung et al., 2018). Thus, each nation or firm is reluctant to take unilateral action that undermines competitiveness. The "regulatory chill," or no change in the emission standard, became a rule rather than the exception (Zarsky, 2002).

4 Carbon leakage and carbon relocation

Unilateral climate policy, represented by carbon pricing, re-sparks the pollution haven debate in the name of carbon leakage (CL). In particular, the European Union Emissions Trading System (EU ETS) has been criticized for threatening the competitiveness of European industry and generating CL or increasing GHG emissions in foreign countries. Two options have been argued to address CL: border carbon adjustments and output-based allocation, and auctioning with border adjustment, which is more efficient, at least theoretically (Monjon and Quirion, 2011). However, the European Commission implemented the grandfathering of CO_2 allowances in proportion to historical GHG emissions in phases 1 and 2. This drew criticism for rewarding higher emitters, not considering firms' early actions, and exempting high trade exposure industries instead of high carbon-intensive industries from auctions, despite the latter's stronger correlation with CL (Martin et al., 2014). In response, the commission employs product-related GHG emission benchmarks in phase 3 and initiates a carbon border adjustment mechanism, that is, putting a carbon price on imports of certain goods from outside the European Union in the EU Green Deal (European Commission, 2020).

To determine the sectors exposed to a significant climate policy-induced CL or strong CL (Michalek and Schwarze, 2015), and thus be grandfathered, the commission provides a formula to calculate the induced carbon costs (European Union, 2015: 63–65). Ex ante modeling analysis has also been conducted, including the computable general equilibrium (CGE) model to assess strong CL at the country level. They suggest a range of 10%–40% of leakage, depending upon the scenario (e.g., a unilateral 0% CO_2 emission reduction by the European Union or Annex I countries in the Kyoto Protocol), scope (fuel combustion or including process emissions), and the extent of sectoral disaggregation (Bednar-Friedl et al., 2012; Caron, 2012).

Ex post empirical studies have demonstrated that EU ETS has induced only a small amount of investment leakage in phases 1 and 2.[2] Although ETS-regulated German firms on average have increased FDI outside the EU, most of them do not operate in the targeted energy-intensive sectors (Koch and Mana, 2019). Relocation can be averted after phasing out the grandfathering scheme only if the permit price triggers sufficient investments into low-carbon technologies or abatement capital that create a lock-in effect that makes relocation unprofitable (Schmidt and Heitzig, 2014).

This finding implies that firms do not always choose among staying inert with grandfathering, investments in low-carbon technologies for compliance, and complete industrial flight or closure and relocation. They may choose to be multilateral corporations that have industrial plants in many countries or unbundle their closed integral production system to form a global value chain (Ezaki, 2018), to optimize their production in accordance with global demand and local regulations. This implies that foreign investors may selectively relocate carbon-intensive *processes* to countries with weak environmental regulations, producing intermediate products there and importing them for the last stage of production at their home (Zhang et al., 2017). The partial relocation enables home countries to reduce domestic CO_2 emissions through a technological effect and an effect on domestic industrial structure and simultaneously increases embodied emissions through the scale effect (Hao et al., 2020).

Partial relocation of carbon-intensive processes can occur in the electricity sector. Sunk investments, high entry barriers, long operating lifetimes, and complementary capital investments justified public ownership, a vertically integrated supply system, and a monopolistic supply of electricity under the price regulation. Foreign companies were allowed to join only as contractors of turnkey projects funded by foreign donors or host country governments. In the 1990s, pressures for cheap electricity, the lack of funding and insufficient investments, inefficient operation and being susceptible to corruption and bribery due to agency problems, and technological development pushed liberalization of the electricity market, unbundling of the vertically integrated supply system, and privatization of electric utilities or public–private partnership (PPP). This change in the supply regime is expected to mobilize additional sources of funding and financing for infrastructure development, enhance project selection, foster efficiency gains, and ensure service delivery (World Bank, 2017). Under the PPP framework, foreign power companies are allowed to join in power projects as independent power producers, and foreign project developers as engineering, procurement, and construction (EPC) contractors. Power companies can invest in switching to gas and RES-E at home, and simultaneously in coal power in foreign countries with weaker regulations when stringent environmental and climate regulations are encountered at home. The selective relocation can be accelerated when cross-border transmission lines are connected between the investing and host countries, and the regulation gap remains intact.

China can not be exempted from the CL risk because it already implemented local carbon emissions trading pilots and a nationwide scheme for the electricity sector. A study identifies 17 four-digit sectors considered at actual risk of CL (Wang et al., 2017).

The above arguments on relocation as firms' responses to stringent carbon-energy policy suggest a specific conceptualization. In this book, we define carbon relocation as the complete *and* partial relocation or FDI of carbon-intensive industrial plants, industry, *and* production processes. Carbon relocation constitutes a part of carbon leakage, which is defined as an incremental increase in CO_2 emissions in host countries induced by more stringent climate policy in investors' countries and generated by both FDI and international trade.

5 Carbon halos

Empirical studies have demonstrated mixed results on the relationship between FDI inflow and CO_2 emissions. Some find the halo effect in CO_2 emissions, or carbon halo effect in China in 1995–2010 (Zhang and Zhou, 2016), in higher emission countries in the five Association of Southeast Asian Nations (ASEAN) countries of Indonesia, Malaysia, the Philippines, Singapore, and Thailand in 1981–2011 (Zhu et al., 2016), and in the Gulf Cooperation Council countries in 1980–2009 (Al-Mulali and Tang, 2013). Others find opposite results in China in 1980–2012 (Sun et al., 2017); in Malaysia in 1970–2008; in middle-income South and Southeast Asian countries in 1980–2012 (Bahera and Dash, 2017); in 15 developing countries in Asia in 1990–2013 (Hanif et al., 2019); and in BRI countries across South Asia, Southeast Asia, East Asia, and Europe in 1985–2017 (Khan and Bin, 2020).

Because of the similarity in countries and regions and the period of years for analysis, and assuming monotonous increases or inverse-U-shaped relations between per capita income and CO_2 emissions, we summarize this research as follows: FDI has generated the carbon halo effect in a limited number of countries, regions, and periods with stringent energy and CO_2 emission regulations, and less carbon-intensive sectors at best (Zheng et al., 2010; Lee, 2013; Lau et al., 2014).

At a micro level, however, greenfield FDI for renewable-energy projects is one of the promising subsectors to generate the carbon halo effect. Such FDI allows both foreign and local companies to engage in the transfer of capital, technology, and expertise through trade and investment (United Nations ESCAP, 2012). India, China, and Indonesia accounted for more than 60% in the amount of renewable-energy investments in Asia in 2013–2016 (OECD, 2017).

Nonetheless, FDI in the clean energy subsector and exports of clean technology can cause repercussions and backlash in host countries. Grid companies may contest against sharply increased RES-E induced by FDI or imports, resulting in a renewable curtailment. A host country government may impose anti-dumping or restrictive measures to protect domestic manufacturers and power producers if foreign companies are perceived too competitive to push them out of the market. However, anti-dumping or restrictive measures are more likely to trigger a vicious cycle of higher costs, lower demand, and lower deployment of clean technology and energy (Burke et al., 2019). These measures reduce the willingness of the industry to reorient innovation or reorganize to take advantage of FDI and exports to gain a profit (McCarthy, 2016). This eventually retards development of regulations, national capabilities to benefit from the technological spillover effect, and industrial structural change. Worse, these measures may simply motivate foreign manufacturers to intensify their efforts to "tariff jump," offsetting the effectiveness of the measures. This increases uncertainty on whether investment can catch up with future demand for power and climate targets.

Connectivity has the potential to prevent carbon relocation and overcome the repercussions of the FDI-induced increase in RES-E. It enables least-cost dispatch, price stabilization, and improving the economies of scale for new renewable-energy supplies, thus significantly promoting the adoption of renewable energy-sourced electricity (Chang and Li, 2015). It is also expected to reduce CO_2, sulfur dioxide (SO_2), and nitrogen oxides (NOx) emissions, and develop clean energy, power, and high-tech industries that will increase GDP (Global Energy Interconnection Development and Cooperation Organization, 2019).

Connectivity can also provide technical benefits, including the reinforcement of system stability, opportunities for sharing ancillary services, and optimization of the energy mix while reducing system vulnerabilities. These benefits will save newly installed capacity for fossil fuel power, reduce fuel import dependencies, and affect resource constraints accordingly (UNESCAP, 2019).

To generate these benefits, United Nations Economic and Social Commission for Asia and the Pacific (UNESCAP) has supported the ASEAN Power Grid and the Trans-ASEAN Gas Pipeline, the two flagship energy connectivity programs in the ASEAN Economic Community "Blueprint 2025."

6 Aims and scope

Against the backdrop, this book defines carbon relocation as a policy-induced complete *and* partial relocation of carbon-intensive industrial plants and industry *and* production processes that generate an incremental increase in CO_2 emissions in host countries. This book also defines carbon halos as a CO_2 emission reduction induced by FDI-brought cleaner technologies and types of energy and better management practices. In this regard, carbon relocation is defined as a specific form of CL, and carbon halos as CO_2-focused pollution halos.

With these definitions, this book aims to answer three research questions.

a How has China's carbon-energy policy incentivized outward FDI in coal power and RES-E projects and exports of these technologies?
b How have Chinese outward FDI in and exports of RES-E technologies generated energy transitions in Asian countries, and caused carbon leakage, relocation, and halos?
c Can regional connectivity be a countermeasure to minimize carbon relocation and enhance the carbon halo effect in the context of China–Asia energy relations?

To answer these questions, this book employs a mixed method of scenario-based simulation analysis and empirical case studies. For the detailed case studies of host countries, we examine Indonesia, India, and Vietnam. These three countries are rich in easily accessible coal and thus initiated a transition to a coal-centered electricity supply system when they foresaw the depletion of other cheaper sources of energy such as oil and hydropower. They have been the largest recipients of China's overseas FDI in coal power projects in Asia throughout the 2010s, along with Pakistan and Bangladesh, who suddenly emerged in the latter half of the decade (referred to in Chapter 5). In addition, this book analyzes Japan as a case to assess the possible repercussions against the increase in the imports of goods for RES-E from China. Japan was the largest manufacturer of solar PV but lost competitiveness amid the global decline in production cost.

Although this book focuses on Asian countries for empirical case studies, it provides a deeper understanding of the contexts and conditions that generate carbon relocation and halos, and implications that go beyond the context of China–Asia energy relations.

7 Book overview

The structure of this book comprises four parts: introduction; China's energy and industrial transformation as a push factor; carbon, leakage, relocation, and halo effects in host countries; and possible countermeasures and future perspectives.

In Chapter 2, Akihisa Mori develops the complementarities in socio-technical systems as an analytical framework to investigate how Asian countries have struggled with the energy-climate conundrum under the Paris Agreement, taking Vietnam, Indonesia, India, and Japan as cases. The chapter finds that they have struggled with the challenges of resistance of influential incumbent regime actors, reconciling compelling narratives, and highly unclear and uncertain benefits of the transformation, and these challenges incentivize incumbent regime actors to retard the restructuring of the existing complementarities, especially when they are backed by international actors such as Chinese investors.

The second part, China's energy and industrial transformation comprises three chapters. The first of the three, Chapter 3 by Jiayang Wang and Kiyoshi Fujikawa investigates how a switch in energy mix from coal to wind and solar can be a driving force for China's outward FDI in coal power projects. By employing a scenario input–output analysis, they analyze impacts on economic activity, employment, and CO_2 emissions of the shift in energy mix.

In Chapter 4, Nobuhiro Horii investigates how Chinese solar PV manufacturers have enhanced sufficient competitive edge as to dominate the global market. Through a retrospective analysis, this chapter explores how Chinese solar PV manufactures have enhanced technological capabilities to overcome the anti-dumping measures by Europe and the United States, and the phase-out of FiT for solar power in China, resulting in a surge of exports.

In Chapter 5, Akihisa Mori investigates the relations between China's stringent environmental, energy, and climate policy; outward FDI in coal power projects; and carbon relocation.

The third part of the book analyzes how Chinese outward FDI and exports have affected energy transitions, causing carbon relocation and halo effects in the electricity sector in host countries, and generating carbon leakage from China.

Chapters 6 and 7 conduct modeling analyses of the impacts in multiple countries. Chapter 6 by Hikari Ban and Kiyoshi Fujikawa investigates the possible impacts on GDP and CO_2 emissions of China's outward FDI in coal power projects in Indonesia, Vietnam, India, and five Central Asian countries of Kazakhstan, Kyrgyzstan, Tajikistan, Turkmenistan, and Uzbekistan. To make the simulation analysis be more realistic, they employ an energy–environmental version of the Global Trade Analysis Project (GTAP-E) model, a global CGE model, and use actual China's development finance in coal power projects compiled by the China's Global Power Database (Gallagher et al., 2019).

In Chapter 7, Yasuhiro Ogura explores possible carbon halo effects through imports of wind and solar PV technologies. The chapter employs matching econometrics to analyze the correlation between renewable-energy policy and the international trade of these technologies, gaining insights on enabling factors of market deployment of these technologies.

Chapters 8–10 adopt a case study of one country as a methodology to explore the dynamics of Chinese outward investments in power projects, exports of wind and solar PV technologies, and policy responses in Indonesia, India, and Japan.

Chapter 8 by Maxensius Tri Sambodo investigates the role of Chinese investments, finance, and contracts in coal power projects in and their exports of RES-E technologies to Indonesia from the energy security perspective.

Nandakumar Janardhanan in Chapter 9 evaluates the opportunities and obstacles of China's role in energy transition in India. Although India set ambitious renewable-energy targets, it suffers from the lack of an internationally competitive domestic RSE-E manufacturers and thus increases dependency on imports from China. Based on a conceptual framework of bilateral energy cooperation, this chapter explores conditions for Chinese large exports of RES-E technologies to generate carbon halo effect.

In Chapter 10, Takashi Hattori and Yi-chun Chen investigate Japan as a case of a host country. Japanese solar PV manufacturers used to be the world's leading ones but lost competition against Chinese ones, resulting in a massive deployment of Chinese solar PV modules in Japanese market. This chapter explores what has brought about this result, and how the losing competitive edge of Japanese manufacturers affects carbon-energy policies in Japan.

In Chapter 11, Tuyet Le Vo and Yiyi Ju investigate how carbon relocation and halo effects in the electricity sector generated by Chinese outward FDI affect the increasing trend of CL in terms of embodied CO_2 emissions in China. They take Vietnam, Indonesia, India, and Japan as cases and employ single-region and multi-region input–output tables to estimate embodied CO_2 emissions of the whole sector as well as by industrial sectors.

The final part explores countermeasures that host countries can take to mitigate carbon relocation and increase carbon halo effects of Chinese investments and export, and enhance energy security to satisfy growing demand, supply electricity around the country at an affordable price at the same time.

In Chapter 12, Budy P. Resosudarmo and Yuventus Effendi investigate if Asian regional electricity market integration can generate the above positive effects, with special focus on macroeconomic and CO_2 emissions. They employ the inter-regional constrained fixed price multiplier (CFPM) method and an inter-regional social accounting matrix (IRSAM)-based microsimulation, and a carbon emission model to make a comparative analysis of the socioeconomic and environmental impacts of regional electricity market integration between ASEAN and Asian Pacific Region covering China, South Korea, Japan, and Australia.

Chapter 13 summarizes the main findings presented in each chapter of this book, discusses implications for carbon leakage, relocation, and halo effects of Chinese outward FDI and exports of RES-E technologies, and suggests that the remaining challenges are topics for further research.

Notes

1 Chapter 5 presents the list of companies in each category.
2 Energy–environment–economy (E3) simulation model also shows that environmental tax reform in EU member states in 1985–2012 induces investment leakage by only 3% at best. This occurs because the reform induces innovation and reduces the energy intensity of the associated industries (Barker et al., 2007).

References

Al-mulali, U., C.F. Tang, 2013. Investigating the validity of pollution haven hypothesis in the gulf cooperation council (GCC) countries, *Energy Policy* 60, 813–819, https://doi.org/10.1016/j.enpol.2013.05.055.

Auer, M., 2000. Pollution havens and industrial flight: Weighing the evidence. In: Bonser, CF (eds.) *Security, Trade, and Environmental Policy*, Springer, Boston, MA. https://doi.org/10.1007/978-1-4615-4399-2_30.

Araya, M., 2005. FDI and the environment: What empirical evidence does- and does not-tell us. In: Zarsky, L. (ed.) *International Investment for Sustainable Development: Balancing Rights and Rewards*. Earthscan, London, 530–548.

Bahera, S.R., D.P. Dash, 2017. The effect of urbanization, energy consumption, and foreign direct investment on the carbon dioxide emission in the SSEA (South and Southeast Asian) region, *Renew. Sust. Energ. Rev.* 70, 96–106, https://doi.org/10.1016/j.rser.2016.11.201.

Barker, T., S. Junankar, H. Pollitt, P. Summerton, 2007. Carbon leakage from unilateral Environmental Tax Reforms in Europe, 1995–2005, *Energy Policy* 35 (12), 6281–6292, https://doi.org/10.1016/j.enpol.2007.06.021.

Beardsworth, J.J. Jr., J.A. Schmidt, 2014. Resource financed infrastructure: Origins and issues, In: Halland, H., J. Beardsworth, B. Land, and J. Schmidt, *Resource Financed Infrastructure, A Discussion on a New Form of Infrastructure Financing*, The World Bank: Washington DC, 11–68, http://dx.doi.org/10.1596/978-1-4648-0239-3.

Bednar-Friedl, B., T. Schinko, K.W. Steininger, 2012. The relevance of process emissions for carbon leakage: A comparison of unilateral climate policy options with and without border carbon adjustment, *Energy Econ.* 34, S168–S180, https://doi.org/10.1016/j.eneco.2012.08.038.

Bokpin, G.A., 2017. Foreign direct investment and environmental sustainability in Africa: The role of institutions and governance, *Res. Int. Bus. Finance* 39, Part A, 239–247, https://doi.org/10.1016/j.ribaf.2016.07.038.

Boocock, C.N., 2002. Environmental impacts of foreign direct investment in the mining sector in Sub-Saharan Africa. In: OECD (ed.) *Foreign Direct Investment and the Environment: Lessons from the Mining Sector*, OECD, Paris, 19–53, https://doi.org/10.1787/9789264199026-en.

Boulle, M., 2019. The hazy rise of coal in Kenya: The actors, interests, and discursive contradictions shaping Kenya's electricity future, *Energy Res. Soc. Sci.* 56, 101205, https://doi.org/10.1016/j.erss.2019.05.015.

Burke, P., J. Widnyana, Z. Anjum, E. Aisbett, B. Resosudarmo, K.G.H. Baldwin, 2019. Overcoming barriers to solar and wind energy adoption in two Asia giants: India and Indonesia. *Energy Policy* 132, 1216–1228, https://doi.org/10.1016/j.enpol.2019.05.055.

Brunnermeier, S.B., A. Levinson, 2004. Examining the evidence on environmental regulations and industry location, *J Environ Dev.* 13 (1), 6–41, https://doi.org/10.1177/1070496503256500.

Caron, J., 2012. Estimating carbon leakage and the efficiency of border adjustments in general equilibrium—Does sectoral aggregation matter? *Energy Econ.* 34, S111–S126, https://doi.org/10.1016/j.eneco.2012.08.015.

Candau, F., E. Dienesch, 2017. Pollution haven and corruption paradise, *J Environ Econ Manage.* 85, 171–192, http://dx.doi.org/10.1016/j.jeem.2017.05.005.

Chang, Y., Y. Li, 2015. Renewable energy and policy options in an integrated ASEAN electricity market: Quantitative assessments and policy implications, *Energy Policy* 85, 39–49, https://doi.org/10.1016/j.enpol.2015.05.011.

Chen, S., 2013. *Energy, Environment and Economic Transformation in China*, Oxon: Routledge.

Cole, M.A., 2004. Trade, the pollution haven hypothesis and the environmental Kuznets curve: Examining the linkages, *Ecol. Econ.* 48, 71–81, https://doi.org/10.1016/j.ecolecon.2003.09.007.

Copeland, B.R., S.M. Taylor, 2003. *Trade and the Environment: Theory and Evidence*, Princeton University Press, Princeton and Oxford.

Dam, L., B. Scholtens, 2012. The curse of the haven: The impact of multinational enterprise on environmental regulation, *Ecol. Econ.* 78, 148–156, https://doi.org/10.1016/j.ecolecon.2012.04.011.

de la Tour, A., M. Glachant, Y. Ménière, 2011. Innovation and international technology transfer: The case of the Chinese photovoltaic industry, *Energy Policy* 39: 761–770, https://doi.org/10.1016/j.enpol.2010.10.050.

Demena, B.A., S.K. Afesorgbor, 2020. The effect of FDI on environmental emissions: Evidence from a meta-analysis, *Energy Policy* 138, 111192, https://doi.org/10.1016/j.enpol.2019.111192.

European Commission, 2020. EU Green Deal (carbon border adjustment mechanism), https://ec.europa.eu/info/law/better-regulation/have-your-say/initiatives/12228-Carbon-Border-Adjustment-Mechanism/, [accessed 22 September 2020].

European Union, 2015. *EU ETS Handbook*, https://ec.europa.eu/clima/sites/clima/files/docs/ets_handbook_en.pdf/, [accessed 22 September 2020].

Eskeland, G.S., A.E. Harrison, 2003. Moving to greener pastures? Multinationals and the pollution haven hypothesis, *J. Dev. Econ* 70 (1), 1–23, https://doi.org/10.1016/S0304-3878(02)00084-6.

Ezaki, Y., 2018. *Deciphering the Current Status on Infrastructure Exports of Japanese Companies*, Bunshindo, Tokyo (in Japanese).

Fawthrop, T., 2019. Myanmar's Myitsone Dam Dilemma: As the unpopular project sits in limbo, the government has to choose between upsetting China and enraging its own people, *The Diplomat* (11 March 2019), https://thediplomat.com/2019/03/myanmars-myitsone-dam-dilemma/, [accessed 4 September 2020].

Gallagher, K.P., R. Kamal, J. Jin, Y. Chen, X. Ma, 2018. Energizing development finance? The benefits and risks of China's development finance in the global energy sector, *Energy Policy* 122, 313–321, https://doi.org/10.1016/j.enpol.2018.06.009.

Gallagher, K.P., Z. Li, X. Chen, X. Ma, 2019. China's Global Power Database, Global Development Policy Center, Boston University, https://www.bu.edu/cgp/, [accessed 25 December 2020].

Global Energy Interconnection Development and Cooperation Organization, 2019. *Research and Outlook on Asian Energy Interconnection*, China Electric Power Press, Beijing.

Hanif, I., S.M.F. Raza, P. Gago-de-Santos, Q. Abbas, 2019. Fossil fuels, foreign direct investment, and economic growth have triggered CO_2 emissions in emerging Asian economies: Some empirical evidence, *Energy* 171, 493–501, https://doi.org/10.1016/j.energy.2019.01.011.

Hao Y., Y. Guo, Y. Guo, H. Wu, S. Ren, 2020. Does outward foreign direct investment (OFDI) affect the home country's environmental quality? The case of China, *Struct. Chang. Econ.* 52, 109–119, https://doi.org/10.1016/j.strueco.2019.08.012.

Hayashi, K., 2006. Conditions for high-performer in international oil and gas upstream industry: A CERA proposal for increasing international competitiveness of Japanese firms, *Oil and Gas Review* 40 (3), 33–41 (in Japanese).

Hervé-Mignucci, M., X. Wang, 2015. Slowing the growth of coal power outside China: The role of Chinese Finance, *A CPI Report*, Climate Policy Initiative, https://climatepolicyinitiative.org/wp-content/uploads/2015/11/Slowing-the-Growth-of-Coal-Power-Outside-China.pdf/, [accessed 20 April 2020].

Horii, N., 2014. The wind turbine industry: the role of policy and markets in the catch-up process. In: Watanabe, M. (ed.) *The Disintegration of Production: Firm Strategy and Industrial Development in China*, Edward Elgar, Cheltenham, 127–148.

Khan, Y., Q. Bin, 2020. The environmental Kuznets curve for carbon dioxide emissions and trade on belt and road initiative countries: A spatial panel data approach, *Singap. Econ. Rev.* 65, 1099–1126, https://doi.org/10.1142/S0217590819500255.

Koch, N., H.B. Mama, 2019. Does the EU Emissions Trading System induce investment leakage? Evidence from German multinational firms, *Energy Econ.* 81, 479–492, https://doi.org/10.1016/j.eneco.2019.04.018.

Koehn, P.H., 2016. *China Confronts Climate Change: A Bottom-up Perspective*, Routledge, Oxon.

Lau, L.S., C.K. Choong, Y.K. Eng, 2014. Investigation of the environmental Kuznets curve for carbon emissions in Malaysia: Do foreign direct investment and trade matter? *Energy Policy* 68, 490–497, https://doi.org/10.1016/j.enpol.2014.01.002.

Lechner, A.M., J.R. Owen, A. Tritto, A.H. Hoong, C. Teo, C.M. Tan, A. Campos-Arceiz, 2020. China's belt and road: An environmental disaster for Southeast Asia? *South China Morning Post* (4 January 2020), https://www.scmp.com/news/hong-kong/politics/article/3044453/digital-silk-road-inspired-chinas-belt-and-road-initiative/, [accessed 27 January 2020].

Lee, J.W., 2013. The contribution of foreign direct investment to clean energy use, carbon emissions and economic growth, *Energy Policy* 55, 483–489, https://doi.org/10.1016/j.enpol.2012.12.039.

Li, M., Q. Wang, 2020. Does industrial relocation alleviate environmental pollution? A mathematical economics analysis, *Environ Dev Sustain.* 22, 4673–4698, https://doi.org/10.1007/s10668-019-00403-7.

Liu, Y., Y. Hao, Y. Gao, 2017. The environmental consequences of domestic and foreign investment: Evidence from China, *Energy Policy* 108, 271–280, https://doi.org/10.1016/j.enpol.2017.05.055.

Ma, J., S. Zadek, T. Sun, S. Zhu, L. Cheng, J. Els, T. Nielsen, D. Ren, I. Granoff, T. Stumhöfer, 2019. *Decarbonizing the Belt and Road: A Green Finance Roadmap*, https://www.vivideconomics.com/casestudy/decarbonizing-the-belt-and-road-initiative-a-green-finance-roadmap/, [accessed 19 September 2020].

Mani, M., D. Wheeler, 1998. In search of pollution havens? Dirty Industry in the World Economy, 1960 to 1995, *J Environ Dev.* 7 (3), 215–247, https://doi.org/10.1177/107049659800700302.

Martin, R., M., Muûls, L.B. de Preuxa, U.J. Wagnerd, 2014. On the empirical content of carbon leakage criteria in the EU Emissions Trading Scheme, *Ecol. Econ.* 105, 78–88, https://doi.org/10.1016/j.ecolecon.2014.05.010.

McCarthy, K.J., 2016. On the influence of the European trade barrier on the Chinese PV industry: Is the solution to the solar-dispute "successful"? *Energy Policy* 99, 154–157, https://doi.org/10.1016/j.enpol.2016.09.055.

Michalek, G., R. Schwarze, 2015. Carbon leakage: Pollution, trade or politics? *Environ Dev Sustain.* 17, 1471–1492, https://doi.org/10.1007/s10668-014-9616-8.

Monjon, S., P. Quirion, 2011. Addressing leakage in the EU ETS: Border adjustment or output-based allocation? *Ecol. Econ.* 70, 1957–1971, https://doi.org/10.1016/j.ecolecon.2011.04.020.

Mori, A., 2018. Sociotechnical and political economy perspectives in the Chinese energy transition, *Energy Res. Soc. Sci.* 35, 29–36, https://doi.org/10.1016/j.erss.2017.10.04.

Mori, A., 2020. Foreign actors, faster transitions? Co-evolution of complementarities, perspectives and sociotechnical systems in the case of Indonesia's electricity supply system, *Energy Res. Soc. Sci.* 69, 101594, https://doi.org/10.1016/j.erss.2020.101594.

Mori, A., M. Takehara, 2018. Revisiting China's climate policy: The climate-energy conundrum point of view. In: Mori, A. (ed.) *China's Climate-Energy Policy: Domestic and International Impacts*, Routledge, 33–51, https://doi.org/10.4324/9781351037587-3.

National Development and Reform Commission (NDRC), 2007. *China's National Climate Change Programme.*

National Development and Reform Commission (NDRC), 2015. Enhanced actions on climate change: China's intended nationally determined contributions, https://www4.unfccc.int/sites/ndcstaging/PublishedDocuments/China%20First/China%27s%20First%20NDC%20Submission.pdf/, [accessed 17 September 2020].

OECD, 2017. *Economic Outlook for Southeast Asia, China and India 2017: Addressing Energy Challenges*, OECD Publishing, Paris, http://dx.doi.org/10.1787/saeo-2017-en/, [accessed 10 October 2017].

Ogura, Y., A. Mori, 2015. Changes in trade and economic structure during the past 25 years, Have green growth, low-carbon strategies made a significant impact in Northeast Asia? In: Yoshida, F., A. Mori (eds.) *Green Growth and Low Carbon Development in East Asia*, Routledge, Abingdon, 77–96.

Schmidt, R.C., J. Heitzig, 2014. Carbon leakage: Grandfathering as an incentive device to avert firm relocation, *J Environ Econ Manage.* 67 (2), 209–223, https://doi.org/10.1016/j.jeem.2013.12.004.

Sun, C., F. Zhang, M. Xu, 2017. Investigation of pollution haven hypothesis for China: An ARDL approach with breakpoint unit root tests, *J. Clean. Prod.* 161, 153–164, http://dx.doi.org/10.1016/j.jclepro.2017.05.119.

Sung, B., W.Y. Song, S.D. Park, 2018. How foreign direct investment affects CO_2 emission levels in the Chinese manufacturing industry: Evidence from panel data, *Econ Syst.* 42, 320–331, https://doi.org/10.1016/j.ecosys.2017.06.002.

United Nations Environment Programme (UNEP), 2019. Emissions Gap Report 2019, UNEP, Nairobi, http://www.unenvironment.org/emissionsgap/, [accessed 5 October 2020].

United Nations ESCAP, 2012. Decentralized energy system, Fact Sheet, United Nations Economic and Social Commission for Asia and the Pacific, http://www.unescap.org/sites/default/files/14.%20FS-Decentralized-energy-system.pdf/, [accessed 23 September 2020].

United Nations ESCAP, 2019. Electricity connectivity roadmap for Asia and the Pacific: Strategies towards interconnecting the region's grids, https://www.unescap.org/sites/default/files/publications/Final-Publication_Electricity_Connectivity_Roadmap.pdf/, [accessed 1 October 2020].

United Nations Framework for Climate Change Convention (UNFCCC), 2015. The Paris Agreement, https://unfccc.int/process-and-meetings/the-paris-agreement/the-paris-agreement/, [accessed 19 August 2020].

United Nations Framework for Climate Change Convention (UNFCCC), 2020. NDC Registry, https://www4.unfccc.int/sites/ndcstaging/Pages/Home.aspx/, [accessed 17 September 2020].

United Nations Statistics Division, n.a. UN Comtrade, https://comtrade.un.org/data/, [accessed 2 October 2020].

Vagliasindi, M., 2013. *Revisiting Public-Private Partnerships in the Power Sector,* World Bank, Washington, DC, https://ppp.worldbank.org/public-private-partnership/sites/ppp.worldbank.org/files/documents/WB%20Study%202013.pdf/, [accessed 1 October 2020].

Vidal, J., 2016. Bangladesh coal plant protests continue after demonstrators killed, *The Guardian* (6 April 2016), http://www.theguardian.com/environment/2016/apr/06/bangladesh-coal-plant-protests-continue-after-demonstrators-killed/, [accessed 19 August 2020].

Wang, D.T., W.Y. Chen, 2014. Foreign direct investment, institutional development, and environmental externalities: Evidence from China, *J. Environ. Manag.* 135, 81–90, https://doi.org/10.1016/j.jenvman.2014.01.013.

Wang, X., F. Teng, S. Zhou, B. Cai, 2017. Identifying the industrial sectors at risk of carbon leakage in China, *Clim. Policy* 17 (4), 443–457, https://doi.org/10.1080/14693062.2015.1104497.

World Bank. 2017. Public-private partnerships: Reference guide version 3. World Bank, Washington, DC, https://openknowledge.worldbank.org/handle/10986/29052/, [accessed 23 September 2020].

World Bank, 2020. DataBank: World development indicators, https://databank.worldbank.org/source/world-development-indicators#/, [accessed 24 September 2020].

Zarsky, L., 1999. Havens, halos and spaghetti: Untangling the evidence about foreign direct investment and the environment. In: OECD (ed.) *Foreign Direct Investment and the Environment*, OECD, Paris, 47–74.

Zarsky, L., 2002. Stuck in the mud? National states, globalization and the environment. In: Gallagher, K.P., J. Werksman (eds.) *Earthscan Reader on International Trade and Sustainable Development*, Earthscan, 45–76.

Zhang, C., X. Zhou, 2016, Does foreign direct investment lead to lower CO_2 emissions? Evidence from a regional analysis in China, *Renew Sust Eenerg Rev.* 58, 943–951, https://doi.org/10.1016/j.rser.2015.12.226.

Zhang, Z., K. Zhu, G.J.D. Hewings, 2017. A multi-regional input–output analysis of the pollution haven hypothesis from the perspective of global production fragmentation, *Energy Econ.* 64, 13–23, http://dx.doi.org/10.1016/j.eneco.2017.03.007.

Zheng S., M.E. Kahn, H. Liu, 2010. Towards a system of open cities in China: Home prices, FDI flows and air quality in 35 major cities, *Reg. Sci. Urban. Econ.* 40 (1), 1–10, https://doi.org/10.1016/j.regsciurbeco.2009.10.003.

Zhu, H., L. Duan, Y. Guo, K. Yu, 2016. The effects of FDI, economic growth and energy consumption on carbon emissions in ASEAN-5: Evidence from panel quantile regression, *Econ. Model.* 58, 237–248, https://doi.org/10.1016/j.econmod.2016.05.003.

2 Struggles for energy transition in the electricity system in Asian countries

A system complementarity perspective

Akihisa Mori

1 Introduction

With rapid population and economic growth, the Asian region has increased its energy consumption. In response, policymakers have facilitated investments in fuel and power supply and infrastructure, focusing also on efficiency to ensure a secure, affordable, and more sustainable energy supply (IEA, 2019). However, an increase in fossil fuel consumption, especially coal consumption has resulted in worsening air pollution and increased greenhouse gas (GHG) emissions, which put heavy stress on local, regional, and global environments. To mitigate the stress the Paris Agreement requires Asian countries to prepare GHG emissions targets, to implement measures and policies as nationally determined contributions (NDCs), and to update pledges with more ambitious targets every five years.

The electricity sector has made the largest contribution to Asia's rising energy consumption and CO_2 emissions. Electricity demand has substantially increased since the 2000s when Asian countries recovered from the 1997 economic crisis. It is projected to more than double by 2040, assuming the current, relatively low per capita electricity consumption, future economic growth, and future universal access to electricity. While a shift from traditional unsustainable and unsafe use of solid biomass to electricity would reduce indoor air pollution and health damage, it may not reduce CO_2 emissions without an accompanying reduction in fossil fuel use within the electricity sector. To achieve more ambitious targets, a large-scale integration of renewable-energy-sourced electricity (RES-E) into the grid system becomes indispensable (Madrigal and Stoft, 2012).

Previous research has analyzed the shift in the energy mix mainly from economic efficiency, security of supply, and lock-ins. They have argued for favorable policy measures to address the high levelized cost of electricity (LCOE) for wider diffusion of wind and solar power (Aguirre and Ibikunle, 2014), such as a feed-in tariff (FiT) and renewable portfolio standard. When the cost of generating this energy becomes competitive around the world (IRENA, 2020) and a FiT is replaced with auctions (Dobrotkova et al.,

DOI: 10.4324/9781003190905-3

2018), the arguments go beyond its generation to address the challenges for network governance, such as integration costs (Hirth et al., 2015), as well as security of supply in order to address shrinking capacity margins. The coal lock-in perspective elucidates interdependent and mutually reinforcing effects among technological, economic, institutional, and behavioral lock-ins, arguing for the involvement and cooperation of actors from different sectors for unlocking (Seto et al., 2016). However, it is not sufficient to analyze the governance of networks in transitions.

Complementarities and competitions within and across a sociotechnical system can bring deeper understanding of the co-evolution of generation and network subsystems. They see a sociotechnical system as elements of complementarities that have their own dynamics, different time horizons, and speed of development (Markard et al., 2016), and technological limitations and asynchronous developments of each element as bottlenecks that slow down or impede a transition (Markard and Hoffmann, 2016).

Against this backdrop, this chapter explores how Asian countries have changed their energy mix in the electricity supply, with special attention to the restructuring of elements of complementarities within and across their electricity systems in energy switch from fossil fuel to RES-E.

The remainder of this chapter is organized as follows. Section 2 makes a literature review to propose an analytical framework for system change in electricity system from complementarity viewpoints. Section 3 overviews changes in energy mix in electricity generation in Asian countries, and Section 4 conducts case studies, taking Vietnam, Indonesia, India, and Japan as representatives of each typology of energy switch. Section 5 discusses commonly observed obstacles and challenges of the restructuring of elements of complementarities, and how foreign actors can accelerate or retard system transitions, causing carbon leakage, relocation, and halos. Section 6 concludes the chapter with perspectives for the following chapters.

2 Analytical framework

2.1 Elements of complementarities in thermal-based electricity supply system

Complementarities and competition in the fuel-intensive thermal electricity supply system can be illustrated as in Figure 2.1. The system has four types of complementarities along the supply chain: infrastructure, organizational, engineering and manufacturing, and institutional. These complementarities are not inherent to the thermal power supply system. Rather, they are built and strengthened to overcome bottlenecks and make the system work effectively.

Infrastructure complementarities are created to secure fuel transportation, and transmission and distribution networks, known as grids, that supply and deliver electricity. Under the centralized electricity system, grids

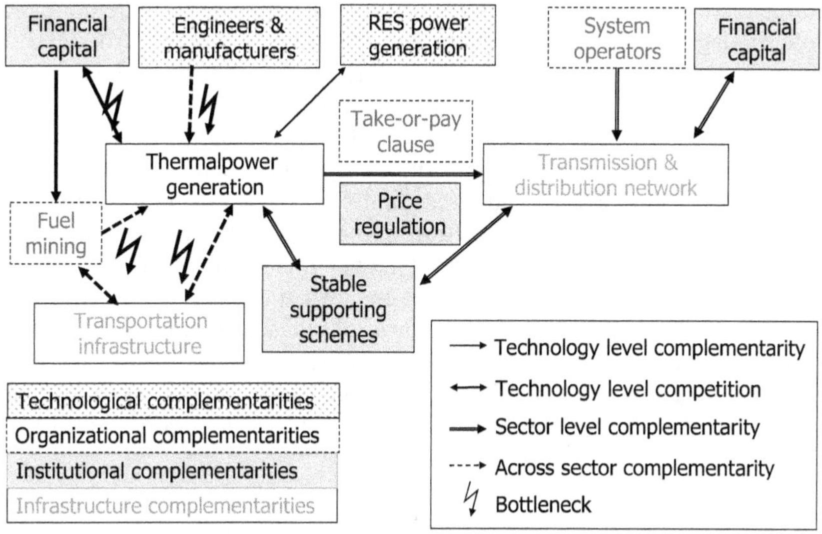

Figure 2.1 Complementarities and their bottlenecks in a fuel-based thermal electricity system

Source: The author.

have mostly been developed in response to individual interconnection requests from large-scale generation plants.

Engineering and manufacturing complementarities are created to engineer design, procure technologies, construct, operate, and maintain plants and grids. Fossil fuel power generation is a proven, standardized technology that requires less testing and qualifying processes (Tushman and Rosenkopf, 1992) and site-specific activities (Steffen et al., 2018). However, some countries do not have enough technological and managerial capabilities, especially for large-scale plants with the latest technologies, such as ultra-supercritical and integrated coal gasification combined cycle plants. Engineering and manufacturing complementarities also help electricity generators upgrade production technologies, provide an arena for testing and qualifying novelties to foster the ability of domestic industries, and establish an industrial network that has a number of technologies and linkages between subsystems (Tushman and Rosenkopf, 1992).

Institutional complementarities are created to secure financial capital. The electricity supply system is characterized by sunk investments, high entry barriers, long operating lifetimes, and complementary capital investments (Schmidt et al., 2017). These characteristics mean investments in the system are perceived as highly risky. To secure a stable revenue stream over the years, vertically integrated monopolistic or oligopolistic supply is employed under network regulations, focusing on short-term efficiency, competition, and a level playing field to restrict exploration of excess rent. Stable institutions, including those with consistent long-term demand-side policies, legitimacy, and alignment with practices in other sectors and regional/local institutions, are key systemic factors for rapid development and diffusion of a type of generation technology (Negro et al., 2012). By confirming institutions for cost recovery, bilateral donors and multilateral development banks provide long-term loans to implement turnkey projects that address technological and institutional bottlenecks simultaneously.

Organizational complementarities are created to minimize commercial risks and avoid sunk cost investments. They include a long-term fuel supply and a transportation contract that ensure a stable fuel supply for power plants at an affordable price, and a power purchase agreement with utilities that ensure stable sales of their products at a pre-determined price. Independent power producers (IPPs) and project developers work to arrange these contracts to close financial packages and to obtain concessions from authorities.

2.2 *Elements of complementarities in distributed, RES-based electricity system*

A substantial change in energy mix requires realignment of these elements of complementarities. The change is radical in the shift to RES-E because the shift requires a transformation not only from fuel-intensive to capital-intensive electricity generation but also from the existing hierarchical and centrally controlled electricity distribution networks toward a smart power grid paradigm, in which unforeseen peaks of distributed local electricity production and uncertainty of RES-E can be properly managed (Abrishambaf et al., 2019).

The electricity system based on the smart power grid paradigm has addressed challenges of cost-effective and proper grid operation and system balancing in three ways: sufficient network capacity and stronger transmission grids; greater storage capacity; and more flexible responses for system balancing (Gulagi et al., 2018; Newbery et al., 2018).

First, ultra-high-voltage, direct-current (UHV-DC) power transmission systems can improve stability, reliability, and transmission capacity. When developed and coupled with region-wide super-grids, the systems can deliver RES-E generators in remote, less populated areas to areas with higher consumption, and thus can reduce RES-E curtailment significantly (Burgholzer and Auer, 2016). Interconnectors can deliver back-up power when variable RES generators are unavailable (Neuhoff et al., 2013). Interconnection exploits differences in wind and solar conditions across regions, reducing supply variability. To develop grid capacity in a cost-effective manner, as well as to attract financing for grid development, existing transmission planning and cost allocation practices have to be revisited to collect network fixed costs in an efficient and equitable manner (Madrigal and Stoft, 2012).

Second, storage offers back-up of RES-E, smoothing out of the variability of RES-E, shaving peak use, and deferring upgrades in transmission and distribution systems. Pumped storage plants have been constructed to deal with inflexible sources of electricity, thus accounting for the majority in the storage capacity. Battery technologies are emerging, offering a grid defection opportunity by mandated installation of rooftop solar photovoltaics (PVs), as well as allowing distributed generation in remote areas where expansion can be very costly and disruptive.

Third, an effective use of the existing network has been pursued to increase flexibility in the transmission grid as well as to reduce the need for network extension (Auer and Haas, 2016). Theoretically, an energy-only competitive wholesale market can satisfy most of the flexibility needs as long as it is equipped with centralized scheduling and efficient dispatch, frequent scheduling and settlement intervals (i.e. five-minute scheduling and settlements), and a make-whole payment guarantee providing incentives for generators that follow the prices (Ela et al., 2016).

Ultimately, smart grids would enhance flexibility, reliability, sustainability, and the efficiency of a distributed electricity supply system by making the grid controllable, automated, and fully integrated (Colak et al., 2016). Several enabling technologies and systems play decisive roles in facilitating the coordination of efficiency in a smart grid, such as smart meters, energy controllers, two-way communication systems, the merger of information and communication technology and electricity grids, intelligent and remote supervision, and Advanced Meter Infrastructure (Camarinha-Matos, 2016). These technologies and systems would constitute a basis for transactive energy systems that can better manage millions of distributed generators, consumers, and prosumers through transactive network management and control, and peer-to-peer management in smart grids without centralized regulators (Abrishambaf et al., 2019). They would enable a shift to more granular temporal and spatial prices and reduce the reliance on politically backed, long-term contracts and the capacity remuneration mechanism.

In practice, however, various market and policy failures make it difficult for a market to operate these programs alone. Generators do not always engage in the electricity market or respond to price signals because they conclude bilateral contracts and provide the market operator or utilities with the scheduled output at a pre-determined price. To incentivize such generators to engage in and offer their flexibility in the market, a number of market-based ancillary service markets have been created in day-ahead and real-time electricity markets. Recent technological developments in smart meters and automated demand controllers enable net metering to work, benefitting prosumers by reducing the charges to pay to the grid operator, and facilitating demand-response programs (Newbery et al., 2018). However, an energy-only market generates price spikes when capacity is tight because incumbent utilities exercise market power to drive up prices. Such a highly volatile electricity market means self-scheduling generators lose substantial profits and credibility from consumers (Ela et al., 2016). Wholesale price caps can limit their market power but reduces profitability of capacity investment, leading to underinvestment in the longer run. Direct load control, such as time-of-use and critical peak pricing, can bring flexibility to the grid by paying incentives to the electricity consumers in exchange for altering their consumption profiles (Siano, 2014). However, demand response is often limited and thus cannot sufficiently address the challenge (Cramton and Ockenfel, 2012).

The capacity remuneration mechanism is an alternative market designed to increase flexibility and to maintain an adequate capacity, simultaneously. It allows utilities to provide pre-specified load reduction in exchange for supplementary revenues. In particular, a forward capacity market with long-term contracts can provide the required adequate level and lower cost to consumers and more stable capacity prices, as compared to a yearly capacity market (Bhagwat et al., 2017). The mechanism is also expected to reduce fluctuations caused by investment cycles, and make market development more predictable (Bublitz et al., 2019).

However, a strategic reserve can have adverse effects on a large-scale integration of RES-E. Even if the capacity is determined by auction, the type and amount of capacity to be procured is critically dependent on government policy and the auction design. Incumbent utilities can exercise market power in capacity auctions (Schwenen, 2015). As a result, strategic reserve can stimulate stand-by generation capacity (Torriti, 2016) and new fossil fuel power plants, preventing existing ones from being decommissioned (Lehmann et al., 2015). In addition, it would make flexibility options, such as the demand-response programs and storage options, redundant (Auer and Haas, 2016).

In addition, both an energy-only market and the capacity remuneration mechanism cannot help centralized system operators manage millions of small-scale, distributed agents such as consumers, producers, and prosumers with distributed technologies such as rooftop solar PVs and electric vehicles (EVs), and are located in large geographical areas and do not have the capability to engage in the market and sophisticated smart grids.

Distributed energy resource aggregators would play a pivotal role in supplying RES-E and ancillary services in the electricity market by grouping such small-scale agents and technologies. They can also manage the uncertain behavior of the RES-Es in the real-time operation by closing information gaps, and coordinating distributed resource operations (Burger et al., 2017; IRENA, 2019). These aggregators are also expected to pool the generation and/or consumption flexibility of customers/prosumers at a low voltage level in the future (Lipari et al., 2018).

Corporate renewable power purchase agreements (PPAs) also help RES-E producers secure a revenue stream and access to project finances. Under a PPA, corporate customers purchase RES-E at a pre-agreed price for a pre-agreed period of time, and transfer environmental attributes. They can hedge against energy price volatility and reduce the cost of carbon in implementing sustainability strategies that go beyond purchasing renewable energy certificates (WBCSD, 2016).

2.3 Challenges to the transitions to RES-E-based system

The aforementioned arguments imply that a large-scale shift in energy mix to RES-E accompanies the restructuring of the elements of complementarities within the electricity system (Figure 2.2).

RES-E generators tend to employ RES-E technologies engineered and manufactured by dedicated manufacturers that are different from thermal power ones. RES-E technologies can generate technological and policy feedback effects (Jordan and Matt, 2014), improving and scaling domestic manufacturing technologies and processes through economies of capacity and scale to gain a competitive edge in both domestic and international markets (Hansen et al., 2019), and mobilizing support from increasing numbers of emerging beneficiaries to modify state capacities and institutions in favor of them (Mori, 2018c). They encourage the installation of storage and batteries to minimize loss from curtailment, and an emergence of business models, such as renewable PPAs and third-party ownership, thereby increasing customer and prosumer bases for RES-E (Ode and Wadin, 2019).

Deepening domestic capital markets enable capital-intensive energy projects to access private financial capital and increase their viability on a commercial basis (Best, 2017). Traditional formal financial institutions are

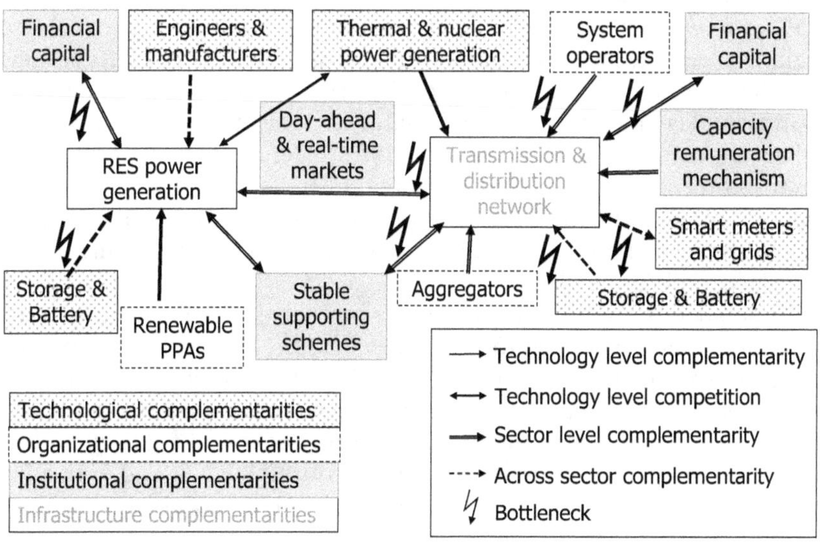

Figure 2.2 Complementarities and their bottlenecks in a RES-based electricity system

Source: The author.

generally less willing to make loans for these new capital-intensive power generation plants, due to longer supply chains and longer pay-back periods (Haskel and Westlake, 2018). In particular, they are unwilling to do so for small and medium-sized energy enterprises, due to the high default risk, insufficient competition, poor guarantees, and a lack of information about their ability to repay loans (Haselip et al., 2013). However, pension funds and green banks are emerging as financial capital providers, thus overcoming financial bottlenecks (Rifkin, 2019).

Grids have to be enhanced to gain complementarities with a variety of types of generations located in wider geographical areas. This requires financial capital for enhancing grid capacity and system balancing. Direct load control, market-based ancillary services, and the capacity remuneration mechanism may be implemented to support centralized system operators to balance the system. Aggregators may emerge as organizations that provide connecting services for a mass of micro prosumers. Storage, batteries, and smart grids may help increase flexibility of grid operation.

On the other hand, a large-scale integration of RES-E will reduce utilization of the capital stock embodied in existing fuel-intensive electricity supply systems, weakening complementarities within and across the fossil fuel-based electricity system. First, coal, oil, nuclear, and combined cycle natural gas plants are required to be used as load following electricity, despite load following use of these power plants or lowering the power output is estimated to increase the LCOE (Hirth et al., 2015). This is particularly the case for nuclear power plants that are designed without having the load following capability and are composed almost entirely of fixed and sunk costs (Nuclear Energy Agency, 2011). The existing installed capacity of thermal power will become idle or spinning reserves, generating extra costs for maintenance. The loss associated with these stranded investments becomes prohibitive for recently installed capacity because they are forced into early retirement, leaving the majority of capital investments unrecovered.

Second, demand for fuel, transport infrastructure, and engineering and manufacture services, and financial capital will decrease as thermal power plants become stranded assets. These goods and service providers are urged to find alternative profit opportunities in other countries or business fields, or risk becoming stranded.

These adverse distributional impacts motivate incumbent utilities and thermal power generators to exercise economic, political, and cognitive power to block thermal power load from being used as a load following generation plants. They may lobby the government to block RES-E generators from obtaining finance in the capital market (Lockwood et al., 2019). Grid companies may impose high fees for transmitting RES-E, and even admit priority access to coal power to RES-E (Mori, 2018c) while deterring investments in grid capacity and flexibility.

Stable institutions can narrow opportunities for change and restrict development of bottom-up solutions (Baker et al., 2014). They enable incumbent regime actors and governing elites to enhance and expand coalitions (Mori, 2019), influencing decisions and political goals in their favor (Meadowcroft, 2011), and create high entry barriers (Stirling, 2014).

In addition, long-term, take-or-pay clauses stand as institutional lock-ins, working to maintain the existing complementarities within and across the fuel-intensive electricity supply system. In particular, take-or-pay clauses in long-term PPAs force grids to offer priority access to coal IPPs, and usually remain unchanged (Burke et al., 2019). They protect thermal power plants from becoming stranded even if RES-E achieves grid parity, thus forcing renewable curtailment.

3 Methodology and case selection

We use the restructuring of elements of complementarities as a framework to explore the choke points of system transformation, and the possible role of foreign actors in accelerating and retarding them. The logic of this selection is that an increasing number of Asian countries encounter renewable curtailment that calls for the transformation of the grid system to fix it, and that a whole system perspective that encompasses interdependencies between generation and network subsystems becomes important to avoid bottlenecks in the acceleration phase of energy transitions (Bauknecht et al., 2020).

We adopt a case study strategy because case studies are rich in context and can track complex developments over time (George and Bennett, 2004). Given that Asian countries are diverse in energy resource endowment and have taken varied pathways to coal-based electricity supply systems, we make a preliminary analysis on energy transitions in these countries for case selection.

4 Transition in energy mix in power generation in Asia

4.1 Cluster analysis

Most of the Asian countries—26 countries in Northeast, Southeast, South, and Central Asia in this chapter—used domestically available energy resources to increase electricity supply at the outset of economic development. Initial endowment of energy resources is varied among them. Some countries are rich in multiple energy resources, others are rich in only one of them, and the rest have to rely almost all their energy resources on foreign countries.

They can be grouped into four categories by domestically available energy resources.

The first group is oil- and gas-rich countries. They are Bangladesh, Brunei, Indonesia, Malaysia, Myanmar, Turkmenistan, and Uzbekistan. Some of them establish state companies to exploit oil and gas, gaining resource rent in the form of resource revenue, and distribute it widely to the public in the form of subsidized prices to maintain the legitimacy of governing elites. Others give concessions to domestic and international companies with ample technological and financial capacity, gaining resource rent in the form of corporate income tax, and spend it in a more transparent manner (Luong and Weinthal, 2010).

Many countries in this group rely on domestic natural gas and oil for electricity generation. Some of them continue to rely on them. In Brunei and Turkmenistan, natural gas and oil account for almost 100%, and Uzbekistan more than 80%, in 2018 (Figure 2.3). Others have switched to other sources of energy due to foreseeing a depletion of domestic oil resources in Malaysia and Indonesia, and to export contracts under resource backed loans or resource backed infrastructure schemes (Beardsworth and Schmidt, 2014).

The second group is water resource-rich countries. They are China, India, Indonesia, Japan, Laos, Malaysia, Pakistan, Tajikistan, and Vietnam, and to a lesser extent Kyrgyzstan and Myanmar (International Hydropower Association, 2020). Hydropower used to be the only source of energy for electricity generation for fossil fuel poor countries. In the 1990s, some countries, such as Laos, Nepal, Sri Lanka, and Tajikistan, relied on hydropower for all of their electricity supply, and others, including Kyrgyzstan, Vietnam, and Myanmar, relied on it for half of their supply. While Kyrgyzstan, Tajikistan, and Nepal still rely mostly on hydropower, Laos has decreased its reliance to two-thirds, and Sri Lanka, and Vietnam to one-third, in 2016–2018 (Figure 2.4). They have increased their installed capacity of coal power to satisfy the growing demand.

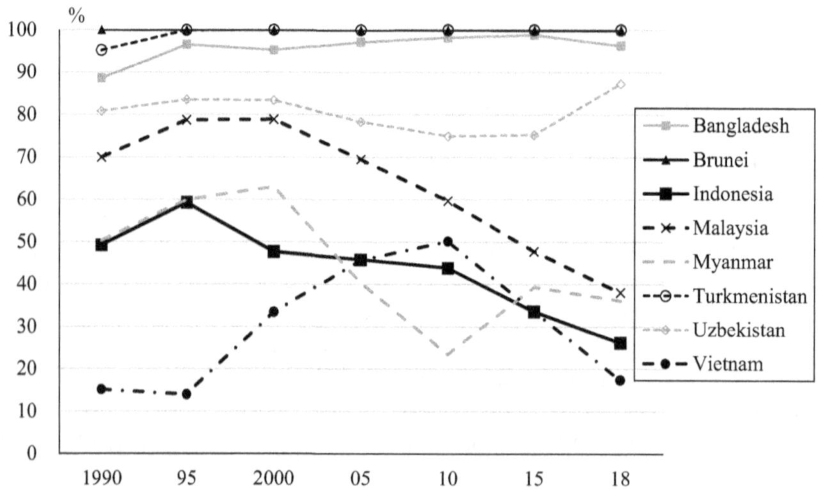

Figure 2.3 Electricity production from oil and gas in total production.
Source: Compiled by the author based on the data from World Bank (2020).

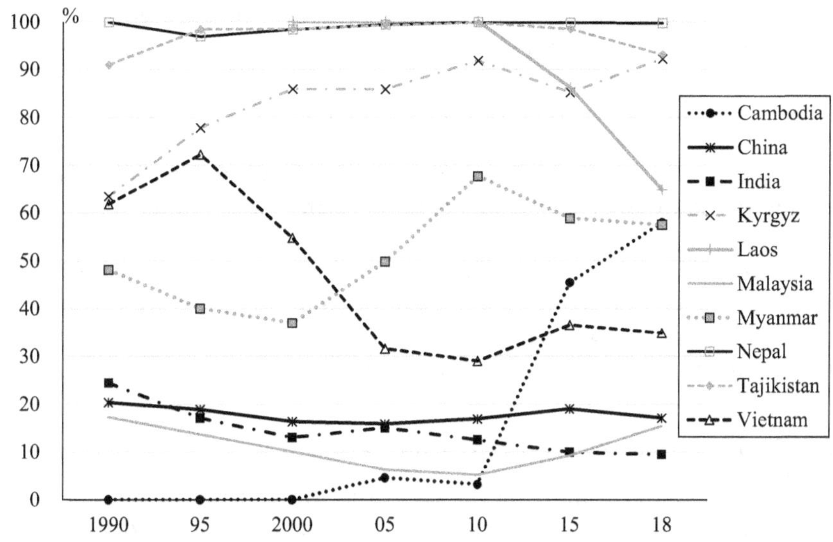

Figure 2.4 Electricity production from hydropower in total production.
Source: Compiled by the author based on the data from World Bank (2020).

Decreasing reliance on hydropower does not imply that these countries will stop hydropower development. China has the largest installed capacity in the world and is competing with Brazil to be the world's leader in new capacity installation. India has also increased new capacity, surpassing Japan in total installed capacity in 2018 (International Hydropower Association, 2020). Vietnam, Laos, and Cambodia have developed hydropower along the Mekong River basin, Myanmar along the Salween River basin, Malaysia in Borneo, and Indonesia in Java, Sumatra, and the Sulawesi Islands (International Hydropower Association, 2018, 2019, 2020).

The third group is coal-rich countries. Although coal is an easily accessible and low-cost energy resource for most of the Asian countries, China, India, and Vietnam are the largest producers. Therefore, it is rational that coal power has played a dominant role in electricity generation in China and India (Figure 1.2). Vietnam experienced a steady increase in the ratio of coal power in the 2000s, from 12% in 2000 to 30% in 2015.

Indonesia joined this group in the 2000s. When perceiving depletion of oil and stagnant development of new natural gas depots, the country shifted the focus on energy development toward coal mining. Coupled with the local autonomy, a number of concessions have been given to domestic developers for exports and domestic consumption (Mori, 2018b). The ratio of coal power in total electricity generation has increased from 24% in 1995 to 36% in 2000, and 56% in 2015 (Figure 1.2).

The last group is modern renewable energy-rich countries. The Philippines, Indonesia, and Japan have large potential for geothermal energy. However, the speed of development has been slow so far, due to high financial, technological, and institutional barriers. Geothermal energy is capital intensive in nature, requiring large amounts of initial capital. Higher development risks in exploring wells and unpredictable quality may create cost overrun, despite recent technological developments and increased accuracy of exploration (West Japan Engineering Consultants, Inc., 2007). Unpredictable and irreversible adverse impacts delay drilling permits, thus increasing financial risks (Kubota et al., 2013), especially where appropriate land use and spatial planning policies, streamlining permitting and environmental impact assessment processes, and studies on environmental and social impacts are lacking (Haukkala et al., 2021).

4.2 Changes in energy mix in electricity sector

The aforementioned mapping indicates that most of the Asian countries have gradually shifted their energy mix from easily accessible domestic energy resources to coal. They have accelerated the shift since the 2000s. Some countries have simultaneously developed hydropower but have turned to coal power much faster and on a much larger scale.

An increased accessibility to coal, financial capital, and engineering and manufacturing capabilities enables Asian countries to accelerate the energy shift. An increase in coal exports by Indonesia, Australia, Mongolia, and Kazakhstan (Mori and Dong, 2018) enables energy-poor Asian countries to access coal for electricity generation at an affordable price. This is particularly the case in Cambodia and Lao that have seen rapid increased coal imports for electricity generation (Figure 1.3). Vietnam has also rapidly increased coal imports since 2015 when it perceived a depletion of its domestic reserve. Other Asian countries added coal imports along with the expansion of coal power plants: India in 2009–2013, Malaysia and Thailand in 2000–2016, and the Philippines and Pakistan since 2014. International IPPs become more active in packaging financial, technological, operational, and fuel supply contracts in order to join the bidding and to gain concessions under PPAs (Mori, 2020).

In the 2010s, an increasing number of Asian countries began to shift their energy mix toward modern RES. In addition to the geothermal energy-rich countries of the Philippines and Indonesia, Thailand, Japan, India, and China have accelerated the shift, becoming top runners in the region. They increased the ratio of RES by around 10% in their total electricity generation in 2018 (Figure 2.5). Mongolia has rapidly increased RES since 2013 to diversify energy mix that had been exclusively relying on domestic coal. Pakistan, South Korea, and Sri Lanka can be categorized as followers with the ratio of RES at around 3%–4%, and Cambodia and Malaysia as laggards with a ratio of 1%.

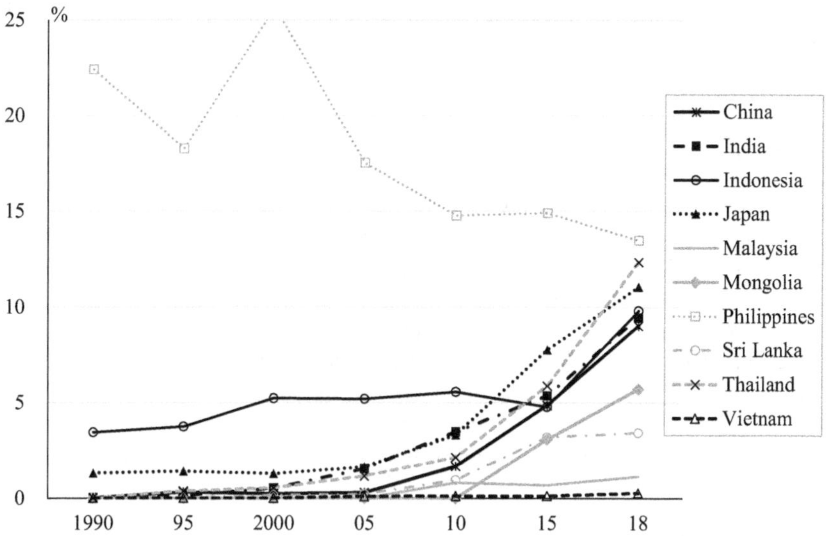

Figure 2.5 Electricity production from RES-E in total production.
Source: Compiled by the author based on the data from World Bank (2020).

Behind the boost of RES-E in Asia, there are favorable renewable energy policies and decreasing LCOE. An increasing number of Asian countries have implemented a FiT, ambitious RES targets including ones specific to wind, solar, and geothermal, and priority grid access (REN21, 2020). LCOE from RES has been going down steadily (REN21, 2018: 119). The global shift to tenders is driving down the cost of wind power for utilities and ratepayers, prompting wind turbine manufacturers to look for ways to further reduce their costs and consolidate the industry (REN21, 2018: 115). The manufacture of components, assembly, and company offices are spreading to be close to growing markets in wind energy. Capacity factors are increased by scaling size of machinery. Combined solar and wind projects at the same interconnection prevail to reduce equipment, siting, grid connection, financing, and operations and maintenance costs (REN21, 2020: 140).

Given the substantial differences between coal-based and RES-based electricity supply systems indicated in Section 2.3, the simultaneous increase in coal and RES in energy mix triggers serious conflicts of interest, resulting in a large-scale curtailment (Mori, 2018c). Although countries with large production capacity of RES-E components increase exports to mitigate the conflict, this strategy has triggered repercussions in the importing countries. The United States imposed anti-dumping duties on Chinese and Taiwanese crystalline silicon solar panels in 2011 and 2015, expanding to uniform tariffs to cover all the imports including those from Malaysia, Korea, and Vietnam in 2018 (Nguyen and Kinnucan, 2019). India also imposed anti-dumping duties on imports of a certain type of sheet used in solar cell making from China, Malaysia, Saudi Arabia, and Thailand for five years to safeguard domestic players against cheap shipments (The Economic Times, 2019).

4.3 Case selection

A varied energy endowment and transition pathway in the preliminary analysis suggest that no country can represent energy transition in Asia. Nonetheless, we pick up four countries as representatives in each cluster that went through the transition pathway from coal-based to RES-based electricity supply systems. Vietnam is selected as a representative of countries rich in water resources and going through an energy shift in a short period of time. Indonesia represents oil- and gas-rich countries going through an energy shift to coal when perceiving depletion. India represents coal-rich countries with strong coal lock-ins, and Japan with strong nuclear lock-ins.

5 Case studies

5.1 Vietnam

Vietnam's electricity sector is dominated by large state-owned enterprises. Vietnam Electricity (EVN) fully controls grid systems and accounts for two-thirds of the installed capacity. Other large state-owned enterprises (Vinacomin and Petrol Vietnam), joint stock companies, and other domestic investors own the rest (Neefjes and Dang, 2017). Energy mix in the sector has been changed from hydropower to natural gas, and then to coal during the last three decades. When the country became a net-importer of coal in 2015, a reduction of the fiscal costs of imported coal (in a state-owned power generation system) became an important policy objective (Zimmer et al., 2015). In addition, serious air pollution triggers local protests against new coal power (Do et al., 2020).

In response, the government set ambitious renewable targets by type of sources, revised the National Power Development Plan VII (PDP-7) to shift the priority on RES-E development, accepted IPPs, and implemented a generous FiT for onshore wind in 2011, biomass in 2014, and scale and rooftop solar PVs in 2017, as well as tax exemptions. The FiT directed investments in RES-E, thus increasing its ratio in installed capacity in 2015 (Figure 2.6a). In particular, it boosted investments in utility-scale installations in 2019, making its installed capacity exceed the rest of ASEAN countries combined (Shani, 2020).

However, RES-E generation has not been scaled to be commensurate with the installed capacity. Except for hydropower and biomass, renewables accounted for less than 1% of total electricity generation by 2018 (Figure 2.6b). The strong control of retail electricity price discourages EVN from offering bankable PPAs and grid access to utility-scale solar project developers

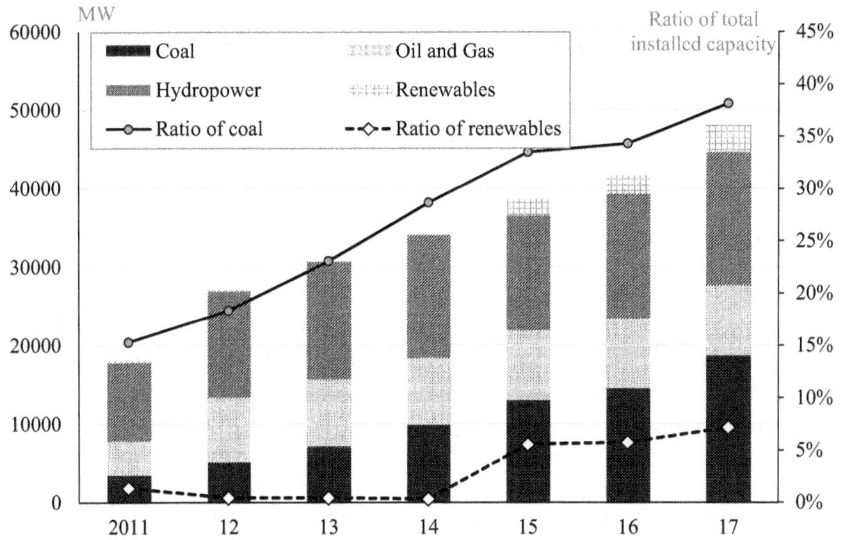

Figure 2.6a Energy mix in installed power generation capacity in Vietnam in 2011–2017.

Source: Compiled by the author based on the data from Vietnam Electricity (2012–2018).

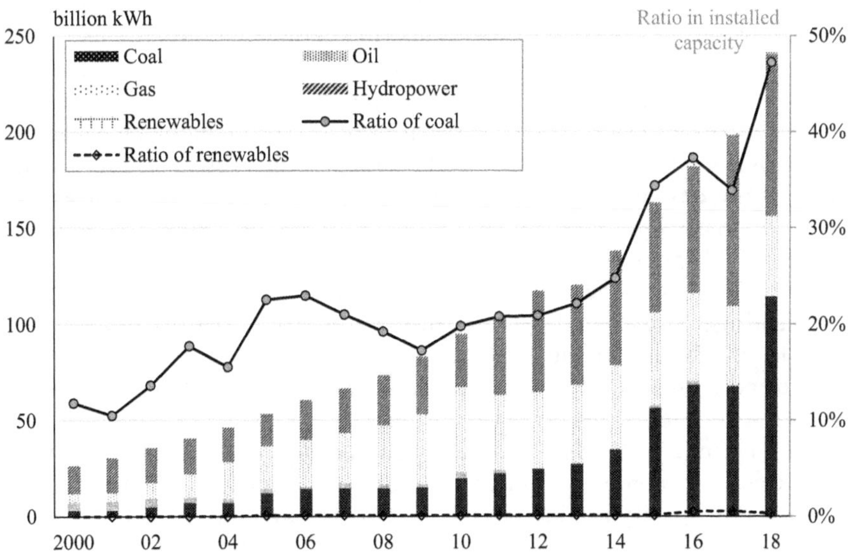

Figure 2.6b Energy mix in power generation in Vietnam in 2000–2018.

Source: Compiled by the author based on data from IEA (2021).

(Breu et al., 2019). Coupled with the geographical imbalance in demand and supply, insufficient financial capital for grid capacity development triggered solar curtailment (World Bank, 2019). Although the government lowered the feed-in tariff in 2019 and planned to replace the FiT with reverse auction (Government of Vietnam, 2020), inflexible updates under the Planning Law of 2019 delays the government's investments in grid capacity. Tightened public borrowing and abolishment of government guarantees make it difficult for the government to access international funding, further exacerbating the incompatibility between RES-E installed capacity and grid systems (Do et al., 2020).

5.2 Indonesia

Indonesia's electricity sector is characterized by the vertically integrated state-owned utility that is permitted monopolistic supply with a number of IPPs. It has four major transmission networks with limited interconnections within and across them.

To address interrelated challenges of insufficient generation causing frequent blackout, peaked oil production, increased energy subsidy squeezing fiscal resources for infrastructure development, and its induced demand growth in the early 2000s, the government released the Fast-Track Program (FTP-I) to increase installed capacity of 10,000 MW by coal power, which was perceived as a readily available, accessible, affordable, and less vulnerable source of energy source (Reshetova, 2019). In the process, the country has strengthened complementarities in the coal-based electricity supply system (Mori, 2020). Initially, the government provided full guarantee to the credit risk of the state-owned utility in engineering, procurement, and construction contracts. To change the unfavorable terms of conditions, it allows foreign shareholding of IPPs with electricity business licenses and accepts take-or-pay clauses in PPAs with IPPs to secure financial packages. It imposes a domestic market obligation regulation, designates low-quality coal as the design coal for coal power plants (Best, 2017), and invests in ports, roads, and railways for coal transport to secure stable coal supply at an affordable price.

These newly created complementarities deter the government from implementing policies and developing institutions for a large-scale integration of RES-E, despite having large potential that could be used for pumped hydro energy storage (Blakers et al., 2018). The accelerated increase in coal power generation triggers power surplus, especially in the Java-Bali grid system (Kennedy, 2018). The take-or-pay clauses in PPAs may force the state electricity company to pay for unnecessary electricity when additional generation capacity is added in the system. The amount of such payments becomes significant once RES-E becomes cheaper than coal power generation. This poses the risk of the state-owned utility becoming incapable of investing in grid management and rationalization of electricity supply across regions (Burke et al., 2019). To save the distress of the state-owned utility, the government implemented a series of policy measures that would make renewable investments unviable (Setyowati, 2020) and the renewable target in the electricity generation in the 2014 National Energy Plan unachievable. These measures include a cap of the RES-E purchase price at 85% of the state-owned utility's average local generation cost; reduction of the price of exports from solar power generators to 65% of the company's applicable retail price (Hamdi, 2019); and replacement of a FiT with reverse auctions under a build-own-operate-transfer basis that impose takeover risks of the land for utility-scale solar power generation (Burke et al., 2019). However, neither the government nor the state-owned utility has enhanced grid capacity.

As a result, installed capacity of coal power increased by 10GW in 2011 and exceeded 30GW in 2019, while that of RES-E did so by 1.5GW in 2013 and has slightly increased since then (Figure 2.7a). Accordingly, coal accounts for a greater portion in electricity generation, exceeding 60% in 2017, replacing oil, while RES-E remains a minor portion (Figure 2.7b).

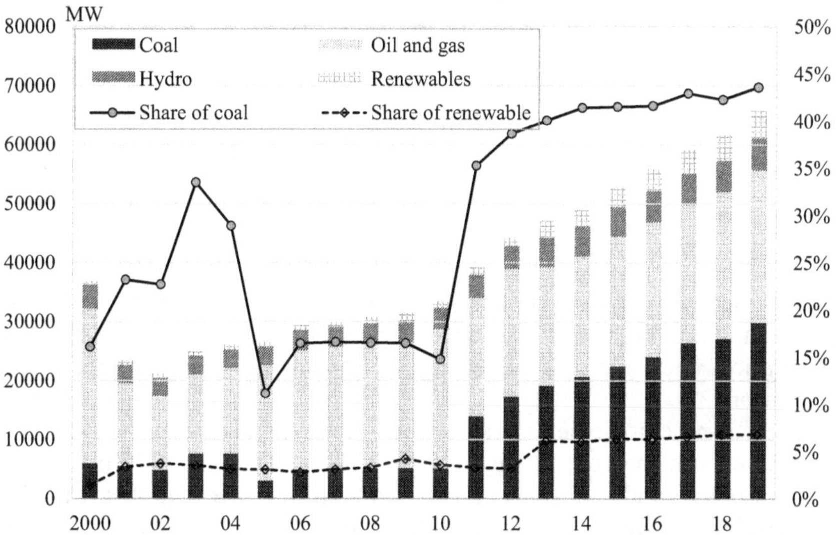

Figure 2.7a Energy mix in installed power generation capacity in Indonesia in 2000–2019.

Note:

1 Renewable includes large, mini and micro hydropower, geothermal, wind, solar PV, and biomass power.

2 In Indonesia, PLN and Ministry of Energy and Mineral Resources publish statistical yearbook of electricity. However, there are slight discrepancies between them, and both update a series of data in later years, which makes it difficult to analyze with consistent data. In addition, PLN annual reports are accessible only in 2014–2018, which is narrower than the scope of this paper. For these reasons, this paper takes the data from the Ministry of Energy and Mineral Resources because it provides disaggregated data for many years, which enables to trace source of energy.

Source: Compiled by the author based on the data from Kementerian Energi dan Sumber Daya Mineral.

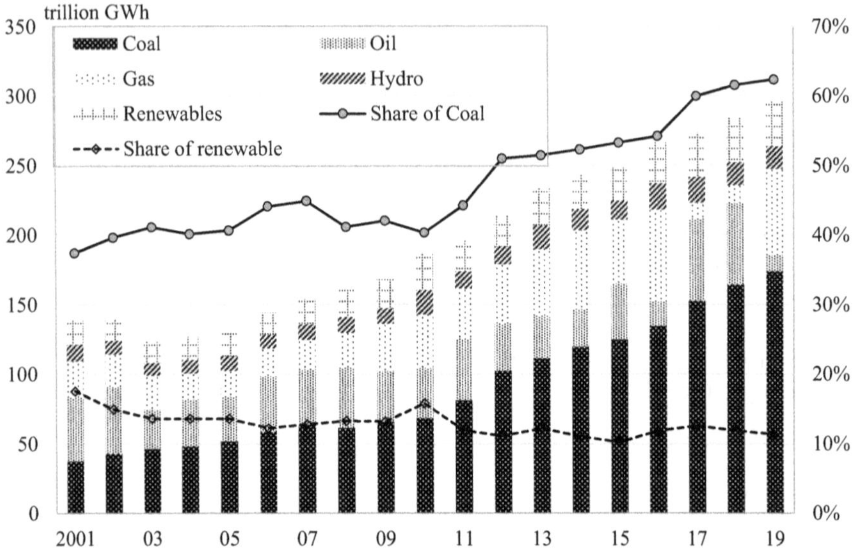

Figure 2.7b Energy mix in power generation in Indonesia in 2001–2019.
Source: Compiled by the author based on the data from Kementerian Energi dan Sumber Daya Mineral.

5.3 India

India's electricity system is characterized by the strong complementarities within and across the coal-based electricity system, rapid growth in RES-E generation, and a nationwide network of transmission lines with inefficient operation.

The strong complementarities within the coal-based electricity system originate from the coal linkage system among domestic coal mining, national railway, and coal power plants. To guarantee fuel supply for the life of coal power plants and complementary capital investments in coalmining, the State Energy Board specifies that coalmining supplies coal to a coal power plant through a fuel supply agreement (Chandra, 2011) and designates national railways for transportation. On top of the system, a large number of coal powers have concluded long-term PPAs with state utilities responsible for distribution and sales, despite the creation of day-ahead and real-time electricity delivery markets. New power plants are designed to accept domestically produced, low-quality coal that generates heavy air pollution and fierce protests against new power plants. Despite this, the country has developed technological capabilities for engineering the latest plants with fewer emissions (Mukherjee and Chakraborty, 2015).

The complementarities have been entrenched by large vested interests. Coal provides not only benefits for energy security but also jobs for a massive number of the labor force, and royalty revenues for most of the central and eastern region states, becoming a source of political support (Vishwanathan et al., 2018). Fossil fuel and on-grid electricity subsidies (Burke et al., 2019) and cross-subsidy to railway passengers (Carl, 2015) are also entrenched to satisfy persistent demands for social gains (Kale et al., 2018). These entrenched complementarities have created large, vested interests, constraining policymakers and state utilities from diverting these subsidies for renovation and upgrade of the deteriorated transmission and distribution networks (Kale et al., 2018).

As a result, the gap between demand and supply rose to 10% in 2009–2010 (Ministry of Power, 2020). The serious gap directed the government to boost RES-E as a politically sustainable option to increase installed capacity. The government has developed institutions and implemented policies favorable for RES-E development. They include establishment and upgrade of dedicated ministry, financial institutions, and research institutes for renewable energy; the Electricity Act 2003 that ensured complete participation of private producers; national wind and solar targets and renewable purchase obligation targets; a FiT and "reserve" power package, and its replacement with reverse auctions to take advantage of technological improvements and economies of scale in global solar PV production; development and operation of solar parks coupled with long-term PPAs to winning bidders (Chawla et al., 2018); and handling environmental impact assessments (EIA) and other administrative procedures as a part of auctions (Dobrotkova et al., 2018) that addressed uncertainties over land access, transmission connections, and regulations. Following Gujarat and Rajasthan, many states implemented their own complementary solar policies (Tarai and Kale, 2018). All of these institutional supports reduce renewable power pricing and financial costs, making access to bank loans easier (Thapar et al., 2018) and incentivize investments in RES-E projects. The repowering policy in 2016 upgraded engineering complementarity by mandating the replacement of aging wind turbines with more modern and powerful units (Kumar and Majid, 2020).

In addition, national grid interconnectivity has been improved under the One Nation-One Grid initiative and a Green Energy Corridor scheme. Utility-scale solar and wind developers are allowed to waive payment of interstate transmission charges (Dibyanshu and Rastogi, 2020). These elements of infrastructural complementarity enable developers to deploy solar and wind power in high-resource locations, and the electricity system to gain more flexibility.

Capitalizing on these favorable institutional and infrastructural environments, developers with access to finance in favorable terms win bids in competitive renewable energy auctions, dominating the RES-E supply (Dutt et al., 2019). As a result, new solar and new wind installations exceeded new coal installations in 2017, and new solar installations exceeded new wind installations in 2019 (Figure 2.8a). The ratio of solar and wind generation

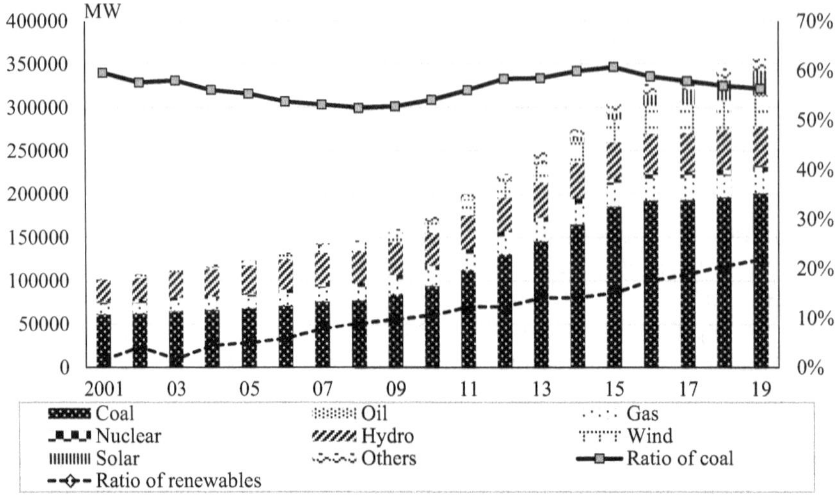

Figure 2.8a Energy mix in installed power generation capacity in India in 2001–2019.
Source: Compiled by the author based on data from Ministry of Power, *Annual Report,* (from 2001–2002 to 2018–2019), https://powermin.nic.in/en/content/annual-reports-year-wise-ministry#/, accessed on 10 October 2020.

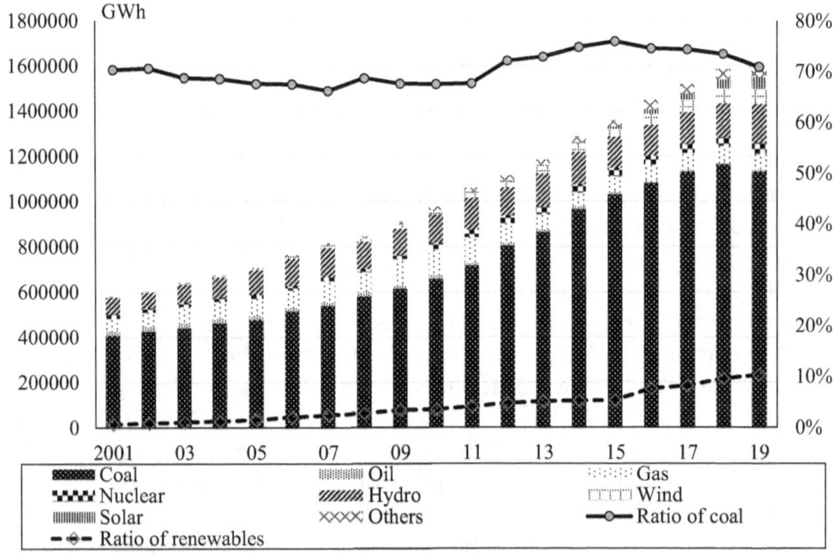

Figure 2.8b Energy mix in power generation in India in 2001–2019.
Source: Compiled by the author based on the data from IEA (2021).

exceeded 10% in 2019, filling the demand–supply gap and making that of coal power hit its peak in 2015 (Figure 2.8b). However, reverse auctions have intensified market concentrations to top developers who can undercut the competition consistently through foreign private equity investments, lower cost foreign debt, balance-sheet strength, or by virtue of being state-owned enterprises. Market uncertainties around the impact of the goods and services tax (GST) and the imposition of trade duties on imported solar modules, and the related impact on tendered projects under construction, reduce the number of developers sanctioning new capacity, further increasing market concentration (Chawla et al., 2018).

5.4 Japan

The Japanese electricity supply system is featured by a vertically integrated, centralized, nuclear, and liquidated natural gas-based one. Ten private electric power companies are permitted regionally monopolistic electricity supply in exchange for responsibility for security of supply and under the price regulations. The country has a nationwide network of transmission lines but is not sufficiently interconnected across their region service areas due to the differences in standard frequency and limited transmission capacity between the islands.

The centralized regionally monopolistic supply system has been reinforced since the 1970s when the oil crises pushed the Liberal-Democratic Party, the party in government for most of the period after World War II, and the ministry in charge, as well as the private electric power companies, to choose nuclear power as an alternative to oil, and to diversify sources of energy. To quell local protests, the government set up a dedicated earmarked fund to subsidize local governments that accepted the location of new nuclear power plants. To secure profit from nuclear business, it developed a nuclear fuel cycle and burdened backend costs, and limited competition among these private electric power companies by deferring investments in grid interconnectivity, leaving the choke points of the nationwide grid system unaddressed. It also encouraged Japanese manufacturers to obtain licenses on reactor engineering and manufacturing in order to enhance technological capabilities, and research institutes to develop technologies (Yamaoka, 2015).

The Party, the ministry, the electric power companies, and reactor manufacturers organized the pro-nuclear coalition, increasing spending for propaganda to tame the media and populace (Honma, 2016), and capitalized on the Kyoto Protocol to justify nuclear power (Mori, 2019). While the country had the largest capacity for solar PV manufacturing in the late 1990s, the coalitions propped up pressures against wider deployment of off-grid rooftop PVs, preventing solar PV manufacturers from taking advantage of scale economy to enhance market competitiveness.

The Fukushima nuclear disaster, coupled with the global financial crisis in 2008–2009, opened a window of opportunity for RES-E to emerge. Nuclear power lost credibility and suspended operations until safety was proved against the more stringent safety regulations, and until the government committee, local governments, and residents living nearby had been convinced to recommission the plants. To reconcile satisfying electricity demand and more stringent climate targets, the government's 2014 Strategic Energy Plan called for RES-E to account for 22%–24% of electricity generation by 2030. The incumbent electric power companies were legally unbundled and the retail market was liberalized to increase competition in generation and distribution. As a result, renewable investments were boosted, and RES-E accounted for 6% in installed capacity and 9% in total electricity generation in 2018 (Figures 2.9a and 2.9b).

However, the country has left the restructuring of complementarities for larger integration of RES-E unaddressed. The levelized cost of wind and solar power remains less competitive due to higher cost of invertor and installation required to satisfy Japanese consumers' high demand for reliability (IRENA, 2020), a lack of clearly defined land use regulations, and unclear

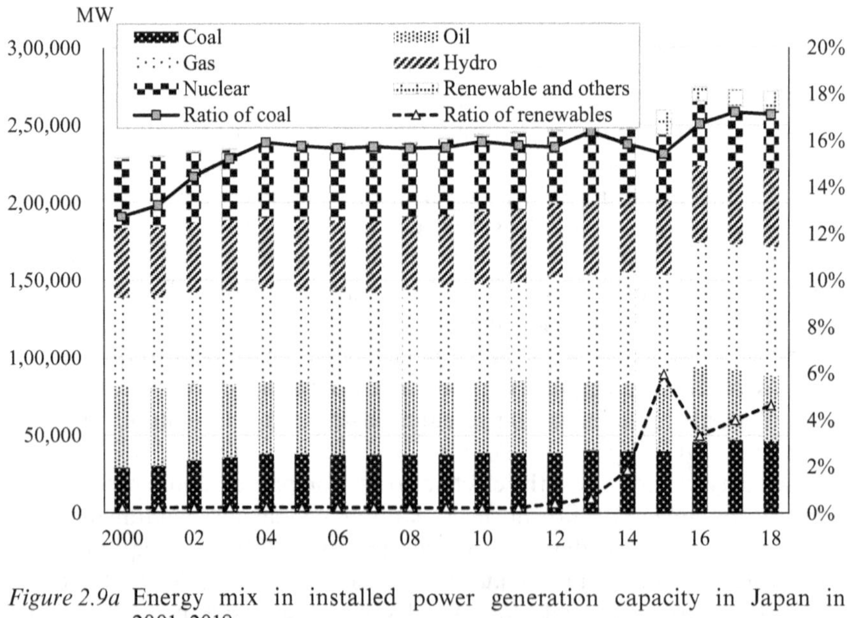

Figure 2.9a Energy mix in installed power generation capacity in Japan in 2001–2018.

Note: There is an inconsistency in dataset between the year 2015 and 2016 due to the difference in the coverage of the original database that the source refers to.

Source: Compiled by the author based on data from Federation of Electric Power Companies of Japan (2019).

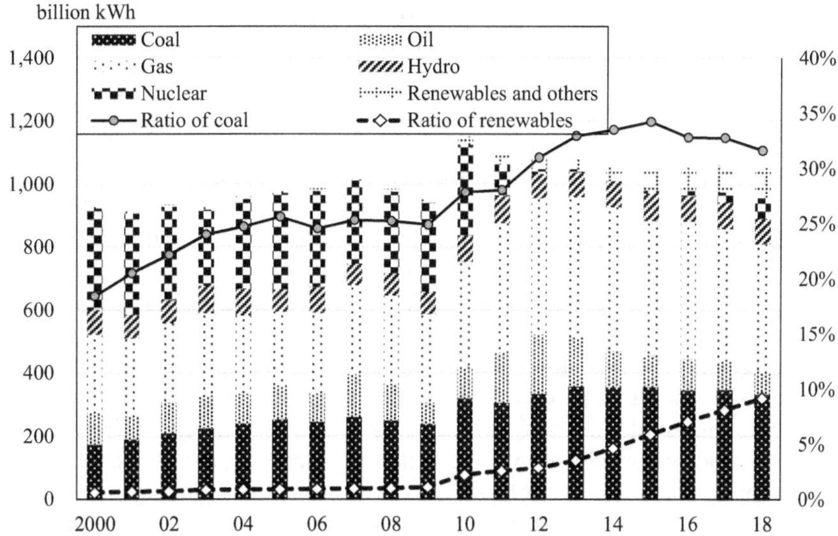

Figure 2.9b Energy mix in power generation in Japan in 2001–2018.
Source: Compiled by the author based on data from Agency for Natural Resources and Energy Japan (2020).

administrative and EIA procedures (Maruyama, 2014), and deference to the incumbent electric power companies for investments in grid capacity and interconnections. These have caused solar curtailment, increased risk of renewable investments, and increased grid access costs. The legally backed priority grid access for the incumbent electricity power companies, and the government's endorsement of their solar curtailment without compensation, further increased risks of investment and grid access costs for RES-E IPPs. The dominance of the incumbent electricity power companies both in the generation and retail market, and insufficient information disclosure collapsed the electricity market in times of emergency, thus disabling independent electricity suppliers, including RES-E producers, from securing stable supply in January 2021 (Hara, 2021). Conversely, incumbent electric power companies are favored in the market design: the capacity remuneration mechanism has been so generous that they can use their obsolete and inefficient fossil fuel power as reserve capacity.

6 Discussion

The above-mentioned country case studies indicate three major challenges in the transition from fossil fuel-intensive, vertically integrated, and hierarchical and centrally controlled electricity supply system toward a capital-intensive, distributed, and smart grid-based electricity system that can achieve a large-scale integration of RES-E.

The first challenge is to tame the incumbent influential regime actors. They are likely to be hit hardest and to lose vested interests, and thus use ample resources to oppose restructuring. In particular, coal and nuclear power generators, coalminers, and dedicated transport companies whose assets have long remaining economic life will protest most fiercely to avoid their assets becoming stranded. In case they are vertically integrated electric power suppliers and dominant in supply, they are likely to work with the government to keep institutional and infrastructural complementarities favoring fossil fuel and nuclear power. These complementarities include investment and consumption subsidies; conservative RES-E generation and renewable purchase obligation targets; priority grid access under utility's monopolistic supply (Yamaka, 2018); curtailment without compensation (Agency for Natural Resources and energy, 2018); and deterred investments in grid capacity and interconnectivity of transmission networks. Some utilities may not address timeliness and reliability of payments for power purchase by state utilities (Chawla et al., 2018), imposing higher investment risks to RES-E generators than coal and gas power providers. Perceiving stagnant future demand, they become reluctant to renovate fossil fuel-based power plants, leaving severe environmental pollution unaddressed.

The second challenge is to reconcile three compelling narratives: "energy for development," that privileges energy as critical to economic growth and long-term strategic security; "energy for industrial development," that fosters the renewable energy industry as a new engine of industrial development; and "energy for all," that prioritizes the role of energy for basic development and ending poverty (Mohan and Topp, 2018; Mori, 2018a). Reverse and competitive auctions have shown effectiveness in the rapid reduction of LCOE and deployment of wind and solar power. However, it can drive out domestic manufacturers and increase international dependence. Further decrease in capital cost and improvements in operation and maintenance can be hardly anticipated in case international suppliers are cartelized and a lack of domestic capacity for commercially deployed renewable energy technology and inadequate built-up capacity are kept unaddressed (Kumar and Majid, 2020). On the other hand, a high local content requirement, limited foreign ownership, and users' preferences for reliable RES generation systems hike the system cost, retarding uptake of RES-E (PwC, 2018) or triggering repercussions from exporting countries (Miles, 2019). A high FiT and priority on utility scale and on-grid RES-E may reconcile the tradeoff but can reduce financial options for small and distributed renewable energy initiatives (Setyowani, 2021). Even such small and distributed initiatives can generate energy injustice by passing through the incremental costs to those consumers who do not have access to the initiatives.

The final challenge is high uncertainty about effectiveness, efficiency, and equity of a capital-intensive, distributed, and network-based electricity system, and those in a transition process. Although several countries such as Germany are going ahead in the transition, they have not yet proved the arrangements and elements of complementarities that ensure effectiveness, efficiency, equity, and sustainability of the novel system. Nonetheless, the transition absolutely requires huge amounts of complementary investments, innovative organizational, financial, and institutional arrangements, and restructuring of elements of complementarities that have significant distributional implications.

International actors can accelerate and retard the restructuring. China has provided subsidized financial capital, engineering, manufacturing, and organizational capabilities for coal power in a package, strengthening complementarities in a coal power-based electricity system (Burke et al., 2019; Mori, 2020). International wind and solar power manufacturers, especially Chinese ones, have played a critical role in declining system costs for RES-E.

7 Conclusions

The change in energy mix in electricity generation from fossil fuel to renewable energy is accompanied by a transformation of electricity systems from fossil fuel-intensive, centrally controlled toward capital-intensive, distributed, and network-based electricity systems. Achieving this transformation goes beyond addressing each type of lock-in separately to restructuring the interdependence of generation and transmission subsystems and fostering collaboration among key stakeholders.

Against this backdrop, this chapter proposes restructuring of elements of complementarities within and across an electricity system as an analytical framework, exploring how Asian countries have struggled with the restructuring, taking Vietnam, Indonesia, India, and Japan as cases. We find that all four case study countries have struggled with the three challenges of resistance from influential incumbent regime actors, compelling narratives of "energy for development," "energy for industrial development," and "energy for all," and unclear and uncertain benefits from the transformation. Coupled with favorable institutions and infrastructure, and easier access to financial capital, engineering, manufacturing, and organizational capabilities for coal power globally, and less uncertainty in coal power technologies, these challenges can incentivize incumbent regime actors to retard the restructuring, causing renewable curtailment and reducing renewable investments. This is especially the case when international actors support to reinforce the incumbent regime.

It is worth investigating how domestic and foreign actors interact to accelerate or retard the restructuring through investments and trade, and meet the compelling quests for energy security, industrial development, energy justice, and climate requirements.

References

Abrishambaf, O., Lezama, F., Faria, P., Vale, Z., 2019. Towards transactive energy systems: An analysis on current trends, *Energy Strategy Rev.* 26, 100418, https://doi.org/10.1016/j.esr.2019.100418.

Agency for Natural Resources and energy, 2018. Renewable curtailment for a large-scale integration of RES-E, (in Japanese), https://www.enecho.meti.go.jp/about/special/johoteikyo/kyushu_syuturyokuseigyo.html/, [accessed 25 January 2021].

Aguirre, M., Ibikunle, G., 2014. Determinants of renewable energy growth: A global sample analysis, *Energy Policy* 69, 374–384, https://doi.org/10.1016/j.enpol.2014.02.036.

Auer, H., Haas, R., 2016. On integrating large shares of variable renewables into the electricity system, *Energy* 115, 1592–1601, https://doi.org/10.1016/j.energy.2016.05.067.

Baker, L., Newell, P., Phillips, J., 2014. The political economy of energy transitions: The case of South Africa, *New Polit. Econ.* 19(6), 791–818, https://doi.org/10.1080/13563467.2013.849674.

Bauknecht, D., Andersen, A.D., Dunne, K.T., 2020. Challenges for electricity network governance in whole system change: Insights from energy transition in Norway, *Environ. Innov. Soc. Trans.* 37, 318–331, https://doi.org/10.1016/j.eist.2020.09.004

Beardsworth, J.J. Jr., Schmidt, J.A., 2014. Resource financed infrastructure: Origins and issues, In: Halland, H., J. Beardsworth, B. Land, and J. Schmidt, *Resource Financed Infrastructure: A Discussion on a New Form of Infrastructure Financing*, The World Bank: Washington DC, 11–68, http://dx.doi.org/10.1596/978-1-4648-0239-3.

Best, R., 2017. Switching towards coal or renewable energy? The effects of financial capital on energy transitions, *Energy Econ.* 63, 75–83, http://dx.doi.org/10.1016/j.eneco.2017.01.019.

Bhagwat, P.C., Marcheselli, A., Richstein, J.C., Chappin, E.J.L., De Vries, L.J., 2017. An analysis of a forward capacity market with long-term contracts, *Energy Policy* 111, 255–267, http://dx.doi.org/10.1016/j.enpol.2017.09.037.

Blakers, A., Stocks, M., Lu, B., Cheng C., Nadolny, A., 2018. Global pumped hydro atlas. http://re100.eng.anu.edu.au/global/index.php/, [accessed 9 February, 2021].

Breu, M., Castellano, A., Frankel, D., Rogers, M., 2019. Exploring an alternative pathway for Vietnam's energy future, https://www.mckinsey.com/featured-insights/asia-pacific/exploring-an-alternative-pathway-for-vietnams-energy-future/, [accessed 5 February, 2021].

Bublitz, A., Keles, D., Zimmermann, F., Fraunholz, C., Fichtner, W., 2019. A survey on electricity market design: Insights from theory and real-world implementations of capacity remuneration mechanisms, *Energy Econ.* 80, 1059–1078, https://doi.org/10.1016/j.eneco.2019.01.030.

Burger, S., Chaves-Ávila, J.P., Batlle, C., Pérez-Arriaga, I.J., 2017. A review of the value of aggregators in electricity systems, *Renew. Sust. Energ. Rev.* 77, 395–405, https://doi.org/10.1016/j.rser.2017.04.014.

Burgholzer, B., Auer, H., 2016. Cost/benefit analysis of transmission grid expansion to enable further integration of renewable electricity generation in Austria, *Renew. Energy* 97, 189–196, https://doi.org/10.1016/j.renene.2016.05.073.

Burke, P.J., Widnyana, J., Anjum, Z., Aisbett, E., Resosudarmo, B., Baldwin, K.G.H., 2019. Overcoming barriers to solar and wind energy adoption in two

Asian giants: India and Indonesia, *Energy Policy* 132, 1216–1228, https://doi.org/10.1016/j.enpol.2019.05.055.

Camarinha-Matos, L.M., 2016. Collaborative smart grids – a survey on trends, *Renew. Sustain. Energy Rev.* 65, 283–294, https://doi.org/10.1016/j.rser.2016.06.093.

Carl, J., 2015. The causes and implications of India's coal production shortfall, In: Thurber, M.C. and R.K. Morse (eds.) *The Global Coal Market: Supplying the Major Fuel for Emerging Economies*, Cambridge University Press, Cambridge, 294–373.

Chandra, R., 2011. India's coal-ed streak, Center for the Advanced Study of India, University of Pennsylvania, https://casi.sas.upenn.edu/iit/rohitchandra/, [accessed 28 November 2019].

Chawla, K., Waldron, M., Dutt, A., Aggarwal, M., Toril, A., Nobuoka, Y., 2018. *Clean Energy Trends: Evolving Investment Landscape for Grid-Connected Renewable Energy Projects in India.* New Delhi: Council on Energy, Environment and Water, https://www.ceew.in/sites/default/files/CEEW-IEA-Clean-Energy-Investment-Trends-Report-PDF-30Jul18.pdf/, [accessed 3 February 2021].

Colak, I., Sagiroglu, S., Fulli, G., Yesilbudak, M., Covrig, C.F., 2016. A survey on the critical issues in smart grid technologies, *Renew. Sustain. Energy Rev.* 54, 396–405, https://doi.org/10.1016/j.rser.2015.10.036.

Cramton, P., Ockenfels, A., 2012. Economics and design of capacity markets for the power sector. Zeitschrift für Energiewirtschaft 36, 113–134, https://doi.org/10.1007/s12398-012-0084-2.

Dibyanshu, Rastogi, S., 2020. India: Waiver of inter-state transmission charges and losses (25 August 2020), Khaitan & Co, https://www.mondaq.com/india/renewables/979040/waiver-of-inter-state-transmission-charges-and-losses/, [accessed 3 February 2021].

Do, T.N., Burke, P.J., Baldwin, K.G.H., Nguyen, C.T., 2020. Underlying drivers and barriers for solar photovoltaics diffusion: The case of Vietnam, *Energy Policy* 144, 111561, https://doi.org/10.1016/j.enpol.2020.111561.

Dobrotkova, Z., Surana, K., Audinet, P., 2018. The price of solar energy: Comparing competitive auctions for utility-scale solar PV in developing countries, *Energy Policy* 118, 133–148, https://doi.org/10.1016/j.enpol.2018.03.036.

Dutt, A., Arboleya, L., Mahadevan, B., 2019. *Clean Energy Investment Trends: Evolving Risk Perceptions for India's Grid-Connected Renewable Energy Projects.* New Delhi; Paris: Council on Energy, Environment and Water; International Energy Agency, https://www.ceew.in/sites/default/files/CEEW-Clean-Energy-Investment-Trends-2019.pdf/, [accessed 3 February 2021].

Ela, E., Milligan, M., Bloom, A., Botterud, A., Townsend, A., Levinc, T., Frew, B.A., 2016. Wholesale electricity market design with increasing levels of renewable generation: Incentivizing flexibility in system operations, *The Electricity J.* 29, 51–60, http://dx.doi.org/10.1016/j.tej.2016.05.001.

Federation of Electric Power Companies of Japan, 2019, *FEPC Inforbase 2019*, https://www.fepc.or.jp/library/data/infobase/pdf/infobase2019.pdf, [accessed 24 October 2020].

George, A.L., Bennett, A., 2004. *Case Studies and Theory Development in the Social Sciences*, MIT Press, Cambridge.

Government of Vietnam, 2020. Decision 13/2020/QD-TTg on Mechanism for Encouragement of the Development of Solar Power in Vietnam, Government of Vietnam, Hanoi, Vietnam.

Gulagi, A., Bogdanov, D., Breyer, C., 2018. The role of storage technologies in energy transition pathways towards achieving a fully sustainable energy system for India, *J. Energy Storage* 17, 525–539, https://doi.org/10.1016/j.est.2017.11.012.

Hamdi, E., 2019. Indonesia's solar policies: designed to fail? IEEFA report, https://ieefa.org/wp-content/uploads/2019/02/Indonesias-Solar-Policies_February-2019.pdf/, [accessed 28 January 2021].

Hansen, E.G., Lüdeke-Freund, F., Quan, X.I., West, J., 2019. Cross-national complementarity of technology push, demand pull, and manufacturing push policies: The case of photovoltaics, *IEEE T Eng. Manage.* 66:3, 381–397, https://doi.org/10.1109/TEM.2018.2833878.

Hara, E. 2021. Japan's crisis after the "confusion in the electricity market," *JB Press* (6 February 2021), (in Japanese), https://jbpress.ismedia.jp/articles/-/63972/, [accessed 6 February 2021].

Haselip J., Desgain, D., Mackenzie, G., 2013. Financing energy SMEs in Ghana and Senegal: Outcomes, barriers and prospects, *Energy Policy* 65, 369–376, https://doi.org/10.1016/j.enpol.2013.10.013.

Haskel, J., Westlake, S., 2018. *Capitalism without Capital: The Rise of the Intangible Economy*, Princeton University Press, Princeton.

Haukkala, T., Holttinen, H., Kiviluoma, J., Mori, A., Penttinen, S.L., Kilpeläinen, S., Talus, K., Aalto, P., 2021. How to accelerate renewable energy production? In: Aalto P. (ed.) *Electrification: Accelerating the Energy Transition*, Academic Press and Elservier, 79–93, https://doi.org/10.1016/B978-0-12-822143-3.00002-0.

Hirth, L., Ueckerdt, F., Edenhofer, O., 2015. Integration costs revisited—An economic framework for wind and solar variability, *Renew. Energy* 74, 925–939, https://doi.org/10.1016/j.renene.2014.08.065.

Honma, R. 2016. *Nuclear Power Propaganda*, Iwanami Shinsho, Tokyo (in Japanese).

International Energy Agency (IEA), 2013. *Redrawing the Energy-Climate Map*, https://webstore.iea.org/download/direct/480/, [accessed 25 January 2021].

IEA, 2019. *Southeast Asia Energy Outlook 2019*/, https://www.iea.org/reports/southeast-asia-energy-outlook-2019, [accessed 26 September 2020].

IEA, 2021. *IEA Data and Statistics*, https://www.iea.org/data-and-statistics/data-tables?country=CHINAREG&energy=Electricity&year=2019/, [accessed 8 January 2021].

International Hydropower Association, 2018. *2018 Hydropower Status Report: Sector Trends and Insights*, https://hydropower-assets.s3.eu-west-2.amazonaws.com/publications-docs/iha_2018_hydropower_status_report_4.pdf/, [accessed 9 January 2021].

International Hydropower Association, 2019. *2019 Hydropower Status Report: Sector Trends and Insights*, https://hydropower-assets.s3.eu-west-2.amazonaws.com/publications-docs/2019_hydropower_status_report_0.pdf/, [accessed 9 January 2021].

International Hydropower Association, 2020. *2020 Hydropower Status Report: Sector Trends and Insights*, https://hydropower-assets.s3.eu-west-2.amazonaws.com/publications-docs/2020_hydropower_status_report.pdf/, [accessed 9 January 2021].

IRENA, 2020. *Renewable Power Generation Costs in 2019*, International Renewable Energy Agency, Abu Dhabi, https://www.irena.org/-/media/Files/IRENA/Agency/Publication/2020/Jun/IRENA_Power_Generation_Costs_2019.pdf/, [accessed 14 January 2021].

Jordan, A., Matt, E., 2014. Designing policies that intentionally stick: Policy feedback in a changing climate, *Policy Science* 47, 227–247, https://doi.org/10.1007/s11077-014-9201-x.

Kale, S.S., Dubash, N.K., Bharvirkar, R., 2018. Introduction: A framework for mapping power. In: Dubash, N.K., Kale, S.S., Bharvirkar R. (eds.) *Mapping Power: The Political Economy of Electricity in India's States*, Oxford University Press, Oxford, 1–27.

Kementerian Energi dan Sumber Daya Mineral, *Statistik Ketenagalistrikan Dan Energi, Tahun 2005, 2009, 2012, 2013, 2014 2015, 2016, 2017, 2018, 2019*, Jakarta, http://gatrik.esdm.go.id/frontend/download_index/?kode_category=statistik/ [accessed 10 February 2021].

Kennedy, S.F., 2018. Indonesia's energy transition and its contradictions: Emerging geographies of energy and finance, *Energy Res. Soc. Sci.* 41, 230–237, https://doi.org/ 10.1016/j.erss.2018.04.023.

Kubota, H., Hondo, H., Hienuki, S., Kaieda, H., 2013. Determining barriers to developing geothermal power generation in Japan: Societal acceptance by stakeholders involved in hot springs, *Energy Policy* 61, 1079–1087, https://doi.org/10.1016/j.enpol.2013.05.084

Kumar, C.R.J., Majid, M.A., 2020. Renewable energy for sustainable development in India: Current status, future prospects, challenges, employment, and investment opportunities, *Energy Sustain. Soc.* 10:2, https://doi.org/10.1186/s13705-019-0232-1.

Lehmann, P., Brandt, R., Gawel, E., Heim, S., Korte, K., Löschel, A., Massier, P., Reeg, M., Schober, D., Wassermann, S., 2015. Capacity payments to secure electricity supply? On the future of Germany's power market design, *Energy, Sustain. Soc.* 5:15, 1–7, https://doi.org/10.1186/s13705-015-0039-7.

Lipari, G., Rosario, G.D., Corchero, C., Ponci, F., Monti, A., 2018. A real-time commercial aggregator for distributed energy resources flexibility management, *Sustain. Energy, Grids Netw.* 15, 63–75, https://doi.org/10.1016/j.segan.2017.07.002.

Lockwood, M., Mitchell, C., Hoggett, R., 2019. Unpacking 'regime resistance' in low-carbon transitions: The case of the British Capacity Market, *Energy Res. Soc. Sci.* 58, 101278, https://doi.org/10.1016/j.erss.2019.101278.

Luong, P.J., Weinthal, E., 2010. *Oil is not a Curse: Ownership Structure and Institutions in Soviet Successor States*, Cambridge University Press, Cambridge.

Madrigal, M., Stoft, S., 2012. *Transmission Expansion for Renewable Energy Scale-Up: Emerging Lessons and Recommendations*, A World Bank Study. World Bank, Washington, DC, http://hdl.handle.net/10986/9375/, [accessed 14 January 2021].

Markard, J., Hoffmann, V.H., 2016. Analysis of complementarities: Framework and examples from the energy transition, *Technol. Forecast. Soc. Change* 111, 63–75, http://dx.doi.org/10.1016/j.techfore.2016.06.008.

Markard, J., Wirth, S., Truffer, B., 2016. Institutional dynamics and technology legitimacy – A framework and a case study on biogas technology, *Res. Policy* 45, 330–344, https://doi.org/10.1016/j.respol.2015.10.009.

Maruyama, Y. 2014. *Socialization of Renewable Energy: Revisiting Renewable Energy from Social Acceptance*, Yuhikaku: Tokyo (in Japanese).

Meadowcroft, J., 2011. Engaging with the politics of sustainability transitions, *Environ. Innov. Soc. Trans* 1(1), 70–75, https://doi.org/10.1016/j.eist.2011.02.003.

Miles, T., 2019. India wins U.S. solar case at WTO but impact disputed, (28 June 2019), https://www.reuters.com/article/us-usa-trade-india-wto-idUSKCN1TS2B0/, [accessed 2 February 2021].

Ministry of Power, 2020. Power Sector at a Glance ALL INDIA, https://powermin.nic.in/en/content/power-sector-glance-all-india/, [accessed 3 February 2021].

Mohan, A., Topp, K., 2018. India's energy future: Contested narratives of change, *Energy Res. Soc. Sci.* 44, 75–82, https://doi.org/10.1016/j.erss.2018.04.040.

Mori, A., 2018a. Climate-energy policy: Domestic policy process, outcome and impacts. In: Mori, A. (ed.) *China's Climate-Energy Policy: Domestic and International Impacts*, Routledge, Abingdon, 3–19, https://doi.org/10.4324/9781351037587-1.

Mori, A., 2018b. Impact of the China-induced coal boom in Indonesia: A resource governance perspective. In: Mori, A. (ed.) *China's Climate-Energy Policy: Domestic and International Impacts*, Routledge, Abingdon, 167–197.

Mori, A., 2018c. Sociotechnical and political economy perspectives in the Chinese energy transition, *Energy Res. Soc. Sci.* 35, 29–36, https://doi.org/10.1016/j.erss.2017.10.04.

Mori, A., Dong. L., 2018. Impact of the resource boom in the 2000s on Asian-Pacific energy exporting countries. In: Mori, A. (ed.) *China's Climate-Energy Policy: Domestic and International Impacts*, Routledge, Abingdon, 123–153, https://doi.org/10.4324/9781351037587-8.

Mori, A., 2019. Temporal dynamics of infrasystem transition: The Case of Electricity System Transition in Japan, *Technol. Forecast. Soc. Change* 145, 186–194, https://doi.org/10.1016/j.techfore.2017.05.00.

Mori, A., 2020, Foreign actors, faster transitions? Co-evolution of complementarities, perspectives and sociotechnical systems in the case of Indonesia's electricity supply system, *Energy Res. Soc. Sci.* 69, 101594, https://doi.org/10.1016/j.erss.2020.101594.

Mukherjee, S., Chakraborty, D., 2015. Walking a thin line between growth and development concerns? Environmental governance in India. In: Mukherjee, S. and D. Chakraborty (eds.) *Environmental Challenges and Governance: Diverse Perspectives from Asia*. Routledge, Abingdon, 49–74.

Neefjes, K., Dang, T.T.H., 2017. Towards a socially just energy transition in Vietnam, http://library.fes.de/pdf-files/bueros/vietnam/13684.pdf/, [accessed 4 February 2021].

Negro, S.O., F. Alkemade, M.P. Hekkert, 2012. Why does renewable energy diffuse so slowly? A review of innovation system problems, *Renew. Sust. Energ. Rev.* 16, 3836–3846, https://doi.org/10.1016/j.rser.2012.03.043.

Neuhoff, K, Barquin, J., Bialek, J.W., Boyd, R., Dent, C.J., Echavarren, F., Grau, T., von Hirschhausen, C., Hobbs, B.F., Kunz, F., Nabe, C., 2013. Renewable electric energy integration: Quantifying the value of design of markets for international transmission capacity, *Energy Econ.* 40, 760–772, https://doi.org/10.1016/j.eneco.2013.09.004.

Newbery, D., Pollitt, M.G., Ritz, R.A., Strielkowski, W., 2018. Market design for a high-renewables European electricity system, *Renew. Sustain. Energy Rev.* 91, 695–707, https://doi.org/10.1016/j.rser.2018.04.025.

Nguyen, L., Kinnucan, H.W., 2019. The US solar panel anti-dumping duties versus uniform tariff, *Energy Policy* 127, 523–532, https://doi.org/10.1016/j.enpol.2018.11.048

Nuclear Energy Agency, 2011. Technical and Economic Aspects of Load Following with Nuclear Power Plants, OECD, Paris, https://www.oecd-nea.org/ndd/reports/2011/load-following-npp.pdf/, [accessed 13 January 2021].

Ode, K.A., Wadin, J.L., 2019. Business model translation-The case of spreading a business model for solar energy, *Renew. Energy* 133, 23–31, https://doi.org/10.1016/j.renene.2018.09.036.

PwC. 2018. *Power in Indonesia: Investment and Taxation Guide, November 2018, 6th edition*, https://www.pwc.com/id/en/publications/assets/eumpublications/utilities/power-guide-2018.pdf/, [accessed 6 April 2019].

REN21, 2018. *Renewables 2018 Global Status Report*, https://www.ren21.net/wp-content/uploads/2019/08/Full-Report-2018.pdf/, [accessed 9 February 2021].

REN21, 2020. *Renewables 2020 Global Status Report*, https://www.ren21.net/wp-content/uploads/2019/05/gsr_2020_full_report_en.pdf/, [accessed 9 February 2021].

Reshetova, E., 2019. Indonesia's energy transition: From oil to coal, *Georgetown J. Asian Affairs* Winter 2019, 18–24, http://hdl.handle.net/10822/1053160.

Rifkin, J. 2019. *The Green New Deal: Why the Fossil Fuel Civilization Will Collapse by 2028, and the Bold Economic Plan to Save Life on Earth*, St. Martins Press, London.

Schmidt, T.S., Matuo, T., Michaelowa, A., 2017. Renewable energy policy as an enabler of fossil fuel subsidy reform? Applying a socio-technical perspective to the cases of South Africa and Tunisia, *Global Environ. Chang*e 45, 99–110, http://dx.doi.org/10.1016/j.gloenvcha.2017.05.004.

Schwenen, S., 2015. Strategic bidding in multi-unit auctions with capacity constrained bidders: The New York capacity market, *RAND J. Econ*. 46:4, 730–750, https://doi.org/10.1111/1756-2171.12104.

Seto, K.C., Davis, S.J., Mitchell, R.B., Stokes, E.C., Unruh, G., Ürge-Vorsatz, D., 2016. Carbon lock-in: Types, causes, and policy implications, *Annu. Rev. Environ. Resour.* 41, 425–452, https://doi.org/ 10.1146/annurev-environ-110615-085934.

Setyowati, A.B., 2020. Mitigating energy poverty: Mobilizing climate finance to manage the energy trilemma in Indonesia, *Sustainability* 12: 1603, https://doi.org/10.3390/su12041603.

Setyowati, A.B., 2021. Mitigating inequality with emissions? Exploring energy justice and financing transitions to low carbon energy in Indonesia, *Energy Res. Soc. Sci*. 71, 101817, https://doi.org/10.1016/j.erss.2020.101817.

Shani, N., 2020. ASEAN solar sector: 2019 Highlights, ASEAN Centre for Energy, https://aseanenergy.org/asean-solar-sector-2019-highlights/, [accessed 4 February 2021].

Siano, P. 2014. Demand response and smart grids—A survey, *Renew. Sustain. Energy Rev.* 30, 461–478, https://doi.org/10.1016/j.rser.2013.10.022.

Steffen, B., Matsuo, T., Steinemann, D., Schmidt, T.S., 2018. Opening new markets for clean energy: The role of project developers in the global diffusion of renewable energy technologies, *Bus. Polit.* 20:4, 553–587, https://doi.org/10.1017/bap.2018.17.

Stirling, A., 2014. Transforming power: Social science and the politics of energy choices, *Energy Res. Soc. Sci.* 1, 83–95, https://doi.org/10.1016/j.erss.2014.02.001.

Tarai, R.K., Kale, P., 2018. Solar PV policy framework of Indian States: Overview, pitfalls, challenges, and improvements, *Renew. Energy Focus* 26, 46–57, https://doi.org/10.1016/j.ref.2018.07.001.

Thapar, S., Sharma, S., Verma, A., 2018. Analyzing solar auctions in India: Identifying key determinants, *Energy Sustain. Dev.* 45, 66–78, https://doi.org/10.1016/j.esd.2018.05.003.

The Economic Times, 2019. India levies anti-dumping duty on solar cell component from four nations, (1 April 2019), https://economictimes.indiatimes.com/news/economy/foreign-trade/india-levies-anti-dumping-duty-on-solar-cell-component-from-four-nations/articleshow/68668956.cms?utm_source=contentofinterest&utm_medium=text&utm_campaign=cppst/, [accessed 25 January 2021].

Torriti, J. 2016. *Peak Energy Demand and Demand Side Response*, Routledge, Abingdon.

Tushman, M.L., Rosenkopf, L., 1992. Organizational determinants of technological change: Toward a sociology of technological evolution, *Res. Organ. Behav.* 14, 311–347.

Vietnam Electricity (EVN), Corporate Profile 2010/11, 2011/12, 2012/13, 2015, 2016, 2017, 2018, https://en.evn.com.vn/d6/news/-Annual-Report-2018-6-13-2118.aspx/, [accessed 10 February 2021].

Vishwanathan, S.S., Garg, A., Tiwari, V., 2018. Coal transition in India: assessing India's energy transition options, IDDRI and Climate Strategies, https://www.iddri.org/sites/default/files/PDF/Publications/Catalogue%20Iddri/Rapport/20180609_ReportCOAL_India.pdf/, [accessed 2 February 2021].

West Japan Engineering Consultants, Inc., 2007. The barriers of geothermal development and necessity of government support. In: Master Plan Study for Geothermal Power Development in the Republic of Indonesia Final Report, Japan International Cooperation Agency and Ministry of Energy and Mineral Resources of the Republic of Indonesia, https://openjicareport.jica.go.jp/pdf/11864576_05.pdf/, [accessed on 10 January 2019].

World Bank, 2019. *Vietnam Solar Competitive Bidding Strategy and Framework.* World Bank, Washington, DC, http://documents1.worldbank.org/curated/en/949491579274083006/pdf/Vietnam-Solar-Competitive-Bidding-Strategy-and-Framework.pdf/, [accessed 5 February 2021].

World Bank, 2020. *World Development Indicators* (Last Updated 16 December 2020), https://databank.worldbank.org/source/world-development-indicators/, [accessed 8 January 2021].

World Business Council for Sustainable Development (WBCSD), 2016. Corporate renewable power purchase agreements: Scaling up globally, https://www.wbcsd.org/contentwbc/download/1810/22670/, [accessed 17 January 2021].

Yamaka, K., 2018. *The Problem of No Vacant Grid Capacity: Electricity Market Is Not Liberalized in Practice in Japan*, NextPublsihing (in Japanese).

Yamaoka, J., 2015. *Japan's Electricity War: History of Struggles over Resources, Interests and Nuclear Power*, Soushisha, Tokyo) (in Japanese).

Zimmer, A., Jakob, M., Steckel, J.C., 2015. What motivates Vietnam to strive for a low-carbon economy? — On the drivers of climate policy in a developing country, *Energy Sustain. Dev.* 24, 19–32, http://dx.doi.org/10.1016/j.esd.2014.10.003.

Part II

China's energy and industrial transformation as push factors

3 Economic and environmental impacts of power supply configuration change in China

An application of scenario input-output analysis

Jiayang Wang and Kiyoshi Fujikawa

1 Introduction

China's energy consumption has increased rapidly in the last decade, and it has become the largest energy consumer and CO_2 emitter in the world. Saving energy and reducing emissions are becoming urgent issues in China. China has declared that CO_2 emissions per GDP will be reduced by 60%–65% (compared with that in 2005) and the total carbon emissions will peak by 2030 as stated in the Nationally Determined Contributions in the Paris Agreement in 2015 (National Development and Reform Committee of China, 2015). Moreover, at the United Nations' 2020 General Assembly, China made an ambitious pledge that China will be a carbon-neutral country before 2060.[1] China's economy is highly dependent on fossil energy, especially on coal. Coal-fired power generation provides approximately 70% of China's total power generation, and the power generation sector accounts for nearly 50% of China's total CO_2 emissions (NBSC, 2020; World Input-Output Database, 2013). China needs to reform its energy structure and reduce coal consumption to achieve these targets.

Although renewable power generation is now rapidly spreading throughout China, there are some issues which deserve discussions. For example, it is not clear how much CO_2 emissions can be reduced when coal-fired power generation is replaced by renewable energies. Moreover, it is not clear, given the replacement of coal-fired power generation with renewable energies, whether energy shifts will have a negative impact on the economy/employment or not, and if it has negative effects on the economy/employment, how large they will be.

Against this backdrop, this chapter applies scenario input-output analysis to estimate the environmental, economic, and social effects by shifting power sources from coal to renewable energies.

2 Model

2.1 Scenario input-output analysis

Input-output analysis is a convenient economic tool to determine the overall effect of demand shift or structural change on production, energy

DOI: 10.4324/9781003190905-5

consumption, or CO_2 emissions. It is important to note that input-output analysis assumes that one kind of commodity is produced by one kind of activity. However, electricity is produced by such plural activities as thermal power, hydropower, nuclear power, wind power, and solar power. Changing the activity share in the power generation structure will produce different economic, environmental, and social effects even if the final energy demand remains the same.

Several methods have been developed to tackle this objective. Yoshioka and Suga (1997) proposed a methodology that rearranged a rectangular input-output table where one product is produced by plural activities into one square so that the Leontief inverse matrix may be defined. Duchin and Levine (2011, 2012) developed a model of Rectangular Choice of Technology (RCOT) with factor constraints that apply linear programming to input-output analysis. The RCOT model allows several input structures in a sector to analyze the economic and environmental effects of technology selection. Fujikawa (2011) applied the RCOT method of Yoshioka and Suga (1997) to analyze thermal and nuclear power substitutability and named this method "scenario input-output analysis." Wang (2016) applied the scenario input-output analysis to estimate economic and environmental effects when the power source shifts from thermal power to renewable-energy power. This analysis used a newly developed input-output table by the Institute for Economic Analysis of Next-Generation Science and Technology, Waseda University, Japan. This chapter will also apply the scenario input-output analysis to estimate how economic, environmental, and social effects differ by changing the power source in China following these previous studies.

The standard input-output table has the comparable industry and commodity names in its rows and columns, respectively. In other words, traditional input-output analysis is based on the standard input-output tables that assume that one commodity is produced by one industry and one industry produces one commodity. Because the input (or technical) structure of each industry is expressed by the corresponding column, one industry name is assumed to be synonymous with "activity." This assumption, however, does not necessarily hold true for all industries in the real economy. The power industry is one of the typical examples where electricity (a commodity in the power industry) is produced by various kinds of activities such as thermal power, window power, solar power, hydropower, and nuclear power. On the other hand, there is only one electricity row on the input side because all activities produce the same good: electricity. However, there are multiple activities (columns) in the electricity industry. The scenario input-output analysis is a method used to combine plural activities into one by giving exogenously the share of the output of each activity.

Figure 3.1 illustrates an input-output table where electric power is generated by five types of energy such as nuclear power, thermal power, hydropower, solar power, and wind power.

		Intermediate Input	Power Generation					Final Demand	Domestic Product
		$j = 1, \cdots, n$	Nuclear Power	Thermal Power	Hydropower	Solar Power	Wind Power		
Intermediate input	$i = 1, \cdots, n$	$\mathbf{X}^{11}$	$\mathbf{x}_1^{12}$	$\mathbf{x}_2^{12}$	$\mathbf{x}_3^{12}$	$\mathbf{x}_4^{12}$	$\mathbf{x}_5^{12}$	$\mathbf{f}^1$	$\mathbf{x}^1$
Power Generation		$\mathbf{x}^{21}$	x_1^{22}	x_2^{22}	x_3^{22}	x_4^{22}	x_5^{22}	f^2	x^2
Value Added		$\mathbf{v}^1$	v_1^2	v_2^2	v_3^2	v_4^2	v_5^2		
Domestic Product		$\mathbf{x}^{1'}$	z_1	z_2	z_3	z_4	z_5		

Figure 3.1 Input-output table with multiple activities in power generation.
Source: Compiled by the authors.

The power generation sector is assumed to be composed of five activities: nuclear power, thermal power, hydropower, solar power, and wind power in this chapter. Changing the shares of the activity mix in the electricity industry will bring different economic and environmental effects even if the level of the final demand is unchanged.

2.2 Production function

In the model equation, the power sector is expressed by a superscript number 2, and the other sectors are indicated with a superscript number 1. The other sectors are collectively referred to as the "normal sector." The power sector is subdivided into five activities. The activity subdivision of the power sector is based on the studies by Fujikawa (2011) and Wang (2016).

The production function of the normal sector is expressed in equation 3-1:

$$x_j^1 = min\left[x_{ij}^{11} / a_{ij}^{11}, x_j^{21} / a_j^{21}\right] \quad (i, j = 1, \cdots, n), \tag{3-1}$$

where

x_j^1 : Output of the normal sector

x_{ij}^{11} : Input from the ith industry (normal sector) to the jth industry (normal sector)

x_j^{21} : Input from the power sector to the jth industry (normal sector)

a_{ij}^{11} : Input coefficient from the ith industry (normal sector) to j^{th} industry (normal sector)

a_j^{21} : Input coefficient from the power sector to the jth industry (normal sector).

The production function of the power sector is expressed in equation 3-2:

$$z_k = min\left[x_{ik}^{12} / a_{ik}^{12}, x_k^{22} / a_k^{22}\right] \quad (i, j = 1, \cdots, n\ ,\ k = 1,\ \cdots,\ 5), \tag{3-2}$$

where

z_k : Output of each activity in the power sector

x_{ik}^{12} : Input from the ith industry (normal sector) to the kth activity (power sector)

x_k^{22} : Input from the power sector to the kth activity (power sector)

a_{ik}^{12} : Input coefficient from the ith industry (normal sector) to the kth activity (power sector)

a_k^{22} : Input coefficient from the power sector to the kth activity (power sector).

The demand-supply equilibrium for the normal and power sectors can be expressed in simultaneous equations 3-3 and 3-4:

$$\mathbf{A}^{11}\ \mathbf{x}^1 + \mathbf{A}^{12}\ \mathbf{z} + \mathbf{f}^1 = \mathbf{x}^1, \tag{3-3}$$
$$\mathbf{a}^{21}\ \mathbf{x}^1 + \mathbf{a}^{22}\ \mathbf{z} + f^2 = x^2, \tag{3-4}$$

where

$\mathbf{A}^{11}$: Input coefficient matrix from the normal sector to normal sector, $\mathbf{A}^{11} = \left[a_{ij}^{11}\right](n \times n)$

$\mathbf{A}^{12}$: Input coefficient matrix from the normal sector to power sector, $\mathbf{A}^{12} = \left[a_{ik}^{12}\right](n \times 5)$

$\mathbf{a}^{21}$: Input coefficient vector from the power sector to normal sector, $\mathbf{a}^{21} = \left[a_j^{21}\right](1 \times n)$

$\mathbf{a}^{22}$: Input coefficient vector from the power sector to power sector, $\mathbf{a}^{22} = \left[a_k^{22}\right](1 \times 5)$

$\mathbf{f}^1$: Final demand ($n \times 1$) vector for the normal sector
f^2 : Final demand for the power sector, which is a scalar
$\mathbf{x}^1$: Output ($n \times 1$) vector for the normal sector
x^2 : Output of the power sector, which is a scalar
$\mathbf{z}$: Output (5×1) vector of each activity in the power sector.

The final demands $\mathbf{f}^1$ and f^2 are exogenous variables that are given from outside the equation system. The number of unknown endogenous variables in the above simultaneous equations is $n + 6$; n in $\mathbf{x}^1$, 1 in x^2, and 5 in z, and the number of equations is no more than $n + 1$. Since the number of equations is less than the unknown endogenous variables, we cannot solve the above simultaneous equation as it is. Therefore, we need to add certain assumptions or "scenarios" to solve the equations.

2.3 Assumptions

We set two assumptions to solve the equations.

Assumption 1: All of the electricity produced through the five different energy sources is supplied and consumed.

$$z_1 + z_2 + z_3 + z_4 + z_5 = x^2, \tag{3-5}$$

where z_1, z_2, z_3, z_4, and z_5 stand for the nuclear power output, thermal power output, hydropower output, solar power output, and wind power output, respectively.

Assumption 2: The power supply configuration is given by exogenous parameters.

$$\begin{cases} z_1 = \alpha_1 x^2 \\ z_2 = \alpha_2 x^2 \\ z_3 = \alpha_3 x^2 \\ z_4 = \alpha_4 x^2 \\ z_5 = (1 - \alpha_1 - \alpha_2 - \alpha_3 - \alpha_4) x^2, \end{cases} \tag{3-6}$$

where α_1, α_2, α_3, α_4 and α_5 stand for the shares of the nuclear power output, thermal power output, hydropower output, solar power output, and wind power output, respectively.

The above two assumptions are summarized in the following matrix equation, which we call the "scenario equation."

$$\begin{bmatrix} z_1 \\ z_2 \\ z_3 \\ z_4 \\ z_5 \end{bmatrix} = \begin{bmatrix} \alpha_1 \\ \alpha_2 \\ \alpha_3 \\ \alpha_4 \\ 1 - \alpha_1 - \alpha_2 - \alpha_3 - \alpha_4 \end{bmatrix} x^2,$$

$$\mathbf{z} - \mathbf{c} x^2 = 0, \tag{3-7}$$

$$\text{where } z = \begin{bmatrix} z_1 \\ z_2 \\ z_3 \\ z_4 \\ z_5 \end{bmatrix} \mathbf{c} = \begin{bmatrix} \alpha_1 \\ \alpha_2 \\ \alpha_3 \\ \alpha_4 \\ 1 - \alpha_1 - \alpha_2 - \alpha_3 - \alpha_4 \end{bmatrix}.$$

As the number of equations increases by 5 because of these assumptions, the total number of unknown variables matches the total number of equations. We can then solve simultaneous equations 3-3 and 3-4.

2.4 Estimating the economic, environmental, and social impacts

Equation 3-7 can be modified into equation 3-7′.

$$\mathbf{z} = \mathbf{c}x^2. \tag{3-7′}$$

Substitution of equation 3-7′ into equations 3-3 and 3-4 gives equations 3-8 and 3-9.

$$\mathbf{A}^{11}\,\mathbf{x}^1 + \mathbf{A}^{12}\mathbf{c}x^2 + \mathbf{f}^1 = \mathbf{x}^1, \tag{3-8}$$
$$\mathbf{a}^{21}\,\mathbf{x}^1 + \mathbf{a}^{22}\,\mathbf{c}x^2 + f^2 = x^2. \tag{3-9}$$

Then, we get equation 3-10.

$$\begin{bmatrix} \mathbf{A}^{11} & \mathbf{A}^{12}\mathbf{c} \\ \mathbf{a}^{21} & \mathbf{a}^{22}\mathbf{c} \end{bmatrix}\begin{bmatrix} \mathbf{x}^1 \\ x^2 \end{bmatrix} + \begin{bmatrix} \mathbf{f}^1 \\ f^2 \end{bmatrix} = \begin{bmatrix} \mathbf{x}^1 \\ x^2 \end{bmatrix}. \tag{3-10}$$

Finally, we obtain equilibrium output equation 3-11. It is important that the input coefficient vector of the power sector is defined as a weighted average of those of five activities in the power sector.

$$\begin{bmatrix} \mathbf{x}^1 \\ x^2 \end{bmatrix} = \left[\mathbf{I} - \begin{bmatrix} \mathbf{A}^{11} & \mathbf{A}^{12}\mathbf{c} \\ \mathbf{a}^{21} & \mathbf{a}^{22}\mathbf{c} \end{bmatrix} \right]^{-1} \begin{bmatrix} \mathbf{f}^1 \\ f^2 \end{bmatrix}. \tag{3-11}$$

We can calculate the outputs of $\mathbf{x}^1$ and x^2 when the final demands $\mathbf{f}^1$ and f^2 are given. The Leontief inverse matrix depends on the scenario or the share of the activities in the power sector.

The total CO_2 emissions (**emi**) can be calculated using the CO_2 emission coefficients $\mathbf{e}_x$ and $\mathbf{e}_z$ for the normal and power sectors, respectively, as shown in equation 3-12.

$$\mathbf{emi} = \begin{bmatrix} \mathbf{e}_x & \mathbf{e}_z \end{bmatrix} \begin{bmatrix} \mathbf{x}^1 \\ \mathbf{z} \end{bmatrix}. \tag{3-12}$$

The total required labor force (**eng**) can be estimated using labor coefficients $\mathbf{l}_x$ and $\mathbf{l}_z$, which are defined as labor input per unit output of the corresponding sector, as shown in equation 3-13.

$$\mathbf{eng} = \begin{bmatrix} \mathbf{l}_x & \mathbf{l}_z \end{bmatrix} \begin{bmatrix} \mathbf{x}^1 \\ \mathbf{z} \end{bmatrix}. \tag{3-13}$$

3 Data

3.1 Input-output tables

We used the "2012 Input-Output Table of China" issued by the National Bureau of Statistics of China (NBSC) for our data. However, the power sector in the input-output table of China is not divided by power generation activity. We estimated an input-output table where the power generation sector is divided into nuclear, thermal, hydro, and renewable energy based on "The Input-Output Table for Analysis of the Next-Generation Energy System for 2005" (Institute for Economic Analysis of Next-generation Science and Technology).[2] We borrowed the input coefficients from the Waseda University table, where we assumed that the input coefficients of the power generation sector are similar between Japan and China.

3.2 Energy consumption and CO_2 emissions[3]

We used the following three-step method when we estimated CO_2 emission coefficient by industry.

i Step 1: Nominal value of fossil energy input by industry
  We calculated the nominal consumption value of three fossil energies such as coal, oil, and natural gas using the "2012 Input-Output Table of China" (NBSC, 2015).

ii Step 2: Calorie-based fossil energy input by industry
  We got calorie-based total fossil energy consumption from the "China Energy Statistical Yearbook 2013" (NBSC, 2013). We calculated the calorie-based fossil energy input by industry by multiplying the calorie-based total fossil energy consumption and nominal consumption share of each industry, which is obtained in Step 1.

iii Step 3: CO_2 emissions by industry
  We used CO_2 emission coefficients in the "2006 IPCC Guidelines for National Greenhouse Gas Inventories" issued by the Intergovernmental Panel on Climate Change (IPCC; Table 3.1).[4] We calculated CO_2 emissions by industry as a product of CO_2 emission coefficients and calorie-based fossil energy consumption by industry, which was obtained in Step 2.

3.3 Required employment

Labor data are based on "Socio Economic Accounts 2016" issued by the World Input-Output Database (WIOD; Timmer et al., 2015). The WIOD labor data are often used in calculating labor coefficients by industry but the sector classification in manufacturing is too approximate to apply to

Table 3.1 CO_2 emission coefficients by fuel type

Fuel type	*Carbon content (kg-C/TJ)*	*Effective CO_2 emissions (kg-CO_2/TJ)*
Coal	25.8	94.6
Oil	20.0	73.3
Natural gas	15.3	56.1

Source: The authors' compilation based on IPCC (2006).

our analysis. We therefore used the share of labor data issued in the China Economic Census Yearbook 2013 (NBSC, 2014), where we retrieved more detailed statistics. Moreover, we used the labor coefficients for power generation activities in the "Renewable Energy-Focused Input-Output Table" (Hienuki et al., 2015).

4 Results

4.1 Scenarios for analysis

China has set a goal of achieving carbon neutrality by 2060. China's non-fossil fuel power generation will need to increase more than 90% by 2050 to achieve that goal (He, 2020). Although significant growth in renewable-energy generation is needed, this study focuses on wind and solar power generation. We excluded hydroelectric power generation as well as nuclear power because both take a long time from planning to operation and their shares are fixed in the current situation. The power supply share in China as of 2012 is as follows: 79% thermal power, 2% nuclear power, 17% hydropower, and 2% new energy of wind and solar power. Therefore, we fixed approximately 20% for nuclear and hydropower, and we distributed the remaining 80% to thermal, wind, and solar power. Then, we implemented the following two simulations: (1) wind power generation replaces thermal power generation, and (2) solar power generation replaces thermal power generation. Finally, we calculated the production, employment, and CO_2 emission effects in each power supply configuration scenario.

4.2 Impacts on economy, CO_2 emissions, and employment by increase of renewable power generation

Tables 3.2 and 3.3 show the estimated impacts when renewable power generation replaces thermal power generation by every 20%. Because the ratio of the hydropower and nuclear power is assumed to be fixed as 20%, the replacement ratio for renewable power can be up to 80%. The first row shows the share of renewable power. The second, the third, and the fourth row show the changes in total production, in CO_2 emissions, and the employees,

Table 3.2 Change of output, CO_2, and employment by the energy switch to wind power

Wind power share	*20 (%)*	*40 (%)*	*60 (%)*	*80 (%)*
Change of total output	−0.4	−0.8	−1.2	−1.5
Change in CO_2 emissions	−9.9	−19.5	−28.0	−35.4
Change of employment	−0.1	−0.2	−0.3	−0.3

Source: The authors' compilation.

Table 3.3 Change of output, CO_2, and employment by the energy switch to solar power

Solar power share	*20 (%)*	*40 (%)*	*60 (%)*	*80 (%)*
Change of total output	0.6	1.2	1.6	2.0
Change in CO_2 emissions	−13.4	−17.7	−25.3	−32.0
Change of employment	0.6	1.0	1.4	1.8

Source: The authors' compilation.

respectively. If the value of the cell is positive, the estimated value is higher than the current status, and vice versa.

Table 3.2 shows the estimated changes when wind power generation replaces thermal power generation by every 20%. CO_2 emissions will decrease significantly as the replacement by wind power increases. If the replacement rate is 80%, CO_2 emissions will decrease by 35.4%. Total output and number of employees will also decrease to some extent when the replacement rate increases as the ratio of wind power increases. If the replacement rate becomes 80%, the total output and the number of employees will decrease by 1.48% and 0.34%, respectively. In short, the replacement of thermal power generation with wind power generation can greatly reduce CO_2 emission but reduce the total output and number of employees only marginally.

Table 3.3 shows the estimated changes when solar power generation replaces thermal power generation by every 20%. The higher replacement by solar power will reduce CO_2 emissions further as we have observed in the case of wind power generation. If the replacement rate is 80%, CO_2 will be decreased by 32%, which is slightly lower than the case of wind power generation. On the other hand, unlike the case of wind power generation, the total output and the number of employees increase when the replacement rate increases. If the replacement rate is 80%, the total output will increase by 2%, and the number of employees will increase by 1.8%. In other words, the replacement of thermal power generation with solar power generation can contribute to a reduction of CO_2 emissions and an increase in total output and the number of employees.

4.3 *Impacts on the thermal power and related industries by increase of renewable power generation*

He et al. (2019) point out that an increased share of renewable energy inhibits such thermal power related industries as mining and coal products though it can promote renewable-energy industry development. Our analysis also shows the same result.

Table 3.4 shows that an energy shift to wind power will significantly reduce the output of thermal power and the related industries. In particular, coal/petroleum/gas, coke/refined petroleum, waste treatment, gas supply, nonmetallic mineral, and transportation will be greatly affected. Also, the

Table 3.4 Output and employment change of thermal power and related industries by the energy switch to wind power

	Wind power share	*20%*	*40%*	*60%*	*80%*
Output Change (%)	Coal, petroleum, and natural gas	−6.67%	−13.16%	−18.82%	−23.80%
	Coke, refined petroleum	−2.70%	−5.33%	−7.62%	−9.64%
	Waste treatment	−1.80%	−3.56%	−5.08%	−6.43%
	Gas supply	−1.41%	−2.79%	−3.99%	−5.05%
	Nonmetallic mineral	−1.28%	−2.51%	−3.59%	−4.54%
	Transport	−0.48%	−0.95%	−1.36%	−1.72%
Employment Change (1000 person)	Thermal power	−899	−1,776	−2,540	−3,211
	Coal, petroleum, and natural gas	−461	−910	−1,301	−1,645
	Transport	−113	−223	−319	−403
	Coke, refined petroleum	−28	−55	−80	−101
	Nonmetallic mineral	−21	−42	−60	−76
	Gas supply	−4	−9	−13	−17

Source: The authors' compilation.

Table 3.5 Output and employment change in thermal power and related industries by the energy switch to solar power

	Solar power share	*20%*	*40%*	*60%*	*80%*
Output change (%)	Coal, petroleum, and natural gas	−5.67%	−11.31%	−16.22%	−20.54%
	Coke, refined petroleum	−1.62%	−3.31%	−4.78%	−6.08%
	Gas supply	−1.16%	−2.33%	−3.34%	−4.23%
	Waste treatment	−0.24%	−0.63%	−0.98%	−1.29%
	Nonmetallic mineral	0.19%	0.30%	0.40%	0.48%
	Transport	1.36%	2.41%	3.31%	4.11%
Employment change (1000 person)	Thermal power	−899	−1776	−2540	−3211
	Coal, petroleum, and natural gas	−392	−782	−1122	−1420
	Coke, refined petroleum	−17	−35	−50	−64
	Gas supply	−4	−8	−12	−15
	Waste treatment	−1	−2	−3	−4
	Nonmetallic mineral	23	41	56	70
	Transport	44	70	93	113

Source: The authors' compilation.

shift to wind power will significantly reduce the labor demand in the thermal power and related industries. If the ratio of wind power becomes 80%, the employment in thermal power generation will decrease by more than 3 million and those in the above-mentioned thermal power related industries will decrease by more than 2 million.

Table 3.5 shows the results of the solar power replacement. Solar power replacement will have positive effect on the economy while it reduces the output and labor demand of thermal power and the related industries such as coal/petroleum/gas, coke/refined petroleum, waste treatment, and gas supply.

However, the impact of the replacement of thermal power generation by solar power generation is different from those of replacement by wind power generation, and the negative impacts on thermal power generation and related industries are not that large. Actually, the production will increase in sectors such as non-metal mineral products and transportation.

5 Discussion

The replacement of thermal power generation with renewable energy will greatly contribute to the reduction of CO_2 emissions in China, but the economic and social effects are not the same between wind power and solar power. In the case of 80% replacement by wind power, China's total output and employment will decrease by 1.48% and 0.34%, respectively. However, in the case of 80% replacement by solar power, China's total output and employment will increase by 2.0% and 1.8%, respectively.

Let us discuss the reasons why wind power and solar power generation have different economic effects. California's Clean Energy Future (CCEF) (2012) shows that the job creation effect of renewable energy is larger than that of thermal power generation, except wind power generation. IRENA (2020) suggests that the required labor force for wind power generation is less than the required labor force for solar power generation, and the relative share for the 'operation & maintenance' that is classified as intermediate inputs of wind power generation is smaller than that of solar power generation as shown in Table 3.6. Similar results have been reported by Wei et al. (2010), Shirley and Kammen (2012), Moriizumi et al. (2017), and He et al. (2019).

The reason why the overall effect of replacement by solar power is positive is that the total of input coefficient for the solar power is higher than that for the wind power. That means, solar power generation requires more inputs from such industries as building repairs, mechanical repairs, transport, and nonmetallic products than wind power.

As a matter of fact, in comparing wind and solar power plants with the same capacity in China, the annual power generation of a wind power plant

Table 3.6 Share of employment by stage of renewable energy value chains

	Planning	*Manufacturing*	*Transport*	*Installation*	*Operation & maintenance*	*Decommissioning*	*Labor requirement**
Solar power	1%	22%	2%	17%	56%	2%	229,055
Wind power**	2%	17%	1%	30%	43%	7%	144,420

* Person days for 50 MW plant.
** Onshore wind power.
Source: The authors' compilation based on International Renewable Energy Agency (IRENA) (2020), p. 63.

Table 3.7 Installed capacity and power generation in renewable energy in China in 2019

	Installed capacity (GW)	*Power generation (TWh)*	*Annual power generation* (kWh)*
Solar power	175	178	1,200
Wind power	184	366	2,000

* Power generation with 1 kW capacity.
Source: CEC (2021).

is much higher than that of a solar power plant. Table 3.7 shows the installed capacity and annual power generation of renewable energies in China. The annual power generation of a wind power plant with 1 kW capacity is around 2,000 kWh, whereas that of a solar power plant is no more than 1,200 kWh (CEC, 2021). In other words, solar power plants require at least 1.5 times capacity compared with wind power plants to generate the same amount of power.

The negative impacts on thermal power and related industries are inevitable when thermal power generation is replaced by renewal energies although there is a difference in the magnitude of impact between wind power and solar power. The labor demand decrease in coal mining is expected to be particularly large. Relocation of workers in the coal mining industry is not easy since the majority of workers in the coal industry are unskilled. Now China introduces wind power generation on a large scale to replace the thermal power generation. The Chinese government has to figure out how to rehire retirees from the coal mining industry.

6 Conclusions

This chapter focuses on China's power industry from the perspective of power supply configuration. The power industry is composed of multiple power generation activities such as nuclear power, hydropower, thermal power, wind power, and solar power. It was therefore difficult to handle the power industry through the traditional framework of input-output analysis. However, scenario input-output analysis makes it possible to analyze the difference in the economic, environmental, and social effects caused by the different power supply configurations. Scenario input-output analysis gives shares of multiple power generation activities in the power sector as parameters that integrate multiple activities into one column in a square input-output table.

We find that the replacement of thermal power generation with renewable energy might greatly contribute to the reduction of CO_2 emissions in China. If all thermal power generation is replaced by renewable energy, China's CO_2 emissions can be reduced by more than 30%. However, the impacts on the economy are different between replacement by wind power and replacement by solar power. Replacement by the wind power has negative effects on the economy while replacement by the solar power might have positive effects on the economy. The reason for this is that equipment for the solar power generation is composed of more parts and requires more time and more labor force for maintenance and repair compared with the wind power. Although wind power replacement has negative effects on the economy, its relative scale is extremely small compared with its CO_2 reduction effect. The results show the possibility of simultaneous realization of economic growth and reduction of CO_2 emissions when the thermal power generation is replaced by renewable-energy power generation.

Moreover, the negative impacts on thermal power and related industries are inevitable when thermal power generation is replaced by renewable power. The negative impacts are especially serious in coal mining and coal products. When China promotes renewable power generation, adjustment policies will be required to mitigate the negative impacts of reduced production and employment in these industries.

7 Acknowledgments

This work was supported by Japan Society for the Promotion of Science, Grants-in-Aid for Scientific Research, under Grant Numbers JP18H03426, JP19K12459, JP20K12291, and Nagoya University.

Notes

1 See UN News dated on 22 September 2020, https://news.un.org/en/story/2020/09/1073052/ [accessed 31 January 2021].
2 See author and title of the website, http://www.f.waseda.jp/washizu/table.html (in Japanese) / [accessed 31 January 2021].
3 Energy consumption or CO_2 emissions in the construction stage of power plants are outside of the scope of this study since this study focuses on the operation stage of power generation.
4 As to the details, see Volume 2 Energy P23–24. Table 1.4, https://www.ipcc-nggip.iges.or.jp/public/2006gl/vol2.html/ [accessed 31 January 2021].

References

California's Clean Energy Future (CCEF) 2012. Preliminary estimates of job creation, http://www.bioin.or.kr/fileDown.do?seq=16187/ [accessed 31 January 2021].

Duchin, F., and Levine, S. H. 2011. Sectors may use multiple technologies simultaneously: The rectangular choice-of-technology model with binding factor constraints, *Economic Systems Research*, 23(3), 281–302. https://doi.org/10.1080/09535314.2011.571238

Duchin, F., and Levine, S. H. 2012. The rectangular sector-by-technology model: not every economy produces every product and some products may rely on several technologies simultaneously, *Journal of Economic Structures*. 1(1), 1–11, https://doi.org/10.1186/2193-2409-1-3

Fujikawa, K. 2011. Input output model to evaluate environmental policies, in Ban K. (ed.), *Model development for comprehensive analysis on Japanese environmental policies and economy* (Final report of Policy Research of Environmental Economics, 2009–2011), 225–267, Ministry of the Environment, Japan, http://www.env.go.jp/policy/keizai_portal/F_research/f-01-03.pdf/ (in Japanese)

He, J. 2020. China's long-term low-carbon development strategy and pathway, the press conference by the Institute of Climate Change and Sustainable Development (ICCSD), https://mp.weixin.qq.com/s/S_8ajdq963YL7X3sRJSWGg/ [accessed 31 January 2021].

He, L., Yang, X., Zhong, Z., and Zhu, J. 2019. On employment effect of renewable energy investment in China: From the overall and industrial perspective, *Journal of Central South University (Social Science)*, 25(3), 84–95, https://doi.org/10.11817/j.issn.1672-3104.2019.03.010. http://www.zndxsk.com.cn/upfile/soft/2019/03_skb/10-p84-19sk03.pdf

Hienuki, S., Kudoh, Y., and Hondo, H., 2015. Life cycle employment effect of geothermal power generation using an extended input-output model: The case of Japan, *Journal of Cleaner Production*, 93, 203–212. https://doi.org/10.1016/j.jclepro.2015.01.008

Intergovernmental Panel on Climate Change (IPCC), 2006. 2006 IPCC guidelines for national greenhouse gas inventories, https://www.ipcc.ch/report/2006-ipcc-guidelines-for-national-greenhouse-gas-inventories/ [accessed 31 January 2021].

International Renewable Energy Agency (IRENA) (2020). *Post-COVID recovery: An agenda for resilience, development and equality,* https://www.irena.org/-/media/Files/IRENA/Agency/Publication/2020/Jun/IRENA_Post-COVID_Recovery_2020.pdf [accessed 31 January 2021].

Moriizumi, Y., Hondo, H., and Nakano, S. 2017. Renewable energy and employment potential: A comparative analysis based on an input-output model, *Journal of the Japan Institute of Energy*, 96(1), 16–27. https://doi.org/10.3775/jie.96.16

National Development and Reform Committee of China, 2015. *Enhanced actions on climate change: China's intended nationally determined contributions.* (in Chinese), https://www4.unfccc.int/sites/ndcstaging/PublishedDocuments/China%20First/China's%20First%20NDC%20Submission.pdf/ [accessed 31 January 2021].

Shirley, R., and Kammen, D. 2012. *Estimating the potential impact of renewable energy*, Renewable and Appropriate Energy Laboratory (RAEL), https://rael.berkeley.edu/wp-content/uploads/2016/03/RAEL-Green-Jobs-Report_-Shirley-and-Kammen_May2012.pdf [accessed 31 January 2021].

Timmer, M. P., Dietzenbacher, E., Los, B., Stehrer, R., and de Vries, G. J. 2015. An illustrated user guide to the World Input-Output Database: The case of global automotive production, *Review of International Economics*, 23, 575–605. https://onlinelibrary.wiley.com/doi/abs/10.1111/roie.12178

Wang, J. 2016. Economic and environmental effects of power generation by renewable energies in China: an application of scenario input output analysis, *Input-Output Analysis-Innovation and I-O Technique* (Pan-Pacific Association for Input-Output Studies), 24(1), 35–48. (in Japanese)

Wei, M., Shana, P., and Daniel, K. 2010. Putting renewables and energy efficiency to work: How many jobs can the clean energy industry generate in the US, *Energy Policy*, 38, 919–931. https://doi.org/10.1016/j.enpol.2009.10.044

Yoshioka, K., and Suga, M. 1997. Application of input output approach in environmental analysis: A study of scenario Leontief inverse, in Ueta, K. et al. *An Econometric Approach to Environmental Problems*, *The Economic Analysis*, 154, 87–132, Economic Research Institute, Economic Planning Agency. (in Japanese)

Data sources

China Electricity Council (CEC) (2021), List of basic data of electricity statistics in 2019, https://cec.org.cn/detail/index.html?3-292822. (in Chinese) [accessed 31 January 2021].

Institute for Economic Analysis of Next-generation Science and Technology (2016), *Input-output table for analysis of next-generation energy system for 2005*, http://www.f.waseda.jp/washizu/table.html (in Japanese) [accessed 31 January 2021].

National Bureau of Statistics of China (NBSC) (2013), *China energy statistical yearbook 2013*, China Statistics Press. (in Chinese)

National Bureau of Statistics of China (NBSC) (2014), *China economic census yearbook 2013*, China Statistics Press (in Chinese)

National Bureau of Statistics of China (NBSC) (2015), *2012 Input output table of China*, China Statistics Press. (in Chinese)

National Bureau of Statistics of China (NBSC) (2020), China statistical yearbook 2019, http://www.stats.gov.cn/tjsj/ndsj/2019/indexch.htm (in Chinese) [accessed 31 January 2021].

World Input-Output Database (2013), Environmental accounts—CHN_CO2, http://www.wiod.org/database/easl13. [accessed 31 January 2021].

4 From latecomer to first-mover advantage

Why Chinese solar PV manufacturers acquire stronger competitiveness in the global market

Nobuhiro Horii

1 Introduction

China has the world's largest installed base of both wind- and solar-power plants. It is noteworthy that in both cases, most of the equipment is supplied by domestic Chinese companies. In this respect, China has achieved green growth as its domestic companies have also grown during the process of emerging as a renewable energy powerhouse. In both wind and solar power, Chinese domestic companies had no presence in the global market prior to the 1990s, but in 2018, more than 36.6% of wind turbines and 72.7% of photovoltaic (PV) solar panels installed worldwide were produced by Chinese companies.[1] How were Chinese companies able to catch up in a period of less than 20 years?

There is a difference in the wind and solar markets as to what triggered the growth of domestic companies. Chinese wind turbine manufacturers started to grow in the late 2000s, by leveraging the introduction of wind turbines into the Chinese domestic market. The world's second-largest manufacturer of wind turbines, Goldwind, with a 13.8% global market share as of 2018, is no newcomer, having been founded in the 1980s. But up until the mid-2000s, when wind power generation in China saw rapid growth, Goldwind's production was limited to small and midsize wind turbines. Although significantly lagging in technology at the time compared with foreign companies, Goldwind began to grow on the back of government policies, mainly the Renewable Portfolio Standard (RPS) policy, to expand the domestic market, and caught up in technology aided by the government's protectionist industrial policies as well as through subsequent acquisitions of second-place foreign companies. (Horii, 2014). Not only Goldwind but several of the many companies founded in the late 2000s also rode the wave of the rapid expansion of the domestic market and now hold positions in the global ranking.

On the other hand, PV manufacturers, similar to wind power players, began to grow in the late 2000s, but initially most of their sales were to the

DOI: 10.4324/9781003190905-6

export market. Although Chinese wind turbine manufacturers now have a large share of the global market, they mainly serve the domestic market with only limited export, while PV manufacturers have been growing in the rough waters of international competition from the very beginning.

From the latter half of the 2000s, latecomer Chinese PV companies expanded their production rapidly, and massive exports by Chinese companies triggered a sharp price decline that led to a series of bankruptcies of formerly leading manufacturers in Europe and the United States. In response, the EU and US governments imposed anti-dumping measures. The Chinese companies abruptly lost their major markets, being placed on the verge of bankruptcy.

The Chinese government made a complete turnaround from its previous cautious stance, deciding to introduce a feed-in tariff (FiT) for solar power to provide a market for Chinese companies to survive. As a result, China's domestic solar market expanded dramatically, and in just a few years, China became the world's leading country for solar power. The Chinese PV industry plunged into a severe recession from 2011 to 2012, which saw the bankruptcy of Suntech, the world's then-largest PV manufacturer. But from 2013 onward, it returned to a growth cycle again.

In May 2018, the Chinese government replaced the FiT with competitive power purchase from all forms of power generation, including coal-fired power. The Chinese government has emphasized economic efficiency in the diffusion of renewable energies as a principle. In fact, the government let wind power, with its superior economic efficiency, be introduced ahead of solar power. A FiT for solar power was implemented as an emergency measure to help domestic companies from the sudden import restrictions, and its replacement can be understood as a return to that principle. The replacement of the FiT forced Chinese PV manufacturers to redevise their development strategies.

Looking closely at individual companies, leading companies have been rapidly changed. Suntech and Yingli Solar, which used to be in the leading position in the world market, went into bankruptcy, or were defeated by another new, fast-growing company. In other words, China's PV industry has achieved rapid development while repeatedly undergoing an active internal metabolism.

Against this backdrop, this paper poses the following three research questions.

1) China's PV industry has been hit by changes in the external environment: import restrictions by Western countries on the grounds of anti-dumping and unfair subsidies in 2011, and the termination of the FiT system in 2018. Has the growth model of the Chinese PV industry transformed in response to these changes? If it has, how?

2) In the PV industry in China (as well as in the world), the ups and downs in the management of PV companies are severe, as companies that were once the world leaders might go bankrupt or disappear from the rankings in just a couple of years. What are the factors behind this?

3) How can the implications of the rise of the PV industry in China and its impact on the world, especially Asia, be evaluated?

Previous research has shed light on the sources of competitiveness of China's PV industry through the early 2010s. Uno and Sakakibara (2009) showed how the global PV industry underwent a structural change in the second half of the 2000s. Under the traditional vertically integrated model, PV production equipment was produced in-house and the value chain was completed in-house, as in the case of Japanese companies. On the other hand, under the new horizontally divided model, PV production equipment was produced separately from downstream PV production as Western companies started to sell their PV production equipment in their process to withdraw from the depressed PV business. Owing to this structural change in the global PV industry, Chinese companies, which were latecomers and had no accumulated technology, came to be able to enter the PV market (downstream) in the late 2000s. In addition, Marukawa (2014) and Chen (2015) found in their detailed case studies that the source of competitiveness of the early Chinese PV industry was low prices, which was made possible by the generous support provided by Chinese local governments, especially in the form of low-cost or free land grants and the provision of low-interest loans. In a sense, competitiveness of Chinese PV industry before 2010 was boosted by the "cunning" approach under the state capitalism, and in this sense, the import restrictions imposed by Western countries were to an extent justifiable.

This chapter is organized as follows. In Section 2, how China's PV industry strengthened its own competitiveness by changing the growth model will be analyzed. In the face of anti-dumping measures by the EU and the United States in 2011, China's PV industry shifted to domestic demand and succeeded in lowering PV prices and improving quality. Section 3, by giving an example of new technology (PERC PV) commercialized in recent years, analyzes the factor that makes the leading companies in the PV industry change so frequently. Then, in Section 4, the overseas development of Chinese PV companies in the 2010s and the recent surge in exports will be analyzed, and how the overseas strategies of Chinese companies are changing and the impact that the development of China's PV industry has had on other countries, especially in Asia will be evaluated.

This chapter analyzes both overall situation of the Chinese PV industry and individual PV companies. Such an approach was necessary because some data and qualitative information of the Chinese PV industry are not available, in which cases we attempted to estimate the overall situation of the industry from the data and qualitative information of individual companies. The data and qualitative information used were obtained from the China Photovoltaic Industry Association (CPIA) and other statistical and annual reports published by the Chinese government and various industry organizations, as well as from papers and articles available on the internet. The sources of the data and qualitative information are clearly indicated.

The contribution of this chapter is to provide novel empirical findings. First, China's PV industry has established a genuine competitive advantage by completing a domestic value chain and driving the development of cutting-edge technologies. Second, anti-dumping measures fostered Chinese PV companies and directed them to locate production plants in Asia. Third, the replacement of the FiT made China's PV exports resurge.

2 Strengthening the competitive advantage of China's PV industry in the 2010s

2.1 Fierce competition among companies in the domestic PV market

In 2011, the EU and US governments began restricting imports of Chinese PV, putting Chinese PV companies at risk of losing the major markets upon which they were relying for nearly 90% of their business. The reason China's PV industry managed to survive and subsequently strengthen its competitiveness was because it succeeded in transforming its previous export-led growth model. In 2011, China's PV production was 19.8 GW, accounting for a 56.6% share of the global market, of which 89.5% was exported. Only approximately 10% went into the domestic market, with China's share of global PV installation standing at only 4.4%. By 2017, however, production had increased to 72 GW, but the export share had fallen to 26.4%, with more than 70% of Chinese PV sold to the domestic market.

Although this shift was made possible by the Chinese government's introduction of the FiT system for solar power, China's PV companies could not have peaceful place by FiT but be thrown into fierce competition. The purchase price set under the FiT was at the lowest level in the world at the time. The FiT purchase price per kWh was RMB 1.15 in 2011, RMB 1.0 in 2012, and RMB 0.9/0.95/1.0 in 2014 (varying by region, considering sunshine conditions and other factors. The same note applies hereafter) and RMB 0.8/0.88/0.98 in 2016. Converted into dollar terms, the purchase price equates to 9.3 cents in 2011, 7.9 cents in 2012, 5.2/5.5/5.8 cents in 2014, and 4.9/5.4/6.0 cents in 2016, respectively, while the global levelized cost of electricity (LCOE) was 28.6, 22.3, 16.4, and 11.4 cents, respectively (IRENA, 2020). The purchase price of FIT in China was 60%–70% lower than that of global solar projects until 2014.[2]

As FiT purchase prices for solar energy were set at a level far below global price levels, power generation companies in China had to place greater importance on price when selecting PV, which in turn encouraged competition among PV producers. In fact, competition for survival among companies was fierce. For example, the domestic average shipment price (monocrystalline PV 156*156 mm, more than 4.3 W) plummeted more than 30% from

RMB 6.4/W in June 2011 to RMB 4.2/W in January 2012. Furthermore, it fell to RMB 2.2/W in January 2013 and RMB 1.4/W in August 2016 (Wang, 2018).

Looking at the market concentration of the PV industry, as of 2011, there were 115 PV producers in China, out of which 14 companies had a production capacity of 1 GW or more and accounted for 53% of the total production capacity. On the flip side, 47% of the production capacity was in a competitive market structure made up of about 100 companies with less than 1 GW of capacity.[3] Meanwhile, as of 2017, the number of companies with more than 1 GW of capacity had grown to 21, with 11 companies having more than 2 GW, and the top three companies with more than 5 GW of capacity (CPIA [2018]). However, if the percentage of production capacity of the top 14 companies against total production capacity is calculated as in 2011, it accounted for 58%, only a slight increase from 2011. There were still many companies with a production capacity of less than 1 GW. While the top firms expanded their production capacity as of 2017, the presence of many midsize firms suggests the continuation of fierce competition.

In addition to a fierce competition among a lot of companies, the purchase price was lowered every few years, leading Chinese PV companies to increase their competitiveness successively. The share of Chinese companies in global PV production increased from 56.6% in 2011 to 69.0% in 2017. In 2005, Japanese companies held a dominant share of the market (Table 4.1a). In 2011, while Chinese companies had increased their presence, there were still powerful companies in both Europe and the United States, as well as three Taiwanese companies (Table 4.1b). Also, Japan's Sharp was barely holding on either. However, by 2017, except for one South Korean company[4] and one Taiwanese company, most of the top companies in global market share had come to be dominated by Chinese companies.

2.2 Domestic production of PV production equipment

The turning point for the development of PV companies in China was the transformation of the traditional vertically integrated industry structure into a horizontal structure with divided functions, and the availability of PV production equipment in the external market. Prior to 2010, it was mostly Western companies such as Meyer Burger (Switzerland) and AMTECH (the United States) that supplied production equipment to Chinese PV companies. Since Western companies were generating revenue through the upstream operations of the supply chain, import restriction by the EU and the United States could impact the upstream business of Western companies. Therefore, there were even arguments for co-existence and co-prosperity with Chinese companies in the United States (Deutch and Steinfeld, 2013).

Later, however, Chinese companies began to enter the market for PV production equipment. Assisted by China's policy to encourage domestic

Table 4.1a Major PV companies in the world market in 2005 (Unit: MW)

	2005
Sharp (JN)	428
Q Cells (DE)	166
Kyocera (JP)	142
Sanyo (JP)	125
Mitsubishi Electric (JP)	100
Shot Solar (US/DE)	95
Suntech (CN)	82
Others	644
Total	1,782

Source: Compiled by the author based on the data from Marukawa (2014).

Table 4.1b Major PV companies in the world market in 2011 (Unit: MW)

	2011
Suntech (CN)	2,070
First Solar (US)	1,981
JA Solar (CN)	1,775
Yingli Solar (CN)	1,684
Trina Solar (CN)	1,604
Motech (TW)	1,120
Canadian Solar (CA/CN)	1,058
Sun Power (US)	922
Gintech (TW)	882
Sharp (JP)	857
Neo Solar (TW)	806
Q Cells (DE)	783
Others	644
Total	32,907

Source: Compiled by the author based on the data from Marukawa (2014).

Table 4.1c Major PV companies in the world market in 2017 (Unit: MW)

	2017
Trina Solar (CN)	7,400
JA Solar (CN)	6,500
Hanwha Q-Ceks (KR)	5,400
Canadian Solar **(CA/CN)**	5,300
Jinko Solar (CN)	5,200
Tongwei (CN)	4,100
Shunfeng PV (incl. Suntech) (CN)	3,900
Aiko Solar (CN)	3,500
Motech (TW)	3,200
Yingh Solar (CN)	3,100
LONGi (CN)	2,000
Rosen Energy (CN)	2,000
Uniex PV (CN)	2,000
Talesun Solar (CN)	2,000
Others	97,400
Total	123,200

Source: Compiled by the author based on the data from CPIA (2018).

Table 4.1d Major PV companies in the world market in 2019 (Unit: MW)

	2019
Tongwei (CN)	13,400
JA Solar (CN)	9,200
LONGi (CN)	8,400
Hanwha Q-Ceks (KR)	7,050
Aiko Solar (CN)	6,950
Trina Solar (CN)	6,850
Canadian Solar **(CA/CN)**	6,500
Jínko Solar (CN)	6,600
Risen Energy (CN)	4,500
Uniex PV (CN)	3,900
Others	66,750
Total	140,100

Source: Compiled by the author based on the data from CPIA (2020).

production of production equipment, Jingsheng Mechanical & Electrical Co., Ltd (JSG), Shenzhen S.C., and other Chinese companies launched production. They initially started with limited equipment and eventually advancing to complete manufacturing on a turnkey basis. For example, in the directory of the world's major PV cell and module companies published on the website of ENF,[5] there were 14 silicon crystalline cell and 20 module turnkey systems suppliers in 2007, of which only one was a Chinese company (Uno and Sakakibara, 2009). By 2020, however, the number of cell turnkey systems suppliers had increased slightly to 16 and the number of modules turnkey systems suppliers increased significantly to 56, with Chinese companies accounting for five of the cell and 33 of the module turnkey systems suppliers. Also, in terms of revenue from the global PV production equipment market as of 2017, the Meyer Burger (US$498 million) was the top runner, followed by Jingsheng Mechanical & Electrical Co., Ltd. (US$281 million) in the second place. Statistics are available for 18 companies, with total sales of US$2.025 billion constituting only 42% of the total market, but of which Chinese companies accounted for $1.12 billion, or a 55% share.

The entry of Chinese companies into the production equipment market is thought to have had a major impact on the cost reduction of production equipment. Figure 4.1 clearly shows a sharp shrink of the PV production equipment market after 2012. Even though PV newly installed capacity has continued to increase after 2012, why the equipment suffered a significant decline in sales? The answer is that Chinese companies started to manufacture production equipment as well, which led to a price destruction causing unit prices to fall significantly. Chinese production equipment manufacturers increased their market competitiveness against Western manufacturers, by lowering prices substantially. Western manufacturers, faced with the low prices offered by Chinese companies, had no choice but to respond to the sharp contraction in sales by also cutting prices.

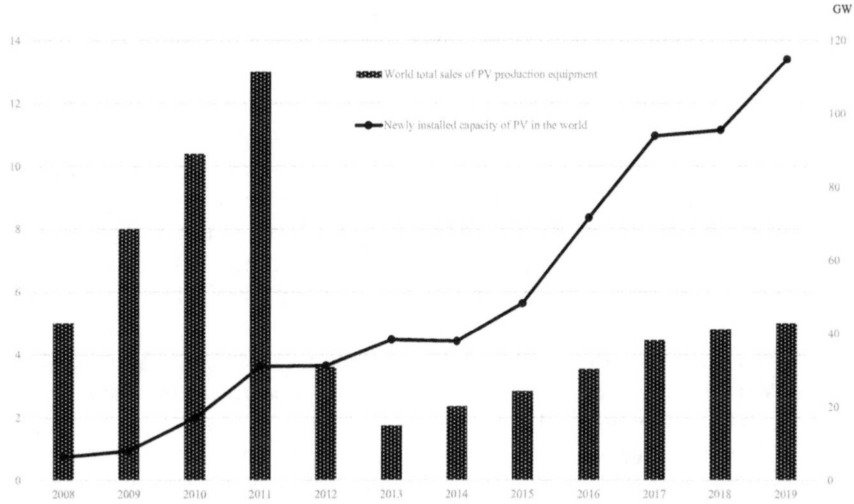

Figure 4.1 The gap between sales of PV production equipment and PV diffusion.
Source: Compiled by the author based on the data from CPIA (2018) and (2020), and BP (2020).

In addition, the Chinese government implemented the "Top Runner system" that resembled the Japanese ones to pursue high-level performance standards. It certified the products of companies that had achieved top-level conversion efficiency for each technology type as Top Runners, and qualified them for government procurement. In particular, adoption in large-scale mega solar projects led by the central government, called Top Runner (领跑者) projects, was highly lucrative to PV manufacturers in terms of sales volume and profit margin. Thus, each company actively invested in technology to obtain certification. As a result, investment in PV with high conversion efficiency—albeit highly priced—was maintained, which led to practical application of PERC PV.

2.3 Short summary

The Chinese government opted to create a domestic market for solar power as an emergency measure against import restrictions imposed by Western countries but set the FiT purchase price at an extremely low level—even by global standards, leading to severe price competition in the domestic market. Although the scale of production of top-ranking firms expanded greatly, many midsize firms remained. Market concentration did not increase much after the shift to domestic demand, and the competitive structure was maintained within the industry organization. In addition, the top companies in the ranking were also in a state of flux, with Suntech and Yingli Solar, once the world's largest PV producers, dropping significantly in the rankings and later disappearing from the list, indicating frequent comings and goings as well as fierce competition among companies.

In addition, during this period, Chinese companies caught up with technology, strengthening their competitive advantage. Chinese companies also entered into the production equipment market, and apparently succeeded in reducing the investment cost of production equipment substantially compared with the situation prior to 2010, when they were relying on supply from Western companies. The government also contributed in the background by operating the Top Runner system, successfully guiding Chinese companies to improve their price competitiveness as well as greatly increasing their technological level.

China's domestic solar installations jumped from only 3 GW in 2011 to 175 GW in 2018, but foreign companies could not easily access the Chinese market. The domestic market thus provided an arena for Chinese companies to foster an overwhelming competitive advantage through economies of scale. As a result, in 2017, most of the top global PV producers were Chinese.

China's PV industry since the 2010s, which shifted to a domestic market driven growth model, has evolved into a completely different nature compared with when it made its first advance in 2010 through a "cunning" approach supported by the industrial policies of local governments. The competitive advantage of Chinese companies is now underpinned by solid factors: the economies of scale through bold and large-scale investment; the value chains comprised purely of Chinese companies, including upstream production equipment; and the advanced technology that is approaching the world's most advanced level.

3 First-mover advantage in PERC PV

In 2018, China's PV industries were forced a shift in the growth model once again. The policy was announced for the phasing out of FiT, which would be revised for solar power to compete with coal-fired power generation on an equal footing. When the reforms were announced in May 2018, the transition to a competitive system was set to take place around 2022, but that timeline is likely to be accelerated. In 2020, tendered projects based on prices referencing the wholesale price of coal-fired power in regions with solar power installations would expand to 33.05 GW, and the average wholesale price of subsidized power of RMB 0.65 per kWh in 2019 would decline to RMB 0.33, and the total amount of subsidies would be halved from RMB 3 billion to RMB 1.5 billion. As a result of this reduction in price subsidies, as shown in Figure 4.2, China's domestic solar market slowed in 2018 and new installations began to decline, with domestic new installations falling by 32% year-on-year to 30.1 GW in 2019.

In 2018 and 2019, significant changes occurred within the industry organization. In just two years, many companies expanded their production volume

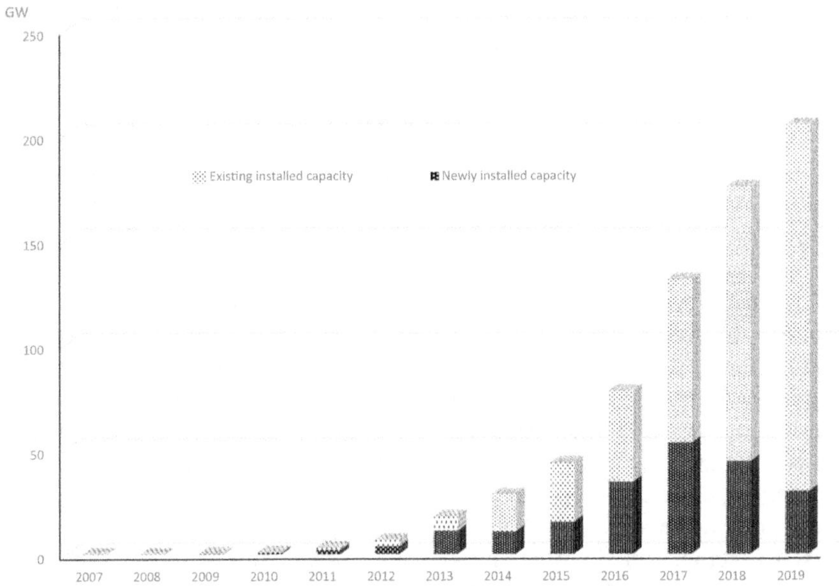

Figure 4.2 Total and newly installed capacity of PV in China.
Source: Compiled by the author based on the data from BP (2020).

dramatically. But two companies, in particular, Tongwei and LONGi, made remarkable strides, growing three and four times, respectively, when comparing their production volumes in 2017 and 2019. On the other hand, Trina Solar, which was in the top spot as of 2017, has not only sunk to sixth place, but its production volume itself has shrunk (Table 4.1c, 4.1d).

Looking back at the development history of the PV industry, the industry saw not only changes between 2017 and 2019, but frequent changes to the companies in the top group as well as their rankings. In the early years, the center of production shifted from Europe and the United States to Japan, and in a short period of time thereafter, Chinese companies drove out non-Chinese companies with their overwhelming competitive advantage. Looking at individual Chinese companies, the leading company has changed rapidly from Suntech to Yingli Solar, then to Trina, and finally to Tongwei. The words "prosperity and decline" and "rise and fall" come to mind, and the cycle is so short. Why do competitive companies in the PV industry get replaced in such a short period of time?

One of the reasons for Tongwei's advance and Trina's decline from 2017 to 2019 can be attributed to the rise of monocrystalline silicon PV with PERC technology. The year 2017 was actually one of significant changes in PV product specification preferences. In China's domestic market, polycrystalline silicon PV had traditionally been the mainstay, but in recent years, there has been a rapid increase in the share of monocrystalline silicon PV. As of 2015, 85% of the market was dominated by polycrystalline silicon PV at 85% against monocrystalline silicon PV at only 15%, but from then monocrystalline silicon PV overtook polycrystalline silicon PV taking a 31% share of the market in 2017 and 62% in 2019. It was almost the first time that monocrystalline silicon PV held a larger share than polycrystalline silicon in solar cells, except for a close call in 2000, and in that sense 2019 was a landmark year. Monocrystalline silicon PV are expected to hold 90% of the Chinese market in 2020.

The difference between monocrystalline and polycrystalline is that monocrystalline silicon PV are produced by directly processing the raw material polysilicon into ingots, whereas polycrystalline silicon PV are produced by melting scrap generated from the manufacture of computer semiconductors and other products that require higher purity than PV and processing them into ingots. Because of these differences in production processes, the conversion efficiency of polycrystalline silicon PV is less than monocrystalline silicon PV because different nanocrystals of silicon are mixed together; on the other hand, they possess an economic advantage because of the significant savings in raw material costs. Monocrystalline silicon PV with high conversion efficiency are preferred for rooftop systems because of the limited installation space, while polycrystalline silicon PV are preferred for mega solar systems because of the reduction in investment costs. The low conversion efficiency is compensated for by production volume. For a long period, polycrystalline silicon PV were by far the mainstream in the Chinese market, as it was mega solar power that drove the introduction of solar power in China.

However, from around 2012, a new type of monocrystalline silicon PV came into play. It is a "Passivated Emitter and Rear Cell (PERC)," which uses a technology to suppress power generation losses caused by the recombination of carriers (electrons and holes) by forming an inactive layer on the back of the cell. While the average conversion efficiency of conventional BSF PV is 18.6%–19.9%, that of PERC PV is 19.6%–21.3%, more than one percentage point higher. The PERC treatment can be used for both monocrystalline and polycrystalline, but the conversion efficiency improvement by PERC is more pronounced in monocrystalline silicon PV. A monocrystalline silicon PV using PERC technology can produce about 10% more power than a polycrystalline silicon PV of the same size.

This 10% difference has fundamentally changed the competitive conditions between monocrystalline silicon PV and polycrystalline silicon PV. Polycrystalline silicon PV were able to save on raw material costs by using scrap, which was the source of its competitive advantage. However, if the difference in conversion efficiency of 10%, or the resultant increase in income is considered, monocrystalline silicon PV are superior in cost performance. The rapid shift from polycrystalline to monocrystalline in recent years, as mentioned earlier, is a natural result reflecting economic efficiency. PERC's production capacity jumped from just 0.5 GW in 2010 to 2.5 GW in 2014 and 28.9 GW in 2017.

Tongwei, which became the leader in the 2019 rankings, is a model example of a company that has grown by rapidly expanding production of new monocrystalline PERC PV. The company, originally a livestock feed manufacturer, entered the PV industry in 2013 through a white knight merger with Saiwei LDK, a one-time powerful PV company that had become insolvent at the same time as Suntech Power. Tongwei has since established production bases in four locations in China: 7 GW in Hefei, Anhui Province (Phase 1 completed in November 2013, Phase 2 in January 2019); 13 GW in Chengdu, Sichuan Province (Phase 1 in June 2016, Phase 2 in September 2017, Phase 3 in November 2018, Phase 4 in November 2019); 15 GW in Meishan, Sichuan Province (Phase 1 in April 2020, Phase 2 under construction); and 30 GW in Chengdu (Jintang County), Sichuan (Phase 1 7.5 GW expected to be completed in Q1 2021). A total investment of RMB 20 billion is expected to be spent on the 30-GW project in Jintang.[6]

Tongwei already has a production capacity of 27.5 GW as of August 2020, which will be expanded to 65 GW with the additional projects under construction. Considering that total global solar installations in 2019 were 115 GW, it appears risky for a single company to have a 65 GW production capacity. However, this is also the strategy that supports Tongwei's competitive advantage.

Tongwei is a new PV company, having only entered the market in 2013, so it has ridden the wave of the rapid rise of monocrystalline PERC PV. Except for Hefei Phase 1, which was acquired through the acquisition of Saiwei LDK, all other production lines are PERC PV production lines. As a result, the company is now largely free of the negative burden of past investment in conventional BSF and polycrystalline silicon PV, which have lost their competitiveness in the market. More importantly, Tongwei's investment in PERC PV production lines is concentrated from2016 onward.

The PERC technology itself was developed in an Australian university laboratory in the 1980s but had since been not paid much attention. It was not until the 2010s that Taiwanese companies and JA Solar first began to commercialize PERC PV. In 2013, JA Solar made other companies realize the potential of PERC PV by surpassing the 20%+ conversion efficiency barrier that conventional BSF PV had been unable to overcome. Since then, companies other than Tongwei have continued their investment aimed at further maturation of PERC PV production technology. It is also important to note that by 2015, domestic companies such as Shenzhen S.C. had become capable of supplying production equipment for PERC, while in 2012, most of the production equipment was procured from Western companies. Taking the example of PECVD (plasma-enhanced chemical vapor deposition) equipment, which is a component of PERC production equipment, Meyer Burger's product price is RMB 17.45 million per unit, while Shenzhen S.C.

priced it at RMB 3.44 million, about one-fifth of the Meyer Burger price (2017, Li, 2020). Tongwei's huge capital investment in the PERC PV production line was made at the time the technology had matured and the economics had improved greatly.

Compared with Tongwei, JA Solar and other companies that had been investing in the commercialization of PERC PV since before 2012 were left with production lines with inferior conversion efficiency, as the investment had been made when the technology was still in its infancy, and at higher investment costs since all the equipment purchases had been made while equipment costs were higher.[7] Moreover, Tongwei's PERC PV production lines are the world's largest at 7.5 GW each, enabling Tongwei to enjoy maximum economy of scale. As a result, Tongwei has been able to significantly lower its production costs and achieve a higher gross margin ratio than other companies. The gross margin ratio of PV production is 4.4% for JA Solar, 11.2% for Hanwha Q Cells, and 11.3% for Jinko, while Tongwei has a gross margin of 18.5% (Yang, 2018). Those are based on 2017 statistics. It is reasonable to assume that the difference in 2019 was even greater.[8]

These are the reasons behind the rapid rise of Tongwei and LONGi (and the decline of Trina left with its BSF battery production facilities). And perhaps the same mechanism has been at work in the past, when league tables changed dramatically, first in Western countries, followed by Japan, and then on to China, and now even among Chinese companies. The PV industry has been investing heavily in capital equipment for PV production, while rapid technological innovation is still underway. As a result of major advances in technology, conventional products become obsolete in an extremely short period of time, and new, overwhelmingly stronger products emerge. At least until now, the rewards for latecomers have been very impressive.

The biggest factor behind this is the FiT system. Although PV was technically immature and could not be expected to grow into a large market without the FiT system, except for some residential applications. Only under the FiT system, it became possible to sell PV at politically set purchase prices that could cover production costs. Since commercialization of the PV industry began at a stage where potential of technological development was still very large, the industry was kept under an environment of rapid technological innovation. Because of the rapid pace of technological progress, politically set purchase prices often fail to reflect this progress and remain relatively high, resulting in excess profit (rent). So, many PV companies entered the market eyeing the rent generated by this policy.

China's FiT system had a smaller policy rent, compared with other countries, by keeping purchase price very low. However, with the sudden loss of the European market, Chinese PV companies were left with no choice other than to hang on the domestic market with fierce competition. There were also new companies to enter into PV industry in pursuit of rent, although rent is not very large, but market entry barrier was low owing to the availability of production equipment from external market. The government reduced the purchase price, and as policy rents shrank, Chinese PV companies sought to secure their competitive advantage through economies of scale by expanding production capacity.

On the other hand, since the Chinese government continued to provide large policy rents for national projects under the Top Runner system, companies continued to invest on innovation as well, aiming for the rents. This was what led the commercialization of PERC technology.

Thus, in the 2010s, China's PV industry saw a race to scale up production capacity and pursue vigorous innovation. As a result, existing facilities became stranded assets within a couple of years, and start-up companies without stranded assets gained market competitiveness.

4 Development of the PV industry in China and its impact on the world and Asia

Facing import restriction measures by the EU and the United States, the Chinese government decided to provide huge domestic market by introduction of FiT system to Chinese PV companies, which rushed to new market, resulting in fierce competition. On the other hand, production in third countries and roundabout export were also attempted, with the aim of evading the import restrictions imposed by Western countries. Overseas production capacity of Chinese companies was 12 GW as of 2018 according to Table 4.2, while China's domestic production capacity was 130 GW. This means that overseas production is less than 10% the size of China's domestic production facilities. In terms of production capacity, it is a minor player, accounting for just less than 10%, but if compared to the 41 GW of exports in 2018, the ratio increases to 30%.

The table also shows that most of the investments in overseas production plants were made by leading companies that appeared in the top corporate rankings throughout the 2000s. According to 2017 data, of the top companies with overseas production, Trina had the largest production volume at 1.9 GW, or 26% of the company's production. Jinko was next with 1.6 GW, accounting for 31% of its production, higher than Trina. They are followed by Canadian Solar with 1.3 GW and JA Solar with 1.2 GW (25% and 18% of the production, respectively). Except for Jinko in South Africa and the United States, and Han-energy in Egypt, most of the countries in which the companies have invested are concentrated in the Asian region. Although dwarfed by the rapid growth in China, installation of solar power is steadily progressing in the Asian region. At present, not only roundabout exports to Western countries but shipments to the Asian region are also thought to be increasing. This trend of Chinese companies should be welcomed by the host countries, as it does create a certain amount of employment. There are

Table 4.2 Overseas production capacity of Chinese PV companies in 2018

Country	*Company*	*Capacity*	*Period to invest*	*Period to start production*
Korea	CNBM	100 MW		2012
South Africa	Jinko	120 MW		2014
Malaysia	JA Solar	400 MW		2015
Thailand	Uniex PV	1.5 GW		2015
Malaysia	Jinko	1.3 GW		2015
Vietnam	Trina Solar	700 MW		2016
Thailand	Chint	300 MW		2016
Vietnam	GCL	600 MW		2017
India	LONGi	2 GW		2018
Vietnam	JA Solar	1.5 GW		2018
India	Trina Solar	1 GW	2018	
Egypt	Han-energy	300 MW	2018	
Malaysia	LONGi	1.25 GW	2019	2020
United States	Jinko	400 MW		2019
Thailand	Trina Solar	500 MW		

Source: Compiled by the author based on the data from Zhu (2019).

also advantages for Chinese companies in terms of labor cost savings and tax exemptions.[9]

On the other hand, China's domestic installation growth started to slow down, following the announcement in 2018 of the policy of phasing out FiT. In response, exports have expanded rapidly since 2018, with exports growing a sharp 61.7% to 66.8 GW in 2019, compared to 41.3 GW in the previous year, and the value of exports regaining the $20 billion mark for the first time since 2012, rising 29% to $20.8 billion. It appears that Chinese PV companies are once again increasing their share of exports to overseas markets.

The largest exporter was Jinko at US$15.3 billion, followed by Risen Energy at US$9 billion, JA Solar at US$8.2 billion, Trina at US$6.3 billion, LONGi at US$6.2 billion, and Canadian Solar at US$5.5 billion. The export ratio of Jinko, Risen Energy, JA Solar, Trina, LONGi, and Canadian Solar ranges from 82%, 80%, 70%, 74%, 63%, and 92%, respectively. It is interesting to note that Suntech, which has almost lost presence in China, is trailing the above major companies with US$5.1 billion in exports. This must be because exports depend not only on price but also brands and sales channels, for which legacy assets still maintain a certain value. It also may explain why Tongwei, a start-up company, supplies most of its products to the domestic market. Jinko and other major companies may have been forced to resort to export, given Tongwei's overwhelming competitiveness.

In addition, exports in 2019 were driven by exports to Europe, where anti-dumping measures against Chinese-made PV have expired, which reportedly accounted for a third of total exports (CPIA [2020]). For developing countries, India accounts for 8.8%, Vietnam 7.3%, and Brazil 7.0%, and even if other countries are included, the proportions remain between 20% and 30%.

The future growth prospects of the expansion by Chinese PV companies into the Asian region are not promising. A value chain is being completed in China[10] and companies have succeeded in significantly lowering production costs in China by enlarging production lines. On the other hand, for example, according to an executive of Chint, which has invested in Thailand, production costs at Thai plants are beginning to rise due to bottlenecks in export logistics, in addition to a shortage of raw material supplies in Thailand. In other words, it can be said that the benefits of consolidating production in China outweigh the benefits of overseas production. As for the anti-dumping and subsidy import restriction measures by Western countries, which triggered the overseas expansion of Chinese companies, EU decided not to renew the measures upon expiry. This may well be because, under the current situation where Chinese PV companies have established overwhelming price competitiveness by building huge PERC factories, restricting imports of Chinese PV will only result in increasing the cost of solar installation. EU had to abandon its FiT because of the cost burden, but on the other hand, it has no choice but to expand the installation of solar power in order to achieve carbon neutrality. It is assumed that Europe can no longer afford to exclude Chinese-made solar cells and give priority to its own expensive solar cells, and therefore Chinese companies no longer need to make roundabout exports.

5 Conclusion

Since 2011, China's PV industry has undergone a major shift in its growth model from an export-driven model to a domestic demand-driven model. During the process, Chinese PV companies further improved their price competitiveness, established a complete value chain encompassing from upstream to downstream, and have taken the lead in developing new technologies. They have evolved from a competitive but "cunning" advantage propelled by state capitalism to a competitive advantage in the true sense of the word.

On the other hand, after the policy to phase out FiT was announced in 2018, the domestic market growth slowed down and exports started to expand. With the slowdown in the growth rate of the domestic market, the future development of Chinese PV companies will be based on both the domestic market and exports. The domestic market is under more severe downward pressure on prices than overseas markets; however, in light of the past history of Chinese companies, even if individual companies repeatedly rise and fall, the industry as a whole is thought to further improve its competitiveness through severe competition. Since overseas markets are more attractive in terms of price,[11] companies will, on the other hand, focus more on branding and sales channels for export. Tongwei, which suddenly jumped to the top spot in 2019, sells almost all of its products to the domestic market; thus, leading companies could avoid competing with Tongwei by increasing export to overseas markets.

With the phasing out of the domestic FiT system, Chinese PV companies are once again looking to export, which has the desired effect of supplying low-cost PV to other countries. The rapid cost reductions realized since the latter half of the 2000s in the global PV market are largely due to the rise of Chinese companies. The development of China's PV industry throughout the 2010s has been an important factor in the constant improvement of the PV quality/price balance and cost performance, which has supported the rapid expansion of global PV adoption. Although PV companies in other countries were hit hard, the decline of the overseas rivals did not result in the reduction of the pressure on Chinese PV companies. Rather, the pressure became more intense by competition in domestic market, which led to innovation and a continuous decline in average production costs.

Another notable change is that Chinese companies are now leading the way in global PV technology innovation. Attempts to commercialize PERC PV were initially started by Taiwanese companies, but Chinese companies eventually overtook them and achieved commercialization in a very short time. An important factor to develop the innovation capability of Chinese PV companies is the incentive system provided by the Chinese government such as the "Top Runner system," that leads PV companies to reinforce their competitive advantage, including not only in price but also in technology.

And newly emerging companies such as Tongwei and LONGi invested heavily in state-of-the-art PERC PV and built massive production capacity. The total production capacity of the top 10 companies in 2019 reached 102.43 GW, and with the transition to PERC PV, the PV industry has become an oligopoly. Almost all of the top companies are dominated by Chinese companies, and the Chinese PV industry is establishing its dominance in the global market.

The concern is that China's domestic production capacity will become excessive. While the total production capacity of the top ten companies in 2019 reached 102.43 GW, there is a considerable gap with the actual production of 73.35 GW. This is not surprising as the total global installed capacity in 2019 was 115 GW. Looking at Tongwei's bullish investment plans, it is highly likely that this gap will become larger in the coming years. If demand does not keep up with the huge investment, concern remains that some companies may suddenly fail. The global economic downturn caused by the Covid-19 pandemic may cool down the enthusiasm for green investment, which is not an unfounded fear.

However, as in the past when Chinese companies responded to anti-dumping and subsidy measures taken by Western countries while using the domestic market as a port of refuge and insurance (the Chinese government is also expected to actively provide support if necessary), as in the semiconductor industry, the huge amount of money invested will itself act as a barrier to entry. Therefore, Chinese companies are expected to maintain their overwhelming international competitiveness. As the Covid-19 pandemic worsens the financial situation in many countries, and difficulties in funding for green investment increase, Chinese companies should contribute to the world by leading the global PV industry and continuing to improve the cost performance of PV.

Overseas investment growth of Chinese PV companies is expected to be sluggish in the future. The PV value chain is complete in China, and its efficiency is high. In addition, backed by the economies of scale brought about by its huge production capacity, Chinese PV companies' price competitiveness is outstanding, thereby offsetting any production cost reduction effects at its overseas plants. In the face of the overwhelming price competitiveness of Chinese PV, shutting out Chinese-made PV would be disadvantageous in advancing climate change measures, and it is also unlikely that the import restrictions imposed by Western countries, which originally triggered overseas investment by Chinese PV companies, will be tightened again in the future. In this respect, Asian countries would benefit a little less afterward from China's green growth than the 2010s.

6 Acknowledgments

The author thanks Dr. Tadashi Hayashi for his comments at the annual conference of the Society for Environmental Economics and Policy Studies (SEEPS) on 27 September 2020, and Prof. Tomoo Marukawa for his comments on the final draft of this chapter.

Notes

1 Wind turbine market share calculated from the list of the world's top 15 companies in a Global Wind Energy Council (GWEC) press release (https://gwec.net/gwec-1-in-5-wind-turbines-are-installed-by-vestas-according-to-new-market-intelligence-report/). The term "36.6%" (the market share of Chinese companies within the top 15) or higher is applied, since it is possible that part of the 6.8% market share of companies other than the top 15 companies might be held by other smaller Chinese manufacturers. The share of Chinese companies in the PV (module) market is an estimate by RTS Corporation (https://solarjournal.jp/solarpower/31599/).

2 However, it appears that local government subsidies were provided separately from FIT, especially in provinces in the eastern coastal areas with higher project costs (land costs and other factors). It is difficult to generalize because the situation differs from province to province, but it may be possible to say at the very least that, even taking these local government subsidies into account, the overall

revenue for developers of PV projects in China was considerably lower than the average revenue of PV projects in other countries.

3 However, as shown in Table 8.1, even at the global level, only the top seven companies have a production volume exceeding 1 GW. Companies with a production capacity of 1 GW were not small as of 2011. It should also be noted that, although there were 14 Chinese companies with a production capacity of 1 GW or more, only five Chinese companies are included in the 2011 ranking in Table 8.1 (whereas companies with a production capacity of less than 1 GW from other countries are included). It is assumed that there were many Chinese companies that had just increased their production capacity in 2011, which were still catching up production levels.

4 Hanwha Q CELLS (acquired by a Korean company after the bankruptcy of Germany's Q-Cells, which used to be the world's largest) is headquartered in South Korea, but most of its main plants are located in China, as is Canadian Solar, which is headquartered in Canada.

5 https://www.enfsolar.com/

6 Obtained from Tongwei's company website, http://www.tw-solar.com/qiye/jianjie.html [accessed on 29 January 2021].

7 For instance, the price of Shenzhen S.C.'s PECVD equipment used by Tongwei decreased by 46% in 2019 compared to 2015. At a time of rapid technology innovation, a difference of just a few years in the timing of introduction can make a huge difference in equipment costs and, ultimately, production costs.

8 For example, Tongwei's capex costs of RMB 420 million per GW in 2018 have fallen to RMB 300 million in 2019. Tongwei commenced operation of a significant amount of additional capacity in 2019, and the fact that costs have fallen so much in just one year suggests that the new, larger facilities are considerably less expensive than older facilities.

9 In Vietnam, for example, labor costs are half of what they are in China, with a four-year tax holiday and tax reduction by 50% for the following nine years.

10 In addition to production facilities, 67% of the world's silicon ingots and 98% of silicon wafers, which are the raw materials for processing, are produced in China in 2019. Although silicon ingots are still a major import item, its degree of dependence on import has fallen from nearly 45% as of 2014 to only 30%.

11 Nevertheless, PV export prices in 2019 were 23.5% lower than in 2017, as major companies competed to increase exports due to slower growth in China's domestic market since 2018.

References

BP. 2020. Statistical review of world energy 2020, https://www.bp.com/en/global/corporate/energy-economics/statistical-review-of-world-energy.html/, [accessed 2021/01/29]

Chen, G. 2015. China's Solar PV manufacturing and subsidies from the perspective of state capitalism, *The Copenhagen Journal of Asian Studies*, 33(1), 90–106, https://doi.org/10.22439/cjas.v33i1.4813.

China PV Industry Association. 2018. *2017–2018 China PV industry annual report*, CPIA（中国光伏行业协会 (2018)『2017–2018年中国光伏产业年度报告』中国光伏行业协会）(in Chinese)

China PV Industry Association. 2020. *2019–2020 China PV industry annual report*, CPIA（中国光伏行业协会 (2020)『2019–2020年中国光伏产业年度报告』中国光伏行业协会）(in Chinese)

Deutch, J., Steinfeld E. 2013. A duel in the sun: The solar photovoltaics technology conflict between China and the United States, *An MIT Future of Solar Energy Study Working Paper*, https://energy.mit.edu/wp-content/uploads/2013/05/MITEI-WP-2013-01.pdf.

Horii, N. 2014. The wind turbine industry: The role of policy and markets in the catch-up process, In: Watanabe. M. eds., *The Disintegration of Production: Firm Strategy and Industrial Development in China*, Edward Elgar, Cheltenham, 127–148.

IRENA. 2020. *Renewable power generation costs in 2019*, International Renewable Energy Agency, https://www.irena.org/publications/2020/Jun/Renewable-Power-Costs-in-2019.

Li, F. 2020. Review on PERC development history and prospect on future PV facility-Analysis on heterojunction PV industry, Industry Research Report by Minsheng Securities (「复盘PERC发展历程，推演设备未来图景—异质结电池设备行业深度报告」民生证券行业研究/深度报告), http://pdf.dfcfw.com/pdf/H3_AP202005131379634913_1.pdf (in Chinese)

Marukawa, T. 2014. China in the global photovoltaic industry, *The Economic Review* (Kyoto University), 188 (2), 15–29, https://repository.kulib.kyoto-u.ac.jp/dspace/bitstream/2433/228019/1/kronso_188_2_15.pdf. (in Japanese)

Uno, T., Sakakibara, K. 2009. Turn-key production equipment to reform PV industry, *SFC Discussion paper*, Keio University, SFC-DP2009-007.（宇野正・榊原清則　(2009)「PV産業を変革する生産設備ターンキーシステム」『SFCディスカッションペーパー』SFC-DP2009-007）， https://gakkai.sfc.keio.ac.jp/dp_pdf/09-07.pdf (in Japanese)

Yang, J. 2018. Gaining the lead by continuing cost reduction and scaling up-Tongwei, *Research by Western Securities.*（杨敬梅 (2018)「成本持续优化，产能扩张剑指龙头—通威股份」西部证券公司深度报告）(in Chinese)

Zhu, G. (eds.), 2019. *2019–2020 China new energy international development report*, China new energy overseas development association/Research institute of Silk road energy finance.（朱共生主编(2019)『2019–2020中国新能源国际发展报告』中国新能源海外发展联盟/丝路能源金融研究院）(in Chinese).

5 Do Chinese power companies employ investments in foreign power projects as a geographical diversification strategy?

Akihisa Mori

1 Introduction

Recent global and national stringent climate policy refuels the debate over its impacts on industrial competitiveness, industrial relocation, and the resultant carbon leakage and haven effects. Industry relocation, the move of industries from one region to another, occurs as a result of economic development, labor cost changes, regional policy discrepancies, and various other factors (Tobey, 1990; Penning and Sleuwaegen, 2000). Environmental and climate policies can be one of the drivers for industrial relocation, and the relocation of emissions. They trigger pollution and carbon havens. If the stringent environmental regulation adversely affects electricity cost and comparative advantage and this effect is sufficiently strong to dominate other sources of comparative advantage, it determines the pattern of trade in pollution and carbon-intensive industries (Cherniwchan et al., 2017; Panhans et al., 2017; Zhao et al., 2020).

Behind the refueling of the pollution haven debate are stringent environmental, energy, and climate policies that have been recently implemented in the European Union (EU), China, and worldwide. Stringent regulations and carbon pricing, as represented in carbon emissions trading schemes, raise concerns about industrial competitiveness and carbon leakage. Perceiving coal power as one of the main sources of global CO_2 emissions, Organization for Economic Co-operation and Development (OECD) member countries have propped up commitments to common standards for coal subsidies and restrictions on international finance for coal power (OECD, 2015). To reaffirm China's firm commitment to the Paris Agreement, the Obama administration initiated a joint statement over China's restriction on public financing for projects with high pollution or carbon emissions in 2015 (White House, 2015).

By contrast, China has increased investments in and financing for foreign coal power projects. China started providing overseas official finance (OOF) in the resource extraction sector in the early 2000s and expanded the scope to infrastructure development, including investments in newly installed capacity (i.e., greenfield investment) in the electricity sector. To reduce country and commercial risks, the country employed the resource-financed

DOI: 10.4324/9781003190905-7

infrastructure in which host country governments pledged their interest in some or all of the revenue flows they will receive from the resource production project to a lender (Beardsworth and Schmidt, 2014). In addition, the Chinese government established bilateral and regional development funds to finance investments in connectivity infrastructure as a part of the Belt and Road Initiative (BRI). These funds combined equal more than US$164.4 billion, of which the Silk Road Fund accounted for the largest share (Gallagher et al., 2018). Subsequently, Chinese companies began brownfield investment, comprising the acquisition of shares of existing power companies and utilities and the generation, transmission, and distribution assets under construction and in operation.[1]

These funds not only provide opportunities for Chinese companies to invest in foreign connectivity infrastructure projects such as high-speed trains and information and communication technologies but also accelerate cross-border relocation of pollution and carbon-intensive industries and displacement of CO_2 emissions in foreign countries with less stringent climate and environmental policies. These investments and financing will not only breach the joint statement but also replace OECD member countries' foreign coal power financing, more than offsetting global commitments to the Paris Agreement.

In addition, Chinese investments and financing in foreign power projects can reconfigure the electricity supply system in host countries toward a carbon-intensive version by making coal power profitable and increasing the number of coal power projects. Even if new coal power generation capacity helps host countries overcome power shortages and provide the electricity necessary for economic development and society in the short run, they can result in stranded assets in the long run, namely, assets that are no longer able to earn an economic return at some time before the end of their economic life (IEA, 2013: 98).

For these reasons, the EU does not hide its cautious stance against China's carbon-neutral pledge by 2060 in the UN Summit in 2020, despite evaluating it as an important step (Xie, 2020).

An increasing number of researchers have investigated China's investments in foreign coal power projects. The first strand of research relates to estimating the scale of China's *finance* for coal power development to identify drivers of the scaling and characteristics of finance. In 2005–2014, China's finance for coal power projects was estimated to be US$21–38 billion, of which two-thirds were allocated to India, Indonesia, and Vietnam. The two policy banks—Export-Import Bank of China (CHEXIM) and the China Development Bank (CDB) financed US$15 billion for foreign coal power projects (Hervé-Mignucci and Wang, 2015). In 2005–2017, the two policy banks financed US$42 billion more than 59 coal plants (Gallagher et al., 2018).

Li et al. (2020) estimated that Chinese power companies invested approximately US$115 billion in 462 foreign power plants in 2000–2017, with a total generation capacity of 81 GW. Among the 81 GW of capacity, coal accounts for 31% or 25 GW. However, they excluded Chinese companies' involvement in power projects as contractors, which may underestimate the scale, especially that of new coal power generation capacity, thus potentially impacting CO_2 emissions. Chinese incumbent generators often start out exploring foreign markets through smaller-scale engineering, procurement, and construction (EPC) contracts through subsidiaries, and after a few years of gaining experience and confidence in operating in the host country, they begin to invest in larger-scale projects (Hervé-Mignucci and Wang, 2015). When including EPC contracts, China is involved in a greater number of foreign coal power projects: 114 coal power projects in operation and 54 projects under construction in the BRI countries in 2001–2016, with a combined installed capacity of 88 GW and 48 GW, respectively (Peng et al., 2017).

The second strand of research concerns environmental and climatic impacts. Chinese foreign coal plants are relatively less efficient than those financed by Japan's export credit agency (Ueno et al., 2014) because the majority of coal power plants deploy subcritical coal technology (Gallagher et al., 2018). This inefficient, pollution-intensive coal power increases the social cost of Chinese foreign power plants, which is US$29.7 billion annually, even by conservative estimates (Gallagher, 2018a). By contrast, NDCs to the Paris Agreement encourage host countries to prop up environmental pressures on foreign coal power investments (Xiong et al., 2019). It is argued that an increasing number of coal power projects have been opposed by fierce local protests and raised political debates, causing substantial delays and cancellations (Boulle, 2019; Vidal, 2016). In response, China has reduced investments and finance for subcritical coal plants (Gallagher et al., 2018). Nonetheless, the total BRI-associated power projects in the 15 countries in 2013–2019 are estimated to generate 37 (range 26–48) gigatonnes (Gt) of committed CO_2 emissions by the end of 2030, which is 4%–11% of the remaining carbon budget for the 1.5°C target (Tao et al., 2020).

However, this strand of research has not yet explored the interaction between domestic environmental and climate policy and foreign direct investment (FDI) in power projects. It has tended to frame Chinese FDI in coal power projects as a response to the "going global strategy" and BRI and recognized domestic coal power overcapacity caused by declining demand as one of the motivations for FDI (Hervé-Mignucci and Wang, 2015). Few researchers have framed such investments and contracts as a response to the stringent domestic environment and climate policies, leading to less attention to the heterogenetic responses within power companies and the electricity industry.

Against this backdrop, this chapter aims to frame their foreign investments *and contracts* in sustainability transitions of the socio-technical regime, to explore the scale of geographical diversification and possible displacement of CO_2 emissions.

The remainder of the chapter is organized as follows: Section 2 develops an analytical framework for identifying and understanding heterogenetic responses to the stringent environment and climate policy within the electricity sector while considering Chinese supporting policies for FDI; Section 3 shows the methodology and data collection strategy; Section 4 provides the results of the analysis; Section 5 discusses the underlying factors of the results to obtain implications of China's investments and contracts in foreign power projects on the displacement of CO_2 emissions; and Section 6 concludes and provides perspectives and remaining challenges for the remaining chapters and further research.

2 Analytical framework

2.1 Direct and indirect effect of stringent environmental and climate policy

Impacts of stringent environmental and climate policy can be categorized as direct and indirect impacts (Zhao et al., 2020). Direct effects of emission reduction refer to emission reduction through exiting or pollution abatement investments by pollution and carbon-intensive industries (Zhao et al., 2020). Indirect effects refer to changes in emissions by inducing the relocation of carbon-intensive industries and the location of new carbon-intensive industries. The relocation of carbon-intensive industries is more likely to occur for industries and companies in highly competitive markets and with few state interventions that benefit them, such as sufficient pass-through rates and larger free allocation of allowances in the emission trading scheme (Zheng and Shi, 2017).

The indirect effects generate two opposing results. On the one hand, they reduce emissions in host countries. Industrial relocation can usher in advanced and/or cleaner technologies for production and generate pollution and the carbon halo effect. Empirical studies have found the less polluting effect (Eskeland and Harrison, 2003), and even halo effect in selected Middle East and North African countries (Asghari, 2013). It is more likely to be generated when host countries have a wide technological gap against countries with stringent environmental and climate policy but a high-skilled labor force (Zugravu-Soilita, 2017) and high learning efficiencies (Dean et al., 2009).

On the other hand, the indirect effects increase emissions. Relocation of pollution or carbon-intensive industries are accompanied by the relocation of emissions, generating pollution, and carbon haven effect. Some empirical tests have shown that the carbon haven effect dominates the carbon halo effect in Latin American countries (Sapkota and Bastola, 2017), sub-Saharan Africa (Kivyiro and Arminen, 2014), Ghana (Solarin et al., 2017), the Association of Southeast Asian Nations' countries (Baek, 2016), and China (Arce et al., 2016; Ren et al., 2014). In China, provinces with worse governance have observed not only relocation of carbon-intensive sectors, increased output and consumption of carbon-intensive sectors, and CO_2 emissions but also the move-out of value added to provinces with better governance, improving the economic performance of the latter (Wang et al., 2019).

An institutional gap can also affect the relative magnitude between pollution and the carbon haven and halo effects because environmental standards, corruption, and democracy can affect the location and environmental behavior of multinational companies (Eskeland and Harrison, 2003; Solarin et al., 2017). In host countries where institutions are more developed and environmental management capabilities are strong, relocated industries and new investors are likely to adopt global environmental standards, invest in more environmentally friendly technology, and act more responsibly in waste generation and management (Christmann, 2004). This results in an improvement in the overall environmental quality of host countries and cities (Wang and Chen, 2014). In contrast, relocated industries, new investors, and political elites in host countries and regions may engage in opportunistic behavior at the expense of the environment (Wang and Chen, 2014), where governance and institutions are weaker because of corruption and financial reasons (Millimet and Roy, 2015). Profit-driven dirty industries are attracted, especially by developed countries (Candau and Dienesch, 2017), while loosened enforcement of environmental regulations can hardly control their polluting practices effectively. Host country governments also do not increase public expenditure for the environment and its contribution to the accumulation of pollution abatement capabilities, as long as they allow foreign firms to control technologies (Dean et al., 2009).

Although the categorization is useful in elaborating how the two opposing results are generated, it does not sufficiently explain the types of incumbent companies and their challenges and perceptions that cause indirect environmental effects through their relocation and investments in foreign countries (Turnheim and Sovacool, 2020). Incumbent companies have important structural differences such as the structure of complexes, regional positioning, and stakeholder structure, which generate different damages from the same external pressures (Kungl, 2015). They pursue their goals and have their decision-making styles, scales of operations, and technologies with their different dynamics, time horizons, and speeds of development (Markard and Hoffmann, 2016). Stringent environmental and climate policies would have different effects on incumbent companies. Incumbent companies with different attributes are expected to show various responses to the policies. Incumbent companies in service sectors may not cause significant environmental effects by their relocation and investments in foreign countries (Al-mulali and Tang, 2013).

2.2 Polices and measures for industrial relocation

The Chinese government's going global strategy and the BRI can be considered strategies for international industrial relocation. Although the BRI is more an economic diplomatic tool to advance these diplomatic and strategic objectives (Blanchard, 2017), both aim to encourage companies to export their products and services in the international market, invest in foreign countries to acquire stakes and assets in resource mining, gain technical know-how, and streamline management capabilities. Among them, coal power is identified as a strategic investment for international development and state support. This is a sector through which Chinese technology, equipment, and services can be exported, particularly as domestic deployments taper off.

By contrast, investors and contractors encounter high country risk and international geopolitics, especially in host countries perceived as a security risk to their invested projects (Feng et al., 2020). This risk ranges from the credit risk of contracted firms, commercial risk, and fuel supply risk to risks associated with political and regime changes and subsequent legal and regulatory changes, local conflicts caused by land appropriation, conflicts of interests among stakeholders, adverse impacts on environment, society and culture, and other *force majeure* such as disasters, wars, riots, and lockouts.

To assist the implementation of the going global strategy and the BRI, the State Council provided guidance in 2015 to provide export credit or other favorable financing terms for EPC contracts or equipment purchases; build, operate, and transfer (BOT) models; and public–private partnerships (PPPs; Hervé-Mignucci and Wang, 2015). CHEXIM and CDB, in coordination with the National Development and Reform Commission, established "special loans" and "equity loans" for foreign investments. Apart from state ownership, the Chinese government capitalizes on the human resources management of the Communist Party of China (CPC) and coordination between its energy-germane and finance-germane bureaucracies, to maintain the alignment between these policy banks and state energy companies (Kong and Gallagher, 2017). Tying financing with business deals for Chinese companies enabled some companies in the declining domestic coal industry to revitalize (Shearer et al., 2019).

Nonetheless, these financial supports are insufficient to motivate FDI in the energy sector. Both Chinese investors and financial institutions are engaged with countries with higher country risk ratings and are thus exposed to higher country and macroeconomic risks. Even the resource-backed infrastructure model has not significantly reduced risks because of the decrease in commodity prices and associated macroeconomic downturns in the developing world (Gallagher et al, 2018).

For these reasons, Chinese investors and banks demanded higher interest payments (LGS Online, 2009) and a full guarantee for the credit risk of a state-owned utility, from the Ministry of Finance (Ali, 2009; Castle and Manuwoto, 2011), as a condition to make loans to coal power projects. However, these unfavorable terms of conditions generated repercussions in host countries, prolonging negotiations. Alternatively, host countries adopted PPPs such as BOT schemes that can shift financial risk to independent power producers (IPPs), in exchange for allowing them to join projects as investors and provide operation and maintenance (O&M) services in the long run.

In response, the Chinese government established standardized procedures for EPC contracts. First, policy banks conclude a framework agreement with a host country's ministry of finance and then ask the ministry for a letter of application, an EPC contract with a Chinese company, a project feasibility study, and an environmental impact assessment. Next, a Chinese importer signs a purchase agreement with the company selling the commodity, and Chinese policy banks sign a loan agreement with the host country government and create an escrow account into which the proceeds from a specified amount of the export are deposited to ensure the repayment of the EPC contract loan in cash, not in commodity (Brautigam, 2009; Brautigam and Gallagher, 2014).

China also employs the common fate and destination model of an infrastructure finance model that underscores common interests between both China and the host country, to manage country and macroeconomic risk in greenfield investments. The key actor in this model is a joint venture established between a Chinese state-owned enterprise and a host company. The venture takes advantage of cost competitiveness and the close relationship with the government to convince the government to host favorable biddings to them, as well as move earlier to address policy changes. When winning a bid, the company mobilizes financing from Chinese institutions by combining export buyer credits and non-concessional loans. These syndicated loans are often tied to the services provided by the company that wins a bid (Lin and Wang, 2017). The company may invite host country counterparts to offer a minor portion of a stake or asset to ensure full ownership of host country governments. Take-or-pay clauses with a state-owned utility have become prevalent to secure the minimum rate of return, assuming that most host countries have a state-owned utility in charge of the transmission, distribution, and supply of electricity and billing to customers.

The Chinese government has also agreed to larger investment framework agreements with an increasing number of host country governments. With Brazil, the government began with the mechanisms of bilateral dialogue and upgraded to the High-Level Concertation and Cooperation Commission in 2004 to enhance the linkage between industries in both countries. In 2009, the two countries signed a Joint Action Plan, which boosted Chinese investments not only in greenfield investments such as steel plants, shipyards, automobile plants, gas pipelines, and railway projects but also in brownfield investments: acquisition of electricity, petroleum extraction, and steel companies (Cardoso, 2013). In 2015, both countries agreed to create the Brazil–China Cooperation Fund for the Expansion of Production Capacity, with envisaged funding of US$20 billion, of which US$15 billion was from the China–Latin America Investment Cooperation Fund (CLAI Fund), expecting that these funds would induce other Chinese companies to make greenfield investments.

In 2015, the Chinese government also agreed to the China–Pakistan Economic Corridor (CPEC), a collection of infrastructure projects in Pakistan supported by Chinese funding; in the same year, it signed the China–Indonesia agreement on the cooperation in the construction of power plants, as well as in the planning, construction, operation, and maintenance of electrical grids (the People's Republic of China and the Republic of Indonesia, 2015).

Perceiving the development of these risk management schemes at the national level, Chinese incumbent power companies increase contracts and make greenfield investments in power projects, including coal power in these countries. Huaneng invests in the Sahiwal coal power plant; State Power Investment Corporation (SPIC) invests in the Hubco power plant in Pakistan; and Huadian, Shenhua, and Datang invest in building and operating coal power plants in Indonesia. As a result, of the 102 GW supported by Chinese finance, 30 GW involve joint ownership arrangements with Chinese state-owned enterprises, and an additional 11 GW are BOT arrangements (Shearer et al., 2019: 7).

3 Methodology and data collection strategy

3.1 Research design and case selection

We adopt a case study strategy with single-case, embedded designs. A case study is more suitable than other methods for studies whose research questions are "how" and "why" and whose focus is more on contemporary, and not entirely historical, phenomena than on other methods (Yin, 2014).

We take the "Big Five" state-owned power generation utility groups: Huaneng, Guodian, Huadian, Datang, and SPIC; two other large state-owned power groups of the State Development and Investment Corporation and China Resources (Huarun); two state-owned grid companies, State Grid Corporation of China and China Southern Power Grid; and two state-owned major coal power-integrated companies, Shenhua and China Coal, as cases of regulated incumbent power companies. The selection logic is that they were mandated to upgrade and renovate coal power plants to either ultra-supercritical plants with the capacity of more than 600 MW or super-critical, fluidized bed plants with the capacity of more than 300 MW, and high efficient fuel gas desulfurization and denitrification equipment in 2014[2] as a part of the 2013 Air Pollution Prevention and Control Action Plan. Because Huaneng becomes the largest shareholder of Shenzhen Energy and the State Grid of Shandong Electric Power Corporation, we treat these two companies as subsidiaries of the Huaneng group.

Readers might at first consider it odd to exclusively select state-owned power groups for comparison because China uses a top-down and non-participatory approach to public policy making (Gilley, 2012). In addition, the CPC can exercise its power over personnel to allocate a higher position in the country's political hierarchy to leaders in state-owned enterprises with better performances, incentivizing them to comply with government priorities (Kong and Gallagher, 2017). Nonetheless, we expect heterogeneity in geographical diversification among the regulated state-owned power utilities because they showed heterogenic responses to the stringent regulations in the domestic market (Mori, 2020).

To analyze the scale of investments and contracts by the regulated incumbents, we compare these "regulated incumbents" with those of other Chinese companies who invest and win contracts in foreign power projects. Chinese power companies are categorized into four groups: (a) incumbent power generators not subject to the stringent regulation (unregulated incumbents); (b) incumbent power equipment manufacturers who organize projects as investors or sign contracts as suppliers (incumbent power manufacturers); (c) renewable energy goods manufacturers who invest not only in greenfield wind and solar power projects but also in new manufacturing plants (renewable energy manufacturers); and (d) developers of coal power plants, that is, engineering and construction companies (project developers; Table 5.1).

Table 5.1 Chinese companies invested and contracted in foreign power projects by types

Incumbent power generators and grids under the stringent regulation	Incumbent power generators not subject to the stringent regulation	Incumbent power equipment manufacturers	Renewable energy manufacturers	Project developers
Huaneng	China Three Gorges (CTG)	Dongfang Electric	Wind power	China Energy Engineering Group Corporation (CEEC)
Shenzhen Energy	China International Water & Electric Corporation	Harbin Electric	Envision Energy	China Power Engineering Consulting Group Corporation (CPECC)
Lancang River Hydropower	China Yangtze Power	Shanghai Electric	Goldwind	China Gezhouba Group
China Energy Investment Corporation	China National Nuclear Corporation	Tebian Electric Apparatus	Ming Yan	Power Construction Corporation of China (POWERCHINA)
Guodian	China General Nuclear Power Group		Solar power	Shandong Electric Power Construction Engineering Corporations (SEPCO I, II, III)
Shenhua			BYD	Sinohydro
Huadian			Comtec Solar	China National Machinery Industry Corporation (SINOMACH)
Huadian Engineering			JA Solar	China Machinery Engineering Corporation (CMEC)
Datang			Jinco Solar	China National Electric Engineering Corporation (CNEEC)
State Power Investment			Longi	China National Heavy Machinery
Corporation (SPIC)				Engineering Corporation (CHMC)
China Power Investment Corporation			Risen Energy	CITIC
Shanghai Electric Power			Solargiga	China Communications Construction
State Nuclear Power Technology Corporation			Suntech	
Huarun/China Resources			Trina Solar	
State Development and Investment Corporation (SDIC)			Zoenergy/ZTE	
State Grid of China			Zongyi	
Shandong Electric Power Corporation				
China Electric Power Equipment and Technology				
Southern Power Grid				
China Southern Power				

Note: Companies located in the second column are subsidiaries in the above first column.
Source: The author's classification.

3.2 Data sources

The Chinese Ministry of Commerce (MOFCOM) releases an FDI database on its website as the official Chinese source; it discloses individual transactions that cover 2,922 investments and contracts and provides the project name, date of transaction, host country, amount of investment, and installed capacity since 2012.[3] However, MOFCOM's annual data are always significantly revised because of unsteady reinvestments (Scissors, 2020); in addition, it does not cover all the projects while uploading projects under a pipeline or bidding process, such as the Ladakh solar project in India. For these reasons, its database is not reliable enough to conduct quantitative analysis.

In response, several institutions and research groups have used various strategies to estimate China's foreign transactions. The China–Africa Research Institute of Johns Hopkins University created a database on Chinese loan commitments to African governments for their analysis of the impacts of China's resource-backed finance in Africa (Brautigam, 2009), and keeps updating the database (Brautigam et al., 2019). However, it covers projects financing exclusively to African countries.

In collaboration with the China–Africa Research Institute, the Global Development Policy Center of Boston University expands the scope of China's energy finance globally by collecting and assembling the energy finance by China's two major policy banks, CDB and CHEXIM, in 2000–2019 (Gallagher, 2018a). The Center's dataset sorts the database into greenfield and brownfield investments to uncover different features within Chinese global energy finance (Kong and Gallagher, 2017). The dataset also estimates the impacts on the carbon footprint of China's global energy finance, by type of investments, by linking the energy finance database with attributes of each power plant described in (Li et al., 2020; Platts, 2015); however, it does not cover energy finance by state commercial banks, an investor's self-finance, and the newly created policy investment funds that aimed to advance the BRI, such as the Silk Road Fund (Gallagher et al., 2018). In addition, the dataset partially covers projects that Chinese companies join as EPC contractors.

By contrast, the College of William & Mary, Development Gateway, and Brigham Young University have developed a more granular and comprehensive dataset on foreign assistance projects worldwide, especially those of China (Dreher et al, forthcoming); however, it covers only the years 2000–2014 and does not release the latest updates.

Finally, the American Enterprise Institute (AEI) has collected and assembled China's global investment and contracts in energy, transportation, real estate, and other major industries from 2005 to 2019 (American Enterprise Institute and the Heritage Foundation, 2020); it is the only fully public record that includes the amount, Chinese parent company, host country, and subsector, and is more reliable than the MOFCOM database. It also classifies Chinese investments into greenfield and brownfield and records the amount of transactions even when Chinese companies are involved only as contractors.[4] However, it covers only those worth US$100 million or more (Scissors, 2020) and does not provide project names and installed capacity. Because the database provides project information only by category of "energy" and "utility" sector, and type of energy, manual classification of projects are required to sort out projects in the electricity sector.

We considered these pros and cons of the database, and their fitness to the purpose of this research, and choose the AEI's China Global Investment Tracker as a core database. We select investments and contracts in the energy and utility sector and manually exclude transactions in resource extraction and transportation. Next, we use the project information in the China Electric Power Yearbook, Gallagher (2018b) and refer to Li et al. (2020), Endcoal (2020), and the Global Energy Monitor and Center for Media and Democracy (2020a) to identify project names, subsector (generation or grid), type of energy, installed capacity, category (greenfield or brownfield investments, contract), and financial institutions supporting the investments. Finally, we cross-check this database with primary sources such as company press reports and quarterly reports; reports from business journals, daily English newspapers such as Reuters, the South China Morning Post, China Daily, the Global Times, the Wall Street Journal, and local English newspapers in host countries to exclude projects that have not been implemented and to add projects not recorded. Documents are collected from online archives by searching for company and project names.

We use the amount of transactions as recorded in the AEI's China Global Investment Tracker. We understand that the differences between the planned and actual costs; delays in land acquisition, insufficient consideration to social and environmental impacts that causes local protests, and corruption are not unusual, and all these factors cause overcharging to host country governments. China Global Investment Tracker records these financial transactions only when it recognizes them as additional transactions. However, we have limited primary and secondary sources to ensure that these transactions are actually made and the recorded transactions are not redundant, because additional transactions are seldom released. This limitation leads us to exclude the recorded transactions with high uncertainty and classify transactions without a detailed description into "unidentified."

4 Results

4.1 Heterogeneous responses among the type of companies

All five types of companies collectively invest in and sign contracts for foreign power projects to the tune of US$234 billion (Figure 5.1a) to increase installed capacity by 164 GW (Figure 5.1b) in 2014–2019. The amount of

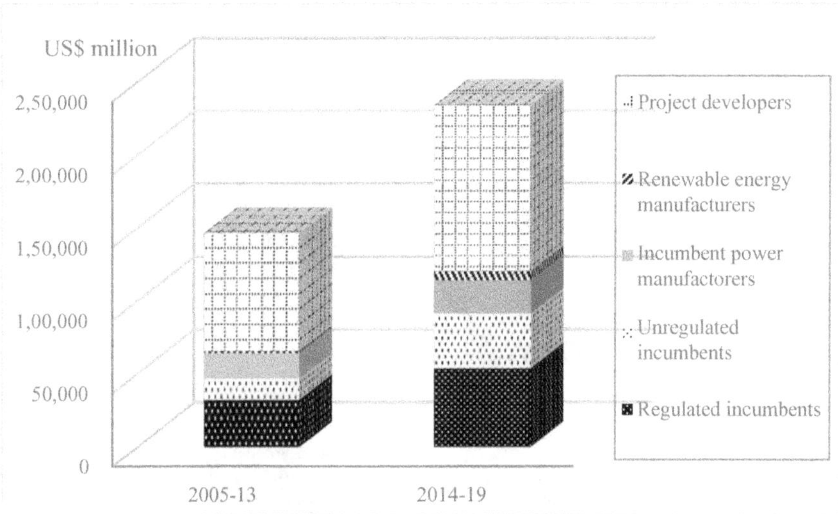

Figure 5.1a Amount of China's investments and contracts in foreign power projects.
Source: Compiled by the author based on sources described in Section 3.2.

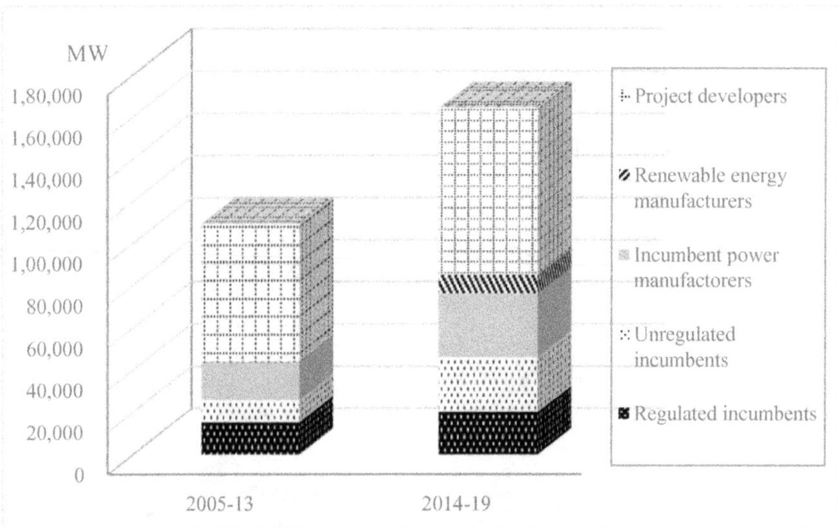

Figure 5.1b Installed capacity by investments and contracts in foreign power projects.
Source: Compiled by the author based on sources described in Section 3.2.

the transaction increases by 60%, and intended newly installed capacity increases by 50% in 2006–2013. The new capacity amounts to 17% of the domestic new installed capacity in China (853 GW) in the same period.[5]

Coal power accounts for 24% in the amount of transaction or US$57 billion (Figure 5.1c), and 33% in the installed capacity or 54 GW (Figure 5.1d), respectively. The new coal power capacity amounts to 21% of the domestic new installed coal power capacity in China (249 GW) in the same period.

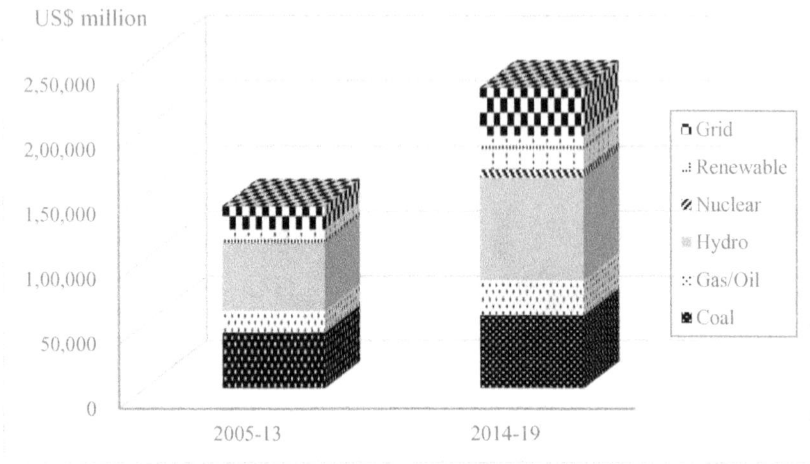

Figure 5.1c Amount of China's investments and contracts in foreign coal power projects.

Note 1: a contract consisting of capacity development of coal and renewable energy sourced power is classified into coal power.

Note 2: excluding transaction that cannot be identified.

Source: Compiled by the author based on sources described in Section 3.2.

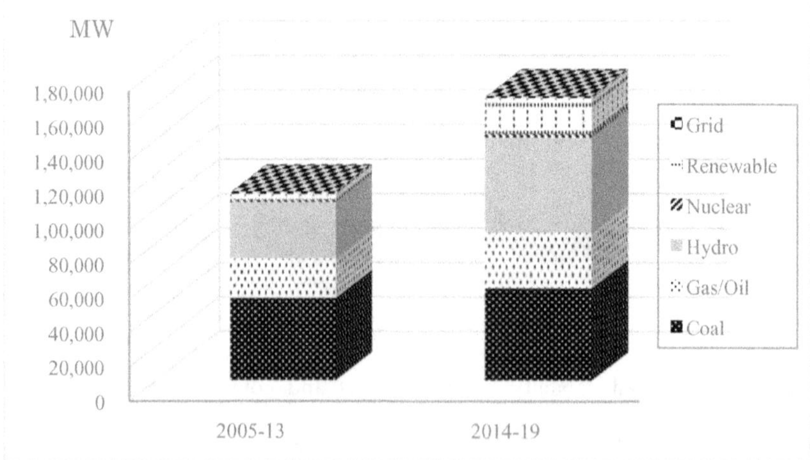

Figure 5.1d Installed capacity by China's investments and contracts in foreign coal power projects.

Source: Compiled by the author based on sources described in Section 3.2.

Among the type of companies, project developers increase the most: US$33 billion and 14 GW. The regulated incumbents are the third largest in the amount of a transaction and fourth in the installed capacity, with US$21 billion and 5 GW, respectively. They increase greenfield investments in coal power (Figures 5.2a and 5.2b) and brownfield investments in grids (Figures 5.2c and 5.2d) and decrease contracts in coal power and grids (Figures 5.2e and 5.2f). As a result, they went through a slight increase in the share of the amount of transaction (from 22% to 23%) but a decrease in the share of the installed capacity (from 14% to 12%) among the types of companies in 2014–2019.

By contrast, the unregulated incumbents increase brownfield investments in hydro and gas/oil power and contracts in nuclear power while slightly reducing greenfield investments in the same period. The incumbent power manufacturers increase contracts in coal power, and renewable energy ones increase greenfield investments in renewable energy (wind and solar power). Project developers increase contracts, especially those for grids, hydropower, and renewable energy. Although they also increase the amount of investments in coal and hydro power, the increased amount of contracts in the three subsectors outweighs the latter.

These results imply that the regulated incumbent utilities are the only type of companies that have shifted from contractors to investors, especially

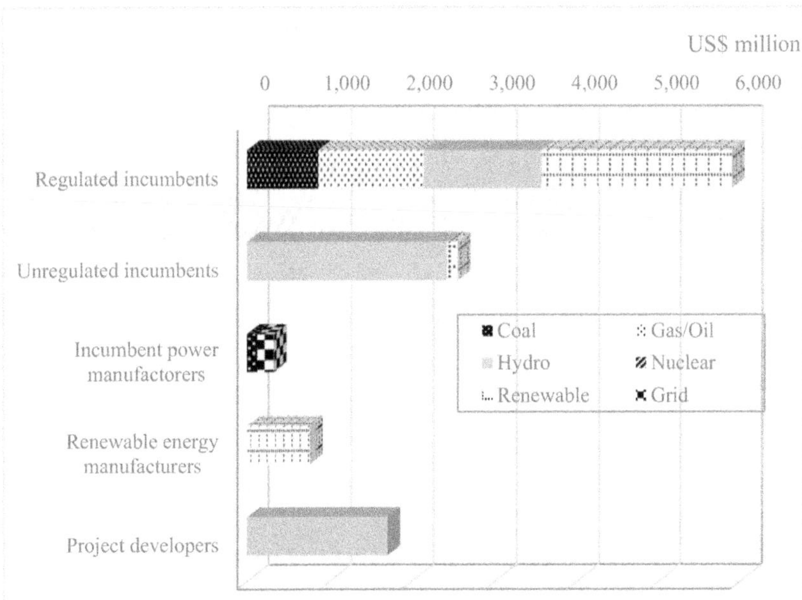

Figure 5.2a Amount of China's greenfield investments by category of companies and by type of energy in 2005–2013.

Source: Compiled by the author based on sources described in Section 3.2.

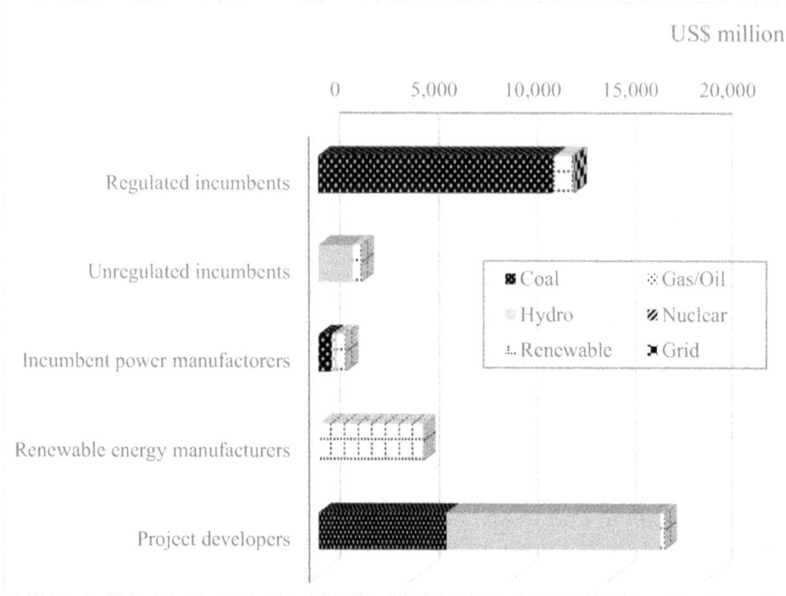

Figure 5.2b Amount of China's brownfield investments by category of companies and by type of energy in 2005–2013.

Source: Compiled by the author based on sources described in Section 3.2.

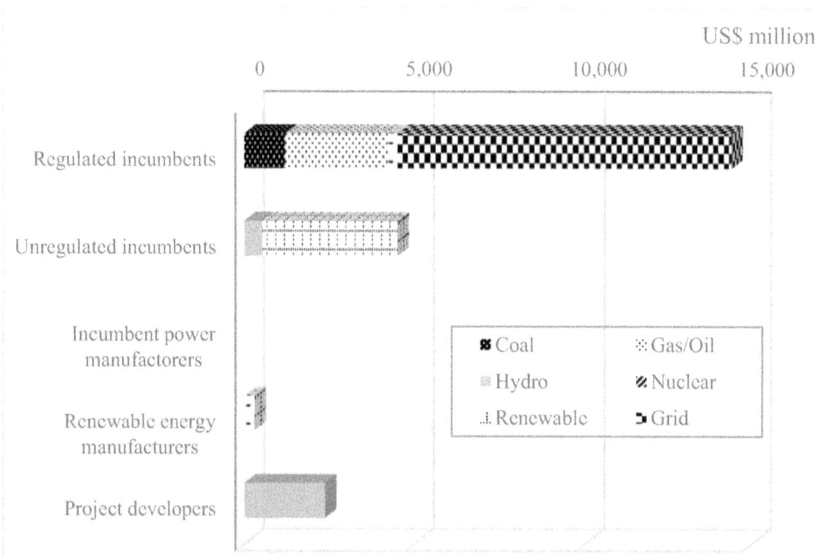

Figure 5.2c Amount of China's contracts by category of companies and by type of energy in 2005–2013.

Source: Compiled by the author based on sources described in Section 3.2.

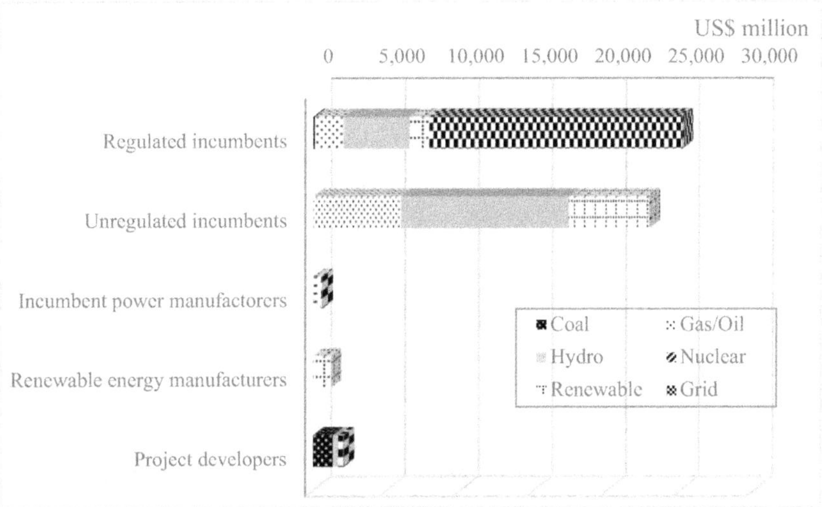

Figure 5.2d Amount of China's greenfield investments by category of companies and by type of energy in 2014–2019.

Source: Compiled by the author based on sources described in Section 3.2.

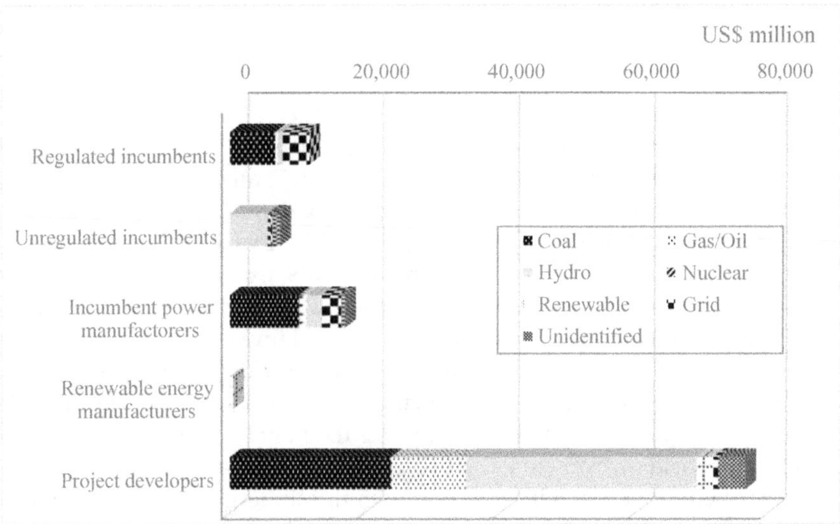

Figure 5.2e Amount of China's brownfield investments by category of companies and by type of energy in 2014–2019.

Source: Compiled by the author based on sources described in Section 3.2.

coal power and grids in 2014–2019. Renewable energy manufacture is another type of company that accounts for a larger amount in greenfield investments in 2014–2019, but they did not win any contracts in 2005–2013.

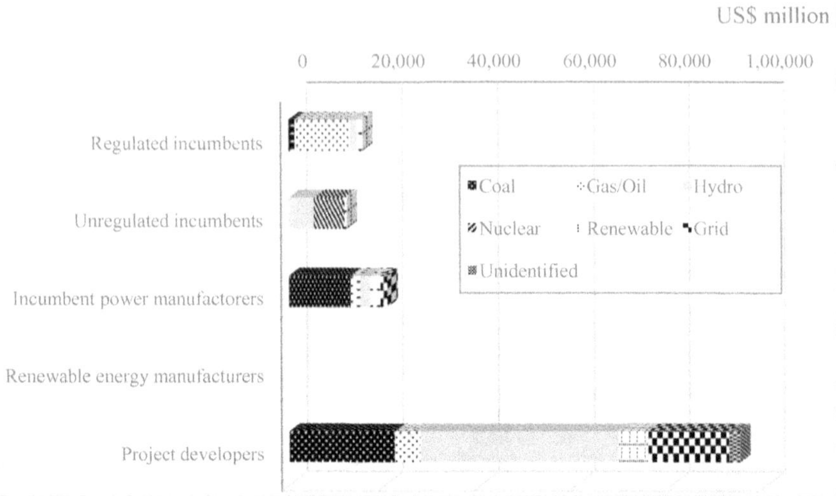

Figure 5.2f Amount of China's contracts by category of companies and by type of energy in 2014–2019.

Source: Compiled by the author based on sources described in Section 3.2.

4.2 Mixed responses within the regulated incumbent power companies

Among the regulated incumbents, SPIC, Southern Power Grid, Shenhua, and Huaneng increase greenfield investments by more than US$1 billion in 2014–2019 (Figures 5.3a and 5.3b). Except for SPIC, all of them invest exclusively in coal power in this period. This finding demonstrates a sharp contrast in contracts, whereby they were awarded in a various types of energy in 2005–2013 while winning nothing in 2014–2019, except for Huadian (Figures 5.3e and 5.3f). These results imply that SPIC, Shenhua, and Huaneng have shifted from being contractors to greenfield investors in coal power.

In contrast, State Grid and Southern Power Grid increase the number of contracts, especially in renewable energy and grid projects (Figures 5.3e and 5.3f). Coupled with the shift of the regulated incumbent power generators to greenfield investments, the two grid companies account for a greater amount of contracts, which exceeds 80% in the amount of contracts held by the regulated incumbents.

State Grid, SPIC, and to a less extent Southern Power Grid, also increase brownfield investments in 2014–2019 (Figures 5.3c and 5.3d). However, they differ in the type of energy: two grid companies increase investments mostly in grids and in installed capacity of gas and renewable energy only when greenfield investment is an integral part of brownfield investment. By contrast, SPIC does so in hydro, gas, and renewable energy.

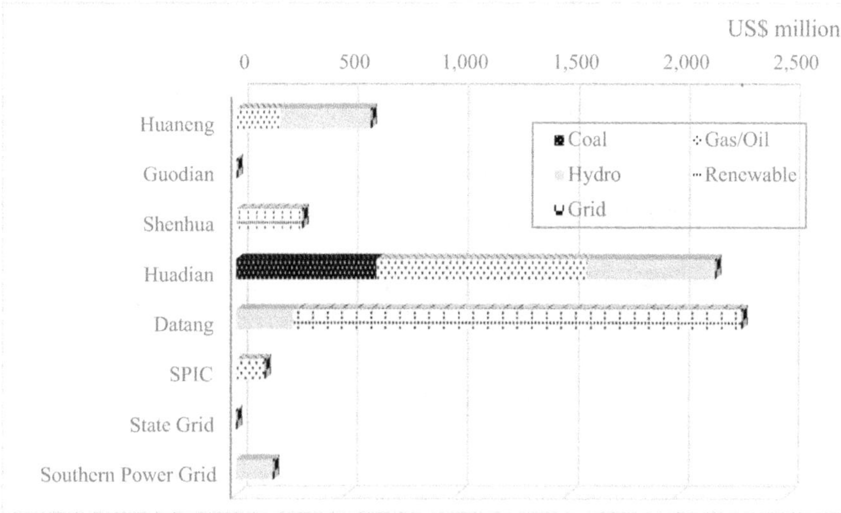

Figure 5.3a Amount of China's greenfield investments by the regulated incumbents and by type of energy in 2005–2013.

Note: Huaneng includes joint investments with Guangdong Yuadian, Datang with China South Industries, SPIC with State Grid, Southern Power Grid and AVIC, and State Grid with Power Construction Corporation.

Source: Compiled by the author based on sources described in Section 3.2.

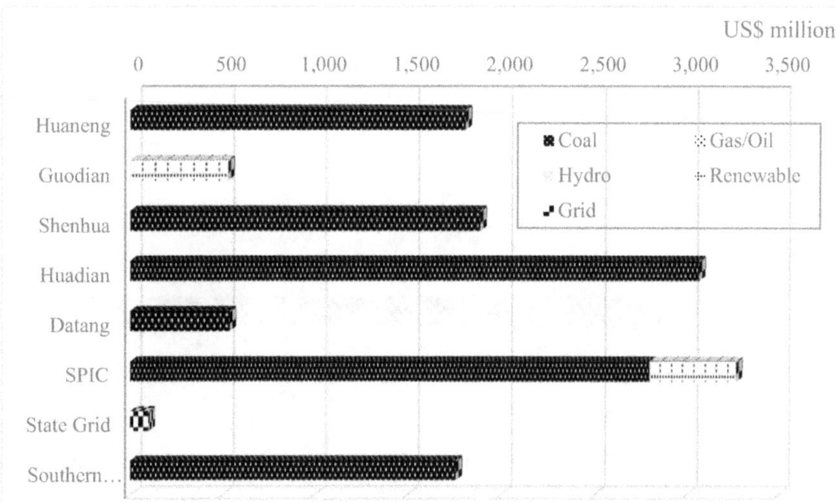

Figure 5.3b Amount of China's brownfield investments by the regulated incumbents and by type of energy in 2005–2013.

Source: Compiled by the author based on sources described in Section 3.2.

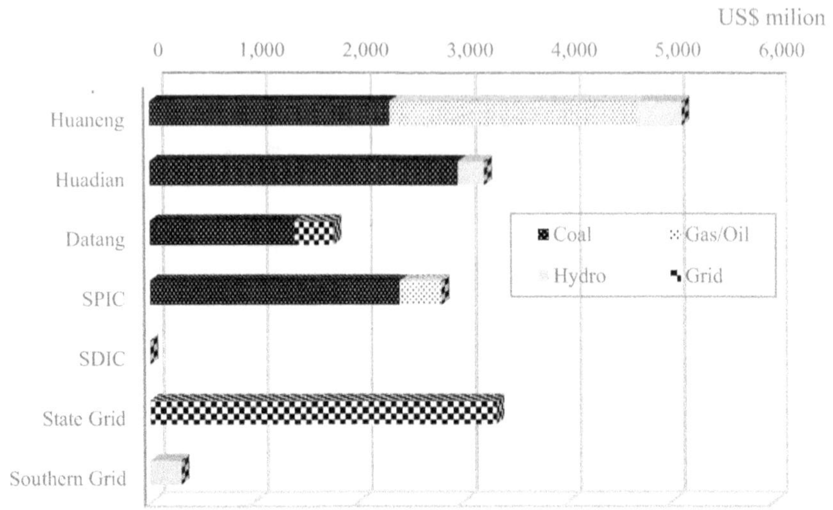

Figure 5.3c Amount of China's contracts by the regulated incumbents and by type of energy in 2005–2013.

Source: Compiled by the author based on sources described in Section 3.2.

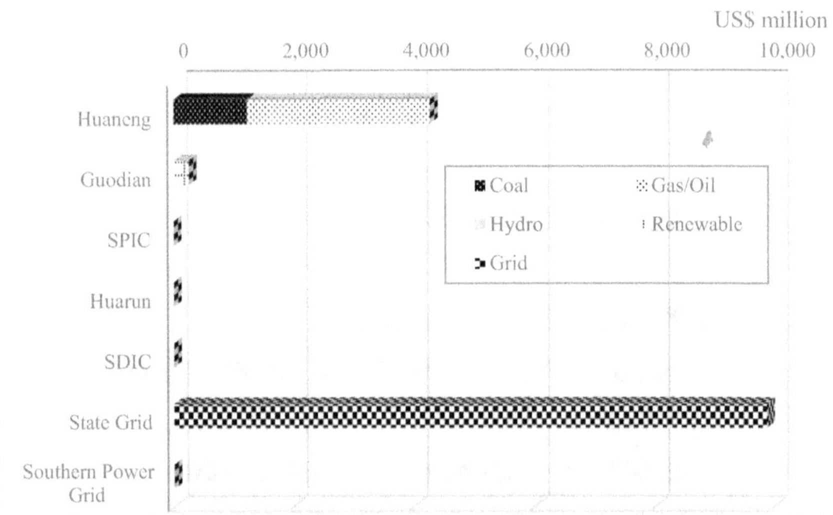

Figure 5.3d Amount of China's greenfield investments by the regulated incumbents and by type of energy in 2014–2019.

Source: Compiled by the author based on sources described in Section 3.2.

By contrast, Datang reduces both greenfield investment and contracts in 2014–2019. The company made the largest amount of greenfield investments in renewable energy in 2005–2013 but a much smaller amount in 2014–2019 because it does not win any contracts in this period.

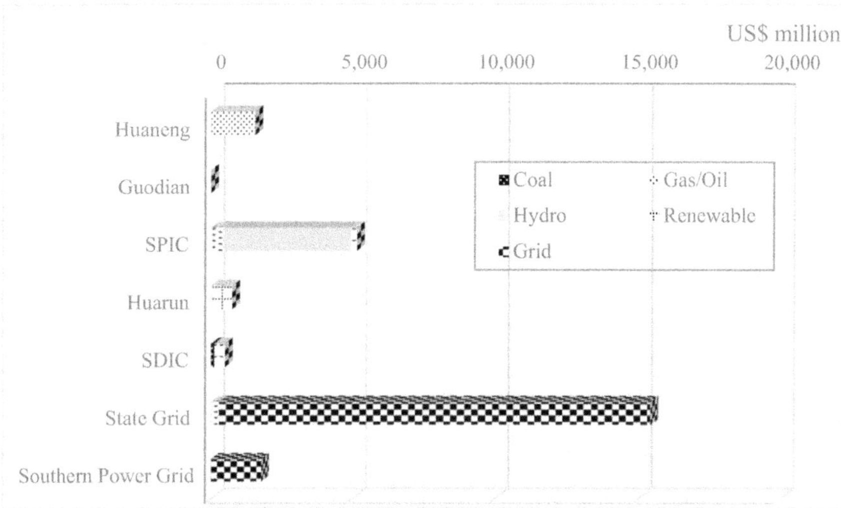

Figure 5.3e Amount of China's brownfield investments by the regulated incumbents and by type of energy in 2014–2019.

Source: Compiled by the author based on sources described in Section 3.2.

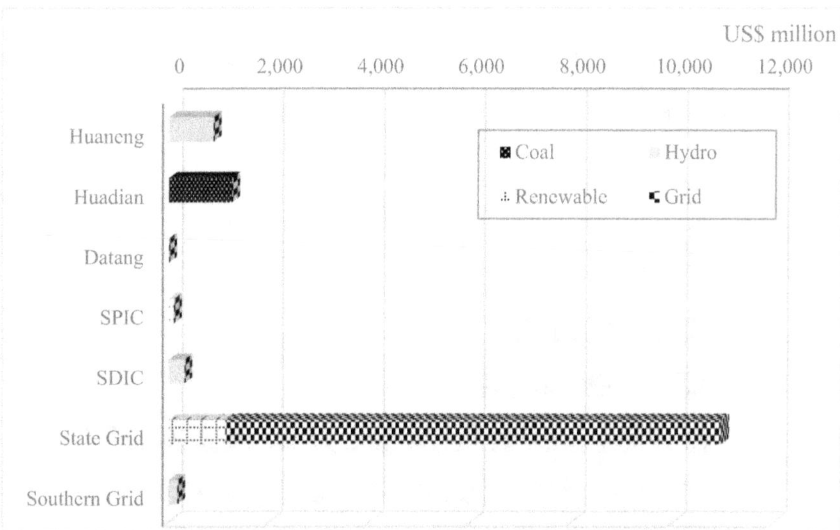

Figure 5.3f Amount of China's contracts by the regulated incumbents and by type of energy in 2014–2019.

Source: Compiled by the author based on sources described in Section 3.2.

4.3 Heterogeneous selection of host countries

The regulated incumbents show heterogeneity in the selection of host countries. The regulated incumbent power generators made greenfield investments and received contracts in a variety of host countries such as India, Turkey, and Vietnam for various types of energy in 2005–2013 (Figures 5.4a and 5.4c). However, they concentrated them in coal power and only in six countries: Indonesia, Pakistan, Vietnam, Turkey, Cambodia, and Bangladesh (Figure 5.4d). This finding sharply contrasts with the regulated incumbent grid companies.

By contrast, the regulated incumbent grid companies made brownfield investments only in Australia, Brazil, the Philippines, and Portugal (Figure 5.4b)

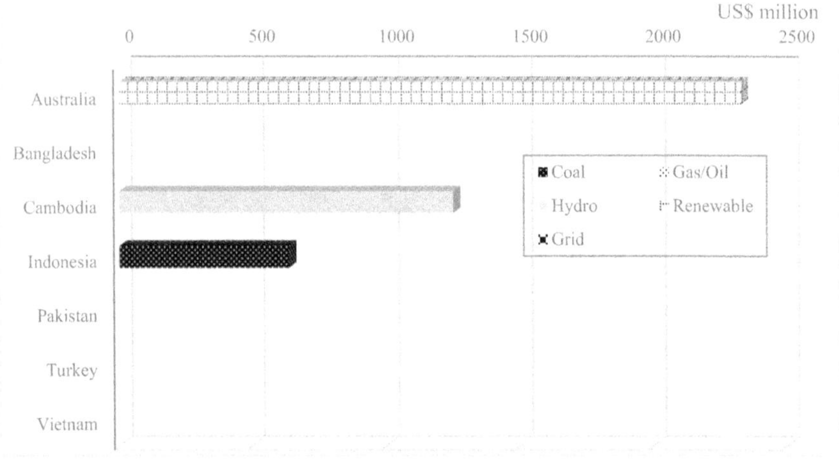

Figure 5.4a Amount of China's greenfield investments by host country and by type of energy in 2005–2013.

Source: Compiled by the author based on sources described in Section 3.2.

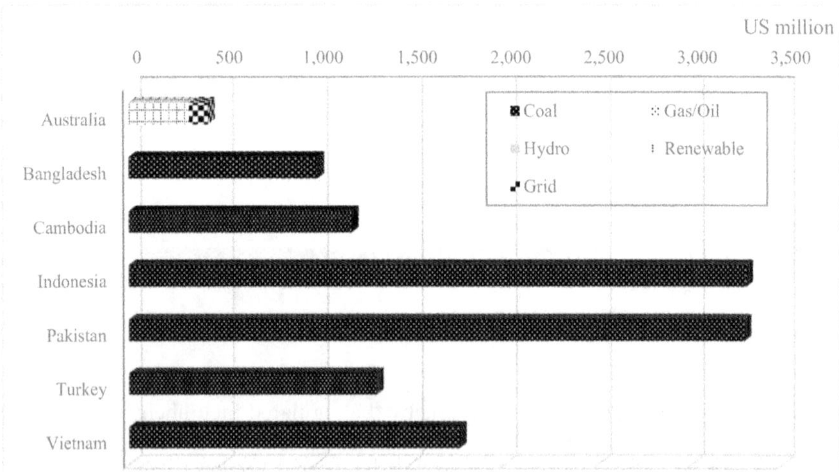

Figure 5.4b Amount of China's brownfield investments by host country and by type of energy in 2005–2013.

Source: Compiled by the author based on sources described in Section 3.2.

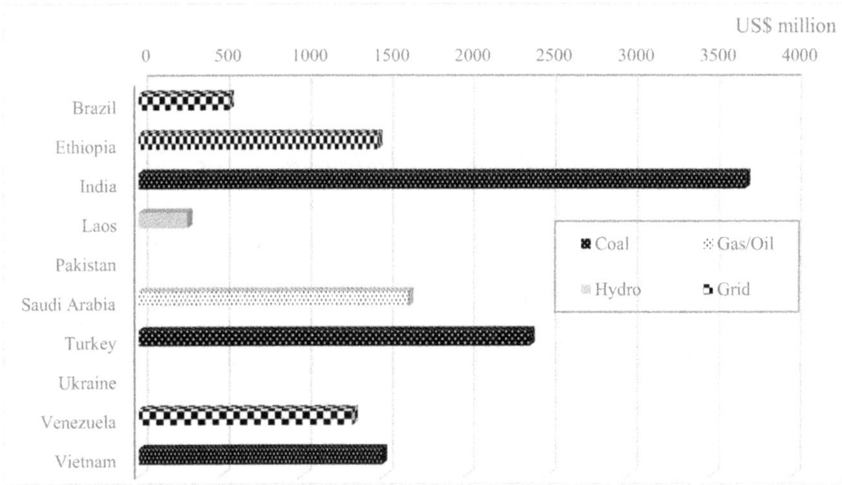

Figure 5.4c Amount of China's contracts by host country and by type of energy in 2005–2013.

Source: Compiled by the author based on sources described in Section 3.2.

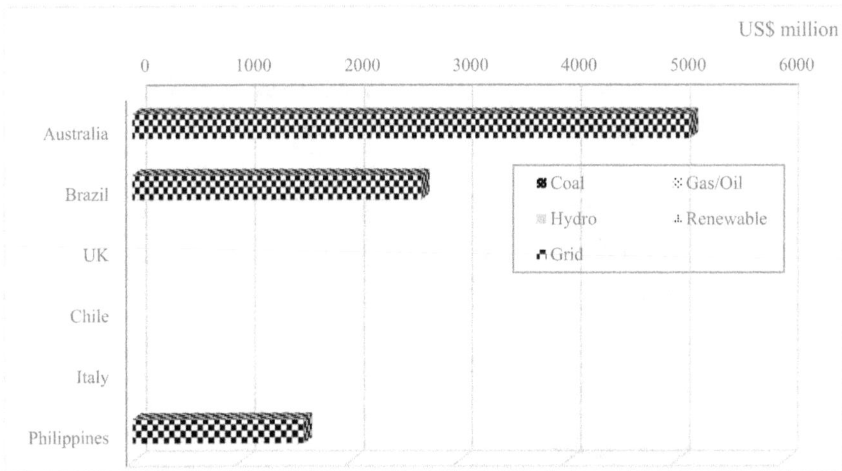

Figure 5.4d Amount of China's greenfield investments by host country and by type of energy in 2014–2019.

Source: Compiled by the author based on sources described in Section 3.2.

and contracts in Ethiopia and Venezuela in 2005–2013 (Figure 5.4c). However, they increase geographical diversification to Brazil, Chile, and Italy in brownfield investments (Figure 5.4e) and to Brazil, Pakistan, and Saudi Arabia in contracts in 2014–2019 (Figure 5.4f).

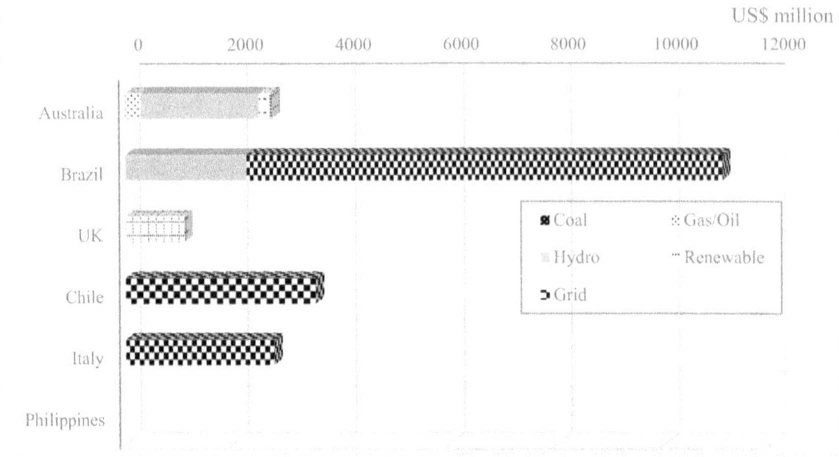

Figure 5.4e Amount of China's brownfield investments by host country and by type of energy in 2014–2019.

Source: Compiled by the author based on sources described in Section 3.2.

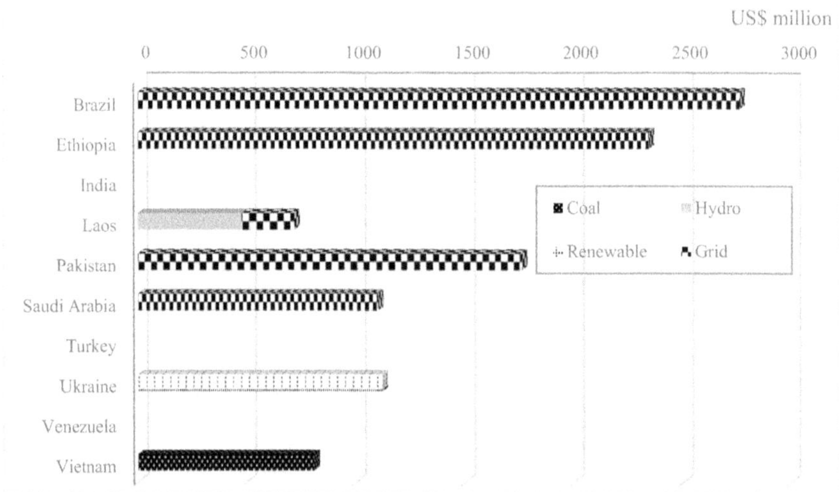

Figure 5.4f Amount of China's contracts by host country and by type of energy in 2014–2019.

Source: Compiled by the author based on sources described in Section 3.2.

4.4 Summary of the findings

We summarize the findings as follows. First, the regulated incumbent generators increased investments and contracts in foreign power projects after the government mandate on the upgrade and renovation of coal power plants in 2014. Second, their investments and contracts are not comparably larger than those of project developers and incumbent power manufacturers, as well as their newly installed capacity in China. Third, the regulated incumbent generators have shifted from contractors to greenfield investors and concentrated investments in a limited number of countries with investment framework agreements. Finally, grid companies increase geographical diversification in brownfield investment and contacts for grids and renewable energy.

5 Discussion

Why have the regulated incumbent generators invested and won contracts smaller than those of the project developers and the incumbent power manufacturers? What generates heterogeneity in a geographical diversification strategy between the regulated incumbent power generators and grid companies and within the regulated incumbent power generators? This section discusses these two questions derived from the results.

5.1 Capabilities for managing country and credit risk

There is a distinguished difference in the capabilities for managing a country and credit risk between the regulated incumbent grid companies and power generators. The regulated incumbent grid companies are capable of purchasing a portion of shares and assets of a state-owned utility in host countries and connecting transmission lines to reduce business risk to power generators. They capitalized on the European debt crisis, which started in 2009, and subsequent privatization of state-owned utilities to purchase them indirectly from their parent companies and foreign stockholders, as well as directly from the utility.

Brazil provides a typical example of how the regulated incumbent grid companies have reduced risks and induced Chinese FDI in power development projects. State Grid acquired seven Brazilian transmission companies from Brazilian Plena Transmissoras (Global Times, 2010), electricity transmission assets in Brazil from Spanish builder Actividades de Construcción y Servicios SA (ACS) (Zhu and Chen, 2012), and a distribution company called Celg Distribuicao SA from state-owned utility Eletrobras (Dezem, 2015). Subsequently, the grid company acquired shares of transmission companies and CPFL Energias, the largest power distributor in Brazil. China Three Gorge Group, one of the unregulated incumbent power generators, also started to acquire a stake in Portuguese utility Energias de Portugal, SA (EDP), establishing a partnership with EDP to obtain half the stakes of the hydropower and wind power projects from its subsidiary EDP Brazil (Macauhub, 2014).

These acquisitions have enhanced Chinese power companies' control over utilities, reducing credit risks for Chinese IPPs. State Grid's investments in transmission lines also reduce curtailment risks of wind and solar power producers. The changes in ownership from European to Chinese companies did not raise fear and protests against foreign ownership, as occurred in Australia (Barrett and Fernandez, 2016) and Europe (De Clercq et al., 2014). Subsequently, State Grid's investments triggered a rush of brownfield investments in the assets of hydro, wind, and solar power, including Ilha Solteira and Jupia hydropower, one of the world's largest hydropower plants.

Learning from the Brazil case, Chinese project developers took over the EPC contract on the transmission line in Kenya from Spanish engineering and construction group Isolux Corsan when the company went bankrupt (Oirere, 2018), securing connectivity of their invested hydropower project.

By contrast, the regulated incumbent generators are not capable of doing the same as the grid companies. They have experienced country risk, suspension of projects, and financial loss, despite their national-level partnership agreements. The Cooperation Framework Agreement on Development of Hydroelectric Resources could not prevent the Thein Sein government of Myanmar from suspending the Chibwe Nge, Myitsone, and Chibwe hydropower projects, which were awarded to SPIC in 2008–2011 because of turmoil, local protests, and armed conflicts (SPIC, n.a). The CPEC agreement does not help Pakistan's government avoid abandoning the proposed Datang coal power project that was assumed to use imported coal to supply electricity at an affordable price because of the violation of the ban on imported fuels (Bhutta, 2020). Pakistan's government leaked to the media Huaneng's alleged overcharging by approximately US$3 billion by using inflated set-up costs and interest payments in a coal power project (Findlay et al., 2020).

These failures partly explain why the regulated incumbent generators consider geographical diversification as a minor option. Only those who have developers with sufficient capability as subsidiaries or organize strong ties with developers outside of their groups have employed it when they find profitable projects in host countries with stable a business environment. Otherwise, they devote themselves to a domestic response strategy, including lobbying for resuming the new installation of coal power in China (Chen and Ge, 2020). Despite the Chinese government's 27 financial assistance deals with Bangladesh that were agreed upon at the time of Xi Jinping's stopover in 2016 (Rogers, 2016), only Huadian has invested in power projects among the regulated incumbents. The project developers make greenfield investments and win contracts for most of the coal power projects in Bangladesh (Figure 5.5a).

5.2 Capabilities for developing and managing greenfield investment projects

The regulated incumbent power generators have heterogeneous capabilities for supplying EPC services and organizing power development projects.

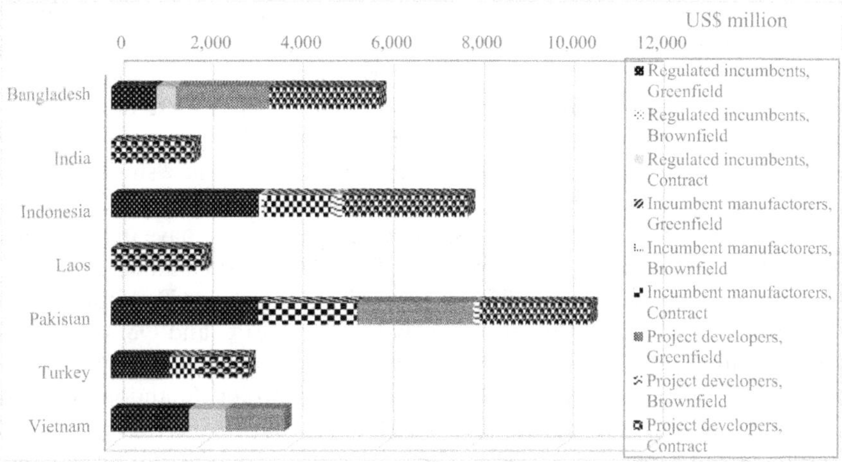

Figure 5.5a Amount of China's investments and contracts in coal power projects by type of Chinese companies in selected host country in 2014–2019.

Source: Compiled by the author based on sources described in Section 3.2.

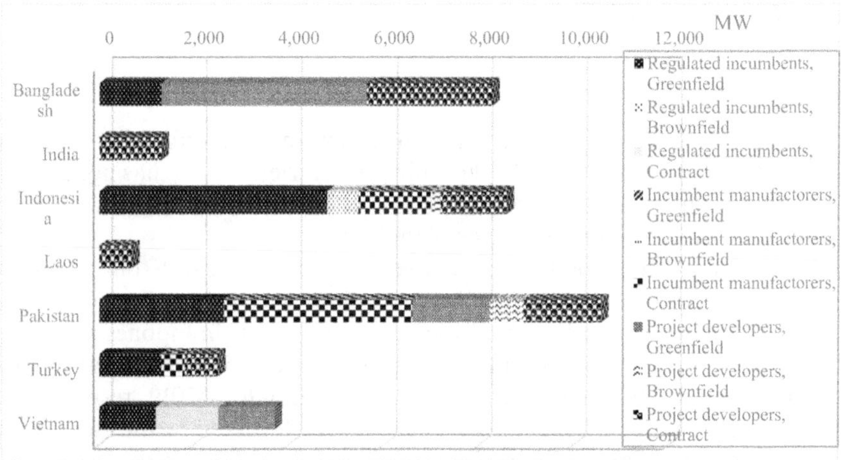

Figure 5.5b Installed capacity by China's investments and contracts in coal power projects by type of Chinese companies in selected host country in 2014–2019.

Source: Compiled by the author based on sources described in Section 3.2.

Host countries that retain vertical integration in their electricity supply system tend to allow participation of foreign companies under EPC contracts and assume that incumbent state electricity companies operate and manage newly developed or renovated generation, grids, transmission, and distribution capacity. Only the host countries awarding O&M contracts or adopting PPP such as a BOT scheme allows foreign power companies to own power generation assets and operate them as IPPs. In host countries that accept bids when selecting developers, to be qualified to join the process, foreign IPPs are required to have sufficient capabilities to develop projects, organize consortiums, and arrange financial schemes.

Thus, the regulated incumbent power companies who have subsidiaries in engineering and/or manufacturing, and take advantage of their close relation with state policy banks (Kong and Gallagher, 2017), have invested in a larger number of foreign power projects. State Grid and Huadian have engineering subsidiaries, China Electric Power Equipment and Technology and Huadian Engineering, capable of providing both EPC and O&M services and organizing consortiums for bidding. SPIC and Huaneng mobilize their subsidiary power generators, Shanghai electric power, Shandong energy, Shenzhen Power, and Lancang River Hydropower, to increase greenfield investments (Table 5.1); however, they are neither capable nor sufficiently innovative to create new schemes to enhance their competitive edge over the project developers. On the basis of the standardized procedures for the EPC contract established by the Chinese government, the project developers have created new business models such as export credit EPC (FEPC), "Planning + FEPC," mixed-ownership investment, and large-scale mixed loan (China Daily, 2019).

5.3 Carbon haven effect

The minor role of geographical diversification in the regulated incumbent generators does not imply that the Chinese electricity sector has not caused the relocation of carbon-intensive plants or the carbon leakage effect in an individual host country and at the plant level.

As analyzed in Section 4.1, regulated incumbents are only one category of Chinese companies who participate in foreign coal power projects. Although they have played a major role in power projects in Indonesia (Figure 5.5a), they account for 20% and 24% in the amount of the transaction for Chinese foreign power projects in 2005–2013 and 2014–2019, respectively. The project developers account for the majority, followed by the incumbent power manufacturers. Chinese companies as a whole will increase coal power capacity by more than 8 GW by 2030 in Bangladesh, Pakistan, and Indonesia, mostly due to greenfield investments and contracts by the incumbent manufacturers and the project developers (Figure 5.5b). Because 3–5 GW of newly installed capacity is large enough for countries either with limited installed capacity or in a power crisis to reconfigure the electricity supply system toward a coal-centered system (Mori, 2020), the parallel investments and contracts in new coal power capacity by the three categories of Chinese power companies can play a decisive role in moving and locking host countries' electricity systems into a coal-centered system.

In this transition, pollution and carbon-intensive plants are relocated across borders. A report demonstrated that the 2 × 300 MW subcritical coal power plants at the Hunan Chuangyuan power station, forcibly closed in China for violating pollution standards (Global Energy Monitor, Center for Media and Democracy, 2020b), were transferred to Cambodia for use in the second phase of the Sihanoukville Cambodia International Investment Development Group (CIIDG) power projects (MOFCOM, 2020; Polaris Thermal Power Network News, 2018).

Given that State Grid played a substantial role in overcoming the conflict of interest between coal power and wind and solar power in China (Mori, 2018, 2020), grid governance and investment choices can affect carbon leakage and displacement of CO_2 emission through Chinese investments and contracts in power projects. If the system actually increases flexibility and network reliability, wind and solar power become profitable businesses. A grid company will probably invest in transmission and wind and solar installed capacity in an integrated manner to maximize profit opportunities (Spring, 2018). By contrast, the grid company may attract coal power investments if it continues to offer an attractive business environment to coal power in a host country with weak grid governance, as in the Philippines after China's State Grid's partial takeover of the National Grid Corporation (Saculsan and Mori, 2020). Which direction to transit depends critically on the good governance of host country; a transparent audit that grids and utilities choose; and developing a secure, flexible, and least-cost system after Chinese companies' takeover (Ahmed, 2020; De Clercq et al., 2014).

6 Conclusions

China has increased investments and finance for foreign coal power projects after the government implemented more stringent regulations on air pollution and CO_2 emissions. The going global strategy and the BRI create opportunities for the power industry to participate in foreign power projects as investors in greenfield projects, the merger and acquisition of shares and assets, and EPC contractors. These investments and contracts can cause carbon relocation. Recent research has estimated the scale and possible adverse impacts on the environment and the climate crisis; however, most of them have framed the environmental impact in the context of the globalization of Chinese companies and the BRI rather than a response to the stringent environmental regulation.

Against this backdrop, this chapter investigates if power companies employ foreign investments and contracts in power projects as a geographical diversification to the stringent regulations and generate carbon relocation.

Our empirical analysis shows that power project developers and to a less extent coal power plant manufacturers have proactively increased contracts and investments in foreign coal power projects. Although power project developers and coal power plant manufacturers are not regulated, they perceive the shrinking Chinese market and seek profit opportunities in foreign countries. The regulated grid companies take advantage of the crises, privatization, and bankruptcies to purchase shares and assets of utilities and national grids, gradually increasing their influence on the direction of power development.

By contrast, the regulated power generators have used foreign power projects as a minor option to circumvent the severe air pollution control regulations at best. The regulated power generators are less capable and innovative enough to compete in international bidding, compared with the project developers and incumbent manufacturers. Although some of them are enhancing the capabilities of developing and managing projects, to shift from contractors to investors and developers, only a few countries accept IPPs, limiting their investment opportunities. Coupled with their initial failure in foreign projects, this results in greenfield investments in a limited number of host countries.

These results suggest that Chinese climate–energy–air pollution control policies, coupled with the going global strategy and the BRI, cause the partial relocation of carbon-intensive processes in the electricity sector. The electricity supply system is more likely to be reconfigured toward a coal-centered system in host countries with weak grid governance and massive investments and contracts from China under investment framework agreements.

A further challenge is to explore how to reconcile environmental and climatic consequences of these Chinese investments and contracts in coal power with the Nationally Determined Contributions to the Paris Agreement in these host countries. We discuss this challenge in the conclusion chapter.

7 Acknowledgments

The author thanks Dr. Gregory Trencher for his comments at the annual conference of the Society for Environmental Economics and Policy Studies (SEEPS) on 26 September 2020. This chapter is financially supported by Murata Foundation H31-GH-31 as well.

Notes

1 An acquisition of assets under construction enables investors to save transaction costs in terms of development of potential projects, administrative procedure, land acquisition, environmental and social impact assessments, and consensus building.

2 National Development and Reform Commission, Ministry of Environmental Protection and National Energy Administration (2014), Notification on the Action Plan for Upgrading and Transformation of the Energy Conservation and Emission Reduction of Coal-fired Power (2014–2020) (Editorial Board of China Electric Power Yearbook, 2016: 669–672).

3 MOFCOM, Foreign investment projects, http://projct.mofcom.gov.cn [accessed 1 September 2020].
4 Project developers often provide equity finance as project owners to organize financial arrangement and may assign themselves as EPC contractors.
5 Author's calculation based on Editorial Board of China Electric Power Yearbook (2015) and China Electric Council (2020).

References

Ahmed, S.J., 2020. IEEFA update: China's state grid group triggers oversight controversy in the Philippines, (18 February 2020), https://ieefa.org/ieefa-update-chinas-state-grid-group-triggers-oversight-controversy-in-the-philippines/, [accessed 17 August 2020].

Al-mulali, U., C.F. Tang, 2013. Investigating the validity of pollution haven hypothesis in the gulf cooperation council (GCC) countries. *Energy Pol.* 60, 813–819. https://doi.org/10.1016/j.enpol.2013.05.055.

Ali, M., 2009. Indonesia power firm signs loan agreements for over $1 bln, *Reuters*, 14 October 2009, https://www.reuters.com/article/indonesia-power-loan/indonesia-power-firm-signs-loan-agreements-for-over-1-bln-idUSJAK54822220091014/, [accessed 14 April 2019].

American Enterprise Institute and the Heritage Foundation, 2020. *The China Global Investment Tracker*, https://www.aei.org/china-global-investment-tracker/, [accessed 20 July 2020].

Arce, G., L.A. López, D. Guan, 2016. Carbon emissions embodied in international trade: The post-China era, *Appl Energy* 184: 1063–1072, http://dx.doi.org/10.1016/j.apenergy.2016.05.084.

Asghari, M., 2013. Does FDI promote MENA region's environment quality? Pollution halo or pollution haven hypothesis. *Int. J.* 1(6), 92–100, http://dx.doi.org/10.12983/ijsres-2013-p092-100.

Baek, J., 2016. A new look at the FDI-income-energy-environment nexus: Dynamic panel data analysis of ASEAN. *Energy Pol.* 91, 22–27, https://doi.org/10.1016/j.enpol.2015.12.045.

Barrett, J., C. Fernandez, 2016. Australian treasurer formally rejects Chinese bids for state-owned Ausgrid, *Reuters*, (19 August 2016), https://www.reuters.com/article/australia-privatisation-ausgrid/australian-treasurer-formally-rejects-chinese-bids-for-state-owned-ausgrid-idUSS9N1AR003/, [accessed 23 August 2020].

Beardsworth, J.J. Jr., J.A. Schmidt, 2014. Resource financed infrastructure: Origins and issues, In: Halland, H., J. Beardsworth, B. Land, and J. Schmidt, *Resource Financed Infrastructure, A Discussion on a New Form of Infrastructure Financing*, The World Bank, Washington DC, 11–68, http://dx.doi.org/10.1596/978-1-4648-0239-3.

Bhutta, Z. 2020, PTI govt abandons K-Electric's coal project, *Tribune* (25 June 2020), https://tribune.com.pk/story/2249796/pti-govt-abandons-k-electrics-coal-projec/, [accessed 3 September 2020].

Blanchard, J.M.F. 2017. Probing China's Twenty-First-Century Maritime Silk Road Initiative (MSRI): An examination of MSRI narratives, *Geopolitics* 22(2): 246–268, https://doi.org/10.1080/14650045.2016.1267147.

Boulle, M., 2019. The hazy rise of coal in Kenya: The actors, interests, and discursive contradictions shaping Kenya's electricity future, *Energy Res. Soc. Sci.* 56: 101205, https://doi.org/10.1016/j.erss.2019.05.015.

Brautigam, D., 2009. *The Dragon's Gift: The Real Story of China in Africa*, Oxford University Press: Oxford.

Brautigam, D., K.P. Gallagher, 2014. Bartering globalization: China's commodity-backed finance in Africa and Latin America, *Global Policy* 5(3), 346–357, https://doi.org/10.1111/1758-5899.12138.

Brautigam, D., J. Hwang, J. Link, K. Acker, 2019. *Chinese Loans to Africa Database*, China Africa Research Initiative, Johns Hopkins University School of Advanced International Studies, Washington, DC, http://www.sais-cari.org/s/LoanData_17July2020.xlsx/, [accessed 23 July 2020].

Candau, F., E. Dienesch, 2017. Pollution haven and corruption paradise, *J. Environ. Econ. Manag.* 85, 171–192, https://doi.org/10.1016/j.jeem.2017.05.005.

Cardoso, D., 2013. China-Brazil: A strategic partnership in an evolving world order, *East Asia* 30(1), 35–51, https://doi.org/10.1007/s12140-012-9186-z.

Castle, J.W., A. Manuwoto, 2011. *Indonesian Business: The Year in Review 2010*, Equinox Publishing (Asia), Jakarta.

Chen, X., Y. Ge, 2020. China fires up coal power plant construction: Surge in first-quarter approvals possibly related to COVID-19 outbreak, (5 May, 2020), *Nikkei Asian Review*, https://asia.nikkei.com/Spotlight/Caixin/China-fires-up-coal-power-plant-construction/, [accessed 26 August 2020].

Cherniwchan, J., B.R. Copeland, M.S. Taylor, 2017. Trade and the environment: New methods, measurements, and results, *Annu. Rev. Econ.* 9, 59–85, https://doi.org/10.1146/annurev-economics-063016-103756.

China Daily, 2019. POWERCHINA forges ahead with innovative international business models, (18 April 2019), http://www.chinadaily.com.cn/m/powerchina/2019-04/18/content_37459891.htm/, [accessed 30 August 2020].

China Electric Council, 2020. *2019 China Electric Industry Economic Performance Analysis*, (in Chinese), http://lwzb.stats.gov.cn/pub/lwzb/gzdt/202005/W020200528770641853077.pdf/, [accessed 7 September 2020].

Christmann, P., 2004. Multinational companies and the natural environment: Determinants of global environmental policy standardization, *Acad. Manag. J.* 47, 747–760.

De Clercq, G., C. Zhu, S. Jewkes, 2014. China State Grid quietly builds Mediterranean power network, (10 August 2014), https://www.reuters.com/article/utilities-mediterranean-china/china-state-grid-quietly-builds-mediterranean-power-network-idUSL6N0QB5NF20140810/, [accessed 23 August 2020].

Dean, J.M., M.E. Lovely, H. Wang, 2009. Are foreign investors attracted to weak environmental regulations? Evaluating the evidence from China, *J. Dev. Econ.* 90, 1–13.

Dezem, V. 2015. Brazil's Eletrobras approves sales of energy distributor Celg-D, Latin America & Caribbean Energy Program, https://www.jsg.utexas.edu/lacp/2016/01/brazils-eletrobras-approves-sale-of-energy-distributor-celg-d/, [accessed 24 August 2020].

Dreher, A., A. Fuchs, B. Parks, A.M. Strange, M.J. Tierney. Aid, China, and growth: Evidence from a New Global Development Finance Dataset, forthcoming in *American Economic Journal: Economic Policy*, https://www.aeaweb.org/articles?id=10.1257/pol.20180631&&from=f/, [accessed on 4 August 2020].

Editorial Board of China Electric Power Yearbook, 2015. *2014 China Electric Power Yearbook*, China Electric Power Press, Beijing (in Chinese).

Editorial Board of China Electric Power Yearbook, 2016. *2015 China Electric Power Yearbook*, China Electric Power Press, Beijing (in Chinese).

Endcoal, 2020. Global coal public finance tracker, https://endcoal.org/finance-tracker/, [accessed on 4 August 2020].

Eskeland, G.S., A.E. Harrison, 2003. Moving to greener pastures? Multinationals and the pollution haven hypothesis, *J Dev Econ* 70: 1-23, https://doi.org/10.1016/S0304-3878(02)00084-6.

Feng, T.T., X.L. Gong, Y.H. Guo, Y.S. Yang, B.B. Pan, S.P. Li, J. Dong, 2020. Electricity cooperation strategy between China and ASEAN countries under 'The Belt and road,' *Energy Strategy Rev* 30, 100512.

Findlay, S., F. Bokhari, S. Yu, 2020. Islamabad wants to renegotiate repayment after claiming costs of power plants were inflated, *Financial Times* (26 June 2020), https://www.ft.com/content/4af8101b-599c-407d-8850-3fd27cd9b31c/, [accessed on 1 July 2020].

Gallagher, K.P., 2018a. China's Global Energy Finance, Boston University Global Development Policy Center, Boston, https://www.bu.edu/cgef/#/all/Country/Global/, [accessed 4 August 2020].

Gallagher, K.P., 2018b. China's Global energy finance: Poised to lead, *Energy Res. Soc. Sci.* 35, 15–16, https://doi.org/10.1016/j.erss.2018.01.001.

Gallagher, K.P., R. Kamal, J. Jin, Y. Chen, X. Ma, 2018. Energizing development finance? The benefits and risks of China's development finance in the global energy sector, *Energy Policy* 122, 313–321, https://doi.org/10.1016/j.enpol.2018.06.009.

Gilley, B., 2012. Authoritarian environmentalism and China's response to climate change, *Environmental Politics* 21(2): 287–307, http://dx.doi.org/10.1080/09644016.2012.651904.

Global Energy Monitor, Center for Media and Democracy, 2020a. International Chinese coal projects, https://www.gem.wiki/International_Chinese_coal_projects/, [accessed on 11 August 2020].

Global Energy Monitor, Center for Media and Democracy, 2020b. Sihanoukville CIIDG power station 2, https://www.gem.wiki/Sihanoukville_CIIDG_power_station_2/, [accessed on 5 August 2020].

Global Times, 2010. State Grid to buy Brazilian power giants, (27 August 2010), http://www.china.org.cn/business/2010-08/27/content_20805031.htm/, [accessed 24 August 2020].

Hervé-Mignucci, M., X. Wang, 2015. Slowing the growth of coal power outside China: The role of Chinese Finance, A CPI Report, Climate Policy Initiative, https://climatepolicyinitiative.org/wp-content/uploads/2015/11/Slowing-the-Growth-of-Coal-Power-Outside-China.pdf/, [accessed 20 April 2020].

International Energy Agency (IEA), 2013. *Redrawing the Energy Climate Map, World Energy Outlook Special Report*, https://webstore.iea.org/download/summary/480?fileName=English-WEO-Climate-2013-ES.pdf/, [accessed 18 August 2020].

Kivyiro, P., H. Arminen, 2014. Carbon dioxide emissions, energy consumption, economic growth, and foreign direct investment: Causality analysis for Sub-Saharan Africa, *Energy* 74:595–606, https://doi.org/10.1016/j.energy.2014.07.025.

Kong, B., K.P. Gallagher, 2017. Globalizing Chinese energy finance: The role of policy banks, *J. Contemp. China* 26:108, 834–851, http://dx.doi.org/10.1080/10670564.2017.1337307.

Kungl, G., 2015. Stewards or sticklers for change? Incumbent energy providers and the politics of the German energy transition, *Energy Res. Soc. Sci.* 8, 13–23, https://doi.org/10.1016/j.erss.2015.04.009.

LGS Online, 2009. PLN may possibly miss target for second 'fast-track' scheme, (26 February 2009), http://www.lgsonline.com/pages/g/lgsimp997/node/lgs4a1d77eb99e7a/, [accessed 14 April 2019].

Li, Z., K.P. Gallagher, D. Mauzerall, 2020. Supplementary information for China's global power, https://docs.google.com/spreadsheets/d/1jPyn4unb06lx0trME4X-BhksiUUJGPSIoLpzLDAelps/edit#gid=0/, [accessed 23 May 2020].

Lin, J.Y., Y. Wang, 2017. *Going Beyond Aid: Development Cooperation for Structural Transformation*, World Bank, Washington DC.

Macauhub, 2014. EDP Brazil completes sale to China Three Gorges of stakes in hydroelectric projects, (30 June 2014), https://macauhub.com.mo/2014/06/30/edp-brasil-completes-sale-to-china-three-gorges-of-stakes-in-hydroelectric-projects/, [accessed 22 August 2020].

Markard, J., V.H. Hoffmann, 2016. Analysis of complementarities: Framework and examples from the energy transition, *Technol. Forecast. Soc. Change* 111, 63–75, https://doi.org/10.1016/j.techfore.2016.06.008.

Millimet, D.L., Roy, J., 2015. Empirical tests of the pollution haven hypothesis when environmental regulation is endogenous. *J. Appl. Econ.* 31, 652–677, https://doi.org/10.1002/jae.2451.

Ministry of Commerce China (MOFCOM), 2020. The first phase of the 2 x 300 MW coal power plant project in the Sihanoukville Special Economic Zone in Cambodia (procurement and construction) (柬埔寨西哈努克斯敦豪经济特区2台300兆瓦燃煤电站一期项目(PC)), http://project.fdi.gov.cn/1800000091_1_111773_0_7.html/, (in Chinese) [accessed 5 August 2020].

Mori, A. 2018. Sociotechnical and political economy perspectives in the Chinese energy transition, *Energy Res Soc Sci* 35: 29–36, https://doi.org/10.1016/j.erss.2017.10.043.

Mori, A. 2020. Foreign actors, faster transitions? Co-evolution of complementarities, perspectives and sociotechnical systems in the case of Indonesia's electricity supply system, *Energy Res. Soc. Sci.* 69: 101594, https://doi.org/10.1016/j.erss.2020.101594.

OECD, 2015. Sector understanding on export credits for coal-fired electricity generation projects, TAD/PG(2015)9/FINAL, https://www.oecd.org/officialdocuments/publicdisplaydocumentpdf/?cote=TAD/PG(2015)9/FINAL&docLanguage=En/, [accessed 19 August 2020].

Oirere, S. 2018. Chinese firms supplant Spanish Group in East Africa power transmission project, *Engineering News-Record* (13 March 2018), https://www.enr.com/articles/44150-chinese-firms-supplant-spanish-group-in-east-africa-power-transmission-project/, [accessed 24 August 2020].

Panhans, M., L. Lavric, N. Hanley, 2017. The effects of electricity costs on firm re-location decisions: Insights for the pollution havens hypothesis? *Environ. Resource Econ.* 68, 893–914, https://doi.org/10.1007/s10640-016-0051-1.

Peng, R., C. Liu, L. Zhang, 2017. China's involvement in coal-fired power projects along the belt and road, Global Environmental Institute, http://www.geichina.org/_upload/file/report/China's_Involvement_in_Coal-fired_Power_Projects_OBOR_EN.pdf/, [accessed 19 August 2020].

People's Republic of China and the Republic of Indonesia, 2015. Joint Statement on Strengthening Comprehensive Strategic Partnership between the People's Republic of China and the Republic of Indonesia, 27 March 2015, http://id.china-embassy.org/eng/zgyyn/zywx/t1249223.htm/, [accessed 14 June 2019].

Penning, E., L. Sleuwaegen, 2000. International relocation: firm and industry determinants, *Econ. Lett.* 67(2): 179–186, https://doi.org/10.1016/S0165-1765(99)00269-4.

Platts, 2015. *Data Base Description and Research Methodology UDI World Electric Power Plants Data Base*, McGraw Hill Financial, Washington DC.

Polaris Thermal Power Network News (北极星电力网新闻中心), 2018. Coal power plant project in the Sihanoukville Special Economic Zone in Cambodia started (柬埔寨西哈努克斯敦豪经济特区燃煤电站项目开工), (20 November 2018), http://news.bjx.com.cn/html/20181120/942881.shtml/, (in Chinese) [accessed 5 August 2020].

Ren, S., B. Yuan, X. Ma, X. Chen, 2014. International trade, FDI (foreign direct investment) and embodied CO2 emissions: A case study of Chinas industrial sectors, *China Econ. Rev.* 28: 123–134, https://doi.org/10.1016/j.chieco.2014.01.003.

Rogers, D. 2016. Bangladesh a "rising tiger" thanks to $40bn in Chinese deals, *Global Construction Review* (18 October 2016), https://pt.globalconstructionreview.com/news/bangladesh-rising-tig7er-than7ks-40bn-chin7ese/#googtrans(en|pt)/, [accessed 1 September 2020].

Saculsan, P.G., A. Mori, 2020. Why developing countries go through an unsustainable energy transition pathway? The case of the Philippines from a political economic perspective. *J. Sust. Res.* 2(2): 1–24, https://doi.org/10.20900/jsr20200012.

Sapkota, P., U. Bastola, 2017. Foreign direct investment, income, and environmental pollution in developing countries: Panel data analysis of Latin America, *Energy Econ.* 64: 206-212, https://doi.org/10.1016/j.eneco.2017.04.001.

Scissors, D., 2020. China's global investment in 2019: Going out goes small, Working Paper, American Enterprise Institute, https://www.aei.org/wp-content/uploads/2020/01/Chinas-global-investment-in-2019-1.pdf/, [accessed 23 July 2020].

Shearer, C., M. Brown, T. Buckley, 2019. *China at a Crossroads: Continued Support for Coal Power Erodes Country's Clean Energy Leadership*, Institute for Energy Economics and Financial Analysis, http://ieefa.org/wp-content/uploads/2019/01/China-at-a-Crossroads_January-2019.pdf, [accessed 22 July 2020].

Solarin, S.A., U. Al-Mulali, I. Musah, I. Ozturk, 2017. Investigating the pollution haven hypothesis in Ghana: An empirical investigation, *Energy* 124: 706-719, https://doi.org/10.1016/j.energy.2017.02.089.

Spring, J., 2018. China's State Grid to invest $38 billion in Brazil power sector, *Reuters* (31 May 2018), https://www.reuters.com/article/us-brazil-power-state-grid-corp/chinas-state-grid-to-invest-38-billion-in-brazil-power-sector-idUSKCN1IV2SR/, [accessed 17 August 2020].

State Power Investment Corporation (SPIC), n.a, Business Networking, http://eng.spic.com.cn/2016SiteEn/SPICGlobal/BusinessNetworking/, [accessed 3 September 2020].

Tao, Y., H. Liang, M.A. Celia, 2020. Electric power development associated with the Belt and Road Initiative and its carbon emissions implications, *Appl Energy* 267, 114784, https://doi.org/10.1016/j.apenergy.2020.114784.

Tobey, J., 1990. The effects of domestic environmental policies on patterns of world trade: an empirical test, *Kyklos* 43(2): 191-209, https://doi.org/10.1111/j.1467-6435.1990.tb00207.x.

Turnheim, B., B.K. Sovacool, 2020. Forever stuck in old ways? Pluralising incumbencies in sustainability transitions, *Environ. Innov. Soc. Transit.* 35, 180–184, https://doi.org/10.1016/j.eist.2019.10.012.

Ueno, T., M. Yanagi, J. Nakano, 2014. Quantifying Chinese public financing for foreign coal power plants, Working Paper GraSPP-DP-E-14-003, Graduate School of Public Policy at University of Tokyo, http://www.pp.u-tokyo.ac.jp/graspp-old/research/dp/documents/GraSPP-DP-E-14-003.pdf/, [accessed 19 August 2020].

Vidal, J., 2016. Bangladesh coal plant protests continue after demonstrators killed, *The Guardian*, (6 April 2016), http://www.theguardian.com/environment/2016/apr/06/bangladesh-coal-plant-protests-continue-after-demonstrators-killed/, [accessed 19 August 2020].

Wang, D.T., W.Y. Chen, 2014. Foreign direct investment, institutional development, and environmental externalities: Evidence from China, *J. Environ. Manag.* 135, 81–90, http://dx.doi.org/10.1016/j.jenvman.2014.01.013.

Wang Z., S. Chen, C. Cui, Q. Liu, L. Deng, 2019. Industry relocation or emission relocation? Visualizing and decomposing the dislocation between China's economy and carbon emissions, *J. Clean. Prod.* 208, 1109–1119, https://doi.org/10.1016/j.jclepro.2018.10.166.

White House, 2015. FACT SHEET: The United States and China Issue Joint Presidential Statement on Climate Change with New Domestic Policy Commitments and a Common Vision for an Ambitious Global Climate Agreement in Paris, https://obamawhitehouse.archives.gov/the-press-office/2015/09/25/fact-sheet-united-states-and-china-issue-joint-presidential-statement/, [accessed 19 August 2020].

Xie, E. 2020. Climate change: Xi Jinping makes bold pledge for China to be carbon neutral by 2060, *South China Morning Post* (23 September 2020), https://www.scmp.com/news/china/diplomacy/article/3102761/climate-change-xi-jinping-makes-bold-pledge-china-be-carbon/, [accessed 20 October 2020].

Xiong, M., X. Yang, S. Chen, F. Shi, J. Yuan, 2019. Environmental stress testing for China's overseas coal power investment project, *Sustainability* 11: 5506, https://doi.org/10.3390/su11195506.

Yin, R.K., 2014. *Case Study Research: Design and Methods, Fifth ed.*, Sage Publications, Thousand Oaks, CA.

Zhao, X., C. Liu, C. Sun, M. Yang, 2020. Does stringent environmental regulation lead to a carbon haven effect? Evidence from carbon-intensive industries in China, *Energy Econ.* 86, 104631, https://doi.org/10.1016/j.eneco.2019.104631.

Zheng, D., M. Shi, 2017. Multiple environmental policies and pollution haven hypothesis: Evidence from China's polluting industries. *J. Clean. Prod.* 141, 295–304. https://doi.org/10.1016/j.jclepro.2016.09.091

Zhu, C., M. Chen, 2012. UPDATE 2-China's State Grid to buy Brazil assets from Spain's ACS, *Reuters*, (29 May 2012), https://www.reuters.com/article/state-grid-brazil/update-2-chinas-state-grid-to-buy-brazil-assets-from-spains-acs-idUSL4E8GT3QM20120529/, [accessed 24 August 2020].

Zugravu-Soilita, N., 2017. How does foreign direct investment affect pollution? Toward a better understanding of the direct and conditional effects, *Environ. Resour. Econ.* 66(2), 293–338, https://doi.org/10.1007/s10640-015-9950-9.

Part III

Carbon, leakage, relocation, and halo effect in host countries

6 The economic and carbon impact of China's outward foreign direct investment in the power sector

Hikari Ban and Kiyoshi Fujikawa

1 Introduction

In 2013, China's outward foreign direct investment (OFDI) totaled US$ 73 billion. However, after the 2013 announcement of the "One Belt and One Road Initiative," it rapidly increased, reaching US$ 216 billion in 2016, making China the second-largest international investor worldwide after the United States of America (USA).[1] Since then, it has declined slightly. Nonetheless, China remains a major global player in OFDI.

In terms of the power sector, the capacity of the power plants that China committed as OFDI in 2013 totaled 6,376 megawatts (MW),[2] which tripled to 18,761 MW in 2017. According to an estimate by Li et al. (2020), Chinese power companies' overall OFDI between 2000 and 2017 reached nearly US$ 115 billion.

One reason for Chinese OFDI in the power sector is that it mitigates air pollution and promotes China's National Determined Contribution to the Paris Agreement and the achievement of carbon neutrality by 2060.

In this chapter, we examine the economic and environmental effects of Chinese OFDI in power sector to other Asian countries and regions since 2014 using China's Global Power Database developed by Boston University (Gallagher et al., 2019). In other words, we determine how China's carbon relocation policy may affect the international economy and global environment.

To quantitatively evaluate these effects, we use a computable general equilibrium (CGE) model. CGE models incorporate the optimization behaviors of each economic agent under budget constraints and determine the output and prices required to clear goods and factor markets. CGE analysis is a suitable tool for investigating the wide-ranging impact of foreign direct investment (FDI) on both input and final goods markets and enables us to examine the environmental impact of FDI by assessing the resultant changes in output, prices, trade, and the energy mix of all industries as well as electricity production.

This chapter has novelty in analytical methodology and empirical evidence. For the analytical methodology, the chapter uses the actual amount

DOI: 10.4324/9781003190905-9

of FDI in coal power to run a CGE model, which has been mostly applied to estimate the impacts of free trade agreements. For the empirical evidence, it quantitatively shows carbon leakage accompanied by the past Chinese FDI in power sector in Asian countries.

2 Model and data

2.1 Model

Despite its suitability as a tool for assessing FDI, fewer studies on FDI using a CGE model exist than studies on free trade agreements, perhaps owing to the lack of available FDI data. Moreover, it seems that even less relevant research on FDI's environmental impact appears in the extant literature.[3]

A conventional means for incorporating FDI into the CGE model is to treat FDI as a change in capital stock. Brown, Deardorff, and Stern (1992) examined the economic effects of increasing Mexican capital stock using FDI from outside of the North American Free Trade Agreement. Ban et al. (1998) determined the economic influence of Japanese FDI on nine Asian countries. Fujikawa and Ban (2016) also investigated the economic and environmental impact of FDI from Japan on Association for South East Asian Nations (ASEAN) countries.

In contrast, this chapter analyzes the economic and environmental effects of FDI specific to the power sector by modifying the Energy–Environmental Version of the Global Trade Analysis Project (GTAP-E) model that considers the links between the economy, the energy sector, and the environment (i.e., as represented by carbon dioxide [CO_2] emissions) to accommodate direct investment by industry.[4] The meaning of the specified factor in this model is explained briefly below.

The GTAP standard model, which is a static model, includes capital, unskilled labor, skilled labor, land, and natural resources as production factors, each of which is constant and does not move internationally at the initially given amount. Because the savings earned during the period are invested in each country according to an expected rate of return on capital, the amount of capital at the end of the period differs from the amount at the beginning. The production factors can be moved between domestic industries. They are classified into three distinct factors: mobile factors, sluggish factors, and specified/fixed factors.

A mobile factor can move freely among domestic industries. There is only one labor market in each country wherein the wage rate fluctuates such that the total demand for labor is equal to the total supply of labor, which is given as an exogenous variable.

Moving a sluggish factor to another industry is difficult, and its supply to an individual industry is less than perfectly elastic. An example of a sluggish factor is land. The total amount of land in a country is an exogenous variable. The supply of land to an individual industry is determined by the total amount of land and the industry-specific returns on the land through a transformation function.[5] If the overall land supply increases or industry-specific returns on land rise, the amount of land allocated to that industry increases. Industry-specific returns on land are determined to balance the supply and demand in each industry's land market.

A specified factor cannot move between industries. If capital is a specified factor, the amount of capital used by industry is treated as an exogenous variable, and there is a capital market by industry. Industry-specific returns on capital are determined such that the supply and demand of each market are balanced. In this study, we modified the GTAP-E model so that capital, land, and natural resources could be treated as specified factors.

Figure 6.1 illustrates the GTAP-E's production function, which has a Leontief structure with zero elasticity of substitution at the top level and a constant elasticity of substitution (CES) structure at the lower level. The Leontief structure implies that the inputs will be used in fixed proportion and the CES structure allows for constant substitutability between the inputs.

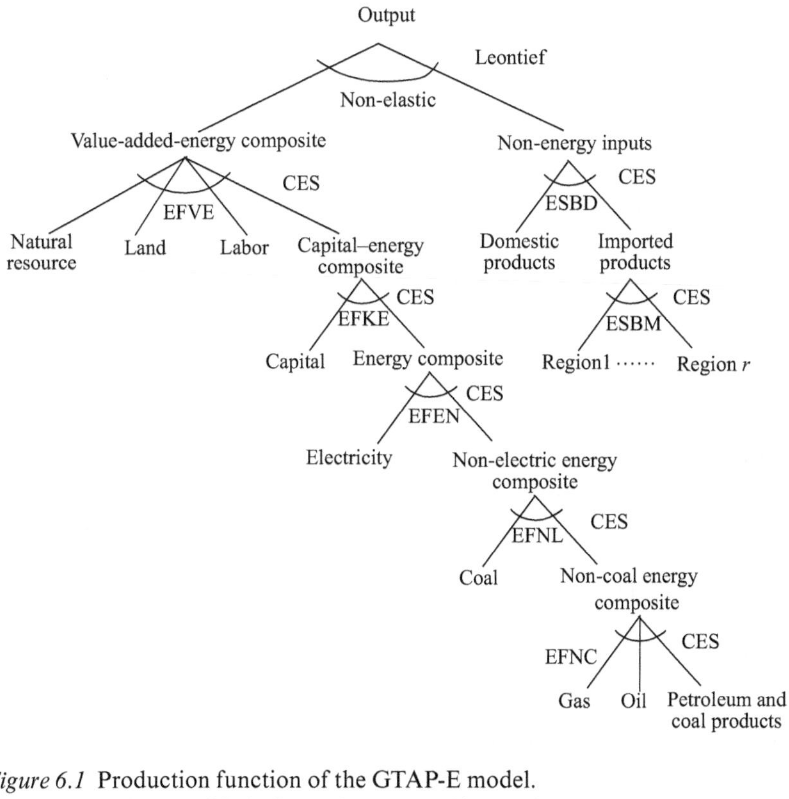

Figure 6.1 Production function of the GTAP-E model.

Source: The authors modified a figure that appeared in Burniaux and Truong (2002).

This production function is structured to enable substitution between capital and energy and substitution between different energy sources. The energy composite is combined with capital and incorporated into the value-added nest to consider energy-capital adjustment to a relative price change. Energy commodities are incorporated into the energy composite at three levels of nested substitution.

The model employs the Armington approach in that firms first determine the source of their imports and then compare the prices of domestic goods and the optimal mix of imports.[6]

2.2 Data

This model uses the GTAP 10A Data Base (Aguiar et al., 2019), which corresponds to the global economy of 2014 with 141 countries/regions and 65 sectors. The production factors include land, natural resources, capital, unskilled labor, and skilled labor. Land, natural resources, and capital are

Table 6.1 Regional classifications

No.	*Country/Region*	*Abbreviation in this chapter*
1	Oceania	Oce
2	China	Chn
3	Japan	Jpn
4	Korea	Kor
5	Mongolia	Mng
6	Taiwan	
7	Other East Asia	
8	Indonesia	Idn
9	Malaysia	
10	Singapore	
11	Thailand	
12	Vietnam	Vnm
13	Rest of ASEAN	
14	India	Ind
15	Other South Asia	
16	Canada	
17	USA	
18	Latin America	
19	European Union (EU) and European Free Trade Association (EFTA)	EUEFTA
20	Rest of Europe	
21	Russia	Rus
22	Turkestan	Trk
23	Middle East and North Africa	
24	Sub-Saharan Africa	

Source: The authors' compilation based on the GTAP 10A Data Base.

Table 6.2 Industrial sector classifications

No.	*Industrial sector*	*Abbreviation in this chapter*
1	Agriculture	
2	Livestock	
3	Forestry	
4	Fishing	
5	Coal mining	Coal
6	Crude oil	
7	Gas and distribution	
8	Petroleum and coal products	P_C
9	Electricity	Ely
10	Other mining	Min
11	Processed food	
12	Textiles and cloth	
13	Paper products and publishing	PPP
14	Chemical products	Chm
15	Non-metallic mineral products	NMM
16	Iron and steel	I_S
17	Automobile	
18	Transport equipment	
19	Electronic equipment	
20	Machine equipment	
21	Other manufactures	
22	Water	
23	Construction	
24	Trade	
25	Water transport	Wtp
26	Air transport	Atp
27	Other transport	Otp
28	Services	Svc

Source: The authors' compilation based on the GTAP 10A Data Base.

assumed to be specified elements that do not move between industries. Only unskilled and skilled labor can move between industries.

The geographic locations were organized into 24 regions located primarily in Asia, as listed in Table 6.1. Here, Turkestan comprises Kazakhstan, Kyrgyzstan, Tajikistan, Turkmenistan, and Uzbekistan, even though Turkmenistan and Uzbekistan are integrated into the GTAP Data Base.

Energy-related and energy-intensive industries were classified into 28 sectors, as listed in Table 6.2.

Table 6.3 exhibits the values for the elasticities of substitution. EFVE to EFNC represent the elasticity of substitution of the composites illustrated in Figure 6.1. ESBD and ESBM represent the Armington parameters for domestic or imported allocation and regional allocation of imports, respectively. The values for the elasticities of substitution, except for EFVE, are common to all countries.

Table 6.3 Elasticity of substitution in the value-added and energy composites

Notation	*Composite*	*Elasticity of substitution*
EFVE	Between value-added components	Common for all countries/regions except for sectors such as Coal, Oil, Gas, and Svc
EFKE	Between capital and energy composite	Coal, Oil, Gas, P_C: 0; Other industries: 0.5
EFEN	Between energy components	Coal, Oil, Gas, P_C, Ely: 0; Other industries: 1
EFNL	Between non-electrical energies	Coal, Oil, Gas, P_C: 0; Other industries: 0.5
EFNC	Between non-coal energies	Coal, Oil, Gas, P_C: 0; Other industries: 1
ESBD	Between domestic and imported products	0.90 (Min)–12.97 (Gas)
ESBM	Between origins of import	1.80 (Min)–32.39 (Gas)

Source: The authors' compilation based on the GTAP 10A Data Base.

3 Simulation scenarios

Table 6.4 displays the power generation capacity of FDI generated by electricity from China by power source. We have picked up the data only after 2014, and this data includes those in operation and under construction. The top 10 countries in terms of power generation capacity for FDI generated by electricity from China are as follows: Pakistan, Vietnam, Indonesia, Malaysia, India, Bangladesh, Laos, Australia, Cambodia, and Turkestan.

However, power source composition varies greatly from country to country. Pakistan accepts FDI into various energy sources such as natural gas-fired power, hydropower, nuclear power, solar power, and wind power in addition to coal-fired power. In Malaysia and Bangladesh, FDI in natural gas-fired power and coal-fired power are substantial. Wind power in Australia and hydropower in Laos and Cambodia account for the majority of the two countries' respective FDI inflows.

Since this chapter considers the impact of FDI in coal-fired power generation from China, we will also cover four other countries/regions: Vietnam, Indonesia, India, and Turkestan.

To conduct a scenario analysis using the GTAP-E model, it is necessary to estimate the amounts of FDI flows from China in US$. This study uses overnight costs for coal plants in China—US$ 813 per kilowatt (kW)—as estimated by International Energy Agency (IEA)/Nuclear Energy Agency (NEA) (2015).[7] Our calculations indicate that China has invested US$ 6.42 billion in Indonesia, US$ 8.96 billion in Vietnam, US$ 3.06 billion in India, and US$ 0.69 billion in Turkestan since 2014 for a total of US$ 19.12 billion.

To investigate the impact of these FDI flows from China, the first stage of this analysis sets scenarios in which the capital stock in the donor country decreases according to conventionally applied scenarios in models with exogenous capital shock. Tables 6.5a and 6.5b summarize the shock values given

Table 6.4 Power generation capacity of FDI from China by power source (in MW)

	Coal	*Gas*	*Hydro*	*Nuclear*	*Oil*	*Solar*	*Wind*	*Total*
Pakistan	4,950	1,999	1,688	2,880	215	500	297	12,530
Vietnam	11,016	0	0	0	0	0	0	11,016
Indonesia	7,895	0	110	0	0	0	0	8,005
Malaysia	1,505	4,540	0	0	0	50	0	6,095
India	3,760	0	0	0	0	0	0	3,760
Bangladesh	1,320	1,088	0	0	256	0	0	2,664
Laos	0	0	2,018	0	0	0	0	2,018
Australia	0	126	30	0	0	160	1,500	1,816
Cambodia	405	0	984	0	0	0	0	1,389
Turkestan	850	0	0	0	0	0	0	850

Note: The value for Turkestan is equal to the sum of Kyrgyzstan, Tajikistan, and Uzbekistan as there was no FDI from China into coal-fired power generation in Kazakhstan during the applicable period.
Source: The authors' compilation based on Gallagher et al. (2019).

Table 6.5a Scenarios simulated for FDI analysis

Scenario name	*Power sector capital change shock*
01E-chn	Capital decrease in China only
02E-idn	Capital increase in Indonesia only
03E-vnm	Capital increase in Vietnam only
04E-ind	Capital increase in India only
05E-trk	Capital increase in Turkestan only
06E-chnidn	Capital transfer from China to Indonesia
07E-chnvnm	Capital transfer from China to Vietnam
08E-chnind	Capital transfer from China to India
09E-chntrk	Capital transfer from China to Turkestan
10E-ivit	Capital increase in Indonesia, Vietnam, India, and Turkestan
11E-chnivit	Capital transfer from China to Indonesia, Vietnam, India, and Turkestan

Table 6.5b Capital change shock of each scenario (%)

	China	*Indonesia*	*Vietnam*	*India*	*Turkestan*
01E-chn	−1.91				
02E-idn		49.19			
03E-vnm			46.57		
04E-ind				2.96	
05E-trk					4.09
06E-chnidn	−0.64	49.19			
07E-chnvnm	−0.89		46.57		
08E-chnind	−0.31			2.96	
09E-chntrk	−0.07				4.09
10E-ivit		49.19	46.57	2.96	4.09
11E-chnivit	−1.19	49.19	46.57	2.96	4.09

Source: The authors' compilation based on the GTAP 10A Data Base.

to the initial power capital for each scenario. The scenarios from *01E-chn* to *05E-trk* are those wherein the capital change shock is given for only one country or region. In the *01E-chn* scenario, China's electricity capital decreases by US$ 19.12 billion. In the scenarios between *02E-idn* and *05E-trk*, Indonesia, Vietnam, India, and Turkestan's electricity capital increases by US$ 6.42 billion, US$ 8.96 billion, US$ 3.06 billion, and US$ 0.69 billion, respectively. The scenarios from *06E-chnidn* to *09E-chntrk* are those in which power capital transfers bilaterally. The shocks to China's electricity capital in these scenarios correspond to the capital increase of each host country. The *10E-ivit* scenario is a scenario in which China's electricity capital does not change and instead overseas electricity capital increases. In the *11E-chnivit* scenario, China's electricity capital is reduced by US$ 19.12 billion, and FDI recipients' electricity capital increases by the above amount.

4 Simulation results

4.1 Impact on power sector

Naturally, by industry, the electrical power sector with the largest changes in capital is the most affected. The effects on output and prices are reported in Table 6.6. Electricity production declines and prices rise in China, and vice versa in capital-receiving countries.

4.2 Impact on gross domestic product (GDP)

Table 6.7 shows how changes in power sector capital impact the GDP of each country or region. GDP decreases in China when the power capital decreases, while it increases in host countries in which the power capital increases. Although the amount of power capital does not change, the decrease in Mongolia's GDP under the *01E-chn*, *07E_chnvnm*, and *11E-chnivit* scenarios is relatively noticeable. In the countries/regions that are not listed in Table 6.7, GDP hardly changes.

4.2.1 The 01E-chn scenario

In Tables 6.5b and 6.7, we can see that in the *01E-chn* scenario, a 1.91% reduction in electricity capital will reduce China's GDP by 0.02%. From Table 6.6, production in China's power sector will fall by 0.55%, and its price will rise by 0.82%. A decrease in electricity production will reduce coal demand, causing China's coal production to decrease by 0.06%. Furthermore, the rise in electricity prices will negatively impact production in most Chinese industries. All of these effects ultimately lead to a decline in China's GDP.

Outside China, the impact on Mongolia's GDP seems relatively large. This is attributable to trade in coal and electricity. The decline in Chinese coal demand will negatively influence coal production in regions other than China. For example, Oceania, Indonesia, and Mongolia's coal exports to China will decrease by 0.10%, 0.10%, and 0.02%, respectively, and production will

Table 6.6 Impact on output and prices in the power sector (% change from the baseline)

		01E-chn	*02E-idn*	*03E-vnm*	*04E-ind*	*05E-trk*	*06E-chnidn*	*07E-chnvnm*	*08E-chnind*	*09E-chntrk*	*10E-ivit*	*11E-chnivit*
Output	Chn	−0.55	0.00	−0.01	0.00	0.00	−0.19	−0.26	−0.09	−0.02	−0.01	−0.57
	Idn	0.00	6.40	0.00	0.00	0.00	6.40	0.00	0.00	0.00	6.39	6.40
	Vnm	0.02	0.00	12.71	0.00	0.00	0.01	12.72	0.00	0.00	12.70	12.73
	Ind	0.00	0.00	0.00	0.26	0.00	0.00	0.00	0.26	0.00	0.25	0.26
	Trk	0.01	0.00	−0.01	0.00	1.51	0.00	−0.01	0.00	1.51	1.49	1.50
	Mng	0.05	0.00	0.00	0.00	0.00	0.01	0.02	0.01	0.00	−0.01	0.04
Price	Chn	0.82	0.00	0.00	0.00	0.00	0.27	0.37	0.13	0.03	0.00	0.82
	Idn	0.00	−7.76	0.00	0.01	0.00	−7.76	0.00	0.01	0.00	−7.75	−7.75
	Vnm	0.02	0.00	−12.70	0.00	0.00	0.01	−12.70	0.00	0.00	−12.71	−12.69
	Ind	0.00	0.00	0.00	−0.35	0.00	0.00	0.00	−0.35	0.00	−0.34	−0.34
	Trk	0.01	0.00	−0.01	0.00	−1.43	0.00	−0.01	0.00	−1.43	−1.44	−1.43
	Mng	0.01	0.01	0.00	0.00	0.00	0.01	0.00	0.01	0.00	0.01	0.02

Source: The authors' compilation based on the GTAP 10A Data Base.

Table 6.7 Impact on the GDP (% change from the baseline)

	01E-chn	*02E-idn*	*03E-vnm*	*04E-ind*	*05E-trk*	*06E-chnidn*	*07E-chnvnm*	*08E-chnind*	*09E-chntrk*	*10E-ivit*	*11E-chnivit*
Chn	−0.02	0.00	0.00	0.00	0.00	−0.01	−0.01	−0.00	−0.00	0.00	−0.02
Idn	−0.00	0.07	−0.00	0.00	0.00	0.07	−0.00	0.00	0.00	0.07	0.07
Vnm	−0.00	0.00	0.49	0.00	0.00	−0.00	0.49	0.00	−0.00	0.49	0.49
Ind	−0.00	0.00	−0.00	0.02	0.00	0.00	−0.00	0.02	0.00	0.02	0.02
Trk	−0.00	0.00	−0.00	0.00	0.06	−0.00	−0.00	0.00	0.06	0.06	0.06
Mng	−0.01	0.00	0.00	0.00	0.00	−0.00	−0.01	−0.00	−0.00	0.00	−0.01

Source: The authors' compilation based on the GTAP 10A Data Base.

Table 6.8 Share of value-added to GDP (%)

	Oce	*Chn*	*Jpn*	*Kor*	*Mng*	*Idn*
Coal sector	2.15	1.20	0.00	0.01	10.79	4.32
Electricity sector	1.36	1.79	0.98	1.69	8.06	0.31
	Vnm	*Ind*	*USA*	*EUEFTA*	*Rus*	*Trk*
Coal sector	1.22	1.43	0.21	0.08	0.80	1.39
Electricity sector	2.97	4.46	1.15	1.41	1.66	2.53

Source: The authors' compilation based on the GTAP 10A Data Base.

also decrease slightly.[8] Because the value-added of Mongolia's coal industry accounts for a relatively high proportion of its GDP, this shock may lead to a decrease in its overall GDP (see Table 6.8).

The rise in electricity prices in China will affect the trade in electricity. In Mongolia, the electricity consumption of industry and households is 1.57 million tons of oil equivalent (Mtoe), of which imported electricity comprises 0.11 Mtoe or 7.21%. Since 51.25% of imported electricity comes from China, the negative effect of rising imported electricity prices on the Mongolian economy is relatively large.

4.2.2 The 02E-idn, 03E-vnm, 04E-ind, and 05E-trk scenarios

GDP increases in capital-receiving countries but not necessarily in proportion to the rate of increase in electricity capital. Comparing the *02E-idn* and *03E-vnm* scenarios, the rate of increase in electricity capital in Indonesia is slightly higher than in Vietnam. However, Indonesia's GDP growth rate in the *02E-idn* scenario seems to be considerably smaller than that of Vietnam's GDP growth rate in the *03E-vmn* scenario. As shown in Table 6.6, the power sector's output will increase by 6.40% in Indonesia and by 12.71% in Vietnam. Electricity prices decrease by −7.76% in Indonesia and by −12.70% in Vietnam. In addition, Vietnam trades power internationally, so its exports will increase by 113.28% in the *03E-vnm* scenario.

One reason for the different responses from these two countries is the capital–labor ratio in the electrical power sector: Indonesia's is 4.23 and Vietnam's is 1.10. Vietnam's electricity sector, wherein capital is a scarce factor, will be able to more efficiently replace labor with cheaper capital, which will lower electricity prices. The rate of change in demand for unskilled and skilled labor in the electrical power sector is −4.52% and −4.54% in Indonesia and −7.91% and −7.77% in Vietnam, respectively.

If the cost of electricity accounts for a large proportion of the total cost, the benefits of lower electricity prices will become greater. Table 6.9 shows the share of electricity costs and the rates of change in prices, production, and exports in the energy-intensive goods sector. Vietnam's energy-intensive goods industry, which bears a higher electricity cost share than Indonesia, exhibits a more substantial rate of price decline and increased production and exports.

Table 6.9 Electricity cost shares and responses in energy-intensive industries (%)

	PPP	*Che*	*NMM*	*I_S*
Initial share of electricity costs in total costs				
Indonesia	1.15	0.83	1.45	5.28
Vietnam	10.78	3.04	9.02	18.25
Change rate in product price				
Indonesia	−0.04	−0.04	−0.11	−0.24
Vietnam	−1.16	−0.20	−1.04	−1.50
Change rate in product output				
Indonesia	0.14	0.17	0.02	0.54
Vietnam	2.66	0.93	1.42	8.10
Change rate in exports				
Indonesia	0.23	0.27	0.58	1.33
Vietnam	6.50	1.27	4.99	8.34

Note: Indonesia's change rates are results for the *02E-idn* scenario and Vietnam's change rates are for the *03E-vnm* scenario.
Source: The authors' compilation based on the GTAP 10A Data Base.

4.2.3 The 11E-chnivit scenario: total effects

The result of the *11E-chnivit* scenario is the sum of the results of the *01-chn* scenario and the *10E-ivit* scenario, and the result of the *10E-ivit* scenario is the sum of the results of the *02E-idn* to *05E-trk* scenarios.

Under the *10E-ivit* scenario, GDP appears to increase in the host countries and remain almost unchanged in other countries. China and Mongolia are affected negatively in the *01E-chn* scenario, which is reflected in their GDP under the *11E-chnivit* scenario. Electricity capital movements from China have a negative impact on China's GDP and a positive impact on the recipient country. Mongolia seems to experience relatively strong effects due to their background of coal and electricity trade with China.

The result of *11E-chnivit* scenario can be considered the sum of the four bilateral scenarios from *06E-chnidn* to *09E-chntrk*. In the bilateral FDI scenarios, the rate of decrease in China's electricity capital is smaller than in the *11E-chnivit* scenario. China's GDP tends to decline by 0.01% only in the *06E-chnidn* and *07E-chnvnm* scenarios in which the shock value on China's power capital is relatively large. A clearly negative effect on Mongolia's GDP is only observed in terms of its FDI against Vietnam.

4.3 Impact on welfare

We now measure welfare changes due to FDI using equivalent variation (EV). EV measures welfare change in terms of income change, assuming that the initial price system remains constant. For example, increased production factors, more efficient resource allocation, and technological progress will enhance economic welfare. Improving the terms of trade also increases economic welfare, as one unit of exports will enable the consumption of more imports.

Table 6.10 displays the EV caused by a change in electricity capital. In the *01E-chn* scenario (i.e., capital decreases), there are negative EV values not only in China but also in other countries. The EV is positive in the capital-recipient country for the *02E-idn* to *05E-trk* scenarios. In any given scenario, changes in economic welfare occur even in countries wherein the amount of capital does not change. Some countries or regions have a positive effect, whereas others have a negative effect. Although the effect on the EV in countries in which the electricity capital is unchanged is extremely marginal, it nonetheless suggests that there are various channels of FDI influence at work.

To understand the effect on EV, we analyzed the term's components. In the GTAP-E model, EV can be decomposed into seven components: resource allocation effects, element endowment effects, technological change effects, population effects, terms-of-trade effects, investment goods price effects, and emissions trading effects.[9] The specific components related to this analysis include the resource allocation, element endowment, and terms-of-trade effects. Resource allocation and factor endowment effects are important in the countries in which the capital stock changes. The terms-of-trade effect is caused mainly by changes in electricity and coal prices.

4.3.1 *The 01E-chn scenario*

In the *01E-chn scenario*, the Chinese EV consists mainly of the resource allocation effect (−US$ 669.9 million), the element endowment effect (−US$ 1,058.6 million), and the terms-of-trade effect (US$ 264.7 million). The rise in the price of electricity causes the prices of Chinese exports to rise, improving the terms of trade in China while worsening them in other countries. The degree of the effect of such deterioration depends on the volume of trade with China. China's export value is US$ 2,499.7 billion; its shares in the exports of EUEFTA, the USA, and Japan are 21.47%, 19.01%, and 8.02%, respectively. Therefore, the reduction in the EV of these countries or regions is relatively large.

Furthermore, there is a decrease in demand for imported intermediate inputs from China's electrical power industry because of a decrease in its production. This worsens the terms of trade for exporting regions by decreasing their prices. For example, Oceania's EV is −US$ 51.2 million, of which the terms-of-trade effect is −US$ 41.5 million. Of the −US$ 41.5 million, −US$ 13.9 million is caused by mining prices and −US$ 9.1 million by coal prices. The same phenomenon can be observed in Indonesia and Mongolia.

4.3.2 *The 02E-idn, 03E-vnm, 04E-ind, and 05E-trk scenarios*

The contribution of the element endowment effect dominates the positive EV of the capital host country in the *02E-idn* through *05-E-trk* scenarios. However, the terms-of-trade effect of the host country is negative. In the

Table 6.10 Equivalent variation (in millions of US$)

	01E-chn	*02E-idn*	*03E-vnm*	*04E-ind*	*05E-trk*	*06E-chnidn*	*07E-chnvnm*	*08E-chnind*	*09E-chntrk*	*10E-ivit*	*11E-chnivit*
Oce	−51	26	10	18	0	9	−14	10	−1	54	3
Chn	−1,474	−4	34	2	4	−492	−646	−234	−49	36	−1,438
Jpn	−16	0	29	−4	−1	−5	22	−6	−2	25	8
Kor	−2	−15	20	−3	−2	−16	19	−3	−2	0	−2
Mng	−4	0	-0	0	0	−1	−2	−0	−0	1	−3
Idn	−15	434	12	15	1	429	5	13	0	462	447
Vnm	−13	2	370	2	0	−2	364	−0	−0	375	361
Ind	−6	−7	6	107	−2	−9	3	106	−2	104	98
USA	−80	28	70	18	−2	2	33	5	−5	113	33
EUEFTA	−103	36	83	25	6	2	36	9	2	150	48
Rus	10	11	−4	7	6	14	0	9	6	19	29
Trk	−2	−0	−0	1	174	−1	−1	0	174	174	172

Source: The authors' compilation based on the GTAP 10A Data Base.

applicable scenarios, the element endowment effects of Indonesia, Vietnam, India, and Turkestan are US$ 507.2 million, US$ 430.4 million, US$ 241.5 million, and US$ 136.8 million, respectively, and the terms-of-trade effects are −US$ 20.2 million, −US$ 221.2 million, −US$ 76.5 million, and −US$ 9.1 million, respectively. Worsening terms of trade result because lower electricity prices lead to lower export prices.

Countries importing at lower prices from the host country, however, will experience positive terms-of-trade effects. This is especially noticeable in the *03E-vnm* scenario. Owing to the increase in electricity capital, the product prices of most industries in Vietnam will decrease. Vietnam's export value is US$ 166.2 billion, and its share of exports to EUEFTA, the USA, China, and Japan is as high as 19.74%, 18.57%, 14.30%, and 9.69%, respectively. A relatively large increase in EV can be seen in these countries and regions.

Lower export prices in host countries negatively impact the terms of trade of the countries that export them. This is particularly remarkable for South Korea's petroleum and coal products in the *02E-idn* scenario. South Korea's EV is −US$ 15.1 million, of which −US$ 15.0 million is attributable to the deterioration in the terms of trade. Of this deterioration, the portion due to the rise in coal import prices is −US$ 4.2 million, followed by the portion due to the decline in the export prices of petroleum and coal products, which is −US$ 3.8 million. South Korea's petroleum and coal exports to Indonesia are as high as US$ 36.4 billion, accounting for 14.71% of its total petroleum and coal exports. Conversely, the share of petroleum and coal exports to Indonesia is low at 1.61% and 1.12% in China and Japan, respectively. Therefore, the terms-of-trade effect of petroleum and coal products in both countries is rather positive.

Increased power generation in the recipient regions also affects the terms of trade. An increase in coal demand due to an increase in power generation in the host countries has a negative impact on the terms of trade of the coal-importing country and a positive impact on the terms of trade of the exporting country. Under the four scenarios, Oceania, Mongolia, and Indonesia experience a positive terms-of-trade effect for coal, while China, South Korea, Japan, and India have a negative effect.

4.3.3 The 11E-chnivit scenario: total effects

Under the *10E_ivit* scenario, the EV of most countries is positive, and an increase in Vietnam's electricity capital contributes to positive EV other than that of the host country. However, in the *11E_chnivit* scenario, the EV in most countries decreases owing to the negative impact of China's decrease in electricity capital. From the perspective of bilateral capital movements, the negative impact of capital movements to Vietnam on China's EVs is the greatest.

4.4 Impact on CO_2 emissions

Tables 6.11 and 6.12 summarize the impact of CO_2 emissions. In this subsection, we focus on China.

Table 6.11 Change in CO_2 emissions (in millions of tons)

	01E-chn	*02E-idn*	*03E-vnm*	*04E-ind*	*05E-trk*	*06E-chnidn*	*07E-chnvnm*	*08E-chnind*	*09E-chntrk*	*10E-ivit*	*11E-chnivit*
Oce	−0.01	0.00	−0.00	−0.01	−0.00	−0.00	−0.01	−0.01	−0.00	−0.01	−0.02
Chn	−4.34	0.11	−0.33	0.06	−0.05	−1.33	−2.33	−0.63	−0.20	−0.21	−4.55
Jpn	−0.01	−0.02	−0.00	−0.03	−0.00	−0.02	−0.00	−0.03	−0.00	−0.05	−0.05
Kor	0.01	−0.02	0.00	−0.02	−0.00	−0.02	0.01	−0.02	−0.00	−0.04	−0.03
Mng	0.00	−0.00	−0.00	−0.00	−0.00	0.00	0.00	0.00	0.00	−0.00	0.00
Idn	−0.00	2.17	−0.00	−0.02	0.00	2.17	−0.00	−0.02	0.00	2.15	2.15
Vnm	0.00	−0.00	1.03	−0.00	−0.00	−0.00	1.03	−0.00	−0.00	1.03	1.03
Ind	0.04	−0.08	−0.03	2.36	−0.01	−0.07	−0.01	2.36	−0.01	2.23	2.28
USA	−0.09	−0.01	0.02	−0.02	−0.02	−0.04	−0.02	−0.03	−0.03	−0.03	−0.13
EUEFTA	−0.04	0.00	−0.06	−0.02	−0.05	−0.01	−0.08	−0.02	−0.05	−0.13	−0.17
Rus	0.01	−0.01	−0.01	−0.01	−0.02	−0.01	−0.01	−0.01	−0.02	−0.05	−0.04
Trk	0.01	−0.00	−0.03	−0.00	1.21	−0.00	−0.03	−0.00	1.21	1.17	1.18
ROW	−0.08	−0.03	−0.09	−0.10	−0.11	−0.05	−0.12	−0.11	−0.11	−0.31	−0.39
Total	−4.50	2.11	0.50	2.19	0.94	0.62	−1.56	1.47	0.78	5.74	1.25

Source: The authors' calculation based on the GTAP 10A Data Base.

Table 6.12 Change in China's CO_2 emissions by sector (in millions of tons)

	01E-chn	*02E-idn*	*03E-vnm*	*04E-ind*	*05E-trk*	*06E-chnidn*	*07E-chnvnm*	*08E-chnind*	*09E-chntrk*	*10E-ivit*	*11E-chnivit*
Coal	0.00	0.01	0.00	0.00	0.00	0.01	0.00	0.00	0.00	0.01	0.01
P_C	−0.01	0.00	0.00	0.00	0.00	0.00	−0.00	0.00	0.00	0.01	0.01
Ely	−8.66	0.03	−0.36	0.04	−0.04	−2.83	−4.35	−1.35	−0.34	−0.33	−8.97
PPP	0.13	0.00	−0.00	0.00	−0.00	0.04	0.06	0.02	0.00	−0.00	0.13
Chm	0.42	0.01	0.01	0.00	−0.00	0.15	0.20	0.07	0.01	0.01	0.44
NMM	0.99	0.02	−0.03	0.01	0.00	0.34	0.42	0.17	0.04	−0.01	0.98
I_S	0.69	0.01	0.01	−0.00	−0.00	0.24	0.32	0.11	0.02	0.01	0.70
Wtp	−0.05	0.00	0.01	0.00	0.00	−0.01	−0.02	−0.01	−0.00	0.01	−0.04
Atp	−0.04	0.00	0.00	0.00	0.00	−0.01	−0.02	−0.01	−0.00	0.01	−0.04
Otp	−0.22	0.01	0.02	0.00	−0.00	−0.06	−0.08	−0.03	−0.01	0.02	−0.19
Svc	0.48	0.01	0.00	0.00	−0.00	0.16	0.22	0.08	0.02	0.01	0.48
Others	1.16	0.01	0.01	0.00	0.00	0.40	0.55	0.19	0.04	0.03	1.19
HHD	0.76	0.00	0.01	−0.00	−0.01	0.25	0.36	0.12	0.02	−0.00	0.76
Total	−4.34	0.11	−0.33	0.06	−0.05	−1.33	−2.33	−0.63	−0.20	−0.21	−4.55

Note: HHD = household.
Source: The authors' compilation based on the GTAP 10A Data Base.

4.4.1 The 01E-chn scenario

In the *01E-chn* scenario, a 1.91% reduction in capital stock in China's power sector will reduce China's CO_2 emissions by approximately 4.34 million tons. CO_2 emissions in the power sector will decrease by 8.66 million tons, whereas emissions will increase in many other sectors. This is especially true in non-metallic mineral products, iron and steel, chemical products, and services—all sectors that have high CO_2 emissions. Household CO_2 emissions will also increase by 0.76 million tons. In this scenario, capital rental costs in China's power sector will increase by 3.62%, thereby increasing electricity prices by 0.82%. Conversely, the price of coal will decline by 0.02%, prompting the replacement of electricity with coal, consequently increasing CO_2 emissions in many sectors other than electricity.

4.4.2 The 02E-idn, 03E-vnm, 04E-ind, and 05E-trk scenarios

The increase in electricity capital stock in Vietnam and Turkestan reduces CO_2 emissions in China, whereas the increase in electricity capital stock in Indonesia and India increases CO_2 emissions in China.

In the *03E-vnm* and *05E-trk* scenarios, electricity trade helps reduce CO_2 emissions from China's electricity sector. Under the *03E-vnm* and *05E-trk* scenarios, Vietnam and Turkestan increase their power exports to China by 113.59% and 8.24%, respectively. In the *03E-vnm* scenario, the CO_2 emissions from China's power reduction are relatively large at approximately 0.36 million tons. Moreover, in these scenarios, China's CO_2 emissions are also reduced in some energy-intensive industries in addition to reductions in the electrical power sector.

In the *02E-idn* and *04E-ind* scenarios, output is virtually unchanged in China's electricity sector, but its CO_2 emissions increase.[10] Furthermore, in the *02E-idn* scenario, an increase in CO_2 emissions from coal, chemical products, iron and steel, and non-metallic mineral products can also be observed in China.

4.4.3 The 11E-chnivit scenario: total effects

The decrease in CO_2 emissions in China is greater in the *11E-chnivit* scenario than in the *01E-chn* scenario because of the reduction in CO_2 emissions in China precipitated by the increase in capital in Vietnam and Turkestan. Most of China's CO_2 emissions reductions in the *11E-chnivit* scenario are attributable to the electricity sector. Further, CO_2 emissions from China's most energy-intensive industries are increasing. This is because of a decrease in Chinese capital rather than an increase in the host country's capital.

In the *07E-chnvnm* bilateral capital movement scenario, the decrease in CO_2 emissions in China exceeds the increase in CO_2 emissions in Vietnam, thereby reducing overall global CO_2 emissions. However, under the other bilateral scenarios, the opposite is true. Global CO_2 emissions increase in the *11E-chnivit* scenario because the effect of the latter outweighs that of the former.

5 Discussion

In this section, we discuss the effects of China transferring their power sector to other Asian countries/regions in the context of carbon relocation using the results of scenarios such as the *06E_chnidn*, *07E_chvnm*, *08E_chnind*, *09E_chntrk*, and *11E_chnivit* scenarios in which electricity capital declines in China and increases in the host country.

Figure 6.2 illustrates the change in CO_2 emissions for each scenario according to China's power and nonpower sectors including households, the host countries' power and nonpower sectors including households, and the rest of the world (ROW). The decrease in CO_2 emissions is attributable to China's power sector, the host countries' nonpower sector, and the ROW. Conversely, the increase in CO_2 emissions is due to China's nonpower sector and the power sector of the host countries. Rising electricity prices in China cause a shift from electricity to coal in the nonpower sector's energy mix, resulting in an increase in CO_2 emissions from the nonpower sector despite its stagnant production. The opposite occurs in the host country.[11] One of the reasons for the decrease in CO_2 emissions in the ROW is the declining production of energy-intensive goods due to international competition with the host country. If the production base is moved to the host country from

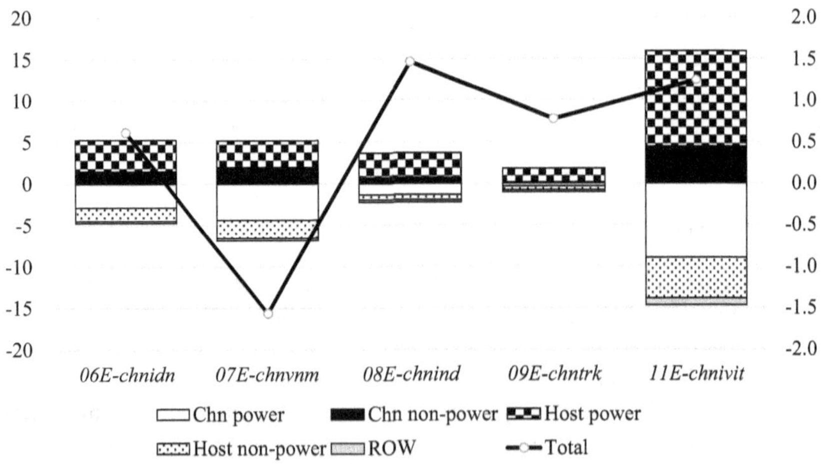

Figure 6.2 Change in CO_2 emissions caused by China's OFDI (in millions of tons).

Note: The left-hand vertical axis is for the bar graph and the right-hand vertical axis corresponds to the line graph.

Source: The authors' compilation based on data from the GTAP 10A Data Base.

a country with relatively lower CO_2 emissions per unit of production, it will cause an overall increase in global CO_2 emissions.

Only in the *07E-chnvnm* scenario do global CO_2 emissions decrease. The first reason is that the decrease in CO_2 emissions in China's power sector is greater than the increase in Vietnam's power sector. Electricity imports from Vietnam are one of the causes underlying declining electricity production in China.

The second reason is that the decrease in the CO_2 emissions of Vietnam's nonpower sector is relatively large. As seen in the section on the impact on power sector, the low capital–labor ratio of Vietnam's electricity sector prompts a significant drop in electricity prices. This causes a shift from coal to electricity in the energy mix of nonpower sectors in the context of Vietnam's high share of electricity costs. In other words, the degree of decline in electricity prices and the progress of electrification in the nonpower sector mitigate carbon leakage.[12]

Figure 6.2 shows that the increase in CO_2 emissions in India's power sector seems to be large considering the increase in its capital. The increase in the power sector capital in India is 48% of those in Indonesia, while the increase in CO_2 emissions in the power sector in India is as much as 78% of those in Indonesia. Possible reason for the relatively larger increase in CO_2 emissions is low efficiency of coal power generation in India. According to the GTAP Data Base, coal energy consumption per billion US$ of electricity capital is 9.90 Mtoe in China, 14.61 Mtoe in Indonesia, 3.05 Mtoe in Vietnam, 18.58 Mtoe in India, and 4.74 in Turkestan. Differences in power generation technology and quality of coal between China and host countries, which is indicated in Chapter 2, may account for carbon leakage.

In the *11E-chnivit* scenario, the increase in CO_2 emissions in the host country's power sector outweighs the decrease in China's electricity sector. Although the decrease in CO_2 emissions from the host country's nonpower sector outweighs the increase in China's nonpower sector, it is not sufficiently large to offset the net increase in CO_2 emissions in the power sector. This results in an increase in Global CO_2 emissions. The carbon leakage rate is 127.4% when calculated as the ratio of the change in CO_2 emissions in countries/regions other than China to the amount of CO_2 reduction in China.[13] In other words, it can be said that since 2014, China's OFDI in coal power generation has taken on the appearance of carbon relocation greater than 100%.

As far as we know, few previous studies have analyzed the environmental effects of FDI using a CGE model. Fujikawa and Ban (2016) treated capital as a mobile factor, while this method could not examine the impact of capital transfer in any particular sector. The CGE model with industry-specific capital used in this chapter makes it possible to establish the effect of FDI in the electricity sector and clarifies the factors for carbon relocation.

Some of the problems encountered in this study and potential future issues are worth noting. First, the productivity of capital (i.e., power generation efficiency, in this study) and the energy mix of electricity generation depend not on the investing country but the recipient country due to the nature of the GTAP-E model. Therefore, it is necessary to distinguish between domestically and foreign-capitalized power plants.[14]

Second, the GTAP-E model used herein does not differentiate between various power generation methods.[15] The capital transfer of coal-fired power generation is assumed; however, for a strict analysis, a model that distinguishes between power generation methods is required.

Furthermore, there are various technologies in coal-fired power generation. It is also necessary to consider the difference in coal-fired power generation technology when estimation the nominal amount of OFDI in China. These are the future challenges for further investigations into this topic.

6 Conclusion

This chapter analyzed the economic and environmental (i.e., CO_2) effects of capital movements of China's electricity sector to Indonesia, Vietnam, India, and Turkestan using the GTAP-E model and China's Global Power Database constructed by Boston University.

We found that the transfer of electricity capital affected not only electricity production and CO_2 emissions in China and the host country but also production by other industries and the economies and environments of other countries/regions. The main conclusions are as follows:

- The overseas movement of Chinese electricity capital reduces China's GDP, and the resultant decline in China's coal demand negatively impacts coal production in coal-exporting countries. The degree of GDP increase in the host country depends on the capital–labor ratio and share of electricity costs as well as the magnitude of the capital increase.
- China's OFDI affects EVs through the terms-of-trade effect in countries and regions other than China and capital-receiving countries. The terms-of-trade effect depends on whether the country is an energy exporter or importer and its trade structure with China and capital-receiving countries.
- The reduction in CO_2 emissions in China's electricity sector is undermined by the shift in demand for coal in the nonpower sectors but is strengthened by electricity imports. The increase in CO_2 emissions from the electricity sector in the host country is mitigated by the shift in demand for electricity in the nonpower sectors.
- With the exception of OFDI to Vietnam, the OFDI of China's power sector increases global CO_2 emissions.

This chapter demonstrates that overseas capital movements from the Chinese power sector increase overall global CO_2 emissions, although the parameters used in this model are not necessarily generalized. If China makes direct investments to reduce domestic emissions (i.e., for domestic optimization), such a decision could ultimately prove globally counterproductive. This result indicates that international society must be cautious about the countries and regions chosen for allocations of capital investment.

7 Acknowledgments

The authors are grateful to Professor Shiro Takeda at Kyoto Sangyo University for the useful comments that he provided at the 25th Annual Conference of the Society for Environmental Economics and Policy Studies. This work was supported by Japan Society for the Promotion of Science, Grants-in-Aid for Scientific Research, under Grant Numbers JP18H03426, JP19K12459, and JP20K12291, and Applied Social System Institute of Asia, Nagoya University.

Notes

1 See Institute for International Trade and Investment (2020) for more information on FDI statistics.
2 See Gallagher et al. (2019). The data includes China's developmental financing of overseas power generation.
3 See Tsutsumi and Kiyota (2002) and Lejour and Romagosa (2006) for surveys of CGE models applied to FDI analysis.
4 See Burniaux and Truong (2002) and McDougal and Golub (2007) for additional details on the GTAP-E model; see Hertel (1997) and Corong et al. (2017) for more information on the GTAP model.
5 A constant elasticity of transformation specification is used in the GTAP model. The change rate of the supply of sluggish factor *i* for use in industry *j* in country *r* $qes_{i,j,r}$ is expressed as follows: $qes_{i,j,r} = qe_{i,r} - \mathrm{ETRE}_{i,r}\ (pes_{i,j,r} - pe_{i,r})$. $qe_{i,r}$, $pes_{i,j,r}$, and $pe_{i,r}$ denote the change rates in the aggregate supply of a sluggish factor, industry-specific returns to the sluggish factor, and aggregate returns to the sluggish factor, respectively. $\mathrm{ETRE}_{i,r}$ represents the transformational elasticity and is negative.
6 The Armington assumption states that products are differentiated according to their countries of origin. See Armington (1969).
7 Overnight costs include direct/indirect construction costs, the owners' costs, and so on. See IEA/NEA (2015, p. 31) for the definition of overnight costs.
8 China's importing-country share of coal is as follows: Oceania, 40.80%; Indonesia, 30.22%; and Mongolia, 5.29%.
9 See Huff and Hertel (2000) for additional details about decomposing welfare changes into the GTAP model.
10 The CES specification in the power sector does not have additive property which assures that the sum of inputs (measured Mtoe) sums to the total output (also in Mtoe). When the substitution between domestic energy and imported energy occurs, simulation results can differ from intuition. In the *02E-idn* and *04E-ind* scenarios, imported coal in China's power sector will be replaced by domestic coal due to the rise in imported coal price. See Peters (2016) for additive property.
11 Since the model assumes that the production function is as shown in Figure 6.1, substitution between electricity and coal in the energy mix could possibly occur.
12 We should note that the power sector is aggregated regardless of power source in the GTAP-E model. While thermal power generation is mainstream in China, the

ratio of hydroelectric power generation is relatively high in Vietnam. Therefore, when simulating an increase in Vietnam's power capital, the increase in CO_2 emissions is suppressed. This is a limitation of utilizing the GTAP-E model for such an analysis.

13 The carbon leakage rate is defined as follows:

$$carbon\ leakage\ rate = \frac{\sum_r Change\ in\ CO_2\ emissions\ in\ r}{Reduction\ in\ CO_2\ emissions\ in\ China} \times 100$$

r= Indonesia, Vietnam, India, Turkestan, and the ROW.
Each country/region's contribution is calculated as follows:

$$contribution = \frac{Change\ in\ CO_2\ emissions\ in\ r}{Reduction\ in\ CO_2\ emissions\ in\ China} \times 100$$

The contributions of Indonesia, Vietnam, India, Turkestan, and the ROW are 47.2%, 22.6%, 50.1%, 25.9%, and −18.4%, respectively.

14 With the recent development of FDI stock data and foreign affiliate sales data, it has now possible to analyze FDI using a GTAP-based FDI model that distinguishes between domestically and foreign-owned companies (Fukui and Lakatos, 2012; Lakatos and Fukui, 2014; Tsigas and Yuan, 2017). Applying such a model to an analysis of FDI's environmental impact is necessary.

15 The GTAP-E-Power model, which is an extension of the GTAP-E model, includes different generating technologies. See Peters (2016) includes different generating technologies.

References

Armington, P. S. (1969) A Theory of Demand for Products Distinguished by Place of Production, *International Monetary Fund Staff Papers, XVI*, 159–178.

Ban, K., Ohtsubo, S., Kawasaki, K., Ono, M., Matsuya, M., Tsutsumi, M., Kitaki, H. and Ono, H. (1998) Applied General Equilibrium Analyses of Current Global Issues: APEC, Foreign Direct Investment, New Regionalism, and Environment, *Economic Analysis*, *156*, the Economic and Social Research Institute. Retrieved June 10, 2020 from http://www.esri.go.jp/jp/archive/bun/bun156/bun156b.pdf (in Japanese).

Brown, D. K., Deardorff, A. V. and Stern, R. M. (1992) A North American Free Trade Agreement: Analytical Issues and a Computational Assessment, *The World Economy, 15(1)*, 11–30.

Burniaux, J. M. and Truong T. P. (2002) GTAP-E: An Energy-Environmental Version of the GTAP Model. *GTAP Technical Paper, 16*. Retrieved June 10, 2020 from https://www.gtap.agecon.purdue.edu/resources/download/1203.pdf

Corong, E. R., Hertel, T. W., McDougall, R. A., Tsigas, M E. and Mensbrugghe, D. (2017) The Standard GTAP Model, Version7, *Journal of Global Economic Analysis, 2(1)*, 1–119. http://dx.doi.org/10.21642/JGEA.020101AF

Fujikawa, K. and Ban, H. (2016) Globalization of the Economy and Load on the Global Environment in Otsubo, S. (ed.) *Globalization and Development, Volume 1*, Oxon: Routledge, 200–227.

Fukui, T. and Lakatos, C. (2012) A Global Database of Foreign Affiliate Sales, *GTAP Research Memorandum, 24*. Retrieved October 16, 2020 from https://www.gtap.agecon.purdue.edu/resources/download/6082.pdf

Hertel, T. W. (ed.) (1997) *Global Trade Analysis: Modeling and Applications*, Cambridge: Cambridge University Press.

Huff, K. M. and Hertel, T. W. (2000) Decomposing Welfare Changes in the GTAP Model, *GTAP Technical Paper, 5*. Retrieved March 7, 2020 from https://www.gtap.agecon.purdue.edu/resources/download/2365.pdf

Institute for International Trade and Investment (2020) *Collection of Direct Investment Statistics of Major Countries in the World, I, Overview* (in Japanese).

International Energy Agency (IEA)/Nuclear Energy Agency (NEA) (2015) *Projected Costs of Generating Electricity, 2015 Edition*, Paris: OECD Publishing. https://doi.org/10.1787/cost_electricity-2015-en

Lakatos, C. and Fukui, T. (2014) The Liberalization of Retail Services in India, *World Development, 59(C)*, 327–340. https://doi.org/10.1016/j.worlddev.2014.01.013

Lejour, A. and Romagosa, H. R. (2006) Foreign Direct Investment in Applied General Equilibrium Models: Overview of the Literature, CPB Memorandum, CPB Netherlands Bureau for *Economic Policy Analysis, 169*. Retrieved October 16, 2020 from https://www.cpb.nl/sites/default/files/publicaties/download/memo1690.pdf

Li, Z., Gallagher, K. P. and Mauzerall, D. L. (2020) China's Global Power: Estimating Chinese Foreign Direct Investment in the Electric Power Sector, *Energy Policy, 136*. https://doi.org/10.1016/j.enpol.2019.111056

McDougall, R. and Golub, A. (2007) GTAP-E: Revised Energy-Environmental Version of the GTAP Model. *GTAP Research Memorandum, 15*. Retrieved February 18, 2020 from https://www.gtap.agecon.purdue.edu/resources/download/4212.pdf

Peters, J. (2016) GTAP-E-Power: An Electricity-Detailed Economy-Wide Model, *Journal of Global Economic Analysis, 1(2)*, 156–187. http://dx.doi.org/10.21642/JGEA.010204AF

Tsigas, M. and Yuan, W. (2017) Addressing Excess Capacity—The Effect of China's FDI in the Iron and Steel Industry in Five Central Asian States: A GTAP-FDI Model Perspective, Conference Paper presented at the 20th Annual Conference on Global Economic Analysis. Retrieved October 16, 2020 from https://www.gtap.agecon.purdue.edu/resources/download/8644.pdf

Tsutsumi, M. and Kiyota, K. (2002) Impacts of Japan's Free Trade Agreement: Analysis by CGE Model, *JCER Discussion Paper, 74*. Retrieved October 16, 2020 from http://www.jcer.or.jp/report/discussion/detail3055.html (in Japanese).

Database

Aguiar, A., Chepeliev, M., Corong, E., McDougall, R. and van der Mensbrugghe, D. (2019) The GTAP Data Base: Version 10, *Journal of Global Economic Analysis, 4(1)*, 1–27. http://dx.doi.org/10.21642/JGEA.040101AF

Gallagher, K. P., Li, Z., Chen, X. and Ma, X. (2019) China's Global Power Database, Global Development Policy Center, Boston University. Retrieved December 25, 2020 from https://www.bu.edu/cgp/

7 Effect of renewable energy policies on the components' exports from Asian countries

Evidence from the trade of PV/wind energy with matching econometrics

Yasuhiro Ogura

1 Introduction

We have seen the global deployment of renewable energy (RE) in the past decade, as seen in the global diffusion of solar photovoltaics (PV), and wind energy. RE has been a part of the climate change mitigation strategy (Stokes, 2016), as it is believed to have considerable potential (IRENA, 2019). Furthermore, the strategy might be intended to tackle the issue of energy security, which evokes the need for less dependence on fossil fuel, especially in countries with scarcity of such energy sources (Fuentes et al., 2020). The vulnerability of the incumbent energy system might also be among the factors affecting the penetration of RE (Mathews and Reinert, 2014), while it has been considered to solve the scarcity of fossil fuel (Pidgeon et al., 2008).

In response, an increasing number of countries perceive RE industry as a new engine of economic growth (Mori and Takehara, 2018). Economic concerns might also have played a role in the penetration of RE (Song, 2015). Organisation for Economic Co-operation and Development (OECD) has set the "green growth" as the agenda for attaining mitigation of climate change or sustainability and the economic growth simultaneously, and RE is placed in "environmental industry" (Jänicke, 2012) that can generate increasing returns (Mathews, 2012).

Owing to the scale economy in production, the global market is dominated by the top ten companies. In wind turbine, Chinese manufacturers account for one-third, followed by other-country manufacturers—Vestas, Siemens, and General Electrics. In solar PV, those in China account for 75%, followed by Korea and Malaysia (REN21, 2020). Accordingly, trade of RE has rapidly grown in this decade (Figures 7.1a and 7.1b), which also indicates that Asian countries have also become the main exporter in the world PV and wind energy components market. This trend might have also

DOI: 10.4324/9781003190905-10

been affected by the growing demand from policies mainly in importing countries, for example, European Union (EU) nations and United States.

During the process, promoting policies, for example, FiT and RPS, have been key to the vast diffusion, as they are in force in an increasing number of countries and regions (Olmos et al., 2012; Smith and Urpelainen, 2013; Shrimali et al., 2015). The trade dispute on RE products between the EU and China shows the significant effect of the policy on demand for the components (Bougette and Charlier, 2018).

RE has been vastly disseminated in the past few decades, as a result of promoting policies such as FiT and RPS. Accordingly, Asian manufacturers of PV and wind energy components have rapidly increased their production. The manufacturers in Asian countries have enhanced the export performance with the growing demand for their products, whereas those in EU with RE policies have dominated the global market. The background suggests that RE policies can impact the overall trade, that is, both export and import of PV and wind energy components. Nevertheless, a limited number of empirical studies on the effect of policies in importing countries exist,

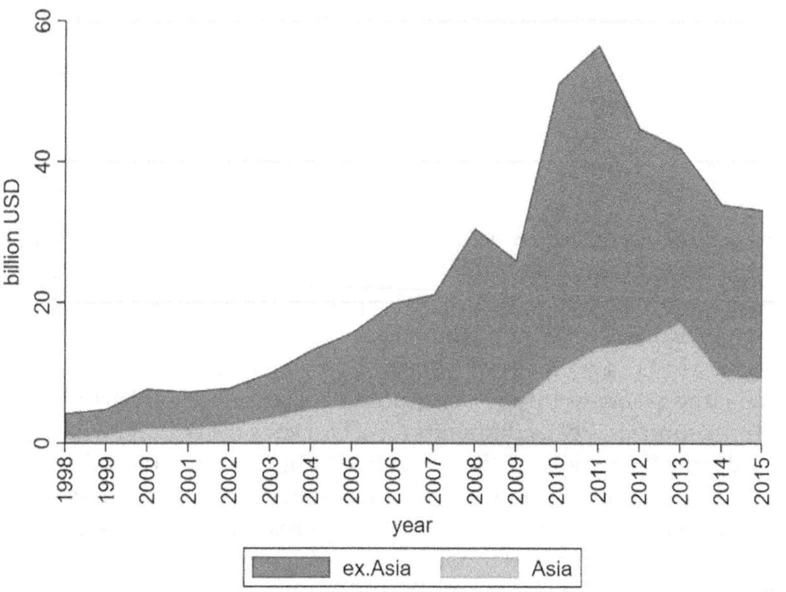

Figure 7.1a Export value and destination of PV components from selected Asian countries: 1998–2015 (CEPII, 2019).

Note: Asian countries: China, India, Indonesia, Japan, Malaysia, South Korea, Thailand (Table 7.A.2).

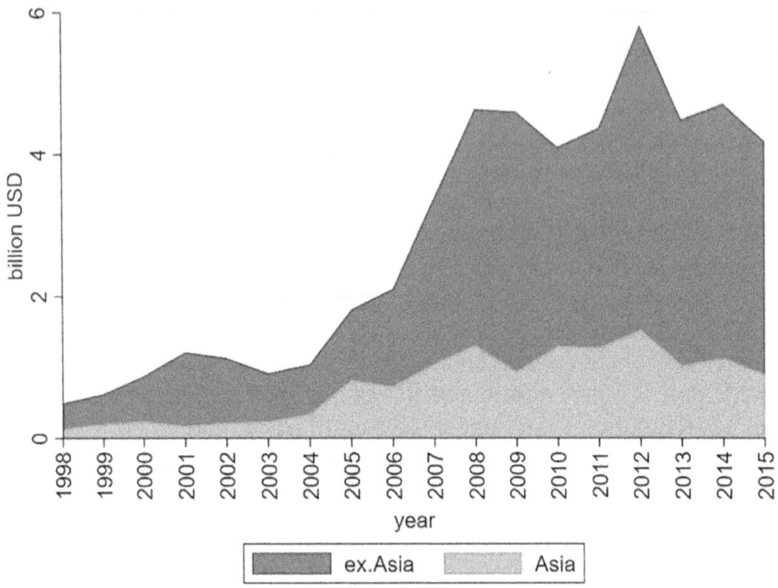

Figure 7.1b Export value and destination of PV/wind energy components from selected Asian countries: 1998–2015 (CEPII, 2019).

Note: Asian countries: China, India, Indonesia, Japan, Malaysia, South Korea, Thailand (Table 7.A.2).

although the literature on the trade of RE components has mainly focused only on those in exporting countries.

Against this backdrop, this chapter analyzes the effect of FiT and RPS on the exports of solar PV and wind energy components from selected Asian countries as the two types of policies have been widely disseminated. We specify and compare the effect of those policies in both exporting and importing countries. Policy dummies are set for each if FiT or RPS had been in force during the periods of the study. In addition to the standard estimation methods in the literature, we apply matching econometrics to control the confounding, that is, mixed effect between gross domestic products (GDP), innovative capacity, and RE policies, in the estimation of the treatment effect of RE policies on PV and wind components' exports.

Section 2 reviews the theoretical and empirical implications on the relationship between RE policy and the exports of PV and wind energy components, and Section 3 specifies the estimated model and the methodology in this chapter. Section 4 shows the estimation results of the standard and matching estimation. Section 5 discusses the estimation results and the implication on the potential carbon halo effect. Section 6 concludes this chapter.

2 Literature review

RE policies such as FiT and RPS can theoretically increase the profit for producers, and they can be incentivized for technological development if they perceive to gain certain level of surplus. The technological development can also benefit the producers. Price-based policies, such as FiT, can provide more incentives to producers, because the surplus from the policy and technological development is basically distributed to themselves. Conversely, the incentives by quantity-based policy may be limited, as the surplus is mainly distributed to consumers or taxpayers (Menanteau et al., 2003). If the additional profit can lead to the increase in the export of the producers, RE policies may enhance the export competitiveness, as suggested by the Porter hypothesis (Porter and van der Linde, 1995).

Additionally, the rent is also available for overseas manufacturers with a higher price level compared to the world market, which might attract the manufacturers to export to countries where the policies are in force. In this case, the manufacturers in countries with the policies in force may be incentivized to supply more to their home countries than exports. Then, the countries with these policies may increase their relative imports of RE components (Ogura, 2020).

The empirical literature on environmental goods (EGs) trade has applied the gravity model for the analyses on the effect of RE policies on the exports (Costantini and Mazzanti, 2012; Costantini and Crespi, 2013; Groba, 2014). In accordance with previous research, this chapter applies the gravity model in international trade.

$$T_{ijt} = \alpha_0 Y_{it}^{\alpha 1} Y_{jt}^{\alpha 2} D_{ij}^{\alpha 3} \tag{7.1}$$

In the basic form devised by Tinbergen (1962), T_{ijt} denotes the trade between country $_i$ and $_j$ in year $_t$. GDP by $_i$ and $_j$ in $_t$ are expressed with Y_{it} and Y_{jt}, respectively. Last, D_{ij} denotes the physical distance between the two. Hence, equation 7.1 shows that the trade between country $_i$ and $_j$ can be explained using the economic scale and the distance. GDP is assumed to have a positive association with the trade, while the distance can be thought to be the cost factor, that is, a negative effect. The equation has been widely used to analyze the effect of trade policies (e.g., Rose, 2004; Baier and Bergstrand, 2007) ever since its theoretical foundation has been confirmed (Anderson, 1979). The literature on the gravity model of international trade indicates the considerable effect of the factors omitted in the model. To deal with the problem, Anderson and van Wincoop (2003) argue that the fixed effects of an exporter, importer, and year have to be considered.

Based on the Porter hypothesis (Porter and van der Linde, 1995), the empirical analyses on EGs trade have examined the relationship of the trade with innovative capacity and environmental policies (e.g., Costantini and Mazzanti, 2012). The model is also applied for the analyses on the effect of RE policies on exports (e.g., Costantini and Crespi, 2013). Among these studies, the duration of FiT is positively associated with the exports, while RPS shows no significant relation (Groba, 2014).

However, the literature has not dealt with the drawbacks. Previous analyses on the trade of EGs and RE components have not considered the theoretical implication on the policy effect, as they assume the positive policy effect on the export based on the Porter hypothesis. Moreover, the empirical literature on the effect of policies in importing countries is limited, while the theoretical implication indicates that the exports can be affected by RE policies in both exporting and importing countries; only Groba and Cao have examined the effect of policies in importing countries as the factors to influence Chinese PV/wind components exports (Groba and Cao, 2014). Furthermore, the literature on the effectiveness of those policies points out the correlation to the innovation (Johnstone et al., 2010), which suggests the potential confounding, that is, mixed effects of GDP, knowledge stock, and RE policies. However, the literature on EGs trade has not yet considered the effect.

3 Methodology

3.1 Standard gravity model

Based on the literature and challenges reviewed in Section 2, we estimate the effect of FiT and RPS on the exports of PV and wind energy components with the model below. Considering the drawback in the literature in Section 2, this study examines the individual effect of the policy; FiT and RPS in both exporting and importing countries are included in the model individually.

$$\ln \mathrm{X}_{ijt} = \alpha 0 + \alpha 1 \ln \mathrm{TGDP}_{ijt} + \alpha 2 \ln \mathrm{D}_{ij} + \alpha 3 \ln \mathrm{P}_{ijt} + \alpha 4 \ln \mathrm{K}_{it} + \alpha 5 \mathrm{REpol}_{ijt} + d_{ij} + d_t + \varepsilon_{ijt} \quad (7.2)$$

where X_{ijt} denotes the exports of PV and wind energy components from country $_i$ to $_j$ in year $_t$. Following Anderson and van Wincoop (2003), the model in this study includes exporter/importer/year fixed effects ($_{di,\ dj,\ dt}$).

Based on the study by Baier and Bergstrand (2009), this chapter examined the effect of the sum of GDP in exporter and importing countries, that is, TGDP_{ijt} in equation 7.3.

$$\mathrm{TGDP}_{ijt} = \mathrm{Y}_{it} + \mathrm{Y}_{jt} \quad (7.3)$$

As already mentioned earlier, D_{ij} denotes the distance between exporter and importer. Dummy variables for sharing the common border and common language: $CNTG_{ij}$ and $LANG_{ij}$ are also included in the model as the cost components of the bilateral trade. Both dummies are assumed to be positively associated with the exports since the feature is likely to be the higher possibility to the relationship in the trade.

The price effect is also considered in this chapter. The variable P_{ijt} is calculated with the trade data by equation 7.4. Q_{ijt} denotes the quantity of traded products annually. Hence, P_{ijt} is the unit value of the exports from $_i$ to j.

$$P_{ijt} = X_{ijt} / Q_{ijt} \tag{7.4}$$

This study also considers the effect of innovative capacity following the suggestion of Porter and van der Linde (1995). In reference to Popp et al. (2011), the knowledge stock variable K_{it} is calculated by equation 7.5 with patent PAT_{it} statistics. This examines the effect on the exports as the proxy for the innovative capacity.

$$K^{it} = \sum_{s=0}^{\infty} e^{-\delta_1(s)} \left(1 - e^{-\delta_2(s+1)}\right) PAT_{i(t-s)} \tag{7.5}$$

3.2 Matching econometrics in the gravity model

Matching econometrics has been applied to the gravity model to analyze the treatment effect of trade policies, for example, free trade agreement (FTA) and accession to World Trade Organization (Baier and Bergstrand, 2009; Kohl and Trojanowska, 2015). This might be partly because the omitted variable bias cannot be fully compensated by the inclusion of fixed effects. Furthermore, FTA can be determined not randomly but affected by other factors, for example, economic mass and the similarity of exporters and importers (Baier and Bergstrand, 2009), which shows the considerable effect of confounding. Matching with these standard gravity variables can control the confounding, and the potential bias with the policy variables can be minimized. Therefore, the matching estimator focuses more on the relationship between export and RE policies, whereas the standard gravity model estimation examines the effect of every regressor in the model. Considering potential confounding that has not been examined in the literature on the trade of EGs including RE components, this chapter applies matching estimator in the analysis.

In the application of matching econometrics in the gravity model, we follow the study by Baier and Bergstrand (2009). Regarding the estimation of the average treatment effect (ATE) and the effect on the treated (ATT), they referred to Abadie and Imbens (2006) considering the large sample properties and the conditional bias with more than one covariate in the model. Since the model in this study has multiple continuous variables, for example, GDP, distance, knowledge stock, and price variables, we also apply the same nearest neighbor matching with robust estimation, adjusting the bias from covariates. Referring to Baier and Bergstrand (2009), the treatment effect on the exports in the matching is explained as follows:

$$X_i^*(0) = \begin{cases} X_i, & \text{if REPol}_i = 0 \\ \frac{1}{M}\sum j \in J_M(i)X_j, & \text{if REPol}_i = 1 \end{cases} \tag{7.6}$$

and

$$X_i^*(1) = \begin{cases} \frac{1}{M}\sum j \in J_M(i)X_j, & \text{if REPol}_i = 0 \\ X_i, & \text{if REPol}_i = 1 \end{cases} \tag{7.7}$$

Also, the ATE and ATT can be expressed as follows:

$$ATE_M = \frac{1}{N}\sum_{i=1}^{N}\left[X_i^*(1) - X_i^*(0)\right] \tag{7.8}$$

$$ATT_M = \frac{1}{N}\sum_{REPol_i=1}\left[X_i - X_i^*(0)\right] \tag{7.9}$$

Missing outcome (export) is imputed from equations 7.6 and 7.7 in the set of indices for the first $_M$ matches, that is, $_{JM(i)}$, based on the index $_j$ in the $_N$ pairs of the countries. After the process, ATE is estimated with the observation $_N$, and the estimators for ATT are obtained only for countries with RE policies in force. Variable REPol_i is also applied to the policies in importing countries REPol_j, as the heterogeneous policy effect is key in this study. Balanced plots of the matching econometrics are shown in the Appendix.

3.3 Data

Trade data (export value and quantity) are extracted from BACI database (CEPII, 2019), and the standard gravity variables, for example, CNTG and LANG, from GeoDist database (CEPII, 2015). Data on GDP are from World Development Indicators database by World Bank (2019). Patent data of the technologies related to PV and wind energy are extracted from OECD statistics (OECD, 2019). The data on the implementation of FiT and RPS are taken from IEA/IRENA (2019).

The period of this study is between 1998 and 2015. A total of 56 countries are examined as they are included in OECD-EPAU (2013), which is listed in the Appendix. For analyzing the trend of exports from Asia, only the exports from seven Asian countries[1] are considered in this study, and the importing countries in this study are 56 countries including seven Asian countries mentioned above (listed in Table 7.A.2). Descriptive statistics is supplied in Appendix (Table 7.A.3).

4 Results

4.1 Results of the standard gravity model

First, the results of the estimation with the standard gravity model are shown in Tables 7.1 and 7.2. In the tables, subscripts *i* of FiT and RPS stand for the policies in exporting countries, and subscripts *j* for those in importing countries.

The result indicates the different effect between FiT and RPS, and between exporting and importing countries. FiT and RPS in exporting countries are negatively associated with the exports of PV components, while the effect is insignificant with fixed effects (columns 5 and 6 in Table 7.1). Conversely, RPS in exporting countries is positively associated with wind component exports in the model with fixed effects (columns 2 and 6 in Table 7.2). Additionally, both FiT and RPS in importing countries indicate their positive effect on the exports of PV and wind energy components (columns 3 and 4 in Tables 7.1 and 7.2).

The positive effect of GDP and the negative effect of bilateral distance are consistent with the assumption in the standard gravity model. The estimation of price effect shows a mixed result, suggesting a positive effect on PV without fixed effects, whereas it shows a negative effect on wind energy components.

Knowledge stock effect is also somewhat mixed. PV export is positively associated with the effect in the estimation with fixed effects. However, the knowledge stock of wind energy is negatively associated with the export (columns 5–8 in Table 7.2). This negative effect of knowledge stock may have been influenced by the stagnation of the exports in 2007–2015 (Figures 7.1a and 7.1b), as no significant effect is detected in the estimation of PV exports. The overall positive effect of knowledge stock is also indicated by Costantini and Mazzanti (2012). Nevertheless, in this study, the robustness of the effect was not seen in the estimation.

4.2 Results of the matching econometrics

The results of the estimation with matching econometrics are shown in Table 7.3. Subscripts *i* and *j* of FiT and RPS in the tables again denote the policies in exporting and importing countries, respectively.

The results show the opposite effects of exporting and importing countries. In exporting countries, FiT has negative effects, while the ATT of RPS

Table 7.1 Results of the standard gravity model: solar PV

	(1)	*(2)*	*(3)*	*(4)*	*(5)*	*(6)*	*(7)*	*(8)*
lnTGDPijt	2.010***	1.980***	1.922***	1.818***	1.034***	1.020***	1.033***	1.036***
	(0.127)	(0.127)	(0.127)	(0.123)	(0.149)	(0.149)	(0.149)	(0.149)
lnDij	−0.496**	−0.500**	−0.495**	−0.527**	−0.750***	−0.752***	−0.749***	−0.750***
	(0.227)	(0.229)	(0.237)	(0.227)	(0.188)	(0.188)	(0.188)	(0.188)
CNTGij	0.756	0.751	0.778	0.870	−0.307	−0.311	−0.305	−0.307
	(0.767)	(0.773)	(0.793)	(0.768)	(0.336)	(0.335)	(0.337)	(0.336)
LANGij	−0.803**	−0.828**	−0.781**	−0.903**	0.843**	0.843**	0.845**	0.842**
	(0.374)	(0.379)	(0.374)	(0.353)	(0.373)	(0.373)	(0.373)	(0.373)
lnPijt	0.328***	0.330***	0.298***	0.292***	0.009	0.010	0.010	0.009
	(0.057)	(0.057)	(0.057)	(0.055)	(0.035)	(0.035)	(0.035)	(0.035)
lnKit	0.007	0.024	−0.003	0.017	0.353***	0.350***	0.353***	0.353***
	(0.038)	(0.039)	(0.038)	(0.036)	(0.054)	(0.054)	(0.054)	(0.054)
FiTit	−0.364***				0.008			
	(0.115)				(0.057)			
RPSit		−0.372***				0.081		
		(0.113)				(0.063)		
FiTjt			0.610***				0.142*	
			(0.162)				(0.083)	
RPSjt				1.309***				−0.026
				(0.181)				(0.116)
Constant	−4.197**	−4.704*	−4.616*	−3.328	7.884***	8.499***	8.301***	9.606***
	(2.442)	(2.450)	(2.521)	(2.408)	(2.094)	(2.110)	(2.121)	(2.328)
Country FE	no	no	no	no	yes	yes	yes	yes
Year FE	no	no	no	no	yes	yes	yes	yes
Observations	5,920	5,920	5,920	5,920	5,920	5,920	5,920	5,920

Robust standard errors in parentheses
***$p < 0.01$, **$p < 0.05$, *$p < 0.1$

Table 7.2 Results of the standard gravity model: wind

	(1)	*(2)*	*(3)*	*(4)*	*(5)*	*(6)*	*(7)*	*(8)*
lnTGDPijt	1.772***	1.660***	1.659***	1.556***	1.250***	1.149***	1.251***	1.248***
	(0.130)	(0.132)	(0.131)	(0.126)	(0.202)	(0.202)	(0.202)	(0.201)
lnDij	−0.697**	−0.653**	−0.659**	−0.683**	−1.260***	−1.267***	−1.262***	−1.263***
	(0.189)	(0.199)	(0.201)	(0.193)	(0.216)	(0.215)	(0.216)	(0.216)
CNTGij	0.549	0.631	0.642	0.740	−0.077	−0.112	−0.076	−0.076
	(0.633)	(0.671)	(0.679)	(0.668)	(0.245)	(0.241)	(0.245)	(0.244)
LANGij	0.652*	0.390	0.446	0.386	1.051***	1.058***	1.049***	1.048***
	(0.386)	(0.384)	(0.382)	(0.318)	(0.337)	(0.337)	(0.337)	(0.337)
lnPijt	−0.232***	−0.234***	−0.236***	−0.237***	−0.291***	−0.288***	−0.291***	−0.291***
	(0.066)	(0.066)	(0.067)	(0.066)	(0.049)	(0.049)	(0.049)	(0.049)
lnKit	0.223***	0.189***	0.203***	0.226***	−0.166**	−0.187**	−0.136*	−0.136*
	(0.038)	(0.040)	(0.039)	(0.038)	(0.078)	(0.076)	(0.077)	(0.077)
FiTit	−0.612***				−0.165**			
	(0.135)				(0.082)			
RPSit		0.217*				0.358***		
		(0.112)				(0.072)		
FiTjt			0.277*				0.042	
			(0.145)				(0.100)	
RPSjt				1.173***				0.068
				(0.175)				(0.137)
Constant	−0.917	−0.817	−0.800	0.256	2.835	3.711	2.884	2.940
	(2.201)	(2.305)	(2.315)	(2.204)	(2.750)	(2.750)	(2.751)	(2.744)
Country FE	no	no	no	no	yes	yes	yes	yes
Year FE	no	no	no	no	yes	yes	yes	yes
Observations	4,915	4,915	4,915	4,915	4,915	4,915	4,915	4,915

Robust standard errors in parentheses
***$p < 0.01$, **$p < 0.05$, *$p < 0.1$

shows weak significance in wind energy. Conversely, both FiT and RPS in importing countries show a positive effect on the export except for insignificant ATE of FiT for wind.

Balance plots of the estimations are displayed in Figures 7.A-1a–7.A-1d and 7.A-2a–7.A-2d in Appendix A.1, which show the density plots of samples before and after matching. As shown in the plots for the continuous variables in the model, price and knowledge stock variables are also included in the estimation to control the effect.

5 Discussion

Overall weaker significance of the policy effect in the standard gravity model estimation might have resulted from the mixed effect with potential bias from other factors than RE policies. The results of the matching estimation are more robust, showing the negative effect of policies in exporting countries and the positive effect of policies in importing countries on the exports. These different results between the two estimations may be associated to the effect of the variables other than RE policies. They may generate bias in the standard estimation and make the results unclear.

The negative effect of the policy in exporting countries is contradictory to previous studies (Costantini and Mazzanti, 2012; Groba, 2014). This contradictory result may be because of the policy-induced higher profitability in home countries than in the global market. The higher profitability motivated the manufacturers of PV and wind energy components to prioritize supplying to their home countries (Jaffe and Palmer, 1997). Since FiT sets the unified policy level on the price, FiT in exporting countries might be the clear sign for the manufacturers to supply to those countries.

Table 7.3 ATE and ATT of FiT and RPS on PV/wind energy components' exports

	PV				*Wind*			
	FiTit	*RPSit*	*FiTjt*	*RPSjt*	*FiTit*	*RPSit*	*FiTjt*	*RPSjt*
	(1)	*(2)*	*(3)*	*(4)*	*(5)*	*(6)*	*(7)*	*(8)*
ATE	−0.564***	−4.352***	0.355***	1.033***	−0.688***	−1.265***	0.068	0.688***
	(0.088)	(0.205)	(0.056)	(0.068)	(0.086)	(0.162)	(0.067)	(0.085)
ATT	−0.697**	−0.653**	−0.659**	−0.683**	−1.260***	−1.267***	−1.262***	−1.263***
	(0.105)	(0.104)	(0.067)	(0.091)	(0.106)	(0.124)	(0.081)	(0.106)
Observations	5,920	5,920	5,920	5,920	4,915	4,915	4,915	4,915

Robust standard errors in parentheses
***p < 0.01, **p < 0.05, *p < 0.1

Nevertheless, the positive effect of FiT and RPS in importing countries is consistent with the results of Groba and Cao (2014), which also seems to be the consequence of the shift in profitability. As foreign manufacturers can obtain the FiT-induced rent, they have been responding to the rent from FiT and RPS (Kwon, 2015), which might have eventually led to more exports to the countries with those policies.

The negative effect of policies in exporting countries and the positive effect of those in importing countries are both consistent with the theoretical implications on the relation between PV and wind energy exports (Ogura, 2020). Therefore, the exports from the selected Asian countries might have fulfilled the growing demand of importing countries with RE policies, and the policies in the Asian countries may have motivated the manufacturers of PV and wind energy components to prioritize supplying to their home countries.

Positive coefficients of price variables in Table 7.1 imply that Asian manufacturers have upgraded quality of the PV components (Wang et al., 2019), while this may be affected merely by the higher price in importing countries caused by the policy effect. In this regard, Asian countries may not necessarily have to offer lower prices to prevail over competition in the global market (Horii, Chapter 8 of this book). In contrast, they are forced to compete in terms of price in the global market of wind energy components, as shown in the negative effect on wind energy in Table 7.2. If the higher price of PV components has resulted merely from the change in the price level by the policy, lower prices can still benefit the manufacturers. However, price competitiveness may not be always beneficial for the manufacturers if the export price reflects the higher quality that is needed in the importing countries.

The upgraded quality of PV components in trade also suggests the shift in the technological capability of Asian countries in the studied period. Positive association between knowledge stock and PV export from Asian countries suggests that the countries have acquired the technology and production capability of PV. If this has been brought by the investment from other countries, Asian countries may have benefited from a part of the carbon halo effect. However, the implementation of FiT and RPS may not lead to the carbon halo effect of the countries, because the growing demand for the components might be fulfilled by the Asian countries' exports rather than the production induced by the investment.

6 Conclusion

Global demand for RE has grown in the period with promoting policies, such as FiT and RPS. Accordingly, Asian manufacturers have rapidly increased the production of solar PV and wind energy components. The exports of RE components from Asian countries have grown rapidly (Figures 7.1a and 7.1b). The background suggests that Asian countries have played a significant role to meet the growing demand in importing countries with RE promoting policies. However, the past literature on the trade of EGs including RE components has focused mainly on the policy effect of exporting countries. Hence, previous studies have not compared the policy effect between exporting and importing countries.

This chapter analyzes the effect of FiT and RPS in both exporting and importing countries on the export of PV and wind energy components. Furthermore, this study is the first to apply matching to the trade analysis of RE components since previous studies have not controlled the confounding, that is, the mixed effect of regressors in the model.

The estimation results show the contrast between the policies in exporting and importing countries. FiT and RPS in the exporting countries show a negative effect on their exports, which is contradictory to the results in the literature on the trade of EGs (Costantini and Mazzanti, 2012) and PV components (Groba 2014). The results indicate that the manufacturers might have prioritized supplying to the home countries than to exports to others. However, FiT and RPS in importing countries show a positive effect on the exports from Asian countries. This suggests the Asian manufacturers' response to the expansion of their profitability generated by the policies in importing countries.

Contrasting results between the policies in exporting and importing countries in this chapter are consistent with theoretical implications (Ogura, 2020), which have not been clearly considered and examined in the empirical literature on the policy effect on the export of RE components. The results are more robust with matching estimators, which has not been applied in previous studies. Positive effect of the price variable in PV estimation indicates the upgraded quality of the products, which suggests that the mitigation of the effect from the price competition, while the negative effect in wind energy suggests the existence. Therefore, these contrasting results between the exporting and importing countries' policy effect, and between the export price of solar PV and wind energy components, constitute the novelty of this study.

Upgraded quality and positive effect of knowledge effect indicate the growing technological capability of Asian countries on their solar PV manufacturing. If those countries acquire the capability through the investment from other countries, it can be a part of the carbon halo effect, that is, FDI-brought RE technology and production capacity that eventually lead to the export of the components. Conversely, FiT and RPS implementation may not lead to the carbon halo effect, since the growing demand for the components might be fulfilled by the Asian countries' exports. As this chapter has not examined the direct relationship between the investment, the deployment of RE, and the shift in the exports of the components, this could be the future scope of research.

Note

1 China, India, Indonesia, Japan, Malaysia, South Korea, and Thailand.

References

Abadie, A., G. W. Imbens (2006). Large sample properties of matching estimators for average treatment effects. *Econometrica*, 74 (1), 235–267, https://doi.org/10.1111/j.1468-0262.2006.00655.x.

Anderson, J. E. (1979). A theoretical foundation for the gravity equation, *American Economic Review*, 69 (1), 106–116.

Anderson, J. E., E. van Wincoop (2003). Gravity with gravitas: a solution to the border puzzle, *American Economic Review*, 93 (1), 170–192, https://doi.org/10.1257/000282803321455214.

Baier, S. L., J. H. Bergstrand (2007). Do free trade agreements actually increase members' international trade?, *Journal of International Economics*, 71 (1), 72–95, https://doi.org/10.1016/j.jinteco.2006.02.005.

Baier, S. L., J. H. Bergstrand (2009). Estimating the effects of free trade agreements on international trade flows using matching econometrics, *Journal of International Economics*, 77 (1), 63–76, https://doi.org/10.1016/j.jinteco.2008.09.006.

Bougette, P., C. Charlier (2018). Antidumping and feed-in tariffs as good buddies? Modeling the EU-China solar panel dispute, *Energy Journal*, 39 (6), 171–188, https://doi.org/10.5547/01956574.39.6.pbou.

CEPII (2015). GeoDist, http://www:cepii:fr/CEPII/en/bdd_modele/presentation:asp?id=6. accessed on July 19, 2018.

CEPII (2019). BACI Database, http://www:cepii:fr/CEPII/en/bdd_modele/presentation:asp?id=1. accessed on August 1, 2019.

Costantini, V., F. Crespi (2013). Public policies for a sustainable energy sector: Regulation, diversity and fostering of innovation, *Journal of Evolutionary Economics*, 23 (2), 401–429, https://doi.org/10.1007/s00191-010-0211-3.

Costantini, V., M. Mazzanti (2012). On the green and innovative side of trade competitiveness?: The impact of environmental policies and innovation on EU exports, *Research Policy*, 41 (1), 132–153, https://doi.org/10.1016/j.respol.2011.08.004.

Fuentes, S., R. Villafafila-Robles, P. Olivella-Rosell, J. Rull-Duran, S. Galceran-Arellano (2020). Transition to a greener Power Sector: Four different scopes on energy security, *Renewable Energy Focus*, 33 (June), 23–36, https://doi.org/10.1016/j.ref.2020.03.001.

Groba, F. (2014). Determinants of trade with solar energy technology components: evidence on the porter hypothesis?, *Applied Economics*, 46 (5), 503–526, https://doi.org/10.1080/00036846.2013.857005.

Groba, F., J. Cao (2014). Chinese renewable energy technology exports: The role of policy, innovation and markets, *Environmental and Resource Economics*, 60 (2), 243–283, https://doi.org/10.1007/s10640-014-9766-z.

IEA/IRENA (2019). Joint Policies and Measures Database, http://www:iea:org/policiesandmeasures/renewableenergy/. accessed on July 31, 2019.

IRENA (2019). Future of Solar Photovoltaic: Deployment, investment, technology, grid integration and socio-economic aspects, https://www.irena.org/publications/2019/Nov/Future-of-Solar-Photovoltaic. accessed on December 10, 2020.

Jaffe, A. B., K. Palmer (1997). Environmental regulation and innovation: A panel data study, *Review of Economics and Statistics*, 79 (4), 610–619, https://doi.org/10.1162/003465397557196.

Jänicke, M. (2012). "Green growth": From a growing eco-industry to economic sustainability, *Energy Policy*, 48, 13–21, https://doi.org/10.1016/j.enpol.2012.04.045.

Johnstone, N., I. Haščič, D. Popp (2010). Renewable energy policies and technological innovation: Evidence based on patent counts, *Environmental and Resource Economics*, 45 (1), 133–155, https://doi.org/10.1007/s10640-009-9309-1.

Kohl, T., S. Trojanowska (2015). Heterogeneous trade agreements, WTO membership and international trade: an analysis using matching econometrics, *Applied Economics*, 47 (33), 3499–3509, https://doi.org/10.1080/00036846.2015.1016211.

Kwon, T.-h. (2015). Rent and rent-seeking in renewable energy support policies: Feed-in tariff vs. renewable portfolio standard, *Renewable and Sustainable Energy Reviews*, 44, 676–681, https://doi.org/10.1016/j.rser.2015.01.036.

Mathews, J. A. (2012). Green growth strategies-Korean initiatives, *Futures*, 44 (8), 761–769, https://doi.org/10.1016/j.futures.2012.06.002.

Mathews, J. A., E.S. Reinert (2014). Renewables, manufacturing and green growth: Energy strategies based on capturing increasing returns, *Futures*, 61, 13–22, https://doi.org/10.1016/j.futures.2014.04.011.

Menanteau, P., D. Finon, M. L. Lamy (2003). Prices versus quantities: Choosing policies for promoting the development of renewable energy, *Energy Policy*, 31 (8), 799–812, https://doi.org/10.1016/S0301-4215(02)00133-7.

Mori, A., M. Takehara (2018). Revisiting china's climate policy: The climate energy conundrum point of view, in *China's Climate-Energy Policy: Domestic and International Impacts*, edited by A. Mori, chap. 3, Routledge, London, https://doi.org/10.4324/9781351037587-3.

OECD (2019). OECD Statistics, http://stats:oecd:org. accessed on July 20, 2019.

OECD-EPAU (2013). Renewable energy policy dataset, version March 2013, https://www:oecd:org/media/oecdorg/directorates/environmentdirectorate/2013-03-04OECD-EPAURenewableEnergyPolicies--FINAL:xls. accessed on September 21, 2018.

Ogura, Y. (2020). Policy as a "porter" of RE component export or import? Evidence from PV/wind energy in OECD and BRICS, *Energy Economics*, 86, 104,630, https://doi.org/10.1016/j.eneco.2019.104630.

Olmos, L., S. Ruester, S.J. Liong (2012). On the selection of financing instruments to push the development of new technologies: Application to clean energy technologies, *Energy Policy*, 43, 252–266, https://doi.org/10.1016/j.enpol.2012.01.001.

Pidgeon, N.F., I. Lorenzoni, W. Poortinga (2008). Climate change or nuclear power-No thanks! A quantitative study of public perceptions and risk framing in Britain, *Global Environmental Change*, 18 (1), 69–85, https://doi.org/10.1016/j.gloenvcha.2007.09.005.

Popp, D., I. Haˇsˇciˇc, N. Medhi (2011). Technology and the diffusion of renewable energy, *Energy Economics*, 33 (4), 648–662, https://doi.org/10.1016/j.eneco.2010.08.007.

Porter, M.E., C. van der Linde (1995). Toward a new conception of the environment-competitiveness relationship, *Journal of Economic Perspectives*, 9 (4), 97–118.

REN21 (2020). Renewables 2020 global status report https://www:ren21:net/reports/global-status-report/. accessed on February 5th, 2021.

Rose, A. K. (2004). Do we really know that the WTO increases trade?, *American Economic Review*, 94 (1), 98–114, https://doi.org/10.1257/000282804322970724.

Shrimali, G., G. Chan, S. Jenner, F. Groba, J. Indvik (2015). Evaluating Renewable Portfolio Standards for in-State renewable deployment: Accounting for policy heterogeneity, *Economics of Energy & Environmental Policy*, 4 (2), 127–142, https://doi.org/10.5547/2160-5890.4.2.gshr.

Smith, M.G., J. Urpelainen (2013). The Effect of Feed-in Tariffs on Renewable Electricity Generation: An instrumental variables approach, *Environmental and Resource Economics*, 1–26, https://doi.org/10.1007/s10640-013-9684-5.

Song, J. (2015). Renewable energy towards green growth, in *Green Growth and Low Carbon Development in East Asia*, edited by F. Yoshida and A. Mori, chap. 1, Routledge, London, https://doi.org/10.4324/9781315695860.

Stokes, L.C. (2016). Electoral Backlash against Climate Policy: A Natural Experiment on Retrospective Voting and Local Resistance to Public Policy, *American Journal of Political Science*, 60 (4), 958–974, https://doi.org/10.1111/ajps.12220.

Tinbergen, J. (1962). *Shaping the world economy; Suggestions for an international economic policy*, Twentieth Century Fund, New York.

Wang, L., R. Zhuang, S. Huang, Y. Zhao (2019). Quality Competition Versus Price Competition: Why Does China Dominate the Global Solar Photo-Voltaic Market?, *Emerging Markets Finance and Trade*, 55 (6), 1326–1342, https://doi.org/10.1080/1540496X.2018.1507905.

World Bank (2019). World Development Indicators, http://databank:worldbank:org/data/reports:aspx?source=world-developmentindicators. accessed on August 7, 2019.

Wu, M., J. Salzman (2014). The next generation of trade and environment conflicts: The rise of green industrial policy, *Northwestern University Law Review*, 108 (2), 401–474.

Yi, H. (2013). Clean energy policies and green jobs: An evaluation of green jobs in U.S. metropolitan areas, *Energy Policy*, 56, 644–652, https://doi.org/10.1016/j.enpol.2013.01.034.

A Appendix

A.1 Balance plot in the matching estimation

Balance plots are shown in Figures 7.A-1a–7.A-1d and 7.A-2a–7.A-2d as a result of the matching estimation.

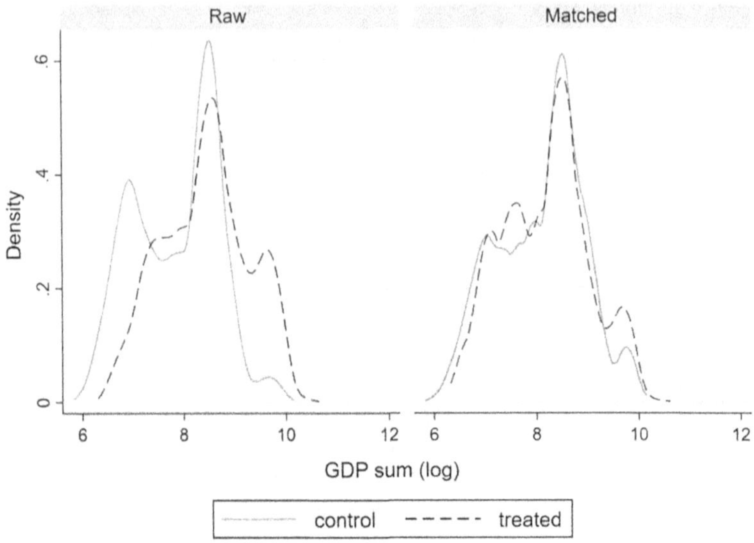

Figure 7.A-1a Balance plot of the sum of exporter and importer GDP: PV.

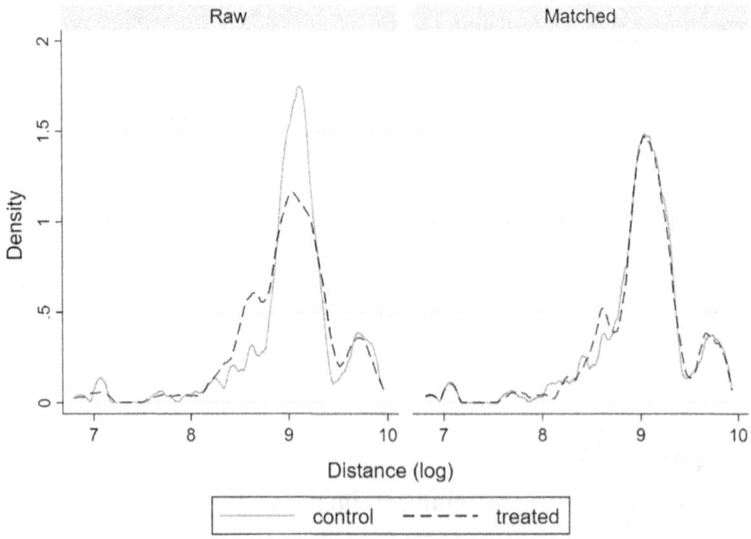

Figure 7.A-1b Balance plot of the distance between exporter and importer countries: PV.

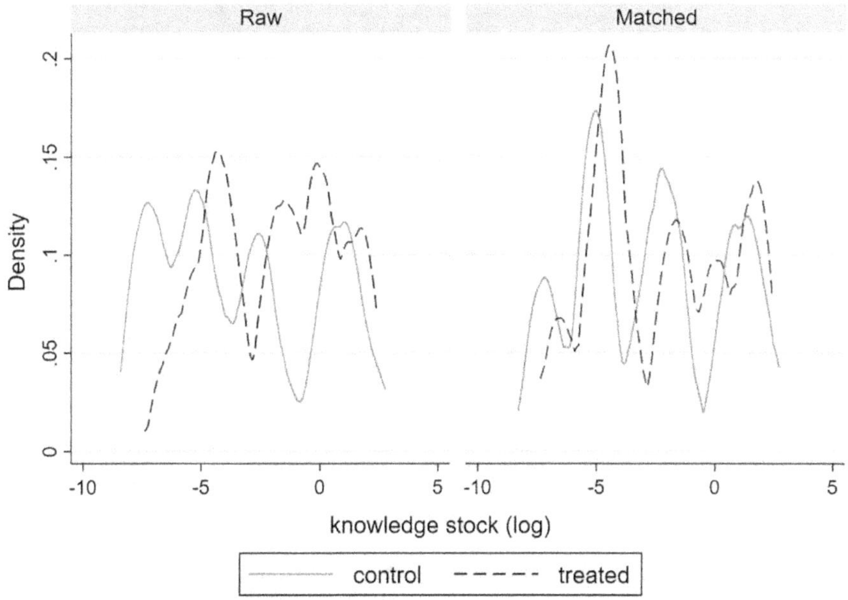

Figure 7.A-1c Balance plot of the exporter countries' knowledge stock: PV.

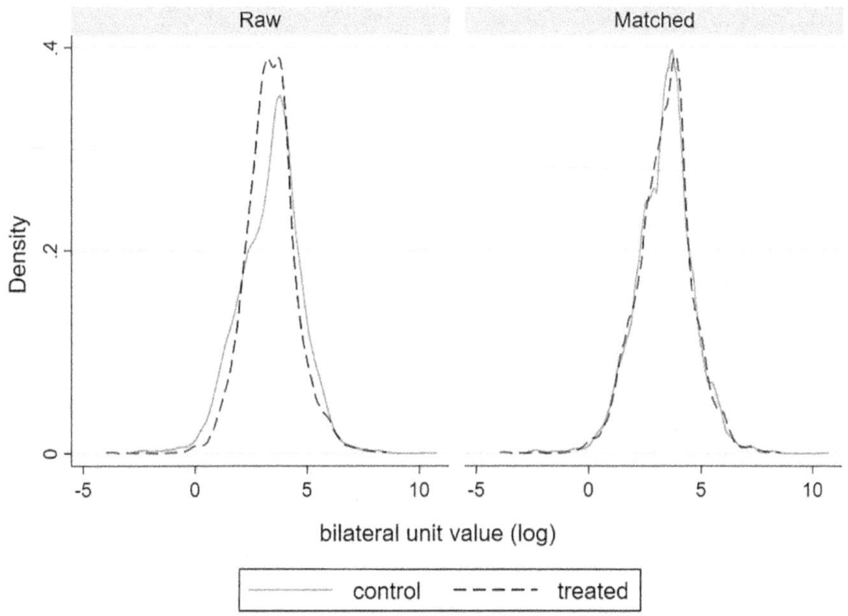

Figure 7.A-1d Balance plot of the bilateral unit value: PV.

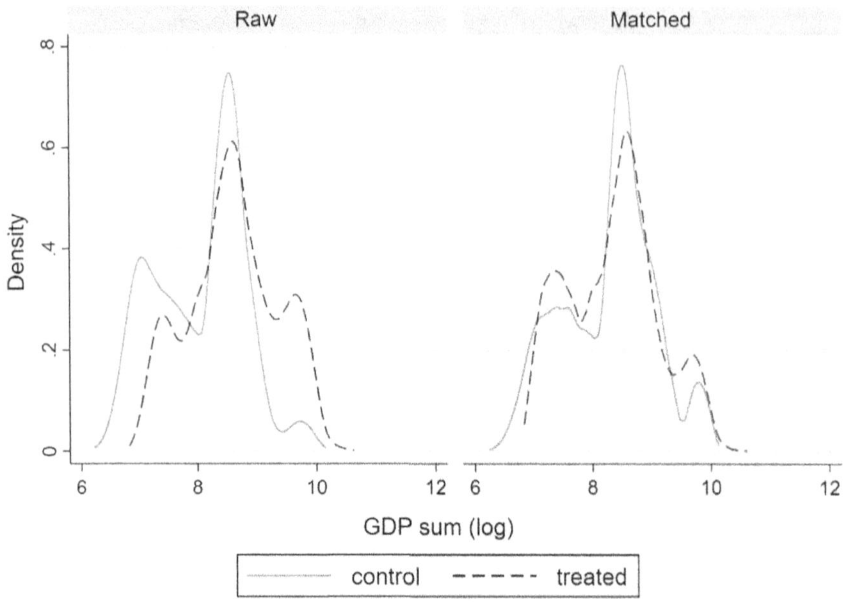

Figure 7.A-2a Balance plot of the sum of exporter and importer GDP: Wind.

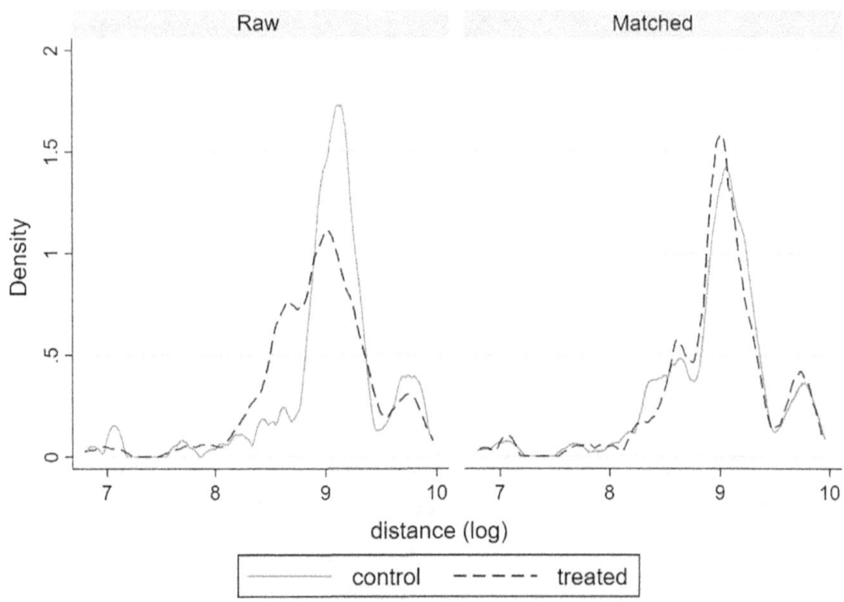

Figure 7.A-2b Balance plot of the distance between exporter and importer countries: Wind.

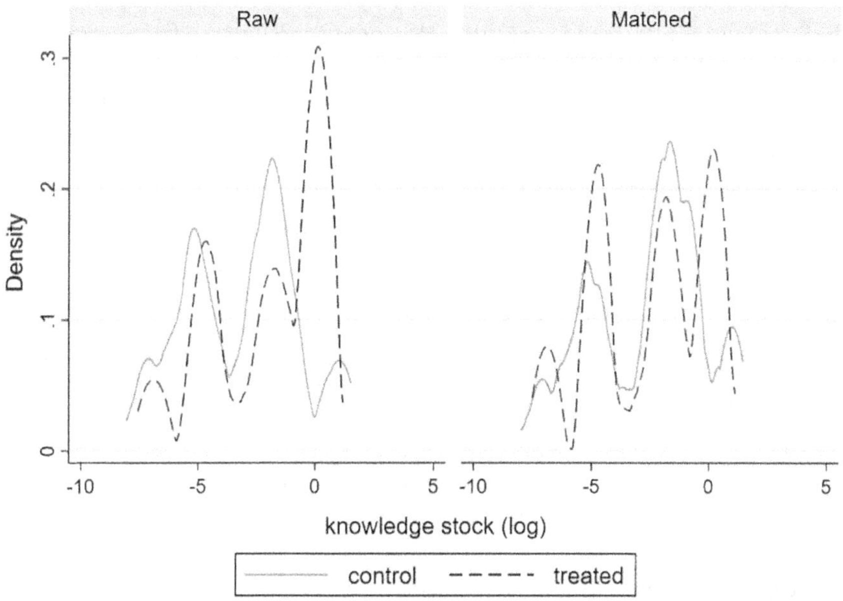

Figure 7.A-2c Balance plot of the exporter countries' knowledge stock: Wind.

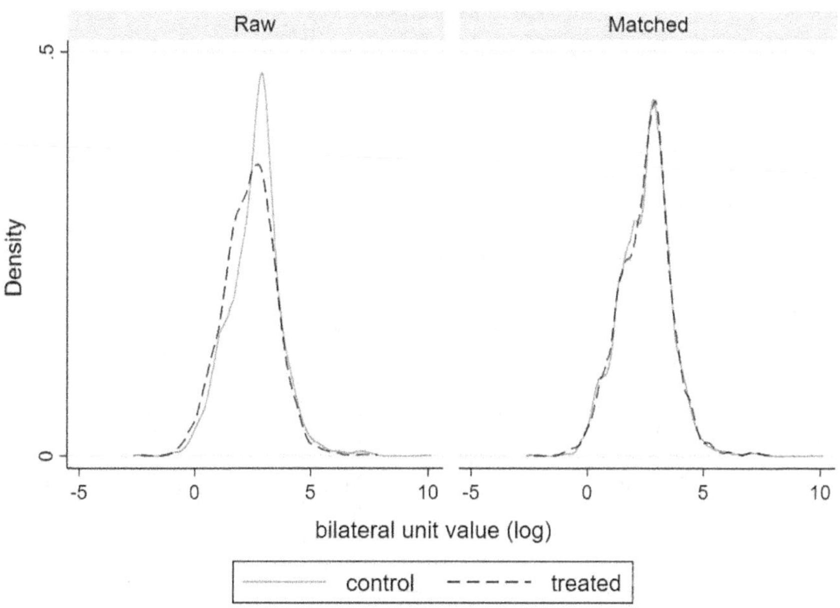

Figure 7.A-2d Balance plot of the bilateral unit value: Wind.

A.2 Complements

Referring to Groba and Cao (2014), HS codes for PV and wind energy components are shown in Table 7.A.1.

The country list in this chapter is shown in Table 7.A.2. A total of 56 countries that were studied have been compiled in OECD-EPAU (2013) regarding the information on their renewable energy policy.

Summary statistics are shown in Table 7.A.3.

Table 7.A.1 HS codes of PV/wind energy components in this study

HS 1996 Code	*Description*
Solar photovoltaics	
850440	Static converters
850720	Other lead-acid accumulators
854140	Photosensitive semiconducter devices, including photovoltaic cells whether or not assembled in modules or made up into panels; light emitting diodes
Wind energy components	
730820	Towers and lattice masts
841290	Parts of hydraulic/pneumatic/other power engines
841381	Other pumps; liquid elevators - Pumps
850231	Other generating sets - Wind-powered
850239	Other generating sets - Other
850240	Electric rotary converters

Source: Groba and Cao (2014)

Table 7.A.2 Classification of countries in this study

Asian Countries				
China	Indonesia	South Korea	Thailand	
India	Japan	Malaysia		
Others				
Algeria	Czech Republic	Ireland	New Zealand	Spain
Argentina	Denmark	Iceland	Norway	Sweden
Australia	Egypt	Israel	Peru	Switzerland
Austria	Estonia	Italy	Poland	Tanzania
Belarus	Finland	Jordan	Portugal	Turkey
Belgium	France	Kenya	Russia	Uganda
Brazil	Germany	Latvia	Serbia	United Kingdom
Bulgaria	Greece	Mexico	Slovakia	United States
Canada	Hungary	Morocco	Slovenia	Urugyay
Chile	Iran	Netherlands	South Africa	

Table 7.A.3 Descriptive statistics

	N	*Mean*	*Std.Dev*	*Min.*	*Max.*	*Unit*
XPVijt	*6930*	*62.15*	*333.82*	*0*	*8820.50*	*million USD*
XWijt	*6930*	*7.291*	*36.17*	*0*	*946.38*	*million USD*
Yit	*6930*	*3330.61*	*3601.90*	*327.30*	*18559.25*	*billion USD*
Yjt	*6930*	*1215.24*	*2463.41*	*9.006*	*18559.25*	*billion USD*
Dij	*6930*	*9074.43*	*3694.90*	*955.65*	*19711.86*	*km*
CNTGij	*6930*	*0.018*	*0.134*	*0*	*1*	
LANGij	*6930*	*0.034*	*0.181*	*0*	*1*	
KPVit	*6930*	*515.35*	*1212.47*	*0*	*5535.58*	
KWit	*6930*	*178.52*	*370.22*	*0*	*1833.08*	
FiTPVit	*6930*	*0.444*	*0.497*	*0*	*1*	
FiTPVjt	*6930*	*0.457*	*0.498*	*0*	*1*	
FiTWit	*6930*	*0.413*	*0.492*	*0*	*1*	
FiTWjt	*6930*	*0.462*	*0.499*	*0*	*1*	
RPSit	*6930*	*0.183*	*0.386*	*0*	*1*	
RPSjt	*6930*	*0.157*	*0.364*	*0*	*1*	

8 The role of China in energy transition in Indonesia

Maxensius Tri Sambodo

1 Introduction

Indonesia started to produce large-scale electricity from steam coal power plants in the mid-1980s. The government has facilitated the development of steam coal power plants by introducing several policies. In 2006, by Presidential Regulation No. 71, Indonesia started to develop a mega project of steam coal power plants, or the first fast-track (FTP-1) program. By November 2018, about 9,647 MW of steam coal power plants were completed, and 280 MW is still under construction (PLN, 2019a). In 2010, the government launched the second fast-track program (FTP-2). In FTP-1, the new capacity was based on the coal power plant, but in FTP-2, the 17,458 MW new power plant consisted of steam coal (10,520 MW), geothermal (4,855 MW), gas (280 MW), and hydropower (1,803 MW). However, by November 2018, about 755 MW of new capacity was operated commercially. Thus, both FTP-1 and FTP-2 will increase the new steam coal power plant to about 20,447 MW. In 2016, the government launched the 35,000 MW project which will be finished in 2028. Coal power plants will contribute about 20,000 MW of the total project.[1] Thus, the three mega projects will further expand the role of coal in the power generating system.

Foreign countries have made significant contributions to developing power plants in Indonesia. By the end of 2015, about 17,300 MW of newly installed power capacity was constructed under the independent power producer (IPP) and engineering, procurement, and construction (EPC) schemes.[2] China is a latecomer to the greenfield coal project, and the first project was constructed in Indonesia by Shenhua Group in 2011, with a capacity of 400 MW (Li, 2019). However, China can move faster than many other countries. Now, China's share of the 17,300 MW is about 46%, with Japan at 30%, while 24% was jointly contributed by South Korea, Turkey, the United States, Malaysia, and Indonesia (Shalati and Simanjuntak, 2019).

Cooperation between Indonesia and China in construction power plants has triggered major changes in terms of business schemes, technology, maintenance, and operation. For example, Java 7 steam coal plant was developed under the IPP model, with a capacity of 2 × 1,000 MW. This project is a

DOI: 10.4324/9781003190905-11

part of the 35,000 MW program. It was implemented by the joint company of Shenhua Guohua and PJB (one of PLN's subsidiary companies). About 70% of stock is owned by China and the rest by Indonesia. This plant uses ultra-supercritical technology, in contrast to FTP-1, which is dominated by subcritical technology. For maintenance and operation, the project involves Guohua Taidian Ltd, PJB Ltd, and Taishan Power Generation Company.

Furthermore, China is aware that Indonesia has a great potential for renewable energy, such as hydropower, geothermal, bioenergy, solar photovoltaics (PV), wind, and ocean wave. Under the first generation of the IPP scheme, China started the development of the hydropower plants Asahan 3 and PLTA Poso. In the case of the Poso hydropower plant in Central Sulawesi, Poso Energy Ltd, part of the Kalla Group business, operated the project under the IPP scheme, but the turbine was imported from China.[3] Chinese companies developed some of the large-scale hydropower plants in East Kalimantan and Sulawesi.[4] In the meantime, China has substantially increased exports of PV components to Indonesia (Chapters 7 and 8 in this book). Considering the position of China, which has been actively involved in developing both coal and renewable energy generation, the energy transition to low-carbon development must not be slack.

Against this backdrop, this paper aims to investigate the role of China in forming the energy transition in Indonesia from the perspective of investment in coal-based and renewable energy power supplies.

2 Framework and method

The analysis in this chapter follows theoretical frameworks of energy security. Energy security is defined as the uninterrupted availability of energy sources at an affordable price (IEA, 2020a). IEA (2020a) defined energy security in the long and short terms. The long-term perspective on energy security refers to investment that aims to achieve economic and environmental development, while the-short term perspective of energy security focuses on the ability of energy systems to respond to any shocks from both the demand and supply side. Then, Sovacool (2011) divided energy security into five dimensions, namely, regulations and governance, availability, technology development and efficiency, environmental sustainability, and affordability.

The World Energy Council (WEC) produces the Energy Sustainability Index. The index covers two major elements, such as energy performance and contextual performance. Energy performance consists of energy security, energy equity, and environmental sustainability, while on the contextual performance, this includes political strength, societal strength, and economic strength. For the transition to low-carbon intensive sources of electricity, it is necessary to develop a higher degree of flexibility in dealing with intermittency of renewable energy (IEA, 2020b). By pursuing energy securities, countries can achieve number 7 of the Sustainable Development

Goals (SDGs), which states that countries should 'ensure access to affordable, reliable, sustainable, and modern energy for all'.[5]

Because energy security is a multidimensional subject (Peimani, 2011), this section focuses on three dimensions of energy security in which Indonesia is relatively successful and less successful. First, from 2010 to 2018, Indonesia provided electricity to an extra 10 million people who had not previously had access to electricity (SEforAll, 2020).[6] This indicates the biggest improvement in the world, after India, Bangladesh, and Afghanistan. Availability and affordability are key factors that open up opportunities for better access to electricity.

Second, Indonesia received a red card for low-carbon electricity generation and CO_2 emissions per capita in 2010–2020 (WEC, 2020). This implies that Indonesia lacks behind in terms of innovation capability toward green energy. Finally, the future performance of the electricity sector depends on how regulation and governance can create business opportunities and economic stability for energy investment (Sambodo, 2016). This area represents elements of political commitment, regulation, and governance. Considering several important elements of energy security in Indonesia, this chapter focuses on accessibility and affordability, sustainability, and governance, and discusses the above three dimensions in relation to energy cooperation with China.

Expert interviews were conducted to confirm and develop robust arguments. The experts covered the perspectives of PLN, private business, and community associations in the energy sector. Secondary data was collected from various sources, such as the Ministry of Energy and Mineral Resources of the Republic of Indonesia, PLN, and data subscribed from BPS. Additionally, information was sourced from major newspapers.

3 A brief review of the power sector development since the Yudhoyono presidency

The development of steam coal power plants has been a government priority since 2006, especially under FTP-1, with support from the Presidential Decree No. 17/2006. The decree aimed to increase the capacity of the steam coal power plan by 80 units, with an additional capacity of 10,000 MW. The regulation also stated the location and number of new units for each province. Then, in 2010, the government extended the program with the implementation of FTP-2 with the Presidential Decree No. 4/2010. The new decree stated that the government hand the assignment to PLN for the development of generating power by utilizing renewables, coal, and gas, with a total capacity of 10,053 MW by 2014. The share of renewable energy in FTP-2 was about 51.5% and consisted of hydropower (1,204 MW) and geothermal (3,977 MW). In sum, FTP-1 promoted only coal power, while FTP-2 provided more space for renewable energy.

In May 2015, the government launched the 35,000 MW program. This was the third accelerated program following the two fast-track programs and will be completed by 2029. The government expected that, by 2020, the construction of new power plants will have reached 8,823 MW, or the highest level of new capacity for the whole project phase.[7] By 2019, the government said that 96%, or 33,856 MW, was under contract and that 19% (6,811 MW) was in operation. Some projects from FTP-2 and regular programs, amounting to 11,872 MW, were carried over under the 35,000 MW program (Sebayang, 2015).

Several ambitious programs are necessary to boost electricity consumption. Installed capacity increased by 38.5 GW from 2004 to 2018 (Table 8.1). The National Electricity General Plans (Rencana Umum Ketenagalistrikan Nasional-RUKN) 2019–2038 stated that the share of new and renewable energy in the power sector needed to reach 23% by 2025. Indonesia produced more electricity, from wider sources of renewable energy, in 2018 than in 2004 (Table 8.1). Considering the target of renewable energy is 39,653 MW by 2025, the annual growth of renewable energy needs to reach about 22% (using the exponential growth model). This target is nigh on impossible, but one that must be pursued. Growth of installed capacity from renewable resources was lower than fossil fuel, and the share of renewable energy slightly decreased from 2004 to 2018 (Table 8.1). Weak institutional architecture, resistance from PLN to adopt premium feed-in tariffs, land access, complicated approval processes, and long negotiation processes, have all

Table 8.1 Installed capacity (in MW) of power plants in Indonesia

Type	*2004*	*2018*	*Change 2018-04*	*Renewable energy target by 2025**
Hydro	3,200	5,370	2,170	17,986.7
Geothermal	820	1,948	1,128	7,241.5
Wind		143	143	1,800
Micro-hydro		105	105	3,000
Mini-hydro		268	268	
Solar		53	53	6,500
Waste		16	16	3,124
Biogas		109	109	
Biomass		1,759	1,759	
Steam coal	9,750	31,578	21,828	
Gas	2,803	5,348	2,546	
Combine cycle	6,846	11,220	4,374	
Diesel	2,994	4,631	1,637	
Gas engine	12	2,358	2,346	
Total	26,424	64,904	38,480	
Share of renewable	0.152	0.151	(0.0016)	

Note: renewable include on grid and off-grid; * based on general planning of national energy (RUEN).

Source: ESDM (2015) and ESDM (2019).

blocked wider deployment (Burke et al., 2019). Since the difficulty in weaning dependency on coal and unsupportive renewable energy has made the Ministry of Energy and Mineral Resources pessimistic about reaching their target, the government has proposed to extend the 23% target of new and renewable energy to 2030.[8]

However, extension of the target on renewable energy may affect the Indonesian government's commitment to reduce greenhouse gas emissions from the energy sector. Indonesia has submitted its Nationally Determined Contribution (NDC) and the government aims to reduce greenhouse gas emissions by 29% under unconditional condition (relying on national strength) and 41% with conditional condition (international cooperation) by 2030. In 2010, the level of CO_2 emissions from the energy sector was the second largest after the forestry sector. However, in 2030, the energy sector will be the largest emitter (Table 8.2). This implies that emissions reduction from the energy sector will have significant impact in terms of the national target. Thus, by considering the existing energy system, energy transformation to low carbon can be promoted by energy efficiency in steam coal power plants or fuel switching.

Coal is showing an increasingly significant role in the electricity generation system and utilization of gas may help Indonesia to reduce carbon dioxide emissions. From 2019 to 2028, the government plan to add 56,394 MW of new capacity, among which 27,063 MW or 48% will be steam coal power (Table 8.3). In 2019, the share of fossil fuels is 59 GW or 85% of total installed capacity. Based on the PLN's business plan, the share of steam coal plants will slightly increase from 46.9% to 47.4% in the same period. Although gas has an important role to play in the transition to low-carbon emissions, its contribution is likely to decline. At the current level of gas consumption, natural gas will run

Table 8.2 Indonesian nationally determined contribution (NDC) by sector

No	*Sector*	*GHG emission level 2010*	*GHG emission level 2030*			*GHG emission reduction*				*Annual average growth BAU (2010–2030)*	*Average growth 2000–2012*
		MtonCO₂e	*(Mton CO₂e)*			*(Mton CO₂e)*		*% of total BaU*			
			BaU	*CM1*	*CM2*	*CM1*	*CM2*	*CM1*	*CM2*		
1	Energy*	453	1,669	1,355	1,271	314	398	11	14	6.7	4.5
2	Waste	88	296	285	270	11	26	0.38	1	6.3	4
3	IPPU	36	70	67	66	3	3	0.1	0.11	3.4	0.1
4	Agriculture	111	120	110	116	9	4	0.32	0.13	0.4	1.3
5	Forestry**	647	714	217	64	497	650	17.2	23	0.5	2.7
	Total	1,334	2,869	2,034	1,787	834	1,081	29	38	3.9	3.2

Note: * include fugitive emissions; ** include peat fire; BaU (not considering climate change mitigation); CM1 (considering emissions target by sector); CM2 (with conditional, more ambitious and considering emissions target by sector).
Source: Ministry of Environment and Forestry, Republic of Indonesia (2017).

Table 8.3 Installed capacity of power plants in Indonesia by source and future direction

Source	*In MW*			*In percentage**	
	Existing capacity 2019	*Added capacity 2019–2028*	*Estimate capacity in 2028*	*Share of installed capacity in 2019*	*Estimate share of installed capacity in 2028*
Fossil based	59,377	39,680	99,057	85.2	78.6
Coal	32,677	27,063	59,740	46.9	47.4
Gas	21,920	12,416	34,336	31.5	27.2
Oil	4,780	201	4,981	6.9	4.0
New and renewable	10,302	16,714	27,016	14.8	21.4
Geothermal	2,131	4,607	6,738	3.1	5.3
Hydro	5,976	6,060	12,036	8.6	9.5
Solar	146	3,483	3,629	0.2	2.9
Other new and renewable	2,049	2,564	4,613	2.9	3.7
Total	69,679	56,394	126,073	100.0	100.0

Note: * Calculated by the authors based on the data.
Source: ESDM (2020) and PLN (2019b).

out in less than 18 years.[9] The contribution of gas tends to decrease. Further, utilization of gas depends on infrastructure. In 2006, Rekayasa Industry Ltd won the contract for the pipe gas network development of about 255 km between Cirebon in West Java and Semarang, Central Java. The project is valued at around US$ 269 million. However, in October 2020, the company backed out of the deal, due to the uncertainty of gas supply. In addition, the Electricity Procurement Plant (Rencana Usaha Penyediaan Tenaga Listrik-RUPTL) also indicated that with a risk of gas supply, then coal and oil will need to substitute any deficit of the gas supply (PLN, 2019a).

Due in part to COVID-19, there was an excess power of 16,675 MW and electricity consumption declined from 243 TWh to 222 TWh in 2020.[10] The excess power occurred in Java-Bali (10,849 MW), Sumatera (3,308 MW), Sulawesi (1,146 MW), Kalimantan (874 MW), and Papua (498 MW). This implies that by 2020, the reserve margin was about 30% and was higher than the target (25%). Because of COVID-19, the government plans to cut power supply from the 35.000 MW project by 15.5 GW, and which will commence at RUPTL from 2020 to 2031.

4 Findings

4.1 Availability and affordability

Due to the economic crisis of 1997/1998, Indonesia started with a low basis of energy access (Sambodo, 2016). This pushed the government to pursue more ambitious programs in order to expand and improve energy access by conducting energy cooperation. On 24 March 2002, President Megawati Soekarnoputri visited China. This brought new projects for steam coal, such as Labuhan Angin, Tapanuli Tengah, and Sumatera Utara.[11] Labuhan Angin was a joint project between PLN Ltd and the China National Machinery & Equipment Corp. (CMEC) with a capacity of 2 × 115 MW. This project was under the EPC scheme and was financed by loans from China and PLN's internal funding. The total investment was about US$ 208.6 million and 232.39 billion rupiahs. Project design and construction were conducted by CMEC. The project was signed on 6 October 2003 and the contract was effective on 15 March 2005. The first and second unit of the project were completed on delivery (COD) in 2009. President Megawati's visit to China was also linked with other projects, such as the steam coal Pangkalan Susu Loan China 2 × 200 MW, steam coal Parit Baru Loan China 2 × 50 MW, and steam coal Jeneponto Loan China 2 × 100 MW. Thus, the 'political lobby' from Megawati was effective in attracting more loans from China into the power sector.

In 2005, both Indonesia and China signed the strategic partnership. The partnership aims to enhance cooperation in trade, investment, and maritime matters. The Indonesian Minister of Mines and Energy, Purnomo Yusgiantoro, indicated China's interest in cooperating in the energy sector. Before the government issued the Presidential Regulation Number 71 Year 2006 (FTP-1), in April 2006, several government officials, such as Vice President, Yusuf Kalla, and the Director of PLN, Eddie Widiono, visited China.[12] This visit aimed to investigate the readiness and ability of Chinese companies to develop steam coal power plants in Indonesia. They then invited Chinese companies to participate in an open tender for FTP-1. At that time, PLN also signed the Memorandum of Understanding (MoU) with five electric companies in China, such as Dongfang Electric Corporation, Harbin Electric Corporation, Shanghai Electric Power Co. Ltd, Huandian, and Chenda.[13]

With the implementation of FTP-1, PLN became the project owner and conducted the open tender or direct bidder. The project's development adopted the engineering, procurement, and construction (EPC) scheme. Chinese companies have capabilities to develop large-scale steam coal power plants, and also for small-scale power plants, such as the 50 MW that was abandoned in China. Many contractors came with technology from China, and many non-Chinese bidders withdrew from the bidding process because they could not compete with low prices offered from China. For example, the average price of 10 GW was about US$ 800/kW, while for non-Chinese products, it was above US$ 1,300/kW.[14] Thus, almost all FPT-1 projects were completed by technology from China, especially on subcritical and supercritical unit (Sambodo, 2012). For the capacity of 100 MW or above, the main contractors were from China, but they needed to cooperate with Indonesian contractors. Then, for capacity below 100 MW, the main contractors were from Indonesia, but electrical and mechanical equipment was supplied by China.

Between 2005 and 2015, Chinese contractors developed 33 coal power projects under EPC (Hervé-Mignucci and Wang, 2015). The total value for the 33 projects was US$ 16,754 million and 40% of the total value consisted of loans from China. The total projects that had been operated were 20, with total capacity 10,070 MW and a total value of US$ 10,683 million (Hervé-Mignucci and Wang, 2015). In most of the FTP-1 projects, the equity was owned by PLN and the debt was provided by China. Almost 80% of FTP-1 projects were allocated in Java (Sambodo, 2012). In addition, nine out of ten projects of FTP-1 in Java were built by EPC contractors from China, with a total capacity of 7,490 MW (Tampubolon, Arinaldo, and Adiatma, 2018). Steam coal capacity in Java was about 16,330 MW in 2016; thus, 46% of coal capacity in Java was related to EPC projects from China.[15] Because most of FTP-1 projects were located in Java, the share of electricity production of coal from PLN power plants in Java was about 88% in 2018. Generally speaking, the operation of power generation followed the long-run marginal cost principle; thus, the most efficient power plant (mostly non-Chinese) went into operation first, followed by the less efficient ones.[16] This applied to Java's system, before 2019, where about 30% of ex-FTP-1 projects contributed to the Java-Bali System.[17]

Steam coal power plants had the lowest percentage change in average cost, because coal had the lowest standard deviation of generating cost. In addition, average elasticity of coal as well as hydropower and geothermal is positive, meaning that energy transition moves toward these two sources. Because the average change in price of geothermal was relatively higher than coal, increasing electricity production from coal was higher than geothermal. Growing coal power generation stabilized generating costs in 2009–2019 (Table 8.4).

Table 8.4 Comparison elasticity, standard deviation, and average of price for different type of power plant 2009–2019

Type of power plant	*Average elasticity**	*Standard deviation of generating cost***	*Average price****	*Average change in price (%)*****
Coal	0.792	113.9	670	3.21
Hydro power	6.089	141.8	241	18.79
Geothermal	0.113	1,708.5	3,298	25.68
Diesel	−0.537	2,472.6	3,486	19.35
Gas	−0.270	591.4	1,099	21.63
Steam gas	−0.742	204.6	1,080	6.95

Note: *The ratio percentage change in electricity production with respect to percentage change in generating cost for respective type of power plant. **Standard deviation of statistical model for period 2009 and 2019 for each respective type of power plant. ***Standard average statistical calculation. ****Calculated by averaging the annual change for the whole period.

Source: PLN (2014, 2019b) and ESDM (2020).

After FTP-1 was launched, PLN substantially increased the number of steam coal power plants. Accordingly, its power generation increased from 47,764 GWh in 2006 to 122,826 GWh in 2019. The increase enabled PLN to supply electricity to 40 million new customers, contributing to an increase in electrification ratio (Table 8.5). Coupled with price stability, these increases bring economic benefits to PLN.

However, it has increased coal consumption from 19 million tons to 67 million tons in the same period (PLN, 2014; PLN, 2019b). Based on PLN's RUPTL 2015–2024, CO_2 emissions will increase from 201 million tons (in 2015) to about 383 million tons (in 2024) and 333 million tons, or 87%, of total emissions will come from coal firing (PLN, 2015). Then, based on the current planning or the RUPTL 2019–2029, CO_2 emissions in 2024 will be about 305.6 million tons and the share of emissions from coal will contribute 88.3% of total emissions (PLN, 2019a). Thus, there has been a reduction in the carbon emissions target, but carbon emissions from coal plants still show a slight increase.

Then, there is the generation cost, which is much higher than the price of electricity sold. As a result, the government needs to provide more electricity subsidies. It is interesting to note the decreasing ratio of electricity production to the number of customers. This indicates two causes. First, the growth in the number of customers is much faster than the level of electricity production. Second, because electricity production per customer hit a peak in 2014 and then declined (Table 8.5), there has been a slowdown in investment growth in the electricity sector.

People realized from FTP-1 projects that operation and maintenance cost from China is more expensive, because it requires increased labor due to the level of automatization, and that the availability factor or level of capacity utilization was relatively low compared to Japan's technology.[18] Also, low quality material was a problem with steam coal power plants from China.[19] Of course, this condition is not ideal, but it is effective to reduce the pressure from increasing generating costs due to the use of fuel oil. As Mori (2020) said, the amount of electricity subsidy increased substantially from 2009 to

Table 8.5 Selected indicators of PLN's performance in 2006–2019

Year	*Number of PLN steam coal power plant*	*Number of PLN customer*	*Price of electricity sold (Rp/kWh)*	*Generating cost (Rp/kWh)*	*Subsidy (kWh)*	*Electricity production (Gwh)*	*Electricity production (KWh)/number of customer**	*Electrification ratio (%)*
2006	43	35,751,224	628	-	-	133,108	3,723.18	63
2009	49	40,117,685	670	768	98	156,797	3,908.43	66
2014	86	57,493,234	940	1,297	357	228,555	3,975.34	84
2019	133	75,705,614	1,130	3,000	1,870	278,941	3,684.55	98.9

Note: The author's calculation from the data.
Source: PLN (2009, 2019b).

2019, and the government gained by reducing total energy subsidy through the switch from oil to coal for power generation.

4.2 Sustainability

Steam coal power plants have contributed a great deal in terms of expanding the national power capacity, promoting price certainty, and increasing the electrification ratio. Furthermore, China has attempted to improve the performance of steam coal power plants by using or licensing boiler, turbine, and generator technology from Japan, the United States, and Europe.[20] Similarly, China has improved significantly its maintenance operator skills and they have a high degree of adaptation in repairs.[21] In addition, steam coal power plants from China can fulfill the existing requirements from the Ministry of Environment and Forestry.[22] For example, steam coal Indramayu 3 × 300 MW in West Java is a consortium project between China (SINOMACH and CNEEC) and Indonesia (Penta Adi Samudera Ltd). In early 2020, this project obtained the 'Green Proper Award'. The Green Proper Award is an appreciation given to firms who manage the environment by government request (the Ministry of Environment). However, China needs to improve assembly capacity and there are many problems on balance of plant (BoP) that causes poor performance of generators, spare parts, quality of works, and generator efficiency.[23]

China has a great interest in developing steam coal power plants. There are three renewable energy sectors in which China has shown its contribution to Indonesia, such as geothermal, hydropower, and solar PV. China attempted to develop geothermal projects, such as those in Ulumbu, Manggarai, and East Nusa Tenggara. There are four units of geothermal in Ulumbu (4x2.5 MW). Units 3 and 4 have operated since 2012, and the plants were imported from China, and were financed by the Indonesian government budget of 2009. Units 1 and 2 were in operation from 2014 and used technology from the United States, with funding from ADB. Units 1 and 2 used back pressure turbine technology, and units 3 and 4 used condensing unit turbines. Utilization of geothermal energy will reduce oil-based power plants that are more expensive in terms of generating cost. In 2013, PLN reduced the consumption of oil to about IDR 75.5 billion (Handoyo and Mychelisda, 2016).

A report indicates that units 3 and 4 very often have problems and that spare parts for repairs are difficult to obtain (Sambodo et al., 2015). The main problem for units 3 and 4 is the Automatic Voltage Regulator (AVR) and PLN is required to independently produce AVRs in Indonesia.[24] After construction was completed, there was no proper takeover process from Chinese engineers to local operators. There were language problems with no manual written in English, which has caused local engineers to have difficulties in fixing electrical and mechanical problems (Sambodo et al., 2015). Because peak load in the Manggarai region was about 9.2 MW, when the two units (3 and 4) failed to operate, it had a substantial impact on power supply in the region.[25] If that is the case, PLN will need to operate diesel power plants that are more expensive.

Another project that China has an interest is hydropower. Currently, investors from China are involved in developing hydropower plants in Batang Toro, Tapanuli Selatan, and Sumatera Utara. The capacity is 4 × 127.5 MW. The projects were developed by North Sumatera Hydro Energy (NSHE) Ltd in cooperation with China's Sinohydro. The Commercial Operation Date (COD) was expected in 2022. This project is part of a 35,000 MW program. NSHE has the rights for about 1,800 hectares, and the open area is about 370 hectares, and 86 hectares will have permanent damage.[26] The Batang Toru project has faced protests by local communities, and by non-government organizations both local and international, because it is the habitat of the Tapanuli orangutan, and also supports other ecosystems. It seems that the project needs to develop more detailed systematic studies to assess and mitigate the environmental impact. Other issues have been raised by the Bank of China and the bank is going to reassess the project.

The Kayan hydropower plant, in North Kalimantan, is another project. Power Construction Corporation of China (PowerChina) has signed a memorandum of understanding (MoU) with Indonesia Kayan Hydropower Energy Ltd (Kayan Hydro Energy/KHE) to jointly build hydropower plants with a total investment of US$ 17.8 billion on the Kayan River in North Kalimantan, by April 2019. The two firms will develop five hydropower plants with a total electricity generation capacity of 9,000 MW. PowerChina began studying the hydropower resources of the Kayan River in 2008 and completed the development plan for the whole basin of the river, as well as the feasibility study and preliminary design of the first hydropower plant, in 2013. Sinohydro Corporation is PowerChina's subsidiary engaged in hydropower plant construction. Kayan hydropower is expected to operate in 2025.

PLTA Kayan seems to work better than Batang Toru. Land acquisition has been prepared, including socialization and negotiation with the local village. There are two permits in process, such as renewing the permit for the utilization of forest areas and a permit from the dam agency. Feasibility studies, environmental assessments, and detail engineering designs (DED) have been completed by KHE. There are 27 permits that need to be prepared and 25 permits have been completed.[27]

Indonesia also has great potential for development of solar photovoltaics (PVs). The first, massive solar home system (off-grid based) program was launched in 2011. PLN launched the Solar PV program or Super Extra Energy Saving (SEHEN), and the Ministry of Energy and Mineral Resources had Solar Home System (SHS).[28] Basically, the programs are similar in terms of technical aspect, but different in terms of business model. The SEHEN model was designed under the management of PLN, while the SHS model was organized by the community. Indonesia has constructed solar PVs, both for autonomous households and the community (communal system). Both SEHEN and SHS have big roles to play in addressing the lack of access to electricity in a fast manner. SEHEN succeeded in increasing customers from 3,984 to about 113,715 in East Nusa Tenggara Province in only one year, between March 2012 and February 2013 (Sambodo, 2015). This strategy helped Indonesia to provide electricity to people who live in the outermost, frontline, and disadvantaged regions that are not economically feasible for grid access. Both SHS and SEHEN have increased the number of households from tier-1 of electricity access to tier-2.[29] However, program and business sustainability are the major challenges for successful PV development (Sambodo, 2015). Program designs that tend to conflict with each other, such as the off-grid models owned by PLN and the Ministry of Energy and Mineral Resources, are different in terms of the amount of payment, even though the benefits are relatively similar (Sambodo, 2015). Also, solar PV components that are damaged are often difficult to replace, especially for imported components, and maintenance services are not yet available, especially to users who live in remote areas (Sambodo et al., 2016).

LEN Ltd is a state-owned enterprise that produces PVs at one of its business units. LEN Ltd started to produce solar PVs in 1997, and the production capacity has increased from 20 MWp to about 45 MWp in 2018. LEN Ltd also developed IPP and the first IPP was a 5 MWp in Kupang of East Nusa Tenggara (the first largest capacity). LEN Ltd also makes solar modules, solar power street lighting systems, solar trees, hybrid solar, grid-connected solar, centralized solar, and bidirectional inverters. However, LEN Ltd cannot fully support the PV program due to capacity constraints and lack of price competitiveness compared to imported goods. As a result, Indonesia imports key components of PVs from several sources, such as China, Hong Kong, Taiwan, Japan, and the United States.[30] The share of PVs in the total imports increased from 0.007% in 2010 to 0.027% in 2018. In particular, imports from China have shown an upward trend, reaching 70% in 2016 (Table 8.6). This indicates that China has become one of the important pillars for the development and utilization of PVs in Indonesia.

Table 8.6 Share of imports of main solar PV components from China (in million US$)

Year	*Total Indonesian imports*	*Imports of Indonesian PV from the world*	*Imports of PV from China*	*Share of PV import to total import (%)*	*Share of import PV from China (%)*
2010	135,663.3	10.2	5.5	0,007	54
2011	177,435.5	13.1	7.8	0,007	60
2012	191,691.0	9.6	6.6	0,005	69
2013	186,628.7	17.5	9.8	0,009	56
2014	178,179.0	16.5	7.6	0,009	46
2015	142,694.8	27.2	15.1	0,019	56
2016	135,652.8	22.7	15.8	0,017	70
2017	156,985.5	33.0	16.2	0,021	49
2018	188,711.2	51.3	34.0	0,027	66

Source: BPS (2018).

The business strategy between LEN Ltd and Chinese companies shows competition and cooperation. LEN Ltd is aware that promoting investment in solar PVs is challenging. The Chinese policy to avoid cell trading and to promote module trading has affected domestic module production. The Chinese government gives support to the solar panel industry, enabling them to sell solar panels below the market price (Purushothaman, 2019). Then, European Union (EC) imposed anti-dumping duties to Chinese solar panels, and other countries, such as the USA and India, implemented similar duties (Purushothaman, 2019). China suspended its subsidies in the second half of 2018 and the government asked companies to bid at competitive prices.[31] This situation has had an impact on Indonesia, which already has low technology capability in PV cell production. LEN Ltd can compete to produce modules with China, if China can export cells at the market price. On the other side, LEN Ltd has developed a business partnership with many of China's companies, such as CETC, CNBM, China Light Solar, Hareon Solar, Hollysys, JA Solar, and ZTE, in order to expand the production of solar PVs. By the end of 2019, President Director of LEN Ltd visited China to find a business partner with total investment of about IDR 1 trillion. However, more than a year later, there has been no significant progress on this investment plan, and it seems the Ministry of Energy and Mineral Resources of the Republic of Indonesia plans to issue a letter to speed up this project.[32]

4.3 Governance

FTP-1 suffered from long delays due to legal issues (land procurement), construction problems (especially from local companies), frequent changes in project location, and lack of awareness of environmental assessment (Sebayang, 2015). It took almost eight years to complete installation of 8,947 MW or 90% of the target 9,975 MW (Sebayang, 2015), compared with 22 months to cover EPC in business as usual.[33] Long delays of project construction on FTP-1 have negatively impacted on Indonesia, both in terms of financial cost and availability of power supply.

First, it increased the external debt position of Indonesia to China. The total debt increased from US$ 735 million in 2006 to US$ 13.66 billion in 2015.[34] The FTP-1 projects amounted to US$ 3,939 million (Shalati and Simanjuntak, 2019).[35] This implies that the FTP-1 project contributed 28.8% of Indonesia's total debt to China. Bank of China, Bank of China Limited, China Development Bank, the Export-Import Bank of China, and Barclay Capital were involved in financing the EPC projects in Indonesia (Shalati and Simanjuntak, 2019). China contributed about 61% of total investment of the first FTP project, while the rest came from Indonesia (especially PLN; Shalati and Simanjuntak, 2019). Because of government guarantees, PLN borrowed loans from domestic banks that covered 39% of the total project investment (Shalati and Simanjuntak, 2019).

Second, the delay increased financial problems for PLN and Indonesian taxpayers. Project delays led to extra cost. The Supreme Audit Agency indicated a financial loss in 2016 of IDR 606 billion or US$ 79 million (Shalati and Simanjuntak, 2019). The Supreme Audit Agency also indicated budget waste due to high project costs of IDR 817 billion or US$ 8.7 million (Shalati and Sumanjuntak, 2019). Then, there were others cost due to poor decision-making that reached 430 billion rupiahs or US$ 36 million (Shalati and Simanjuntak, 2019). Thus, the total cost was 1.85 trillion rupiahs or US$ 124 million. As a result, PLN imposed penalties on the EPC contractors of 705 billion rupiahs or US$ 102 million (Shalati and Simanjuntak, 2019). However, both Indonesia and China were responsible for the delays, caused by land procurement, environmental concerns, incapability of domestic project contractors, planning and design, lack of best practices, poor quality of project conditions, and delay in project financing. This is why EPC contractors bore a portion of the penalty, and PLN and taxpayers were obliged to burden the rest.

One of the Indonesia-China IPP projects stumbled into a legal case. In the case of coal-mine mouth Riau-I (2 × 300 MW), PT PJB (Pembangkit Jawa Bali, subsidiary of PLN) appointed PT PLN Batu Bara, BlackGold, PT Samantika Batubara (subsidiary of BlackGold), and China Huadian Engineering, to form a consortium. By January 2018, they signed a letter of intent (LoI) to obtain agreement on power purchase. In July 2018, the Corruption Eradication Commission (KPK) arrested Eni Maulani Saragih. Eni was a member of parliament and KPK also arrested Idrus Marham, who was a Social Affairs Minister. Eni, for receiving a bribe from Johannes Kotjo, who was one of the owners BlackGold. The bribe was related to coal-mine mouth Riau-I.[36]

The government was also aware that the quality of the projects was below standard. President Joko Widodo, in his speech to 300 entrepreneurs in Beijing (November 2014), mentioned the poor quality of steam coal power plants from China due to problems on both from Chinese and Indonesia sides.[37] In his discussion with President Xi Jinping, to measure the problem of the poor quality of steam coal power plants, President Xi Jinping suggested the leaseback solution and President Joko Widodo agreed to this. However, the trade union of PLN refused the proposal and said that the systemic failure of steam coal power plants was a form of fraud from EPC contractors.[38] Due to the poor quality of steam coal power plants from China, since 2015, China could not compete for any open EPC tender from PLN. Only OECD countries were able to join the tender, such as the expansion of steam coal Teluk Naga which was completed by Japan.[39] However, for IPP projects, China are allowed to join the tender because risks become the responsibility of the developer over the project for about 20–25 years.

Learning the lessons of FTP-1, the government adopted IPP in FTP-2 and the 35,000 MW Program. Although Chinese investors have actively participated in many IPP projects, they do not request government guarantees for financing and investment, despite the fact that other countries do.[40] The perspective of the business sector from Indonesia indicates that there is still a lack of transparency and openness in the financial process and sometimes it is hard to implement.[41] Inaccurate actions in calculating risk, and good understanding of the local bureaucratic context, has caused great harm to both the Indonesian and Chinese sides. For example, some projects have caused corruption in collaboration with Indonesian coal oligarchs or mobilized political power to accept joining tenders with poor quality projects. Finally, low technology standards and the lack of maximized utilization of local content and employment have been criticized by Chinese investors.[42]

5 Discussion

The above analysis reveals that Chinese power investments in Indonesia generate two types of dilemmas. The first is a trade-off between availability, affordability, and sustainability. On the one hand, China has provided affordable technology, more simple procedures, and taken risks for host countries in order to enhance availability.[43] Due to the broad range of technology options, Chinese contractors tend to be more flexible in technological choice, taking financial, technical, and other constraints in host countries into account.[44] Since Sate-Owned Enterprises (SOEs) account for most of the investments, they face no problem with financial resources, and even in taking more risky projects, as long as host country governments offer credit guarantee.[45] Furthermore, China can offer more interesting business proposals, with affordable prices and international standards.[46] Marketing and representative officers from China were more aggressive in delivering business proposals both to government and the business sector in Indonesia.[47] China also develops large-scale hydropower plants. As a result, Indonesia has increased availability at a lower generation cost than oil power plants.

On the other hand, China reduced its commitment to finance the FTP-1 program from US$ 3 billion to about US$ 1.5 billion, due to unclear reasons, and did not listen to claims from the Indonesian government. The resulting delay imposed non-trivial burdens to electric utilities and taxpayers in the host countries, risking the financial sustainability. In addition, China has developed steam coal power plants at a time when OECD member countries raised environmental concerns and reduced financing for steam coal power.[48]

Second, the dilemma is a trade-off between domestic industrial development, availability, and sustainability. The Indonesian government imposed local content requirement for the FTP projects: 70% for below 8 MW; 50% for 8–25 MW; 45% for 25–100 MW; and 40% for larger than 100 MW.[49] By November 2014, China had committed to developing 70 units of steam coal power plants with total capacity of 10,575 MW and a range of capacity between 7 and 600 MW per unit.[50] Among them, 91.5% was larger than 100 MW and thus were subject to 40% local content requirements. Most of the small-scale projects are outside Java, and local developers used technology from China, such as steam coal Embalut, Kalimatan Timur 2 × 3 MW, Palu Tawaeli 2 × 17.5 MW, and many small-scale plants below 20 MW in Kalimantan and Sumatera.[51] However, many small-scale coal power plant (less than 50 MW) projects have been delayed and some units canceled (PLN, 2019). Then, for the sake of efficiency, small-scale coal power plants have been constructed with a capacity of at least 50 MW. As a result, local content requirements for steam coal power plants were satisfied at the sacrifice of low efficient coal power plants generating a higher intensity of emissions.[52]

In contrast, the requirement for hydropower and geothermal did not.[53] In addition, the Ministry of Industry Regulation No. 4 5/2017 imposed higher local content requirements for solar PVs, at 60%. However, this was not realistic for two reasons.[54] Local industry has insufficient capability to supply components, and insufficient product branding or quality, trust or loyalty, and switching costs did not raise the willingness to use local components. Meantime, China shows up as developers of large-scale hydropower projects, and as suppliers of solar PV components, so that Indonesian manufacturers, such as LEN Ltd, can be available for upscaling renewable energy, at the sacrifice of increasing imports and adverse environmental impacts.

6 Conclusions

Rising China has motivated leaders in developing countries to invite China to help them realize ambitious electricity programs, despite lagging behind in its investments in power projects in foreign countries. Against this backdrop, this chapter has focused on accessibility and affordability, sustainability, and governance, and has discussed the above three dimensions in relation to energy cooperation with China. The findings of this chapter can be summarized as follows.

First, Chinese investments in coal power plants enabled Indonesia to switch from an oil-based to a coal-based power supply, enhancing energy availability and affordability. China has offered a variety of technological options suited to economic conditions and natural resources. China has played a significant role in the provision of power supply through bilateral agreements which proactively invite China to invest in coal and renewable energy.

Second, China has strengthened ties with Indonesia in green investment and trade. The Indonesian government has also shown a strong desire to involve more national business actors in these fields while suffering from a trade-off between domestic industrial development and greening energy supply.

Finally, Chinese investments have generated challenges of governance, including huge economic losses due to delays in project implementation, and corruption that has accrued due to local business patterns and weak enforcement of regulations.

China's involvement in the supply of electricity to clean energy is still not optimal. The energy security analysis framework shows that the position of Indonesia has been trapped in high carbon emissions. This is because the government has taken a more compromising stance in pursuing the dimensions of availability and affordability and China can easily grasp the urgent need. Meanwhile, long-term consequences have not received adequate attention from the government.

7 Acknowledgments

The author would like to thank all members of this project for fruitful discussions during the project. My appreciation also goes to Paul Burke from the Australian National University for his useful feedback on the draft. I would like to thank Rio Novandra, a junior researcher at the Economic Research Center, and LIPI for calculating component imports of PVs. Finally, my appreciation to all experts for their interviews.

Notes

1 https://iesr.or.id/batubara-dominan-pemerintah-diminta-evaluasi-bauran-energi-untuk-program-listrik-35-000-mw [accessed 5 December 2020].
2 Shalati and Simanjuntak (2019).
3 Interview with Nasri Sebayang (former Director of Regional Business, PLN), 14 August 2020.
4 Interview with Nasri Sebayang (former Director of Regional Business, PLN), 14 August 2020.
5 By 2030, countries agree to ensure universal access to affordable, reliable, and modern energy services; to increase substantially the share of renewable energy in the global energy mix; and to double the global rate of improvement in energy efficiency.
6 This information was obtained from https://www.seforall.org/system/files/2020-10/Analysis-SDG7-Progress-2020.pdf [accessed 7 February 2021].
7 https://www.esdm.go.id/id/berita-unit/direktorat-jenderal-ketenagalistrikan/tahun-2020-puncak-program-35000-mw [accessed 5 December 2020].
8 https://katadata.co.id/febrianaiskana/energi/5ee22239ddc05/kementerian-esdm-pesimistis-bauran-energi-ebt-23-tercapai-pada-2025 [accessed 5 December 2020].
9 Kompas 15 December 2020.
10 Kompas, 14 January 2021.
11 Interview with Nasri Sebayang (former Director of Regional Business, PLN), 14 August 2020.
12 Ibid.
13 https://majalah.tempo.co/read/laporan-khusus/133356/carilah-listrik-sampai-ke-cina.
14 Interview with Nasri Sebayang (former Director of Regional Business, PLN), 14 August 2020.
15 It is based on the following calculation: 7,490: 16,330 = 46%.
16 Interview with Nasri Sebayang (former Director of Regional Business, PLN), 14 August 2020.
17 Ibid.
18 Ibid.

19 Interview with Zainal Arifin, Division of Engineering and Procurement Planning – PLN, 14 August 2020.
20 Interview with Nasri Sebayang (former Director of Regional Business, PLN), 14 August 2020.
21 Interview with Adrian Lembong, Director of Energy Technology, ADARO, 14 August 2020.
22 Ibid.
23 Interview with Nasri Sebayang (former Director of Regional Business, PLN), 14 August 2020.
24 AVR helps to regulate, adding, and stabilizing power voltage.
25 https://www.floresa.co/2016/10/05/operator-ulumbu-mesin-made-in-china-jadi-biang-pemadaman-bergilir-di-manggarai/.
26 https://www.mongabay.co.id/2020/03/06/nasib-orangutan-tapanuli-dengan-kehadiran-proyek-plta-batang-toru/ [accessed 6 July 2020].
27 https://www.antaranews.com/berita/1633246/lima-investor-berencana-bangun-plta-kayan-di-kaltara.
28 For detailed discussion, please refer to Sambodo (2015), http://efi.ui.ac.id/index.php/efi/article/view/505/530.
29 According to ESMAP, there are six tiers of electricity access (0 to 5). Tier 1 is a cut point for non-energy poverty condition. Under Tier 1, minimum hours available per day is 4 hours; minimum power is 50 W, and minimum daily power capacity is 200 Wh.
30 HS 854140200, photocells, including photodiodes/photo- transistors; HS 854140290, Oth photocells, including photodiodes and phototransistors; HS 854140210, photovoltaic cells, not assembled; HS 854140220, photovoltaic cells, assembled in modules or made up into panels; HS 85414021, photovoltaic cells, not assembled; HS 85414022, photovoltaic cells, assembled in modules or made up into panels; HS 85414029, Oth photocells, including photodiodes & phototransistors.
31 Ibid.
32 Information was obtained from discussion with one of PT. LEN's staff by WhatsApp chat, 6 March 2021.
33 https://media.neliti.com/media/publications/202361-analisis-percepatan-pekerjaan-fondasi-da.pdf [accessed 5 December 2020].
34 Data from the External Debt Statistic of Indonesia, Ministry of Finance, February 2021. We assumed that by 2015, all loans that are related to FTP-1 had been given.
35 This number is derived from Shalati and Simanjuntak (2019), Table 10.
36 https://www.cnnindonesia.com/ekonomi/20180719123945-85-315366/proyek-pltu-mulut-tambang-antara-efisiensi-dan-penyimpangan [accessed 5 November 2020].
37 https://finance.detik.com/energi/d-2743804/jokowi-sindir-kualitas-pltu-buatan-tiongkok-proyeknya-mana-saja [accessed 5 November 2020].
38 https://www.dunia-energi.com/pltu-6-ribu-mw-buatan-china-mangkrak-bpk-diminta-audit-pln/ [accessed 5 November 2020].
39 Interview with Nasri Sebayang (former Director of Regional Business, PLN), 14 August 2020.
40 Interview with Nasri Sebayang (former Director of Regional Business, PLN), 14 August 2020.
41 Ibid.
42 Interview with Nasri Sebayang (former Director of Regional Business, PLN), 14 August 2020.
43 Interview with Adrian Lembong, Director of Energy Technology, ADARO, 14 August 2020.

44 Interview with Yudi Hidayat, Power Generation Technology & Renewable Energy Research PT. Indonesia Power, 14 August 2020.
45 Interview with Paul Butarbutar, Regional Director South Pole Group, 14 August 2020.
46 Interview with Zainal Arifin, Division of Engineering and Procurement Planning – PLN, 14 August 2020.
47 Ibid.
48 Interview with Yudi Hidayat, Power Generation Technology & Renewable Energy Research, Indonesia Power, 14–16 August 2020.
49 https://www.kemenperin.go.id/artikel/499/Pembangunan-PLTU-Batubara-Harus-Memaksimalkan-Produksi-DN [accessed 5 November 2020].
50 https://finance.detik.com/energi/d-2743804/jokowi-sindir-kualitas-pltu-buatan-tiongkok-proyeknya-mana-saja [accessed 5 November 2020].
51 Interview with Nasri Sebayang (former Director of Regional Business, PLN), 14 August 2020.
52 https://katadata.co.id/arnold/berita/5e9a5576a6e61/selama-2018-hanya-pltu-yang-penuhi-target-penggunaan-produk-lokal [accessed 5 November 2020].
53 https://katadata.co.id/arnold/berita/5e9a5576a6e61/selama-2018-hanya-pltu-yang-penuhi-target-penggunaan-produk-lokal [accessed 5 November 2020].
54 https://katadata.co.id/febrianaiskana/energi/5e9a50d693216/kirim-surat-ke-darmin-asosiasi-minta-empat-regulasi-ebt-direvisi.

References

BPS. (2018). *Statistik Perdagangan Luar Negeri Impor 2018* [Trade Statistics of Foreign Import, 2018]. BPS.

Burke, P., Widnyana, J., Anjum, Z., Aisbett, E., Resosudarmo, B., Baldwin, K.G.H. (2019). Overcoming barriers to solar and wind energy adoption in two Asia giants: India and Indonesia. *Energy Policy*, 132: 1216–1228. https://doi.org/10.1016/j.enpol.2019.05.055.

ESDM. (2015). *Handbook of Energy & Economic Statistics of Indonesia 2014*. ESDM.

ESDM. (2019). *Handbook of Energy & Economic Statistics of Indonesia 2018*. ESDM.

ESDM. (2020). *Handbook of Energy & Economic Statistics of Indonesia 2019*. ESDM.

Handoyo, F., Mychelisda, E. (2016). Potensi Sumber Daya Energi di Nusa Tenggara Timur [Potential Energy Resources in East Nusa Tenggara]. In: Maxensius Tri Sambodo, Siwage Dharma Negara, Ahmad Helmy Fuady (eds.), *Akses Listrik dan Kesejahteraan Masyarakat* [Electricity Access and People Welfare]. Jakarta: LIPI Press, 17–57.

Hervé-Mignucci, Wang, X. (2015). *Slowing the Growth of Coal Power Outside China: The Role of Chinese Finance*. Climate Policy Initiative.

International Energy Agency/IEA. (2020a). Energy Security Reliable, Affordable access to all fuels and energy sources. https://www.iea.org/topics/energy-security [Accessed 1 March 2021].

International Energy Agency/IEA. (2020b). Electricity Security. https://www.iea.org/areas-of-work/energy-security/electricity-security [Accessed 1 March 2021].

Li, Y. (2018). China's going out policy a review on China's promotion policy for outward foreign direct investment from a historical perspective. Center for Economic and Regional Studies HAS Institute of World Economics Working Paper, 224: 1–44, https://ideas.repec.org/p/iwe/workpr/244.html.

Ministry of Environment and Forestry, Republic of Indonesia. (2017). *Implementation of Nationally Determined Contribution Strategy*. Direktorat Jenderal Pengendalian Perubahan Iklim [Directorate General of Climate Change Control]. http://ditjenppi.menlhk.go.id/reddplus/images/resources/ndc/terjemahan_NDC.pdf. [Accessed 1 January 2020].

Ministry of Energy and Mineral Resources. (2020). Langkah Pemerintah dalam Implementasi Aksi Mitigasi untuk NDC di Sektor Kelistirkan [Government Action in Implementing Mitigation Action for NDC in Electricity Sector]. Ministry of Energy and Mineral Resources.

Mori, A. (2020). Foreign actors, faster transitions? Co-evolution of complementarities, perspectives and sociotechnical systems in the case of Indonesia's electricity supply system. *Energy Research & Social Science* 69: 101594. https://doi.org/10.1016/j.erss.2020.101594.

Peimani, H. (2011). Introduction. In: Hooman Peimani (ed.), *The Challenge of Energy Security in the 21st Century: Trends of Significance*. Singapore: Institute of Southeast Asian Studies, 1–7.

PLN. (2014). Statistics PLN 2014. Jakarta: PLN.

PLN. (2015). The Electric Power Supply Business Plan (RUPTL) 2015–2024. Jakarta: PLN.

PLN. (2019a). The Electric Power Supply Business Plan (RUPTL) 2019–2028. Jakarta: PLN.

PLN. (2019b). Statistics PLN 2019. Jakarta: PLN.

Purushothaman, C. (2019). China's big push for solar energy. IDSA Issue Brief. https://idsa.in/system/files/issuebrief/ib-china-solar-energy-cpurushothaman.pdf [Accessed 1 February 2021].

Sambodo, M.T. (2012). Mathematical Modeling Analyses for Investigating the Future Expansion of the Electric Power System in Indonesia [Unpublished Dissertation]. National Graduate Institute for Policy Studies.

Sambodo, M.T. (2015). Rural electrification program in Indonesia: Comparing SEHEN and SHS program. *Economic and Finance in Indonesia* 61(2): 107–119. http://efi.ui.ac.id/index.php/efi/article/view/505/530.

Sambodo, M.T. (2016). *From Darkness to Light: Energy Security Assessment in Indonesia's Power Sector*. Singapore: Institute of Southeast Asian Studies.

Sambodo, M.T., Negara, S.D., Fuady, A.H., Dwiastuti, I. (2015). *Kemiskinan Energi Listrik Memberi Terang Wilayah Terpencil Indonesia* [Electrical Energy Poverty Shines Light on Remote Areas of Indonesia]. Jakarta: LIPI Press.

Sambodo, M.T., Negara, S.D., Fuady, A.H. (2016). Catatan Akhir: Agenda Pembangunan Listrik Perdesaan [Final Notes: Rural Electricity Development Agenda]. In Maxensius Tri Sambodo, Siwage Dharma Negara, Ahmad Helmy Fuady (eds.), *Akses Listrik dan Kesejahteraan Masyarakat* [Electricity Access and People Welfare]. LIPI Press, 111–143.

Savacool, B.K. (2011). Evaluating energy security in the Asia Pacific towards a more comprehensive approach. *Energy Policy* 39: 7472–7479. https://doi.org/10.1016/j.enpol.2010.10.008.

Sebayang, N. (2015). Percepatan Pembangunan Infrastruktur Ketenagalistrikan Pengalaman PT. PLN (Persero) Pada Proyek Regular FTP-1 dan FTP-2 [Fast Track Infrastructure in Electricity Experiences from PT. PLN in the First and Second Fast Track Program]. In: Felix Handoyo, W., Mychelisda, E. (eds.), *Telaan Kebijakan Ketenagalistrikan Presiden Joko Widodo: Tantangan dan Prospek*

[Investigation of Electricity Policy under Joko Widodo Presidency: Challenges and Prospect]. Jakarta: LIPI, 27–39.

SEforAll. (2020). SEforAll Analysis of SDG7 Progress – 2020: SDG7 Data 2010–2018. https://www.seforall.org/system/files/2020-10/Analysis-SDG7-Progress-2020.pdf [Accessed 14 February 2021].

Shalati, S.N., Simanjuntak, J. (2019). Kajian Investasi Tiongkok di Sektor Pembangkit Listrik Batubara di Indonesia [China Investment in Generating Power Plant in Indonesia]. AEER. http://aeer.info/wp-content/uploads/2019/12/Laporan-FDI-Batubara-Tiongkok-Akhir.pdf. [Accessed 14 February 2021].

Tampubolon, A.P., Arinaldo, D., Adiatma, J.C. (2018). Coal Dynamics and Energy Transition in Indonesia. http://iesr.or.id/v2/publikasi_file/COMS-PUB-0015_Coal-Dynamics-and-Energy-Transition-in-Indonesia-1.pdf [Accessed 14 August 2020].

World Energy Council (WEC). (2020). World Energy Trilemma Index. https://www.worldenergy.org/assets/downloads/World_Energy_Trilemma_Index_2020_-_REPORT.pdf [Accessed 14 February 2021].

9 India's energy transition

Is China an inhibitor or a catalyst?

Nandakumar Janardhanan

1 Introduction

The Paris climate agreement has upheld India's commitment to climate mitigation and clean energy development. As part of its Nationally Determined Contributions, India has committed to reducing the emission intensity of its GDP by 30%–35% compared to the levels in 2005 and develop 40% of its electricity installed capacity from non-fossil fuel sources (Government of India, 2015). These commitments have given considerable momentum to the energy transition initiatives by the country.

Energy transition targets in India are multi-pronged and include both supply-side as well as demand-side measures. On the supply side, one of the most important areas is the development of renewable energy installed capacity in view of the country's long-term energy security as well as emission reduction goals. National targets on renewable energy development, which includes the development of 175 GW of installed capacity by 2022 and further expansion to 450 GW by 2030 (PIB, 2019), have emerged as key pillars. The renewable targets have also aimed to ensure that clean energy is affordable and accessible to all sections of the population. Regarding the demand-side measures for transition, India has been taking several initiatives that address the energy efficiency needs of industry, the residential sector, transport, and other key sectors responsible for major shares in energy consumption and emissions. This has not only generated larger public interest and acceptance toward renewable power sources but also contributed to dispelling inherent apprehension about the feasibility of non-traditional sources. As the government supported several renewable energy development programs and rural electrification programs, several households began renewable energy installation. The country's total potential for renewable installed capacity is estimated to be over 1000 GW as of March 2017 (NITI Aayog, 2015), which is a promising factor that catalyzes the energy transition initiatives. Additionally, India has a large energy efficiency program that focuses on the domestic industrial sector. The program is known as Perform Achieve and Trade (PAT) and aims to improve efficiency in various energy-intensive industries using a domestic market mechanism. Through

DOI: 10.4324/9781003190905-12

this program, India aims to enhance the energy efficiency of heavy industries and medium enterprises, which together constitute a major proportion of industrial energy consumption in the country.

One of the major challenges India has been facing with regard to expanding its renewable energy sector is the lack of adequate manufacturing facilities that could supply necessary machinery and equipment (Chaudhary et al., 2014; Behuria, 2020; Kumar and Majid, 2020). The demand for power generation facilities in terms of several critical components, including mounting systems, storage systems, solar panels, and charge controllers, indicates that it is imperative to have a cost-efficient supply channel that ensures adequate availability in the domestic market. Prior to setting the ambitious goal of renewable energy development, the supplies from domestic industry were sufficient to meet most of the sector's needs. However, the growing installed capacity targets and faster adoption of renewable energy for industrial as well as residential usage have led to a significant rise in demand for equipment and machinery. To fill the supply gap, the country eventually had to depend on external supply sources, mostly based in China (Bhattacharya and Jana, 2009). China's rapid emergence as the leading renewable energy equipment market (Wang et al., 2019) and its position as a major industry complemented India's search for external supply chains.

By the end of 2019, India imported approximately 85% of the renewable energy equipment and machinery (PTI, 2020) that is required domestically, with China being the major supplier. Similarly, other equipment and machinery needed to meet the energy efficiency improvement targets in the construction and residential sectors have also been sourced from the import market, conventionally dominated by Chinese suppliers. However, the supply chain was unfavorably affected by the economic lockdown brought about by the COVID-19 pandemic (Eroğlu, 2020; Pradhan et al., 2020), as well as by geopolitical tensions between the two countries originating from an ongoing border dispute. Interestingly, and surprisingly, despite historical hostility over border demarcation, India's dependency on China has been substantially increasing in all aspects of trade for several years. Two reasons can be attributed to this dependency: First, it was necessary to meet domestic demand for expanding the renewable energy target and cater to the energy transition, and second, support was required for India's larger global plan for renewable energy development in developing countries, which is widely known as the International Solar Alliance (Deo, 2018).

This chapter provides insights into how China has been both an inhibitor and catalyst for India's domestic energy transition, and it examines a possible change in the trajectory of India's collaboration with China on the renewable energy front. It also examines the extent to which a mutually beneficial approach toward technology ties can be developed between the two countries.

2 Role of China in India's energy transition: catalyst or inhibitor?

China's competitive advantage over other countries in the energy industry and equipment market has been one of the critical factors that help its industries dominate the overseas market. China has a positive trade balance with several leading world economies, indicating their dependency on China. In 2017, China's overall trade balance with the United States was US$ 275 billion, and it was estimated to be US$ 51 billion with India (World Bank, 2018). This also is reflective of the advantage China has in terms of trade with these partners. India's imports of renewable energy equipment and component supply from China were US$ 2.81 billion and US$ 3.41 billion in 2017 and 2018, respectively (ETEnergyWorld, 2020). It is often argued that imports from China are vital for India to meet its renewable energy development goals as the equipment and components are more cost-effective and efficient than those available in India or from other countries. By early 2020, over 80% of the total solar cells and modules used in India were from China (ETEnergyWorld, 2020).

It is widely noted that to defend and further its economic and political interests, China interferes with the political systems of developing economies (USCC, 2018; Shullman, 2019; Ferchen, 2020). While China seeks to ensure its presence in the domestic markets of other countries as well as the regional or global markets for renewable energy, it has often been perceived as pushing its economic interests. As China searches for renewable energy markets in the Asia-Pacific region, it has found itself at cross purposes with India on several occasions (Janardhanan, 2017).

This section discusses the perception of China as it engages with the Indian renewable energy market as a supplier of services and equipment or machinery. The specifics of the discussion highlighted the conflicting but often dominant strands of two sets of perceptions on China among Indian scholars. First, China's competitive advantage and its persisting market interest are perceived as a threat to the growth of domestic industries in India. This is further intensified by the historical animosity of the two that stems from the border conflict of 1962 as well as Beijing's political proximity to Pakistan. However, because of the gap between supply and demand of energy equipment and machinery needs for the expansion of the renewable energy industry, continued dependence on China seems inevitable. This section aims to examine this dialectics of China's role as a catalyst and an inhibitor to India's energy transition. The analysis is based on several studies as well as public statements and reports from the government and industry.

2.1 China as a catalyst in India's energy transition

China has played a significant role in India's energy transition by making available cost-effective equipment and machinery (Bhowmick, 2020;

ETEnergyWorld, 2020) needed for the installation of renewable energy facilities, thus leading to the perception by a section of Indian industry that China is a catalyst in India's energy transition. Collaboration with China has been important from different perspectives, namely, in terms of India's ambitious target, a cost-sensitive domestic market, and the ease of availability of equipment and machinery.

Indian commodity market (Kukarni and Anil, 2018; Rao and Charles, 2021) has undoubtedly been cost-sensitive, and this has been one of the many challenges faced by international firms and companies that intend to tap into the country's vast market and consumer base. Hence, subsidies have been essential in the promotion of the renewable energy sector as well as for energy efficiency equipment (Acharya and Sadathb, 2017; Shrimal et al., 2017). Price sensitivity plays a determining role for both large and small manufacturers. Costs have been highly competitive, which has also influenced the price of all equipment and machinery. Although India has seen a significant rise in demand for advanced technologies, many domestic and overseas companies in the renewable energy equipment industry have not been able to supply this advanced equipment at a sufficiently low cost. For this reason, Chinese companies have gained an advantage, as they have been able to produce and supply equipment and machinery at a lower cost to Indian consumers (Liming, 2007; Yang et al., 2016), and at a much more competitive level in comparison to other leading domestic or overseas players. Furthermore, China has a major market presence because of the aggressive marketing strategies of its companies, which have gained remarkable access in India due to lower costs, easy availability, and good after-sales service.

Another noticeable development is the role of the informal sector in promoting renewable energy equipment. Small and medium businesses have been involved in importing Chinese-manufactured industrial equipment and machinery, and these businesses have been able to benefit largely from the proactive policies and subsidies to promote renewable energy in India. Nevertheless, China's growing market presence in India's renewable energy equipment market was also unfavorably affecting the growth of the domestic industry.

2.2 China as an inhibitor to India's energy and strategic interests

Another point of view that drives the debate on China's role in India's energy transition is that Chinese companies do more harm than good for India's economy and long-term strategic interests. This view is largely founded on a mix of factors that include economic, political, and historic perceptions of China. India–China border disputes remain an unforgettable historical hindrance for both countries. This is also a reminder that there is an urgent need for both countries to work on their differences and find a feasible solution to amicably settle this dispute. Although bilateral cultural relations between India and China have been strong for centuries, recent engagement has been largely shaped by the 1962 border conflict over a disputed geographical boundary. While the conflict did not turn into a full-scale war, this incident led to mistrust on the side of China as regards the Indian political perception (Hansen, 1967; Mansingh, 1994; Das, 2007). It is important to note that the persistent mistrust between the two countries has been undeniably affecting modern-day relations. Notably, the Indian media takes every opportunity to refer to the border conflict with China, bringing the topic into public focus, which also adds to intensified anti-China public sentiments. However, the root cause of the perception of China as an inhibitor to India's energy transition lies elsewhere. China's political proximity to Pakistan, which has been supporting cross-border terrorist activities, and a widespread opinion that China has been conducting direct and indirect espionage activities to limit India's strategic ambitions in the region, are also influencing India's perception of China. Considering India's import dependency on China, the Indian Minister for renewable energy stated that, "power systems are vulnerable to malware attacks, which can shut down our communications, databases and defense systems. Due to this vulnerability, all power sector imports need to be inspected and some countries need to be banned" (Singh, 2020). Against this backdrop, China is often seen as an unreliable partner in energy sector collaboration.

Similarly, the border standoff between the two countries has also been a critical hurdle in taking the diplomatic dialogue with regard to economic policies forward. Instances of border skirmishes escalated into political problems and also affected the economic ties drastically. Despite both sides making efforts to resolve these matters, complete disengagement from India–China geopolitical standoff cannot be envisioned.

One of the critical questions here is to what extent India and China can continue to collaborate on economic and trade relations. While bilateral trade relations are largely shaped by China's economic ambitions, the two countries need to work together to build a much more constructive collaboration. As the Indian market has been sensitive to any predatory economic approaches by China, there will be limited opportunities for both to collaborate using traditional pathways. However, China has made technological progress in the industrial and manufacturing sector as well as in energy efficiency, and these will be critical areas where India can collaborate. With regard to China's export of equipment and machinery damaging the Indian market, it is essential to explore ways to develop a mutually beneficial mechanism that is not founded in an exploitative or predatory approach. In this context, "co-innovation" can be seen to be highly relevant.

However, this perception does not explain why and how China plays the role of an inhibitor to India's energy transition. Conversely, the perception of China as an inhibitor is based primarily on three factors: the impact it creates on the domestic industry in terms of the threat it poses to local manufacturers (Álvarez and Claro, 2009; Chakraborty and Henry, 2019), the perception that Chinese products are unreliable (Narang, 2016), and a lack of space for healthy competition (Srinivasan, 2004; Chakraborty and Henry, 2019) due to low-priced Chinese goods.

The growth of the domestic manufacturing sector focusing on the renewable energy industry has been severely affected due to low-priced Chinese equipment flooding the market. From being one of the major exporters of solar energy-related equipment and machinery to the global market between 2006 and 2011, India is now a major importer of equipment due to low-priced supplies from China. It is estimated that this has not only affected the industry economically but also resulted in a loss of approximately 200,000 jobs (TNN, 2018), as imports from China began dominating the Indian market. A Parliamentary Committee prepared a report on this issue noting that "the implementation of anti-dumping regulations have not been able to witness expected results as most imports from China have been misclassified under different product categories" (Parliament of India, 2018). The strongly worded report also states that "at a time when there is an urgent need to stimulate our manufacturing sector to at least 25 percent of country's GDP, Chinese imports have been adversely affecting India's manufacturing sector" (ET Now, 2018; Parliament of India, 2018).

While some believe that the influx of low-priced equipment and machinery required for the renewable energy sector has helped in clean energy development (Liming, 2007), there is also another prominent perception that the Chinese renewable manufacturing export-oriented industries were benefiting from subsidies handed out by the Indian government. It is estimated that in 2018–2019, India imported power equipment worth INR 710 billion, of which INR 210 billion was from China (ETEnergyWorld, 2020; Singh, 2020).

The influx of low-priced imports from China was also perceived by policymakers in India (Parliament of India, 2018) to have long-term impacts on the domestic renewable energy industry, thereby limiting opportunities for healthy market competition that is necessary for industry development and integration of advanced technology. This view highlights that the Chinese export market deliberately engages in a predatory strategy to sideline other industries in host countries. It is often noted that with state sponsorship, China's state-owned enterprises not only blocked entry into China's key industrial sectors by international business but also flooded the international markets with their inexpensive products and services, gaining a competitive edge over global companies (Oh, 2015). A statement by Rex Tillerson, former US Secretary of State, in 2017 in which he accused China of "financing schemes for large infrastructure projects that saddle recipient countries with unsustainable debt and could even compromise their sovereignty" (Goodman, 2017) echoed in China's engagement with Sri Lanka (Wignaraja et al., 2020). These business practices have been seen as a wider strategy of the predatory business by China with the objective of dominating the host country market. Indian Parliamentary Standing Committee on Commerce has submitted a report (India, 2018) to the government in 2018, highlighting the impact of Chinese goods import on domestic industry, and therefore supporting the view that the overdependence on Chinese imports is unfavorably affecting the domestic industry (Kondapalli, 2021).

While China continues to be the major exporter of renewable energy equipment to India, this has also had a significant adverse effect on domestic industrial production. Despite concerns by the Indian industry about the overdependence on equipment supplies from Chinese manufacturers, the clean energy development target has been forcing the country to continue its dependence on importing equipment from China. It is estimated that India imported (Chandrasekaran, 2017) almost 87% of the total number of solar panels required to meet its domestic demand in 2017, with the majority imported from China. This overseas dependence eventually turned domestic manufacturers into retailers of Chinese goods. While many see China's role as an inhibitor to India's energy industry growth as well as strategic ambitions, the import of low-priced energy equipment and machinery has substantially helped the development of the renewable energy sector. In this context, one of the critical questions that arise is how India and China can develop a possible pathway that respects mutual economic interest and strategic priorities.

2.3 *India's energy transition and COVID-19 impacts*

The COVID-19 economic lockdown revealed the vulnerable spot of India's energy transition. The over-reliance on external supply lines, especially the dependence on China, turned out to be detrimental for meeting renewable energy development targets. As India imported more than 85% of its solar cells and modules from overseas (PIB, 2020a), disruptions to supply have presented a long-term challenge. It is estimated that due to this impact, there will be a minimum 3 GW delay in the target planned for 2022 (Energy World, 2020). As indicated earlier, a significant share of the supplies for solar energy installation is from China (Economic Times, 2020). The current disruptions are opening up opportunities for domestic companies to consider manufacturing locally or diversifying their imports. The post-COVID policies of the Indian government will also be directed toward encouraging domestic industry (Chaudhary et al., 2020; PIB, 2020).

3 A possible framework for India–China collaboration on energy transition

In order to explore the possible future pathway for collaboration between India and China in the former's energy transition plans, this section presents a broader framework on the concept of co-innovation. The section also deals with the potential implementation of co-innovation identifying key areas that require policy attention.

3.1 A concept of co-innovation framework

India is estimated to have about 63.05 million micro industries, 0.33 million small enterprises, and approximately 5,000 medium enterprises (ET Rise, 2019). Hence, the pandemic-related stimulus package that has been offered by the government will be contributing to a revival of the industry. As supplies from China have been affected, domestic industries will slowly fill this gap. Notably, India could attract global companies as a destination for relocation, which will provide further support to ensure progress on the manufacturing of renewables (Inambar, 2020). However, the inability of the manufacturing sector to meet the domestic demand in the short term will continue to be a critical challenge, that is, the supply and demand gap with regard to renewable energy equipment and machinery.

This chapter proposes a renewed approach toward bilateral trade and technology collaboration between China and India, which is based on the concept of co-innovation. Co-innovation is "a collaborative and iterative approach by two or more partners for jointly innovating, manufacturing and scaling up technologies" (Janardhanan et al., 2020). This is also seen as "a shared work of generating innovative and exceptional design conducted by various actors from firms, customers, and collaborating partners" (Saragih and Tan, 2018). Co-innovation also reflects the continuous exchange of knowledge among all the stakeholders including scientists, manufacturers, and the end-users of technology, with the aim of improving the product. Co-innovation brings in profound changes in the industrial world's operating rules (Maniak and Midler, 2008).

The framework shown in Figure 9.1 explains the phases of co-innovation as well as the role of each partner and the associated benefits to each stakeholder. To explain the process better, the framework is divided into three main phases: collaboration, co-innovation, and outcome. The first phase of the process includes both (or more than two) partners identifying the needs and benefits of cooperation. For the source country and the recipient country, there should be a mutual agreement to enter into a collaborative initiative. In this phase, partners may be able to identify the purpose of collaboration, benefits, and the required inputs in terms of soft skills and hard skills for designing a joint venture. One of the most critical elements here is the effort made by stakeholders in planning the financial resources or entering into agreements for securing adequate monetary means for the collaborative initiative. This phase also provides an opportunity for partners to design adequate legal boundaries that are necessary to carry forward the required collaborative work. In cases where both parties decide to institutionalize their collaboration, whereby their respective soft skills and hard skills need a common platform for fine-tuning, the stakeholders can consider the possibility of collaboration laboratories, or technology CoLabs.

The next phase assumes the central role in the process. This phase explains the broad steps involved in the co-innovation process. The first step of

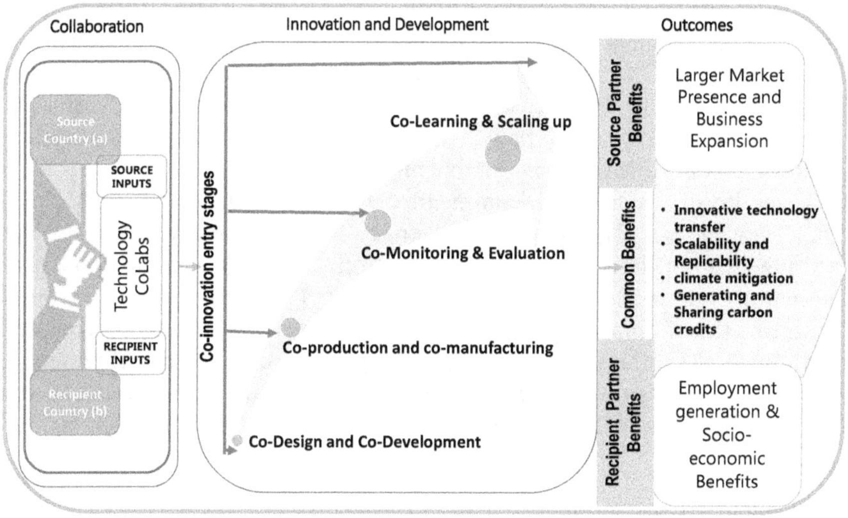

Figure 9.1 Co-innovation framework
Source: Janardhanan, et al. (2021)

this phase is co-design and co-development. This step explains the process that includes ideation, conceptualization, and developing a product design based on mutual agreement among stakeholders. Translating the concept into designing a particular piece of machinery or equipment demands significant joint efforts. The next important step involves co-production or co-manufacturing, which broadly indicates the industrial-level joint production of the machinery or equipment by the stakeholders. The third important step for co-innovation is co-monitoring and evaluation, which are critical processes that include preliminary field testing as well as operational product revision up to and including final product revision, based on co-monitoring activities. This step also can involve processes ranging from product testing to marketing and sale on a commercial scale. The last phase in the process is about co-learning and scaling-up, which involves product revision based on market knowledge, capacity building, as well as further scaling-up of the product for other potential markets. Although there are four possible phases, it is important to point out that co-innovation does not necessarily have exactly all these four steps; rather, co-innovation can be initiated at any stage depending on the agreement between the collaborators.

3.2 Implementation of co-innovation in India–China engagement

Co-innovation has often been discussed in the context of technology collaboration with the aim of overcoming traditional barriers. However, in the India–China context, this is also one of the possible models where both countries can explore developing a collaborative framework for more constructive engagement. While China offers promising benefits in terms of easy availability of raw materials and smaller components, India cannot keep its manufacturing sector away from industrial production activities. For both countries, it may be worth exploring collaboration to strengthen bilateral trade while offering notable mutual benefits.

Three border steps are recommended by experts (Jacob, 2021; Mohan, 2021; Varghese, 2021) as possible avenues for engagement, and they are contingent upon how these proposed options are valued in the context of mutual economic as well as strategic interests. These options are proposed assuming that China's export of equipment and machinery may be accepted in India if the latter's security and strategic interests are not threatened. However, Chinese companies will benefit significantly from access to the huge Indian market. The phased collaboration should be in three steps.

3.2.1 First step: encouraging a material supply for production in India

One of the most important areas of collaboration between India and China pertaining to clean energy is material supply. Critical raw materials including tellurium, gallium, indium, and the rare earths neodymium and dysprosium (Rabe et al., 2017) needed for the clean energy industry have been tightly controlled by state-owned enterprises in China, which is partly due to the environmental and health problems associated with extracting these materials and also to ensure a domestic supply for its own, growing renewable energy industries (Rabe et al., 2017). Considering the long-term plans for clean energy development, this constitutes a potential area for bilateral cooperation.

3.2.2 Second step: engaging the Indian manufacturing sector

It is important for India to consider the development of its domestic industry, which is critical for employment generation as well as for strengthening local economies. This has been an important consideration for the country and has often played a significant role in deciding against overdependence on importing finished equipment and machinery. This area opens up avenues for both countries to engage in joint production and manufacturing utilizing co-innovation in industry.

3.2.3 Third step: promoting joint ventures in host countries

India–China joint production and manufacture of equipment and machinery seems to be a bare possibility in the current geopolitical circumstances. However, if the two countries are able to overcome their challenging border issues, there is every potential for an India–China co-innovation framework to flourish. This will not only help meet the demand for renewable energy equipment and machinery in India but can also play a critical role in meeting the growing demand for renewable sector development in countries where India has been promoting the International Solar Alliance (ISA). Over 50 countries are involved in this alliance and most of the developing countries in the network will be beneficiaries of renewable energy development programs by the India-led initiative. China's closer collaboration with the network as a joint producer and supplier of renewable energy equipment and machinery could be a remarkable contribution to the developing economies.

4 Conclusion

In the past several years, China has been playing an active role in India's energy transition as a supplier of equipment and machinery needed for renewable energy sector as well as for energy efficiency improvement. However, recent months have seen the role of China in India's energy transition rapidly diminish as a result of the pandemic-induced break in bilateral trade and the persisting political volatility between the two countries.

This chapter aims to take stock of the three specific aspects regarding China's role in India's energy transition. First, the factors that give leverage to China in gaining dominance over the overseas market; second, the role China plays as a catalyst and inhibitor to India's energy transition; and third, a potential roadmap for India–China bilateral engagement in the clean energy equipment and machinery sector. Two specific elements are most noticeable throughout the discussions. First, the engagement of India and China in the clean energy domain can be beneficial to both. China's advantage in terms of its ability to supply cheaper equipment and machinery is important for India's stricter target for renewable energy development. However, the political differences founded in geopolitical issues and historical border clashes continue to unfavorably affect bilateral relations, and this is reflected in the energy sector collaboration as well.

The chapter presents a possible conceptual framework for future collaboration based on an innovative approach to co-innovation. The approach facilitates greater involvement of both countries in the manufacturing and production of equipment and machinery, rather than completely depending on imports from one to the other. The conceptual framework indicates that co-innovation can be mutually beneficial given that China's access to the Indian market enables the latter to engage its manufacturing sector to jointly develop and produce equipment and machinery with its Chinese counterparts. Although this proposed approach may appear to lack viability, this addresses one of the most critical and contentious perceptions of Chinese businesses in India as predatory and overly mercantilist. The relevance of co-innovation is also emphasized because strengthening bilateral trade ties will be one of the critical approaches that can build confidence among the two countries and bring about appeasement in their political interactions. This chapter is an attempt to examine China's contribution in India's energy transition and what role it can potentially continue to play in the coming years.

References

Acharya, R. H. & Sadathb, A. C., 2017. Implications of energy subsidy reform in India. *Energy Policy*, 102, pp. 453–462.

Álvarez, R. & Claro, S., 2009. David Versus Goliath: The Impact of Chinese Competition on Developing Countries. *World Development*, 37(3), pp. 560–571.

Behuria, P., 2020. The politics of late late development in renewable energy sectors: Dependency and contradictory tensions in India's National Solar Mission. *World Development,* 126, p. 104726.

Bhattacharya, S. C. & Jana, C., 2009. Renewable energy in India: Historical developments and prospects. *Energy,* 34(8), pp. 981–991.

Bhowmick, S., 2020. *Sino-Indian transitions in the energy sector.* [Online] Available at: https://www.orfonline.org/expert-speak/sino-indian-transitions-energy-sector-64894/ [Accessed 14 January 2021].

Chakraborty, P. & Henry, M., 2019. Chinese competition and product variety of Indian firms. *Journal of Comparative Economics*, 47(2), pp. 367–395.

Chandrasekaran, K., 2017. *China is biggest exporter of solar equipment to India with 87 per cent market share.* [Online] Available at: https://economictimes.indiatimes.com/news/economy/foreign-trade/china-is-biggest-exporter-of-solar-equipment-to-india-with-87-per-cent-market-share/articleshow/58450137.cms?from=mdr [Accessed 20 March 2020].

Chaudhary, A., Krishna, C. & Sagar, A., 2014. Policy making for renewable energy in India: lessons from wind and solar power sectors. *Climate Policy,* 15(1), pp. 58–87.

Chaudhary, M., Sodani, P. R. & Das, S., 2020. Effect of COVID-19 on Economy in India: Some Reflections for Policy and Programme. *Journal of Health Management*, 22(2), pp. 169–180.

Das, D. K., 2007. *China and India: A Tale of Two Economies.* 1st ed. London: Routledge.

Deo, A., 2018. *The International Solar Alliance's China conundrum*. New Delhi: Observer Research Foundation.

Economic Times, 2020. *India imported solar power equipment worth $1,180 mn from China in Apr-Dec FY20.* [Online] Available at: https://energy.economictimes.indiatimes.com/news/renewable/india-imported-solar-power-equipment-worth-1180-mn-from-china-in-apr-dec-fy20/74493914 [Accessed 12 April 2020].

Energy World, 2020. *India's renewables installation could fall by a fifth due to lockdown: Wood Mackenzie.* [Online] Available at: https://energy.economictimes.indiatimes.com/news/renewable/indias-renewables-installation-could-fall-by-a-fifth-due-to-lockdown-wood-mackenzie/75027294 [Accessed 12 August 2020].

Eroğlu, H., 2020. Effects of Covid-19 outbreak on environment and renewable energy sector. *Environment, Development and Sustainability*, June 2020, pp. 1–9.

ETEnergyWorld, 2020. *India imported solar power equipment worth $1,180 mn from China in Apr-Dec FY20.* [Online] Available at: https://energy.economictimes.indiatimes.com/news/renewable/india-imported-solar-power-equipment-worth-1180-mn-from-china-in-apr-dec-fy20/74493914 [Accessed 18 December 2020].

ET Now, 2018. *Parliamentary panel expresses concern over Chinese imports.* [Online] Available at: https://economictimes.indiatimes.com/news/economy/foreign-trade/covid-drugs-india-south-africa-seek-waiver-of-ipr-patents/videoshow/78463117.cms [Accessed 12 July 2020].

ET Rise, 2019. *How structured trade finance solutions help MSME exporters & importers.* [Online] Available at: https://economictimes.indiatimes.com/small-biz/trade/exports/insights/how-structured-trade-finance-solutions-help-msme-exporters-importers/articleshow/70153295.cms?from=mdr [Accessed 2 May 2020].

Ferchen, M., 2020. *How China is reshaping international development.* [Online] Available at: https://carnegieendowment.org/2020/01/08/how-china-is-reshaping-international-development-pub-80703 [Accessed 20 July 2020].

Goodman, M. P., 2017. Peredatory economics and the China challenge. *Global Economics Monthly*, VI(II), pp. 1–2.

Government of India, 2015. *India's intended nationally determined contribution.* [Online] Available at: https://www4.unfccc.int/sites/ndcstaging/PublishedDocuments/India%20First/INDIA%20INDC%20TO%20UNFCCC.pdf [Accessed15 January 2021].

Hansen, G. E., 1967. The impact of the Border War on Indian perceptions of China. *Pacific Affairs*, 40(3/4), pp. 235–249.

Inambar, N., 2020. *Coronavirus: Can India replace China as world's factory?.* [Online] Available at: https://www.bbc.com/news/world-asia-india-52672510 [Accessed 21 May 2020].

India, P. o., 2018. *Impact of Chinese Goods on Indian Industry.* [Online] Available at: http://164.100.47.5/committee_web/ReportFile/13/97/145_2018_7_13.pdf [Accessed 20 December 2020].

Jacob, J. T., 2021. *India China Engagement on Clean Energy Trade* [Interview] (25 January 2021).

Janardhanan, N., 2017. India–China energy geopolitics: Dominating alternative energy market in Pacific Asia. *International Studies*, 52(1–4), pp. 66–85.

Janardhanan, N., Ikeda, E., Zusman, E. & Tamura, K., 2020. *Co-innovation for Low Carbon Technologies: The Case of Japan-India Collaboration,* Hayama: Institute for Global Environmental Strategies.

Kumar, C.R.J., & Majid, M. A., 2020. Renewable energy for sustainable development in India: current status, future prospects, challenges, employment, and investment opportunities. *Energy, Sustainability and Society*, 10(1), pp. 1–36.

Kondapalli, S., 2021. *Prof. Srikanth Kondapalli's assessment about the prominant perception of India's overdependence on China* [Interview] (27 January 2021).

Kukarni, S. H. & Anil, T. R., 2018. Renewable energy in India—Barriers to wind energy. *Strategic Planning for Energy and the Environment,* 38(2), pp. 40–69.

Liming, H., 2007. A study of China–India cooperation in renewable energy field. *Renewable and Sustainable Energy Reviews*, 11(8), pp. 1739–1757.

Maniak, R. & Midler, C., 2008. Shifting from co-development to co-innovation. *International Journal of Automotive Technology and Management,* 8(4), pp. 449–468.

Mansingh, S., 1994. India-China relations in the Post Cold War era. *Asian Survey*, 34(3), pp. 285–300.

Mohan, M. P. R., 2021. *Indian China Clean Energy Trade* [Interview] (22 January 2021).

Narang, R., 2016. Understanding purchase intention towards Chinese products: Role of ethnocentrism, animosity, status and self-esteem. *Journal of Retailing and Consumer Services*, 32, pp. 253–261.

NITI Aayog, 2015. *Report of the Expert Group on 175GW RE by 2022,* New Delhi: NITI Aayog.

Oh, S.-Y., 2015. How China outsmarts WTO rulings in the wind industry. *Asian Survey*, 55(6), pp. 1116–1145.

Parliament of India, 2018. *Impact of Chinese Goods on Indian Industry.* [Online] Available at: http://164.100.47.5/committee_web/ReportFile/13/97/145_2018_7_13.pdf [Accessed 12 August 2020].

PIB, 2019. *PM Modi addresses Climate Action Summit.* [Online] Available at: https://pib.gov.in/PressReleasePage.aspx?PRID=1585979 [Accessed 12 July 2020].

PIB, 2020. *Finance Minister announces Aatma Nirbhar Bharat 3.0 Stimulus worth ₹ 2.65 Lakh Crore.* [Online] Available at: https://pib.gov.in/PressReleseDetailm.aspx?PRID=1672529 [Accessed 12 January 2021].

PIB, 2020a. *MNRE gives major push towards setting up RE Equipment Manufacturing Parks in India.* [Online] Available at: https://pib.gov.in/PressReleasePage.aspx?PRID=1615611 [Accessed 10 May 2020].

Pradhan, S., Ghose, D. & Shabbiruddin, 2020. Present and future impact of COVID-19 in the renewable energy sector: a case study on India. *Energy Sources,* August 2020, pp. 1–11.

PTI, 2020. *Covid-19: Need to focus on improving domestic solar manufacturing, says official.* [Online] Available at: [Accessed 12 February 2021].

Rabe, W., Kostka, G. & Stegen, K. S., 2017. China's supply of critical raw materials: Risks for Europe's solar and wind industries?. *Energy Policy*, 101(2017), pp. 692–699.

Rao, U. & Charles, V., 2021. An empirical examination of the efficiency of commodity markets in India. *International Journal of Banking, Accounting and Finance*, 12(1), pp. 1–15.

Saragih, H. S. & Tan, J. D., 2018. Co-innovation: a review and conceptual framework. *International Journal of Business Innovation and Research*, 17(3), pp. 361–377.

Shrimali, G., Srinivasan, S., Goel, S. & Nelson, D., 2017. The effectiveness of federal renewable policies in India. *Renewable and Sustainable Energy Reviews*, 70, pp. 538–550.

Shullman, D.O., 2019. *Protect the Party: China's growing influence in the developing world.* [Online] Available at: https://www.brookings.edu/articles/protect-the-party-chinas-growing-influence-in-the-developing-world/ [Accessed 13 July 2020].

Singh, S.C., 2020. *Ban on power equipment imports from China, Pak; Can't give jobs to country that transgresses into India: R K Singh.* [Online] Available at: https://energy.economictimes.indiatimes.com/news/power/ban-on-power-equipment-imports-from-china-pak-cant-give-jobs-to-country-that-transgresses-into-india-r-k-singh/76765596 [Accessed 23 August 2020].

Srinivasan, T.N., 2004. China and India: economic performance, competition and cooperation: An update. *Journal of Asian Economics*, 15(4), pp. 613–636.

TNN, 2018. *Chinese imports shut MSMEs down, lead to job losses: Parliamentary panel.* [Online] Available at: https://timesofindia.indiatimes.com/business/india-business/chinese-imports-shut-msmes-down-panel/articleshow/65157017.cms [Accessed 27 December 2019].

USCC, 2018. *USCC 2018 Annual Report,* Washington: USCC.

Varghese, S., 2021. *India-China engagement on clean energy equipment trade* [Interview] (28 January 2021).

Wang, Q. et al., 2019. A study on the spatial distribution of the renewable energy industries in China and their driving factors. *Renewable Energy,* 139, pp. 161–175.

White House, 2018. *How China's Economic Aggression Threatens the Technologies and Intellectual Property of the United States and the World,* Washington D.C.: White House Office of Trade and Manufacturing Policy.

Wignaraja, G., Panditaratne, D., Kannangara, P. & Hundlani, D., 2020. *Chinese Investment and the BRI in Sri Lanka,* London: Chatham House.

World Bank, 2018. *China trade balance, exports and imports by country 2017.* [Online] Available at: https://wits.worldbank.org/CountryProfile/en/Country/CHN/Year/2018/TradeFlow/EXPIMP/Partner/by-country [Accessed 12 July 2020].

Yang, X. J., Hua, H., Tan, T. & Li, J., 2016. China's renewable energy goals by 2050. *Environmental Development*, 20, pp. 83–90.

10 Impact of Chinese renewable technology exports on Japan's energy transition

The case of the solar photovoltaic industry

Takashi Hattori and Yi-chun Chen

1 Introduction

Triggered by the need for renewable energy, the installation of solar photovoltaic (PV) systems has increased in the past decade. The cumulative capacity in the world increased from 15 GW in 2008 to 505 GW in 2018 (REN21, 2019). Although advanced countries such as the United States, Japan, and Germany led in its research and development (R&D), application, and diffusion, PV technology has experienced a major change in the past decade, such as the emergence of new players from emerging countries, such as China, Taiwan, and South Korea, in manufacturing, and the remarkable price drop in PV cells and modules (Carvalho, Dechezleprêtre, & Glachant, 2017; Wu & Mathews, 2012). This also intensified industry competition and bankruptcy of some PV manufacturers in the previous leading countries in PV (Carvalho et al., 2017; WIPO, 2017). As of 2018, China's share of world solar cell production was approximately 74%, and its PV system installation was approximately 44% of the world annual installation (RTS, 2019). These findings reveal that a certain portion of Chinese solar products has been exported overseas to maintain this production. Facing the pouring of the Chinese PV products into other countries' markets, some countries such as the United States and those in the European Union have imposed anti-dumping and anti-subsidy tariffs as countermeasures. In summary, China is the main player in the global PV market, and other governments must tackle its "power" when promoting solar PV installation in their countries.

Feed-in tariff (FiT) is a policy tool frequently employed when promoting the diffusion of renewable energy. The implementation of FiT, which creates business incentives for renewable energy installation, starting with the European countries such as Germany and Spain, has also supported the emergence of these new players, such as China and Taiwan. From the 1990s to the early 2000s, Japan ranked first in PV installation and manufacturing in the world, with its PV manufacturers such as Sharp and Kyocera, as global major PV firms. Japan as the leader was replaced by Germany, which introduced FiT to facilitate PV diffusion. In addition, Japanese manufacturers' PV products exported to Europe competed with the aforementioned

DOI: 10.4324/9781003190905-13

emerging players. Where FiT was executed, Chinese and other overseas PV products entered these markets. Japan introduced FiT in 2012 as well, which resulted in the rapid diffusion of PV, and became 3rd in the cumulative PV capacity in the world (as of 2018; ISEP, 2019). Perhaps not surprisingly, as reported in the mass media, this diffusion has been, to a certain extent, supported by the large import of foreign PV cells and modules, particularly those of China, into Japan's market, which is competition for Japanese PV manufacturing. Additionally, this quick solar PV diffusion has been driven by the FiT mechanism; hence, an increasing financial burden to citizens has become a concern in Japan's discussion on energy policies.

As stated in its FiT law,[1] the Japanese government intended that the FiT mechanism would not only facilitate renewable energy diffusion but also contribute to "...promotion of Japanese industry and the revitalization of local communities" (Article 1). However, if the situation does not progress as the policy intended, as the media has reported, negative feedback may be observed or at least an adjustment will be necessary. Thus, we pose this question: How has the import of Chinese PV products affected Japan's PV industry and its related policies?

Regarding the solar PV deployment in Japan during recent years, the aforementioned reports in the media have provided some simple numbers, situations, and voices from the industry but neither a comprehensive picture of the detailed data nor analyses based on it. Some researchers have investigated Japan's high cost of PV system installation (Kimura, 2019; Kimura & Zissler, 2016). Others have investigated problems related to the quick diffusion of utility-scale PV systems (Fraser & Chapman, 2018; Yamashita, 2018) or community power in Japan (Yamashita & Fujii, 2016). Additionally, still other work, such as that of Muhammad-Sukki et al. (2014), has indicated that FiT in Japan ensures an increasing installation of solar PV in the following years.

Covering the suggestions for Japan, analysis of the Chinese PV industry has attracted interest. Marukawa (2012) analyzed the development of the Chinese PV industry and suggested that it is not a smart move to exert a protectionist procedure on the Chinese PV products. Moreover, based on the China case, Marukawa (2014) indicated that the FiT scheme has caused negative competition in the PV industry. These studies have demonstrated some aspects and perspectives on the recent PV market and installation in Japan but cannot portray the real condition of the impact of Chinese PV products on Japan.

Therefore, in this chapter, we fill this gap in the literature and explore two research questions:

1 What is the actual importation of Chinese and foreign PV products into the Japanese market and its impact on the PV industry, and how have the Japanese PV manufacturers responded to this?
2 What is the impact on Japan's renewable energy-related policies responding to the situation on the importation of Chinese PV products and reflecting the impact on the Japanese PV industry?

The remainder of this chapter is structured as follows: Section 2 presents the methodology and data used in this research; Section 3 discusses our first research question, and we briefly review the development of Japan's PV industry and investigate the situations of the PV industry after FiT was introduced; Section 4 provides the feedback from the government and examines adjustments in energy policy, answering our second question; Section 5 discusses the results from Sections 3 and 4; and Section 6 concludes the chapter.

2 Methodology and data collection

To understand the changes in Japan's PV market and the penetration of Chinese products, we collected numerical data and plotted charts to understand the trends between Japanese and Chinese/foreign PV products. We compiled the number of shipments of solar cells/modules from the Japan Photovoltaic Energy Association (JPEA), and data of production value from the Optoelectronics Industry and Technology Development Association (OITDA) to present annual changes in Japan's PV market in domestic and overseas production. Because the data show only Japanese and overseas production, information from news articles that indicated the shares of PV system brands in the market was compiled to verify the influence of Chinese manufacturers in the market.

Regarding the response from Japanese manufacturers, we focused on the five major Japanese PV firms: Sharp, Kyocera, Panasonic, Mitsubishi Electric, and Solar Frontier. We traced their moves after the introduction of FiT by searching news articles from the database of the Nihon Keizai Shimbun (Nikkei), mainly from 2012 to early 2020, with some solar PV-related articles from Smart Japan as supplementary information. A chronological completion of the main events was then summarized to a table to understand the companies' business strategies.

For the second research question on the response from the Japanese government, we conducted interviews with Japanese government officials at the Agency of Natural Resource and Energy, Ministry of Economy, Trade and Industry (METI) on February 8 and November 11, 2019, and attempted to analyze major characteristics of the Japanese government's policy-making to manage the penetration of overseas PV products in Japan's market. The interviews were, among others, with the Director and Director-General in charge of renewable policy at METI.

3 Import of Chinese solar modules and its impact on Japan's PV market

3.1 Solar PV diffusion in Japan

Renewable energy (conventional hydropower included) in Japan's power generation increased from 10.5% (2011) to 17.4% (2018), among which 6.5% is from solar power (ISEP, 2019). The cumulative PV capacity of Japan

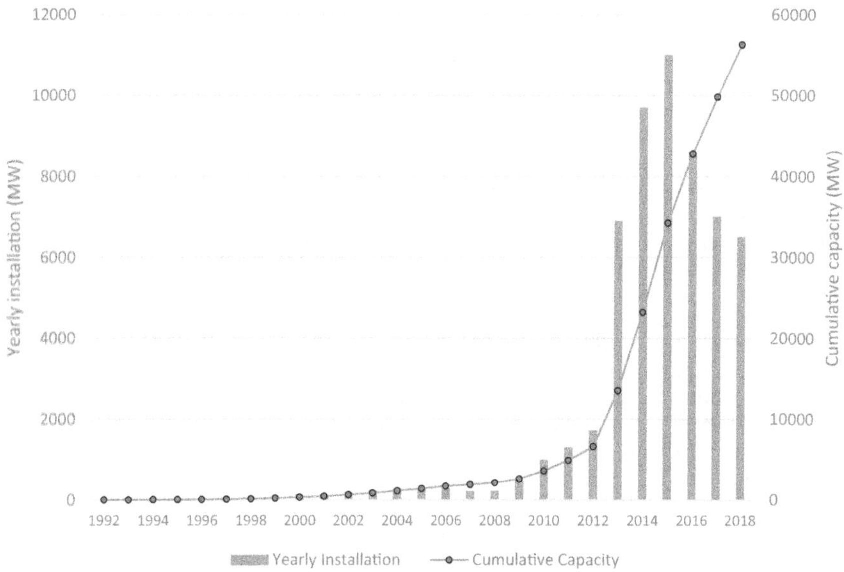

Figure 10.1 Annual and cumulative installed PV capacity in Japan.
Sources: Charted by the authors based on the data compiled from the IEA, "Japan National Photovoltaics Status Report 2012," and Snapshot of Global PV Markets 2014–2019.

reached 55 GW (Figure 10.1), which ranks third in the world, behind China and the United States.

The R&D of PV in Japan has a long history. Because of the oil crisis, the Japanese government launched the Sunshine Program (1974–1992) to support the R&D for searching for alternative energy sources, among which solar power was included (Table 10.1). This induced private companies to join the R&D of solar energy technology. Japan succeeded in initiating and practicing the world's first connection of residential photovoltaic power generation to feed-in to the grid to the utility (reverse power flow). With the subsidy support, Japan promoted the earliest residential use PV diffusion (NEDO, 2007). This leading position was triggered by the government's support, and Japan has ranked first in PV installation and manufacturing in the world since the late 1990s. Subsequently, regarding policy measures promoting renewable energy, Japan introduced a renewable portfolio standard (RPS) instead of FiT in 2003, which is one reason why Japan lost its leading position in solar PV (Muhammad-Sukki et al., 2014; Taki, 2018).

The Fukushima nuclear disaster in 2011 highlighted Japan's power system problems and was a driver for the Japanese government to reconsider its energy policy. A comprehensive FiT scheme was introduced in July 2012 to promote the diffusion of renewable energy in Japan. The scheme, particularly because of its preferential rates during the first three years, ensured a diffusion of renewable energy and a prosperous renewable energy market

Table 10.1 Development of solar PV in Japan

Year	*Events*
1974	Sunshine Program
1992	– Surplus electricity purchase for residential solar panels; initiated the idea of reverse power flow – End of Sunshine Program
1993	Kyocera launched Japan's first residential solar power generation system
1994	Subsidy for residential PV system
1997	Japan ranked first in PV installation in the world (1997–2004)
1998	Kyocera ranked first in solar PV manufacturing
1999	Japan surpassed the United States, ranked first in solar PV manufacturing
2000	Sharp ranked first in solar PV manufacturing
2003	Introduction of RPS
2005	– Germany surpassed Japan as first in PV installation – Abolition of subsidy for residential PV system (revival in 2009) – Top 5 PV manufacturers in the world: Sharp, Q-Cells, Kyocera, Sanyo, and Mitsubishi
2007	Q-Cells (Germany) ranked 1st
2009	FiT for residential solar PV (only for surplus electricity)
2010	Four of the Top 5 of PV manufacturers in the world are Chinese firms
2011	Fukushima nuclear disaster
2012	Introduction of FiT for all renewables

Sources: NEDO (2007); Shimamoto (2012); Taki (2018); summarized by the authors.

(Muhammad-Sukki et al., 2014). Because PV has a short lead time, unlike wind power, whose deployment is subject to environmental impact assessments, a rapid growth subsequently occurred in solar power installation after FiT was introduced.[2] The total installation of PV was approximately 4,900 MW in 2011 but soon reached 13,500 MW at the end of 2013. The average annual installation was approximately 8,200 MW in recent years. This rapid diffusion caused Japan to surpass Germany in the cumulative PV capacity, and to rank the third, only behind China and the United States (ISEP, 2019). However, rates of FiT decreased rapidly, from 40 JPY/kWh in 2012 to 21 JPY/kWh in 2017, that is, reduced by half (the case for 10 kW–2 MW; Table 10.2). The auction scheme started in 2017.

Different from Japan's history of being the leader in PV and Germany's growth in PV installation, the global PV industry has a different outlook now. That is, in 2006, four of the top 10 global major solar cell manufacturers were Japanese and one was Chinese, and in 2011, one Japanese manufacturer remained in the top 10 list, and the Chinese manufacturers accounted for six in the top 10, becoming the main global players (Movellan, 2016; Shimamoto, 2012, p. 101). This result reveals a more complicated policy planning process other than the old measure of "diffusion triggers the PV industry" might be necessary.

The introduction of FiT has rapidly diffused PV in Japan. The cost for PV system installation has reduced 32%, from JPY 421,000 in 2012 to JPY 286,000 in 2018 (Procurement Price Valuation Committee, 2019, pp. 9–10).

Table 10.2 Rates of FiT in Japan

Fiscal year	*>2,000 kW*	*500–2,000 kW*	*10–500 kW*	*<10 kW (no obligation to install output control compatible devices)*	*(Double power generation)*	*<10 kW (obligation to install output control compatible devices)*	*(Double power generation)*
2012	40	40	40	42	34	42	34
2013	36	36	36	38	31	38	31
2014	32	32	32	37	30	37	30
2015	27	27	27	33	27	35	29
2016	24	24	24	31	25	33	27
2017	17.2–21*	21	21	28	25	30	27
2018	14.25–15.45*	18	18	26	25	28	27
2019	*	*	14	24	24	26	26

Note: Rate represents 1 kWh/JPY (Japanese Yen). * means "via auction."

However, issues such as grid connection and the financial burden on the citizens, which resulted from the FiT scheme, particularly the preferential rates for the first three years of FiT introduction, became the concerns. Although the rate of FiT has been halved after its introduction, the cost of installing a PV system in Japan remains higher than that in other countries; thus, the call to further reduce the price. In addition, attracted by favorable FiT rates, foreign PV manufacturers' entrance into the Japanese market has threatened Japan's manufacturers and its PV industry. Hence, although a useful measure to promote the diffusion of renewable energy (Morotomi, 2015), FiT has become a target of criticism in Japan.

3.2 Penetration of China's PV products into Japan's market

Introducing FiT changed Japan's PV industry from exporting PV overseas to domestic selling and importing foreign cells and modules (JPEA, 2012, 2013, 2015). The domestic consumption of PV shifted from mainly for residential use to nonresidential use (large scale). The domestic shipment of PV increased from approximately 1,000 MW in 2011 to over 9,000 MW in 2014 (Figure 10.2). Among them, domestically produced PV increased three times, from 1,034 to 3,688 MW. Additionally, Japanese manufacturers imported cells from overseas, such as from China and Taiwan, as original equipment manufacturers, to fulfill domestic need (JPEA, 2013). In the beginning stage of FiT, namely, around 2013–2014, there were over 50% imported products in the market, and foreign brands owned approximately 30% share of the market (Figure 10.2). Both domestic and overseas products reached their peak of shipment in 2014 (Figure 10.2). In terms of brands in shipment, the share of Japanese brands (overseas production included) was approximately 70% in 2014 and has been below 50% since 2018; thus, foreign brands possess more of the market share than Japanese brands do. We further examined manufacturers' production location: approximately 37.42% of modules shipped to the domestic market were manufactured in Japan by Japanese manufacturers in 2014, but this share gradually decreased to less than one-fifth (17%) of the total market in 2019 (Figure 10.3).

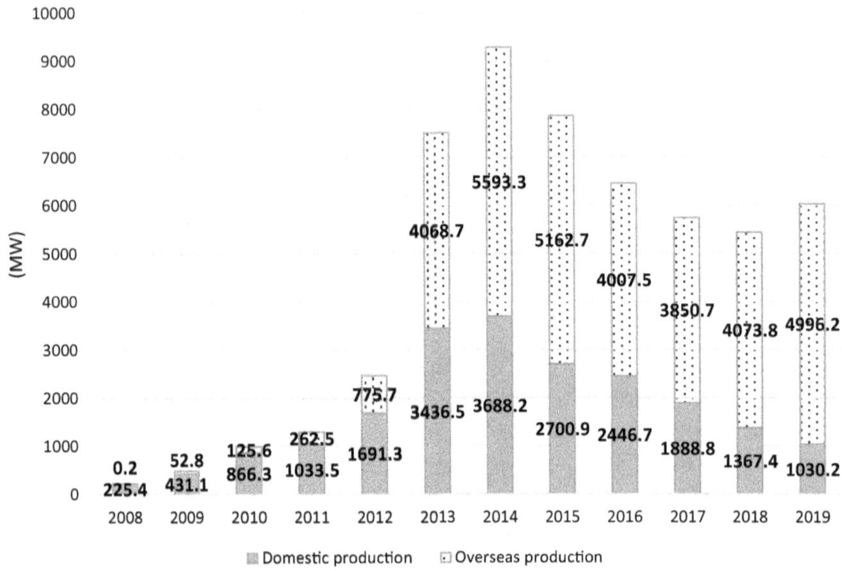

Figure 10.2 Shipment of domestic and foreign solar cells/modules in Japan's PV market.

Note: The data present the shipment of cells and modules during 2008–2012 and modules after 2013.

Sources: Compiled by the authors based on the data from JPEA (2009–2020).

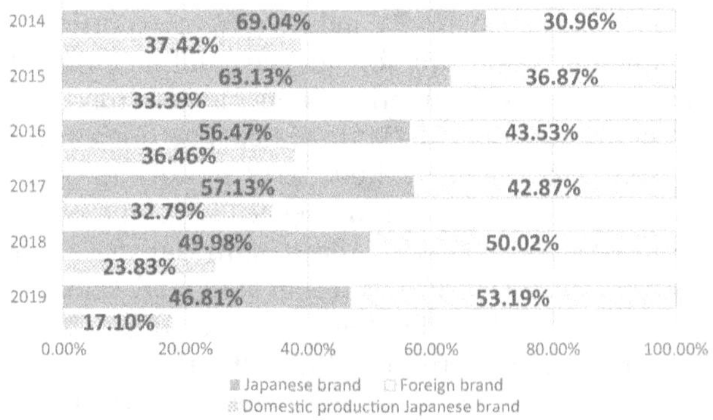

Figure 10.3 Share of Japanese brand and foreign brand PV modules in Japan's market.

Source: The authors charted the information based on the data from JPEA (2014–2020).

In terms of production value, the peak of Japan's PV industry value was in the fiscal year (FY) of 2014, accounting for JPY 3.01 trillion, and continued to decrease; in 2018, the figure was almost half that (1.58 trillion; Figure 10.4). The introduction of FiT only benefitted domestic production value in solar cells/modules in the beginning (FY 2012, 2013), with a margin smaller than that of FY 2011 (Figure 10.5). The overseas production value soon surpassed the domestic production value, in FY 2013, revealing that the Japanese firms relied on the imported products.

Although the decline in FiT rates led to the downsizing of the market scale, foreign brands produced overseas maintained a steady shipment of modules after 2014 and have had recent growth (2018–2019; Figure 10.6). The domestic module production of Japanese brands continued to decline, and finally, the overseas production surpassed domestic production, namely, the Japanese manufacturers produced more modules overseas than domestically. In addition, this finding reveals that Japanese PV manufacturers rely not only on imported cells but also on modules manufactured overseas.

Regarding the major PV cell and module manufacturers, 90% of the market share belonged to the major Japanese manufacturers, for example, Sharp, Kyocera, and Panasonic (Figure 10.7a–g). In the early stage after introducing FiT (FY 2013), the top five manufacturers, all Japanese, maintained approximately 64% of the market share. In FY 2014, foreign manufacturers entered the top five, where JA Solar (Chinese) was third and Canadian Solar

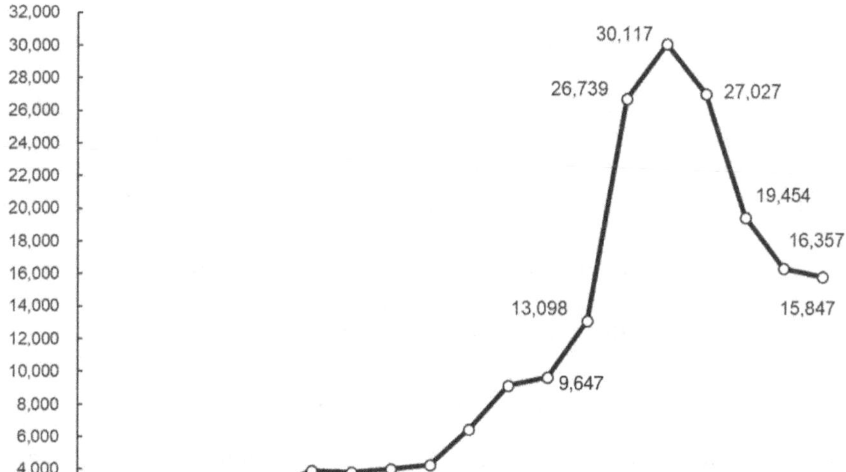

Figure 10.4 Domestic production value of PV industry in Japan.
(Unit: JYP hundred million; fiscal year)
Note: FY 2018 is expected value.
Sources: Adapted from OITDA (2019:12).

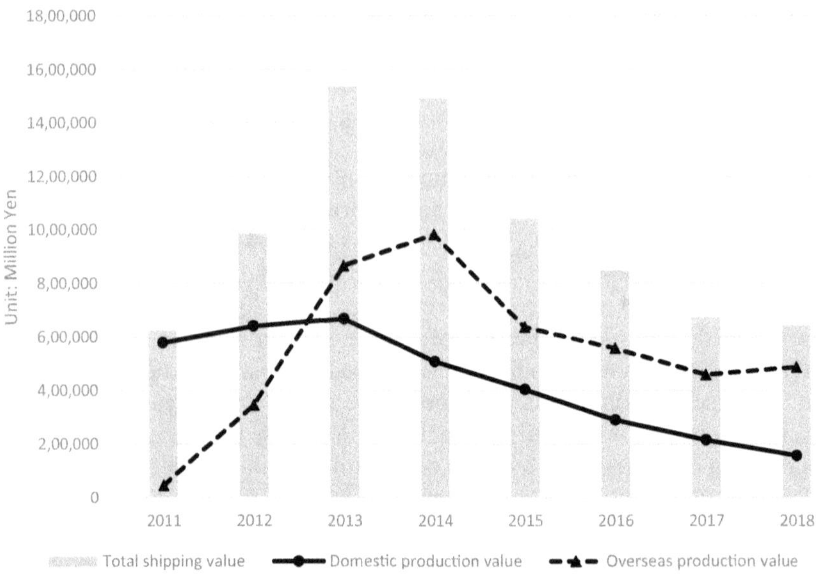

Figure 10.5 Production value of solar cells and modules in Japan (Japanese manufacturers).

Note: X-axis presents the fiscal year. FY 2018 is the expected value.

Sources: Compiled and charted by the authors based on data from OITDA (2014–2019).

(Canadian) was fifth. Since FY 2015, three of the top five manufacturers have been from Canada, China, and South Korea. In FY 2018, for the first time in Japan's history, a foreign brand, Hanwha Q-Cells (Korean), ranked first in the Japanese market. In addition, the Japanese manufacturer that had ranked first obtained approximately 30% of the market share, but this decreased to approximately 10% for the top five firms after FY 2015, revealing the fierce competition in the PV market.

These compiled data and figures and the aforementioned analysis show that the manufacturing and deployment of PV in Japan is increasingly relying on overseas production and foreign brands.

3.3 Impact on and response from the Japanese PV manufacturers

The data and analysis demonstrate that Japanese manufacturers could have maintained their market shares at the initial stage of introducing FiT, although they provided more expensive products than foreign manufacturers did. This result could be attributed to the preferential rates of FiT during the first three years. However, as the rates decreased, increasingly more foreign brands and overseas products entered the market. The marketing battle then shifted from large-scale PV to residential PV, which was where

Japanese companies had the advantage. Some even referred to the battlefield as the last stronghold for the Japanese PV manufacturers competing with the prevailing Chinese solar modules (Matuki, 2019). This advantage for Japanese manufacturers can be attributed to several reasons. One reason is that Japan has promoted residential PV domestically and advanced

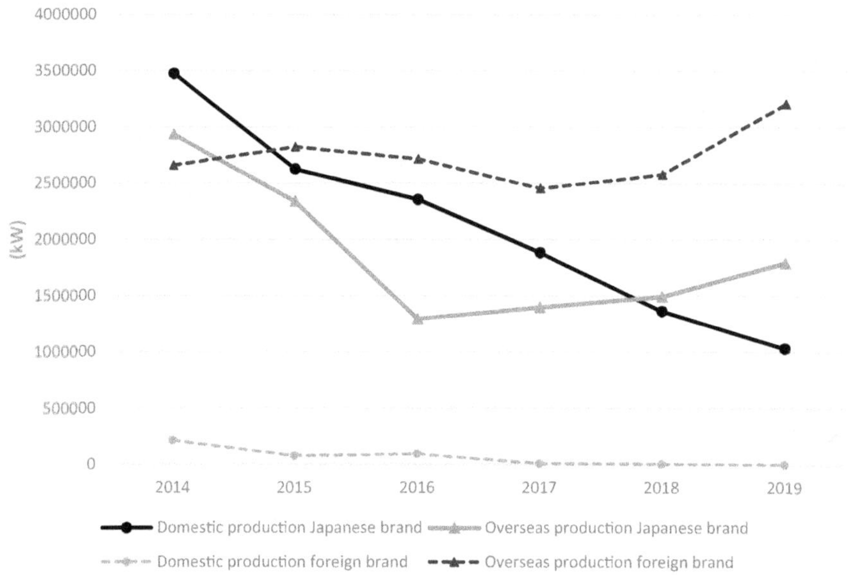

Figure 10.6 Shipment of Japanese brand and foreign brand PV modules with different production locations.

Source: The authors charted the information based on the data from JPEA (2014–2020).

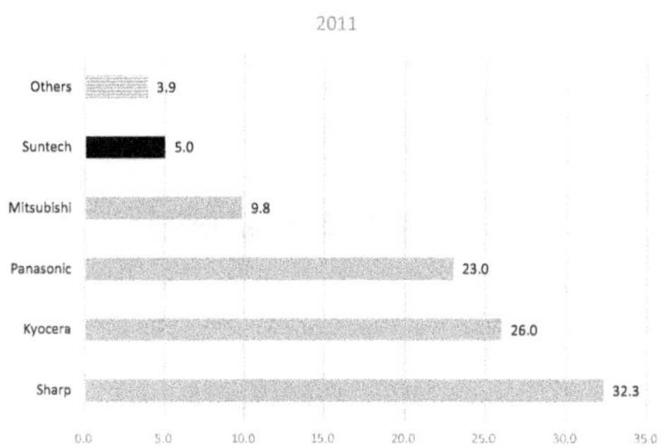

Figure 10.7a Top five PV manufacturers in Japan's market (2011 fiscal year).

(Unit: %)

Sources: Data compiled from Nikkei Sangyo (2012) and charted by the authors.

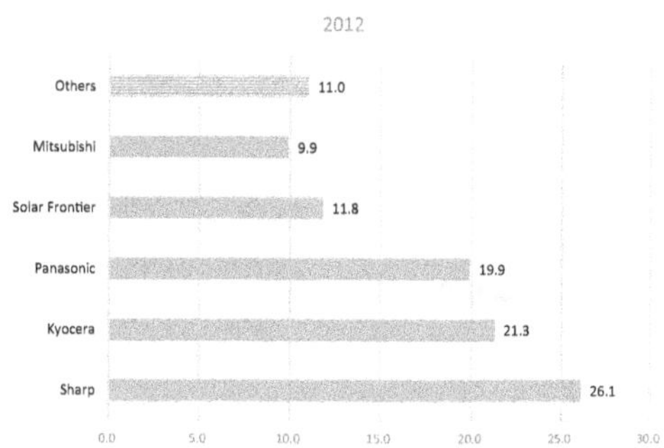

Figure 10.7b Top five PV manufacturers in Japan's market (2012 fiscal year).

(Unit: %)

Sources: Data compiled from Nikkei Sangyo (2013a) and charted by the authors.

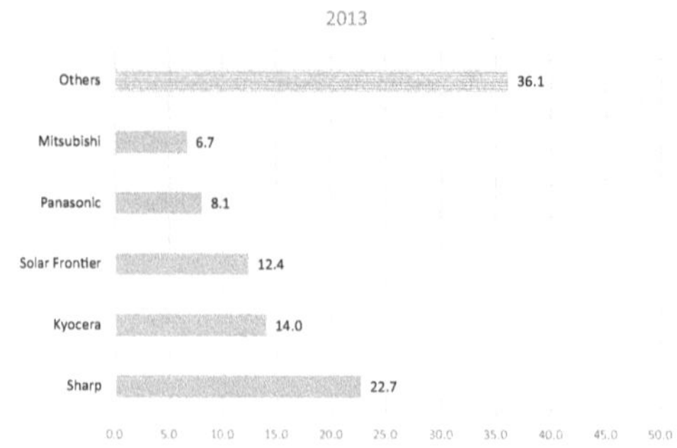

Figure 10.7c Top five PV manufacturers in Japan's market (2013 fiscal year).

(Unit: %)

Sources: Data compiled from Nikkei Sangyo (2014) and charted by the authors.

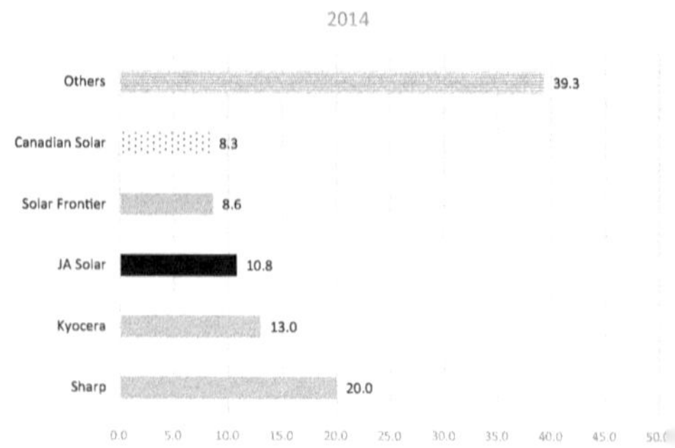

Figure 10.7d Top five PV manufacturers in Japan's market (2014 fiscal year).

(Unit: %)

Sources: Data compiled from Nikkei Sangyo (2015) and charted by the authors.

Figure 10.7e Top five PV manufacturers in Japan's market (2015 fiscal year).

(Unit: %)

Sources: Data compiled from Nikkei Sangyo (2016) and charted by the authors.

Figure 10.7f Top five PV manufacturers in Japan's market (2016 fiscal year).

(Unit: %)

Sources: Data compiled from Nikkei Sangyo (2017) and charted by the authors.

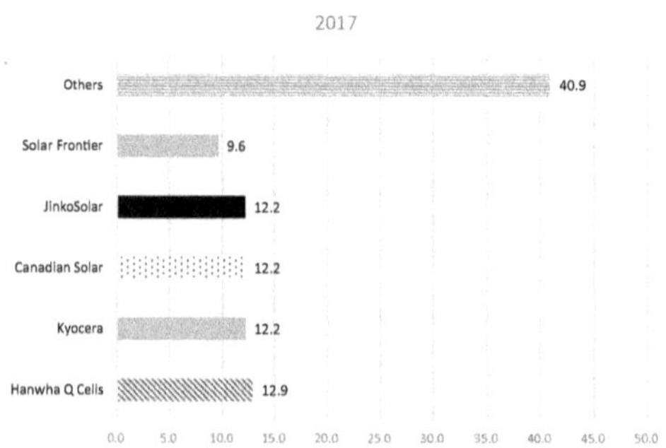

Figure 10.7g Top five PV manufacturers in Japan's market (2017 fiscal year).

(Unit: %)

Sources: Data compiled from Nikkei (2018) and charted by the authors.

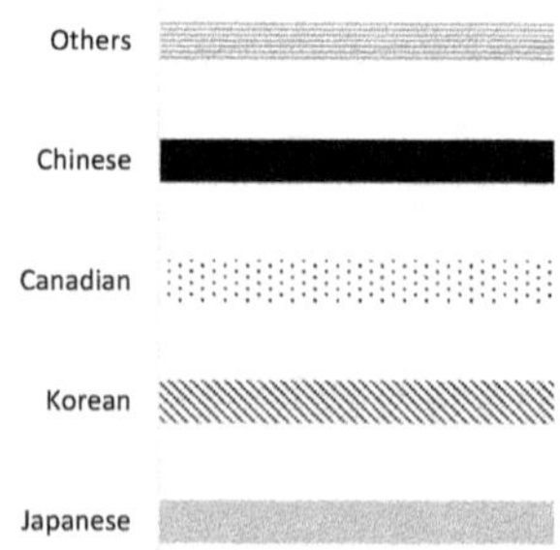

Legend of Figure 10.7

Note: Different patterns in the legend represent the nationalities of the PV manufacturers.

its R&D. A second reason is that Japanese PV manufacturers have their sales channels such as through house builders to market their PV systems. Furthermore, the Japanese brand is highly accepted in the domestic market because of its high quality. Some have even indicated a "tacit rule" in the Japanese market: the adoption of made-in-Japan PV panels is a condition for solar financing (Nikkei Sangyo, 2013b).

On the basis of the shipment data according to PV usage (Figure 10.8), Japanese brands prevail over foreign brands by holding 70%–80% of the residential PV market. However, this share is declining, decreasing from 87% in 2015 to 76% in 2019. By contrast, the share of foreign brands almost doubled its growth (from 12.64% to 23.28%). Regarding nonresidential PV, the Japanese manufacturers possessed more than half the market share (56.59%) in 2015, but that decreased to approximately 40% in 2019. Thus, Japanese manufacturers are losing their market shares in not only nonresidential PV but also in residential PV. Thus, we would not be surprised if the penetration of foreign brands becomes more obvious in the market, as long as the FiT rates continue decreasing or the government adjusts the scheme while the foreign manufacturers continue their marketing in Japan.

Because of the introduction of FiT and the foreign PV manufacturers that thus entered into the market, the Japanese manufacturers have implemented strategies and adjusted their businesses to respond to this change (Table 10.3). In the beginning, because FiT was passed, the emerging needs of PV systems were expected, and hence, manufacturers expanded their production. The resulting competition from cheap Chinese solar modules also propelled them to attempt to reduce the cost, causing them to adopt actions

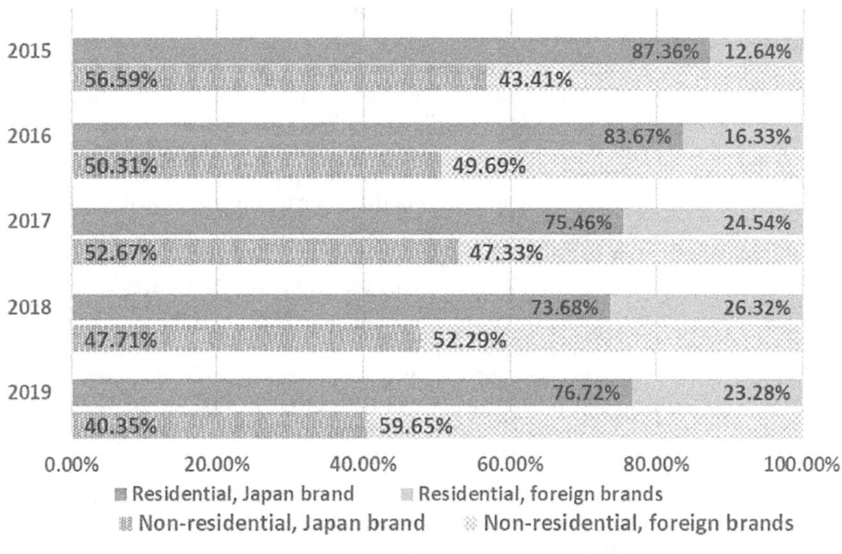

Figure 10.8 Share of Japanese brand and foreign brand PV modules in Japan's market according to usage.

Sources: The authors charted the information based on the data from JPEA (2015–2020).

Table 10.3 Moves/business strategies of the major Japanese PV manufacturers during recent years

Manufacturers	*Moves*
Sharp	• increased staff to manage mega solar power generation business • reduced the production of solar cells at its Katsuragi factory and consolidated them at its Sakai factory • started manufacturing a new type of solar cell with a power generation efficiency 20% higher than the conventional types at the Sakai factory • expanded sales via their joint company with LIXIL (a manufacturer of building materials and housing equipment) • procured cells from foreign companies • provided services from construction to operation of solar power generation • continual development of solar technology (combination of InGaP, GaAs, and InGaAs) and realized the world's highest level of conversion rate
Kyocera	• manufactured cells in Japan and shipped them to its factory in Europe to assemble panels to reduce cost and fulfill needs • improved existing facilities rather than increasing manufacturing lines • sold PV with its other energy-efficient products • in 2017, terminated panel assembling at its Ise factory, switched to outsourcing and producing at group companies in China • accelerated the shift to business in Southeast Asia • consolidated manufacturing at its Yasu factory • increased automation of its production • developed business in "providing [a] service" other than selling products, such as leasing PV systems
Panasonic	• focused on residential PV • sold solar power storage systems • marketed through the sales channels of Panasonic and the former Panasonic Electrical Works Co. • in 2012, adjusted its overseas solar panel production system: reducing overseas panel assembling and setting up its first overseas factory that realized vertically integrated production in Malaysia • in February 2016: – stopped operating the Hama factory, one of the three domestic factories producing residential PV, because of sluggish demand. – increased profitability by increasing sales of storage batteries and other system products in addition to panels – expanded sales in emerging markets such as that in India by using its main production facility in Malaysia • in August 2017: cooperated with Tesla (US) to set up a factory in Buffalo manufacturing solar cells, which is planned to provide products to Tesla exclusively • in FY 2017: – terminated assembling at its Shiga factory

	– ceased silicon material manufacturing at its Oregon factory – focused on cell manufacturing and overseas sales • in 2018: announced switching the exclusive supply contract with Tesla for solar cells to supply them to other companies within the United States • in 2019: – announced the selling of its Malaysia factory to GS Solar (China) but will continue procuring modules from it – sold cells made in its Buffalo factory to Japanese housebuilders • in February 2020: ended the cooperation of joint production of solar cells with Tesla • in July 2020: announced the termination of the contract with GS Solar (i.e., not selling Malaysia factory)
Mitsubishi Electric	• strengthened sales for nonresidential PV by using the group's sales channels • terminated production of cells, kept solar panel manufacturing and roof installation in 2018 • ceased manufacturing and sales of its brand of solar power systems by the end of March 2020 (i.e., total withdrawal from the manufacture and sale of own-brand equipment related to solar power generation); formed a partnership to introduce Kyocera's products, if necessary
Solar Frontier	• in 2013: – restarted its Miyazaki 2nd factory to fulfill domestic needs – developed and produced PV cells that maximize the efficiency under the Japanese weather conditions • in 2015: – operated its new factory (Tohoku factory) with the newest mass-production technology, aimed at acquiring overseas production and sales – promoted Build-operate-transfer business domestically and overseas – achieved 22.3% conversion efficiency for CIS thin-film solar cells (a new world record for thin-film solar cells) • in 2017: – halted new orders in overseas markets, including the countries where profitability was deteriorating – reduced panel production at its domestic factories by 30% – focused on developing high value-added products by focusing on domestic residential and factory-use • in 2018: – announced "no initial cost" business of solar PV system installation – withdrew from overseas and mega solar markets – cooperated with house builders to provide PV and storage batteries as a combined unit

Sources: Compiled and summarized from news articles (Nikkei, Smart Japan) by the authors.

such as decreasing the number of factories in operation and consolidating production in only one or several factories, procuring cells or assembling modules overseas, renewing manufacturing facilities to improve efficiency, and abandoning vertical integration of production or upstream material manufacturing. As the competition in the domestic market becomes more severe for manufacturers, some of them expand their businesses overseas; moreover, they must adopt new business models or expand their scopes to maintain an adequate share of this industry, for example, by combining other energy appliances with PV systems in their marketing packages, providing operation and maintenance service, selling electricity, or providing solar panel leasing services.

Based on Japan's actions in recent years (Table 10.3), we observe that these Japanese PV manufacturers can only continue adjusting their strategies to maintain their PV business in the increasingly severe market circumstances. However, as demonstrated in the list of the top five manufacturers in Japan's PV market (Figure 10.7), Japanese manufacturers have not revived themselves and returned to the top-share seats. Finally, one of the main players, Mitsubishi Electric, withdrew from the PV system business, including sales and production.

4 Impact on Japan's renewable energy-related policies

How the government perceives and thinks about the current situation of the PV industry, market, and power supply will decide its feedback on the ongoing energy transition, affecting its energy and industry policies. We conducted interviews with several Japanese government officials on February 8 and November 11, 2019, to analyze major characteristics of the Japanese government's policy-making to manage the penetration of overseas PV products in Japan's market.

Major events regarding renewable energy and FiT policies are summarized in Table 10.4. According to the authors' interviews with the Director-General and the Director in charge of renewable energy policy at METI, the Japanese government understands the situation of Chinese PV products' penetration in Japan's market. However, the current PV cell/module production has been commodified, and the Japanese government did not change their renewable energy-related policies to drastically reverse this situation.

Although some countries such as the United States and those in the European Union have attempted to leverage tariff duties as a measure to stop the dumping of Chinese PV products into their markets, the Japanese government has not been working toward this direction. Regarding trade disputes, they will be difficult to resolve; whether a favorable result can be obtained is difficult to predict. According to the interviewees, the Japanese PV manufacturers did not strongly ask the government to do so, and the government did not impose the import restriction.

Table 10.4 Major events regarding renewable energy/FiT policies

Time	*Policies and events*
2011.03	3.11 Fukushima nuclear disaster
2012.07	Introduction of FiT
2014.04	4th Strategic Energy Plan: 3E+S
2015.07	"Long-term energy supply-demand outlook:" increase renewable energy to 22%–24% in power generation by 2030
2017.04	Revision of FiT: introduction of bidding
2017.08–2018.04	METI Roundtable for Studying Energy Situations
2018.07.03	5th Strategic Energy Plan: sophisticated 3E+S: technology self-sufficiency; Renewable energy as a major power source

Source: Made by the authors.

The decrease in FiT rates does not mean that the Japanese government has abandoned PV technology. According to the interviewees, the Japanese government thinks that the current adjustment of FiT is appropriate, with a speed that is not too fast. Regarding the call for price decline to reduce the cost of electricity from renewable energy, in the case of solar PV, the interviewees explained that panels account for only part of the price in deployment. Whether the modules are made in Japan or not, how fierce the competition is between Chinese and Japanese manufacturers is a secondary issue, compared with avoiding high energy costs in Japan.

The interviewees confirmed that the thriving of Japanese PV manufacturers was a crucial aspect when considering its renewable energy-related policies. However, for the government's policy and stance, to maintain the long-term stability of the energy supply is more important, rather than using a single technology. The interviewees emphasized that the Japanese government is promoting the development of new, next-generation PV technologies.

In addition to energy self-sufficiency, the concept of "technology self-sufficiency" was emphasized in the 5th Strategic Energy Plan (SEP; METI, 2018). Because of the changing PV market and the response to the global energy situations and global warming countermeasures, the fifth SEP was announced in 2018, which set the basis for Japanese energy policy, namely, changes to tackle these situations. In the 5th SEP, there is no definition of "technology self-sufficiency," but this concept was used to highlight the importance of domestically developed and maintained "technology."

One side of the PV diffusion in Japan presents a situation of the import of foreign PV products, the impact on the local PV industry, and the national wealth flowing overseas (because of FiT). This is against the government's goal, which pursues increasing energy self-sufficiency. Such concerns were raised in the METI Roundtable for Studying Energy Situations and were the emphasis of the "technology self-sufficiency" to be included in the 5th SEP, namely, the stress of "the amount of energy supply which is covered by Japan's technologies with respect to domestic energy consumption."

The government realized the dependency on China's PV panels and hence emphasized the need to ensure Japan's obtaining core technologies in the energy supply chain. Moreover, the current situation cannot satisfactorily promote the green industry necessary to improve the economy, because its intention is written in the FiT law, "...contributing to the strengthening of the international competitiveness of Japan and the sound development of the national economy, including the promotion of Japanese industry and the revitalization of local communities."

In addition, the call for a diversity of energy sources in power generation, the search for the next promising technology, and the improvement of power generation efficiency have been highlighted in this regard. These demonstrate the strategic consideration from the government as it manages the domestically and internationally changing situation in energies.

Furthermore, the 5th SEP introduced "efforts for the utilization of renewable energy as the major power" as a policy response. The introduction of FiT undoubtedly facilitated the PV diffusion in Japan. The import and penetration of foreign PV products, with the continued decrease in FiT rates, also decreased the PV diffusion cost. Although this intensified competition in the industry and downsized the share of domestic manufacturing, the continued cost reduction and growth in installed capacity led renewable energy to become a "major power source" in the long term. For the Japanese government, long-term planning of the development of energy technology and maintaining stable energy supply are more important than that.

5 Discussion

The introduction of FiT in 2012 caused the importation of Chinese PV products into the Japanese market. The original purpose of FiT was to reduce the risk for investors to enter the renewable energy industry and power generation. With the decrease in FiT rates, which fosters innovative activities to reduce the cost of renewable energy, finally, renewable energy can compete economically with mainstream, conventional energy sources. Some appropriate protection and nurturing of an infant industry could be justified. However, Japan has had a high-quality PV industry. The preferential rates of FiT in the beginning were greater, such as protecting the Japanese PV manufacturers to allow the Japanese PV manufacturers to find a means to sustain themselves and maintaining the industry while diffusing renewable energy, rather than helping nurture an infant renewable energy industry. The policy makers probably realized the situation of the global PV industry and the "vulnerability" of Japan's manufacturers under such a situation and hence adopted the preferential rates in the beginning as a balanced policy.

After the first three years, the Japanese government continued to adjust the FiT rates, did not restrict the importation of Chinese products, and allowed market penetration according to the market mechanism. Japanese PV manufacturers did not find their new position in developing this industry in time and hence were unable to stop the penetration of Chinese PV products. This further continues the dilemma in PV diffusion in Japan, where the request for a decrease in the cost of PV installation has continued, and by contrast, a concern for the penetration of Chinese PV modules in its market has been indicated.

Nevertheless, the competition with the Chinese manufacturers did urge Japanese companies to develop their downstream business and diversify their sales to maintain their profits. Additionally, despite the fierce competition and losing the dominant position in the current global market, the Japanese manufacturers continue developing next-generation PV technologies, with a vision to again acquire the market share.

Considering Japan's industry as a whole, PV manufacturers are small, and the impact on the Japanese economy has been limited. Additionally, PV manufacturers in Japan are merely a branch of electronics companies. The industrial policy was not applied to protect domestic PV manufacturers when much cheaper PV products were manufactured in China. Energy security through allowing cheaper PV products from China might have been prioritized compared with maintaining the commercialized PV production within Japan. Regarding domestic PV manufacturing, the Japanese government promoted developing new PV technologies. This manner of seeking a balance between energy and industry, and exploring promising technologies, has become a background and a challenge in Japan's energy transition.

6 Conclusion

In this chapter, we investigated the impact of the introduction of FiT and the import of Chinese solar modules and cells on Japan's PV industry and its related policies. The results show the rapid diffusion of PV in Japan led to the quick penetration of Chinese and other foreign countries' PV cells and modules in Japan's market; and with the decrease in FiT rates, the situation became more serious. These have caused the Japanese manufacturers to withdraw from cell or module manufacturing and to adjust their business models and strategies dynamically. However, the Japanese government continued to allow the drop in FiT prices while continuing the promotion of renewable energy in Japan's energy mix. The Japanese government has focused on new technology development rather than protecting the domestic manufacturing of commercialized products. These resulted in adjustments in energy policy, which emphasizes technology self-sufficiency, diversification of energy choices, and searching for the next energy technology while facilitating renewable energy to be promoted as the main power supply in Japan's energy mix. Instead of protecting the current PV commodity manufacturing, the Japanese government is applying a long-term vision and a holistic energy policy principle to tackle this challenge during its energy transition.

7 Acknowledgments

The authors thank Professor Sung-In Na for his comments at the annual conference of the Society for Environmental Economics and Policy Studies on September 27, 2020. The authors also thank the interviewees for taking their time to answer our questions and sharing their insights.

Notes

1 The full name of the legal basis for FIT is the "Act on Special Measures Concerning Procurement of Electricity from Renewable Energy Sources by Electricity Utilities."
2 However, the environmental impact assessment for large-scale solar power generation began in April 2020.

References

Carvalho, M., Dechezleprêtre, A., & Glachant, M. (2017). *Understanding the Dynamics of Global Value Chains for Solar Photovoltaic Technologies*. Retrieved from https://www.wipo.int/edocs/pubdocs/en/wipo_pub_econstat_wp_40.pdf

Fraser, T., & Chapman, A. J. (2018). Social equity impacts in Japan's mega-solar siting process. *Energy for Sustainable Development, 42*, 136–151.

ISEP. (2019). *Renewables 2018/2019 Japan Status Report (Summary)*. Retrieved from https://www.isep.or.jp/archives/library/category/japan-renewables-status-report (in Japanese)

JPEA. (2009–2020). Solar Cell/Module Shipment Statistics. Retrieved from http://www.jpea.gr.jp/document/figure/index.html (in Japanese)

JPEA. (2012). *JPEA PV OUTLOOK 2030 (August 2012 revision)*. Retrieved from Tokyo: http://www.jpea.gr.jp/pdf/t120925.pdf (in Japanese)

JPEA. (2013). *JPEA PV OUTLOOK 2030 (Summary) (December 2013 revision)*. Retrieved from Tokyo: http://www.jpea.gr.jp/pdf/pvoutlook2013-2.pdf (in Japanese)

JPEA. (2015). *JPEA PV OUTLOOK 2030: A Certain Progress toward 2030-Aiming for Smart Country Japan-*. Retrieved from Tokyo: http://www.jpea.gr.jp/pdf/pvoutlook2015-1.pdf (in Japanese)

Kimura, K. (2019). *Costs of Solar Power Generation in Japan: Current Situation and Future Estimates*. Retrieved from Tokyo: https://www.renewable-ei.org/pdfdownload/activities/Report_SolarCost_201907.pdf (in Japanese)

Kimura, K., & Zissler, R. (2016). *Comparing Prices and Costs of Solar PV in Japan and Germany: The Reasons Why Solar PV Is More Expensive in Japan*. Retrieved from Tokyo: https://www.renewable-ei.org/images/pdf/20160113/JREF_Japan_Germany_solarpower_costcomparison.pdf (in Japanese)

Marukawa, T. (2012). *The Compressed Development of China's Photovoltaic Industry and the Rise of Suntech Power*. Retrieved from https://www.rieti.go.jp/jp/publications/dp/12e051.pdf

Marukawa, T. (2014). China in the global photovoltaic industry. *The Economic Review, 188*(2), 15–29. Doi: 10.14989/228019 (in Japanese)

Matuki, T. (2019, April 5). Domestic solar cell manufacturers at the corner of the ring, making a last-ditch effort to recover their profits. *Nikkan Kogyo Shimbun*. Retrieved from https://newswitch.jp/p/17139 (in Japanese)

METI. (2018). *The Fifth Strategic Energy Plan.* Tokyo Retrieved from https://www.enecho.meti.go.jp/category/others/basic_plan/pdf/180703.pdf (in Japanese)

METI. (n.d.). Feed-in tariff scheme: Purchase price and period, etc. Retrieved from https://www.enecho.meti.go.jp/category/saving_and_new/saiene/kaitori/kakaku.html (in Japanese)

Morotomi, T. (2015). Electrical system and distributed electrical system. In T. Morotomi (Ed.), *Electrical System Reform and Renewable Energy* (pp. 1–30). Tokyo: Nippon Hyoron Sha. (in Japanese)

Movellan, J. (2016, April 25). Japanese manufacturers have disappeared from the world's top 10 solar cells in 2015. *Nikkei xTECH.* Retrieved from https://xtech.nikkei.com/dm/atcl/column/15/286991/041900018/ (in Japanese)

Muhammad-Sukki, F., Abu-Bakar, S. H., Munir, A. B., Yasin, S. H. M., Ramirez-Iniguez, R., McMeekin, S. G., Stewart, B. G., Sarmah, N., Mallick, T. K., Rahim, R. A., Karim, M. E., Ahmad, S., and Tahar, R. M. (2014). Feed-in tariff for solar photovoltaic: The rise of Japan. *Renewable Energy, 68*, 636–643.

NEDO. (2007). *How Did Japan Become the World's Number One Solar Power Generation?* Kawasaki: New Energy and Industrial Technology Development Organization. (in Japanese)

Nikkei. (2018, July 10). Solar panels: A domestic predicament. *Nihon Keizai Shimbun,* p. 14. (in Japanese)

Nikkei Sangyo. (2012, July 30). Domestic market share of 100 products. *Nikkei Sangyo Shimbun,* p. 13. (in Japanese)

Nikkei Sangyo. (2013a, July 29). Domestic market share of 100 products. *Nikkei Sangyo Shimbun,* p. 15. (in Japanese)

Nikkei Sangyo. (2013b, August 7). Part 4: The Solar Bubble (3) Japan's strength and search for ways to utilize technology (Energy Evolution). *Nikkei Sangyo Shimbun,* p. 2. (in Japanese)

Nikkei Sangyo. (2014, July 28). Domestic market share of 100 products. *Nikkei Sangyo Shimbun,* p. 13. (in Japanese)

Nikkei Sangyo. (2015, July 27). Domestic market share of 100 products. *Nikkei Sangyo Shimbun,* p. 19. (in Japanese)

Nikkei Sangyo. (2016, July 25). Domestic market share of 102 products. *Nikkei Sangyo Shimbun,* p. 19. (in Japanese)

Nikkei Sangyo. (2017, July 24). Domestic market share of 100 products. *Nikkei Sangyo Shimbun,* p. 19. (in Japanese)

OITDA. (2014–2019). Optical Industry Trend Survey (Technological Information Report), FY2013–2018. (in Japanese)

Procurement Price Valuation Committee. (2019). *Opinions on Procurement Prices and Other Issues in and after FY2019.* Tokyo. (in Japanese)

REN21. (2019). *Renewables 2019 Global Status Report.* Retrieved from Paris: http://www.ren21.net/gsr-2019/

RTS. (2019). Global solar market maintains 100 GW. How was the impact of China's control measures offset? *Solar Journal.* Retrieved from https://solarjournal.jp/solarpower/31599/ (in Japanese)

Shimamoto, M. (2012). Can the Japanese PV industry revive? *Hitotsubashi Business Review, 59*(4), 98–114. (in Japanese)

Taki, J. (2018, November 3). Electricity utilities became barriers toward renewables diffusion: Low purchase targets, dislike high costs. *Nihon Keizai Shimbun,* p. 8. (in Japanese)

WIPO. (2017). *World Intellectual Property Report 2017 – Intangible Capital in Global Value Chains.* Retrieved from https://www.wipo.int/publications/en/details.jsp?id=4225

Wu, C.-Y., & Mathews, J. A. (2012). Knowledge flows in the solar photovoltaic industry: Insights from patenting by Taiwan, Korea, and China. *Research Policy, 41*(3), 524–540.

Yamashita, H., & Fujii, K. (2016). Japanese municipalities' policies on renewable energies as they stand, and their needed changes. *Research on Sustainability, 6*, 57–70. (in Japanese)

Yamashita, N. (2018). Lessons learned from local issues with solar PV to promote local projects. *Kagaku: Science Journal, 88*, 1015–1022. (in Japanese)

11 Generating or receiving carbon leakages?

An examination of China's CO_2 emissions in Asia

Le Tuyet Vo and Yiyi Ju

1 Introduction

After opening up and economic reforms in 1978, China's development was remarkable with a gross domestic product (GDP) growth rate of almost 10% per year, and it became the world's second-largest economy. In 2018, China became the world's number-one export country and was second in imported goods. In the meantime, decades of rapid economic growth have dramatically expanded China's energy needs. As a result, China is now the world's largest CO_2-generating country. China's fossil fuel consumption accounted for 87.6% of total energy consumption in 2014 (China Energy Group at Lawrence Berkeley National Laboratory, 2014). Along with increased international trade, the production of goods and services has become multinational. This indicates the possibility of environmental pollution also being exported overseas.

In the context of globalization's remarkable rise, the relationship between trade and the environment has also been discussed in the literature. Among the debates on the impact of trade globalization on the environment, there are discussions on the pollution haven hypothesis (PHH) and carbon leakage terms (Cole, 2004; Dietzenbacher & Mukhopadhyay, 2007; Gill et al., 2018; Mani & Wheeler, 1998; Taylor, 2004; Wiebe & Yamano, 2016).

Conventionally, the PHH and carbon leakage were terms related to environmental regulation and production activities. Relatively strict environment regulation in developed countries forced entrepreneurs to save energy and to introduce energy-saving technology, which raised the cost of the product when produced in developed countries. As a result, multinational companies tried to reduce costs by moving production bases to developing countries with lax environmental policies. Carbon leakage refers to the movement of carbon through the market mechanism. For instance, Copeland and Taylor (1994) considered the PHH in north-south trade under the North American Free Trade Agreement. Their research showed the connection between stringent environmental regulations and trade patterns in terms of a country's pollution. The research found that enterprises in highly

DOI: 10.4324/9781003190905-14

regulated systems such as the United States or Canada were directly competitive with those operating in poorer countries with weak environmental standards like Mexico. In the globalization and liberalization era, developing countries could become PHHs for the pollution-intensive industries of advanced countries. Therefore, carbon leakage occurs because of the trade between developing countries and developed countries.

Yang (2001) tested the impacts on Taiwan's environment and CO_2 emissions after Taiwan joined the World Trade Organization (WTO). The author applied computable general equilibrium (CGE) to see the interaction among the economic sectors and then employed the Laspeyres index to decompose the change in CO_2 emissions after Taiwan joined the WTO in 1996. The results showed that, along with trade liberalization, CO_2 emissions also increased. The net change in emissions was focused on some carbon-intensive sectors such as on-metallic mineral products, metal products, and electricity sectors. Yang's (2001) paper supported the PHH in Taiwan after it joined the WTO.

Dietzenbacher and Mukhopadhyay (2007) examined India's PHH. Their study estimated CO_2 and SO_2 emissions released into the environment when they assumed that exports and imports would increase by the same amount of 1 billion rupees. Although the authors expected that India would export pollution-intensive goods, they found the opposite results in the case of India. The amount of CO_2 and SO_2 emissions generated to produce one unit of exports were smaller than the pollution amounts avoiding being generated by one unit of imports. Consequently, India exports relatively clean goods and gains from the extra trade. This means that India was not a pollution haven in the 1990s.

Similar to Dietzenbacher and Mukhopadhyay (2007), Temurshoev (2011) employed the same methodology to examine the PHH or the factor endowment hypothesis for the United States and China for 1992 and 1997. This empirical research examined three cases of trade: (1) China's trade with the rest of the world; (2) U.S. trade with the rest of the world; and (3) the bilateral trade between China and the United States. It was revealed that a PHH does not exist in the case of bilateral trade and that China gained in terms of emissions. The author also found that, over time, the gains from trade with the United States are more beneficial in terms of CO_2 emissions than the same increase in trade with the rest of the world.

Chen et al. (2011) found that China's export-oriented economy from 1993 to 2007 was good for the environment. Employing the simultaneous equation model, the authors investigated the interaction among economic growth, foreign trade, foreign direct investment (FDI), and the environment. The results of this research did not support the PHH. However, it could be interpreted that China was causing the rise of CO_2 emissions in the rest of the world under its export-oriented economy.

On the other hand, in Jayanthakumaran and Liu's (2016) research, the result was the opposite for bilateral trade between China and Australia. Using the sector input–output (IO) model to calculate the CO_2 emissions embodied in trade between China and Australia, the net CO_2-embodied emissions transferred from Australia to China had a negative value. It can be shown that the Australian trade caused the rise of Chinese emissions in the period of 2008–2011. This research found that global CO_2 emissions could increase by 39.13 million tons when Australia consumes China's export goods, but China's consumption of Australia's products could slow world emissions by 20.19 million t-CO_2. The authors suggested that the composition of more bilateral trade may help reduce global emissions.

Fan et al. (2019) also tested the CO_2 embodied in Chinese trade in 2010 and 2011. The author created a panel data model to examine the impact of trade on CO_2 emissions, using the single-region input–output (SRIO) model to decompose the industrial sector and carbon dioxide emissions. In general, the more open the trade, the more reduction in carbon intensity and gross emissions.

Carbon relocation is another environmental term. It occurs through FDI. Shahbaz et al. (2015) showed the change in emissions through FDI. The paper demonstrated the effects of FDI on the environments of low-, middle-, and high-income countries. The author used panel data from 1975 to 2012 and employed panel co-integration techniques. The results when economic growth gains 1%, energy use and environmental pollution increase by 0.07% and 0.65%, respectively. In turn, FDI decreases the CO_2 emissions in high-income countries in every period, but this does not happen in low-income countries. In low-income countries, FDI speeds environmental degradation. The result supports the PHH. Carbon leakage is the movement of carbon through the market mechanism, but carbon relocation refers to the redirection of carbon according to policies of carbon-intensive countries like China. There is a significant difference between carbon leakage and carbon relocation. However, carbon leakage and carbon relocation cannot be distinguished in terms of phenomena.

After specifying the differences in carbon leakage and carbon relocation definitions, this chapter aimed to estimate the international carbon leakage that considers the differences in technology levels of imported goods and services between countries. Previous studies used the SRIO table (Dietzenbacher and Mukhopadhyay, 2007; Temurshoev, 2011) assuming the technology levels of imported goods and services same between the home countries and the rest of the world due to unavailability of international intermediate trade data. The results calculated by such an SRIO approach disregarded the CO_2 emissions from importing goods and services and thus may underestimate the international carbon leakage. As a supplementation, we used the multi-region input–output (MRIO) approach in addition to the SRIO so that technology levels of both domestic and importing countries can be included for the carbon leakage examination.

This chapter also focuses on the emissions induced by international trade. It examines whether China has been transferring CO_2 emissions to

Asian countries through bilateral trade or receiving overseas CO_2 emissions. Further, the chapter investigates whether the pattern of China's bilateral emissions transfer has changed from 2005 to 2015. We selected four trade partner countries in Asia to use when considering the range of economic development level, specifically by the indicator GDP per capita (China US $4,550 in 2010). These countries include Vietnam (US $1,318), India (US $1,358), and Indonesia (US $3,122) with GDP per capita smaller than China, as well as Japan (US $44,508, GDP per capita in 2010, World Bank, 2011), larger than China. This chapter contributes to a better understanding of the role of one country in the global carbon transaction. It examined different carbon leakage hypnosis by the application of two examination approaches: SRIO and MRIO analyses. The latter one distinguishes emission intensities of imports and domestic production, which is a feature of international trade that has not received enough attention in the previous literature.

2 Methodology

This chapter adopts input–output methodology to calculate embodied emissions and to further examine whether China has been transferring CO_2 emissions to Asian countries through bilateral trade or has been receiving overseas CO_2 emissions. The literature has applied various methodologies to evaluate the interaction between global business and the environment, such as CGE (Yang, 2001) and econometric models (Chen et al., 2011). However, use of the econometric models may involve the endogeneity of explanatory variables. In addition, the model may test for only a single country and may lack data for developing countries. One of the advantages of input–output (IO) analysis is that it does not depend on the availability of long-term series data to track emissions. Moreover, it can also distinguish the demand for various fuel types in economic sectors that show the interrelation of production sectors in the economy. Computer generated equilibrium models can also become the extension of IO models. However, the disadvantage of CGE is the complexity of their computation and the validation difficulty. Therefore, the IO approach can be considered as appropriate.

We further applied both the SRIO and MRIO approaches to cover the importance of intermediate goods and services in this chapter.

2.1 The structure of the single-region input–output table

The structure of an SRIO table is shown in Figure 11.1. The vector $\mathbf{x}_r$ represents the total input (output) for all sectors in region r. The matrix $\mathbf{A}_r\widehat{\mathbf{x}_r}$ displays the flow between domestic sources (rows) and domestic destinations (columns) by sectors in region r and the import intermediate demand. The

	Intermediate demand	Final demand	Total output
Intermediate input	$\mathbf{A}_r\widehat{\mathbf{x}_r}$	$\mathbf{y}_r$	$\mathbf{x}_r$
Value added	$\mathbf{v}_r$		
Total input	$\mathbf{x}_r'$		

Figure 11.1 Structure of a single-region input–output table in region *r*.
Source: Authors.

matrix $\mathbf{y}_r$ represents the final demand for goods and services in region r. The matrix $\mathbf{V}_r$ represents the value added in region r.

2.2 The structure of the multiple-region input–output table

The structure of an MRIO table is shown in Figure 11.2. Compared with that of the SRIO table, the total input (output) for all sectors is expanded to all k regions; e.g., $\mathbf{x}_k$ represents the total input (output) for all sectors in region k.

The intermediate demand matrix is expanded to all k regions; e.g., $\mathbf{A}_{k2}\widehat{\mathbf{x}_k}$ represents the input of intermediate goods and services for all sectors from region k to region 2. Similarly, the final demand matrix and the value-added matrix are also expanded to all k regions; e.g., $\mathbf{y}_{k2}$ represents the input of final products and services for all sectors from region k to region 2, and $\mathbf{v}_k$ represents the value added in region k.

2.3 Analysis by a single-region approach

The emission coefficient of the ith sector in the rth region, c_{ir}, is formulated in Equation 11-1.

$$c_{ir} = p_{ir} / x_{ir} \quad (i=1,\cdots, n;\ r=1,\cdots, k), \tag{11-1}$$

where p_{ir} represents the direct CO_2 emissions of sector i; x_i represents the total output of sector i; c_{ir} is one of the elements of the direct-emission coefficient vector $\mathbf{c}_r$ for all n sectors in region r; and $\mathbf{c}_r$ is also one of the elements of the direct-emission coefficient vector $\mathbf{c}$ for all n sectors in all k regions.

The total output $\mathbf{x}_r$ of all n sectors in region r meets the production balance in Equation 11-2.

$$\mathbf{x}_r = [\mathbf{I} - \mathbf{A}_r]^{-1} \mathbf{y}_r, \tag{11-2}$$

		Intermediate demand				Final demand				Total Demand	Total Output
		Region 1	Region 2	...	Region k	Region 1	Region 2	...	Region k	$\mathbf{y}$	$\mathbf{x}$
Intermediate input	Region 1	$\mathbf{A}_{11}\hat{\mathbf{x}}_1$	$\mathbf{A}_{12}\hat{\mathbf{x}}_1$		$\mathbf{A}_{1k}\hat{\mathbf{x}}_1$	$\mathbf{y}_{11}$	$\mathbf{y}_{12}$		$\mathbf{y}_{1k}$	$\mathbf{y}_1$	$\mathbf{x}_1$
	Region 2	$\mathbf{A}_{21}\hat{\mathbf{x}}_2$	$\mathbf{A}_{22}\hat{\mathbf{x}}_2$		$\mathbf{A}_{2k}\hat{\mathbf{x}}_2$	$\mathbf{y}_{21}$	$\mathbf{y}_{22}$		$\mathbf{y}_{2k}$	$\mathbf{y}_2$	$\mathbf{x}_2$
	⋮			...				...			
	Region k	$\mathbf{A}_{k1}\hat{\mathbf{x}}_k$	$\mathbf{A}_{k2}\hat{\mathbf{x}}_k$		$\mathbf{A}_{kk}\hat{\mathbf{x}}_k$	$\mathbf{y}_{k1}$	$\mathbf{y}_{k2}$	...	$\mathbf{y}_{kk}$	$\mathbf{y}_k$	$\mathbf{x}_k$
Value Added	$\mathbf{v}$	$\mathbf{v}_1$	$\mathbf{v}_2$	...	$\mathbf{v}_k$						
Total input	$\mathbf{x}$	$\mathbf{x}_1'$	$\mathbf{x}_2'$	...	$\mathbf{x}_k'$						

Figure 11.2 Structure of a multi-region input–output table.
Source: Authors.

where $\mathbf{A}_r$ represents the $n \times n$ intermediate input coefficient matrix of region r and $\mathbf{y}_r$ represents the final demand of region r. The final demand consists of household (and non-profit institutions serving households) final consumption, final government consumption, gross fixed-capital formation, changes in inventories, and the acquisitions less disposals of valuables.

Total CO_2 emissions induced by the export from region r to region s, $\mathbf{ct}_{rs}$, are formulated as

$$\mathbf{ct}_{rs} = \widehat{\mathbf{c}_r}\,[\mathbf{I} - \mathbf{A}_r]^{-1}\,\mathbf{y}_{rs} \ \ (r = 1, \cdots, k;\ s = 1, \cdots, k), \tag{11-3}$$

where the direct-emission coefficient vector in the rth region $\mathbf{c}_r$ is diagonalized; $\mathbf{y}_{rs}$ represents the goods and services exported from region r to region s, and both intermediate and final exports are included. Total CO_2 emissions induced by the imported goods of region r from region s can be calculated in Equation 11-4, which is similar to that of Dietzenbacher and Mukhopadhyay (2007):

$$\mathbf{ct}_{sr} = \widehat{\mathbf{c}_r}\,[\mathbf{I} - \mathbf{A}_r]^{-1}\,\mathbf{y}_{sr} \ \ (r = 1, \cdots, k;\ s = 1, \cdots, k), \tag{11-4}$$

where $\mathbf{y}_{sr}$ represents the export of final demands from region s to region r. However, in this equation, the direct-emission coefficient vector in the r th region $\mathbf{c}_r$ is utilized, which means Dietzenbacher and Mukhopadhyay (2007) assumed that imported goods from the rest of the world have the same technology as that of region r. Thus, the result indicates that the total CO_2 is avoided in region r through its imports. This estimation approach is limited by the data access at the time and may lead to large uncertainties in results. This can be improved with Equation 11-5, where total CO_2 emissions induced by importing from region s to region r can also be calculated by

$$\mathbf{ct}_{sr}^{*} = \widehat{\mathbf{c}_s}\left[\mathbf{I} - \mathbf{A}_s\right]^{-1} \mathbf{y}_{sr} \quad (r = 1, \cdots, k;\ s = 1, \cdots, k), \tag{11-5}$$

where the direct-emission coefficient vector in region s, $\mathbf{c}_s$, is utilized.

In this chapter, both intensity vectors, namely, the vector of the receiving regions of the imported goods (used in $\mathbf{ct}_{sr}$) and the vector of the original regions of the imported goods (used in $\mathbf{ct}_{sr}^{*}$), were examined.

The trade balance of total CO_2 emissions, tb_{rs}, if

$$tb_{rs} = \iota\left[\mathbf{ct}_{rs} - \mathbf{ct}_{sr}\right] < 0 \quad (r = 1, \cdots, k;\ s = 1, \cdots, k), \tag{11-6}$$

region r caused the rise of emissions in region s. Also, if

$$tb_{rs} = \iota[\mathbf{ct}_{rs} - \mathbf{ct}_{sr}^{*}] < 0 \quad (r = 1, \cdots, k;\ s = 1, \cdots, k), \tag{11-7}$$

region r avoided domestic CO_2 emissions by the imports from region s. In other words, region r caused the rise of emissions in region s.

However, in a one-country IO table, it is not possible to obtain the direct-emission coefficient vector $\mathbf{c}_s$ and matrix $\mathbf{A}_s$. Therefore, the second examination can be improved with a multi-region approach, as shown in the next section.

2.4 *Analysis through a multi-region approach*

The total output of all n sectors in all k regions, $\mathbf{x}$, meets the production balance in Equation 11-8:

$$\begin{bmatrix} \mathbf{x}_1 \\ \vdots \\ \mathbf{x}_k \end{bmatrix} = \left[\mathbf{I} - \begin{bmatrix} \mathbf{A}_{11} & \cdots & \mathbf{A}_{1k} \\ \vdots & \ddots & \vdots \\ \mathbf{A}_{k1} & \cdots & \mathbf{A}_{kk} \end{bmatrix}\right]^{-1} \begin{bmatrix} \mathbf{y}_{11} + \cdots + \mathbf{y}_{1k} \\ \vdots \\ \mathbf{y}_{k1} + \cdots + \mathbf{y}_{kk} \end{bmatrix}, \tag{11-8}$$

where $\mathbf{A}_{rs}$ represents the $n \times n$ intermediate coefficient matrix of region r's imports from region s. The final demands for goods and services are separated by country and sector in $\mathbf{y}$ (e.g., $\mathbf{y}_{1k}$ represents the $n \times 1$ vector of final goods and services from region 1 to region k).

The total CO_2 trade emissions in all *n* sectors in all *k* regions, $\boldsymbol{C^t}$, can be formulated as

$$C^t = \hat{\mathbf{c}}\left[\mathbf{I} - \begin{bmatrix} \mathbf{A}_{11} & \cdots & \mathbf{A}_{1k} \\ \vdots & \ddots & \vdots \\ \mathbf{A}_{k1} & \cdots & \mathbf{A}_{kk} \end{bmatrix}\right]^{-1} \begin{bmatrix} \widehat{\mathbf{y}_{11}} & \cdots & \widehat{\mathbf{y}_{1k}} \\ \vdots & \ddots & \vdots \\ \widehat{\mathbf{y}_{k1}} & \cdots & \widehat{\mathbf{y}_{kk}} \end{bmatrix}, \tag{11-9}$$

where the direct-emission coefficient vector of all *k* regions **c** is diagonalized.

The total CO_2 trade emissions between regions *r* and *s*, $\mathbf{C}^t$, can be considered as

$$\mathbf{C}^t = \begin{bmatrix} \mathbf{C}_{11}^t & \cdots & \mathbf{C}_{1k}^t \\ \vdots & \ddots & \vdots \\ \mathbf{C}_{k1}^t & \cdots & \mathbf{C}_{kk}^t \end{bmatrix}. \tag{11-10}$$

The trade balance of total CO_2 emissions from region *r* to region *s*, $tb_{rs}$is:

$$tb_{rs} = \imath[\mathbf{C}^t{}_{rs} - \mathbf{C}^t{}_{sr}]\imath' < 0 \; (r = 1, \cdots, k; \; s = 1, \cdots, k), \tag{11-11}$$

If $tb_{rs} < 0$, region *r* caused the rise of emissions in region *s*.

In this chapter, the *k* regions include Vietnam, Indonesia, India, Japan, and the rest of the world. All 26 *n* sectors include agriculture, mining and quarrying, and electrical and machinery, as shown in Table 11 Appendix, Sectors.

2.5 Data sources

This chapter employs the IO tables from the Eora Global Supply Chain Database (EORA database) for the years 2005, 2010, and 2015 with the basic prices. The EORA database is the global supply chain database that provides the time series IO tables for 190 countries with environmental satellite accounts. Currently, this database has three formats: the individual country IO tables, EORA26, and full EORA. EORA26 will be employed in this chapter because all industries were aggregated into 26 sectors. With the different numbers of industries or commodities among 190 countries, using EORA26 will be more suitable and easier to analyze and compare among country sectors.

The EORA database also offers both basic and purchase prices. However, in this research, the basic price will be used because it has already deducted the tax payable and has included the subsidy for one unit of goods and services output. This keeps the transaction value between producers and consumers as homogenous as possible. In terms of sector-level emissions, the study also includes the CO_2 emissions from EORA26 for the years 2005, 2010, and 2015.

Three data providers were used to create the CO_2 and greenhouse gas satellite account rows in the EORA database: the Emission Database for Global Atmospheric Research (EDGAR), the Carbon Dioxide Information Analysis Center (CDIAC), and the PRIMAPHIST model. However, this chapter used the Potsdam Real-time Integrated Model for the Probabilistic Assessment of Emission Paths (PRIMAP) to obtain the total CO_2 generated by sectors in all countries because it included the EDGAR and CDIAC data.

3 Results

3.1 National CO_2 emissions during 2005–2015

Figure 11.3 represents the total national CO_2 emissions of China and selected Asian countries from 2005 to 2015 based on the EORA database. In general, China is the highest CO_2 emitter among the six countries. China's carbon emissions increased from 6.2 billion t-CO_2 in 2005 to 10.8 billion t-CO_2 in the period from 2005 to 2015. National CO_2 emissions in Vietnam and India are relatively insignificant compared with China's; however, they increased significantly from 2005 to 2015. Vietnam's CO_2 doubled from 99 million t-CO_2 in 2005 to 203 million t-CO_2 in 2015. Similarly, India's emissions increased from 1.2 to 2.3 billion t-CO_2 in the same period. Emissions in Indonesia also increased by 36% from 2005 to 2015. The only decrease in total national CO_2 occurred in Japan, which had a 4% drop over ten years.

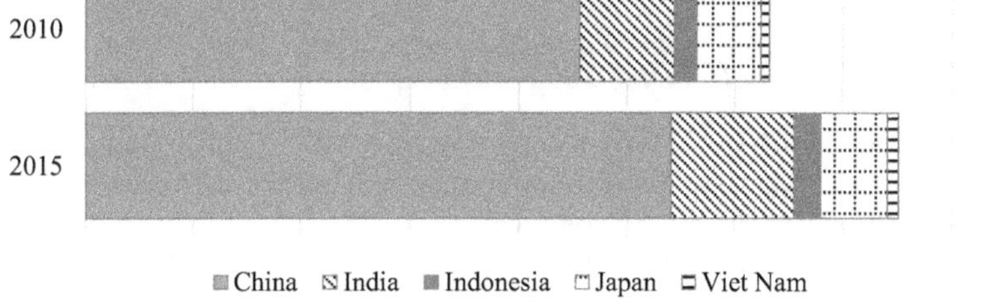

Figure 11.3 Total national CO_2 emissions, 2005–2015.
Source: EORA database.

Table 11.1 Direct-emission coefficients of main industrial sectors in selected Asian countries (Unit: million t-CO_2/US$ billion)

	2005					*2015*				
	CHN	*IDN*	*IND*	*JPN*	*VNM*	*CHN*	*IDN*	*IND*	*JPN*	*VNM*
Agriculture	0.81	1.03	1.20	0.16	1.06	0.58	0.59	1.00	0.12	0.82
Fishing	0.77	0.84	0.83	0.15	0.97	0.58	0.55	0.95	0.10	0.47
Mining	1.35	1.12	2.22	0.18	2.49	0.63	0.70	1.40	0.08	2.66
Food	0.44	0.40	0.75	0.20	0.57	0.22	0.24	0.72	0.16	0.48
Textiles	0.71	0.41	0.79	0.25	1.38	0.40	0.29	0.75	0.23	1.75
Pet. & Chemical	1.07	1.61	1.03	0.17	0.67	0.48	0.60	0.73	0.10	0.45
Metal	0.99	1.44	0.99	0.15	1.31	0.32	0.49	0.56	0.08	0.58
Machinery	0.93	1.35	0.87	0.18	1.19	0.39	0.61	0.58	0.14	0.62
Transport Equipment	0.20	0.09	0.12	0.07	0.37	0.13	0.04	0.09	0.05	0.15
Other Manufacturing	0.91	0.86	0.90	0.18	1.51	0.52	0.47	0.65	0.14	0.71
Electricity	17.01	18.27	16.11	5.13	32.12	6.28	11.60	14.18	3.50	34.54

Source: The authors' calculations are based on the EORA database.

The direct-emission coefficients of the main sectors are shown in Table 11.1. The results were divided into the non-electricity sectors and the electricity sector from 2005 to 2015. Generally, the direct-emission coefficient slowed from 2005 to 2015. However, there are some differences in outcomes among these countries. Among the main sectors, the electricity sector has the highest emission coefficient, followed by the mining sector. Japan had a low direct-emission coefficient in both the electricity sector and the non-electricity sectors. In contrast, China, Vietnam, India, and Indonesia have a relatively large volume of emissions per monetary unit. However, China and India decreased their emission coefficients by year and by sector, but Vietnam tended to enhance its emission coefficients from 2005 to 2015, especially in the mining sector.

The emission coefficient expresses the volume of emissions per unit of GDP, the reduction of which can be interpreted as less pollution released per unit of GDP. Countries with small emission coefficients may have better technology or more efficient energy consumption than those with high coefficients.

3.2 Bilateral CO2 trade during 2005–2015

Table 11.2 shows the trade balance and corresponding embodied emissions between China and the selected Asian countries. The results are listed using both the SRIO and MRIO approaches.

According to the IO table, China was the net exporter of final demands to Vietnam, India, Indonesia, and Japan in both selected years. Following a similar pattern, the emissions that China transferred to Vietnam, India, Indonesia, and Japan through the export of final demands also overweighed

Table 11.2 China's bilateral trade with selected Asian countries and the corresponding embodied emissions using the single-region I-O (SRIO) and multi-region I-O (MRIO) approach

	Bilateral trade, Unit: US$ billion							
	2005				*2015*			
	VNM	*IDN*	*IND*	*JPN*	*VNM*	*IDN*	*IND*	*JPN*
CHN's export to	0.9	2.3	3.1	49.4	5.2	9.3	12.9	99.0
CHN's import from	0.4	0.9	0.5	16.3	0.9	5.9	3.1	53.1
	Bilateral CO_2 trade (SRIO base), Unit: million t-CO_2							
	2005				*2015*			
	VNM	*IDN*	*IND*	*JPN*	*VNM*	*IDN*	*IND*	*JPN*
CHN's export to	1.7	4.6	7.2	105.2	4.7	9.1	14.6	105.6
CHN's import from	0.5	0.2	0.8	4.7	1.4	0.3	4.3	12.0
	Bilateral CO_2 trade (MRIO base), Unit: million t-CO_2							
	2005				*2015*			
	VNM	*IDN*	*IND*	*JPN*	*VNM*	*IDN*	*IND*	*JPN*
CHN's export to	1.9	5.1	8.2	116.3	5.1	9.8	15.9	113.5
CHN's import from	0.6	1.1	0.9	8.1	1.6	3.4	4.7	20.4

Source: The authors' calculations are based on the EORA database.

those that arrived through imported goods. The gaps between the bilateral emission export and import between China and Japan (105.6 vs. 12.0 million t-CO_2 by the SRIO approach or 113.5 vs. 20.4 million t-CO_2 by the MRIO approach) were far larger than the gaps between the bilateral export and import (US$99.0 billion vs. US$53.1 billion). China has been exporting more "dirty goods" (pollution-intensive goods) to Japan.

Comparing the results in 2005 and 2015, the emissions that China transferred to Vietnam, India, and Indonesia largely increased (by 176.5%, 97.8%, and 102.8%, respectively, using the SRIO approach). The bilateral emissions exported from China to Japan over those ten years remained nearly the same. On the other hand, the emissions that China imported from Vietnam, India, and Japan largely increased (by 180.0%, 437.5%, and 155.3%, respectively, using the SRIO approach). The increase in bilateral emissions imported from Indonesia to China during those ten years was slight.

When the results of the SRIO and MRIO approaches are compared, the bilateral emission trade results calculated by the MRIO approach are larger than the results calculated by the SRIO approach. All indirect emissions, namely, the emissions generated in the domestic production activities in all sectors, are considered. Moreover, under the SRIO approach, the emissions that China transferred to Japan slightly increased from 105.2 to 105.6 million t-CO_2; however, under the MRIO approach, such an increase turned into a slight decrease from 116.3 to 113.5 million t-CO_2. The SRIO approach, without considering intermediate imports and indirect domestic emissions, underestimated such growth. This can only be revealed by conducting the MRIO approach.

The difference in total net bilateral CO_2 trade results based on the single-region and multi-region approaches is shown in Figure 11.4.

Under both approaches, China was net exporting CO_2 induced by final demand exports to all selected countries in both 2005 and 2015, especially to Japan. Japan has been causing the rise in emissions in China. However, the number has decreased from 2005 to 2015 (−6.9 million t-CO_2 by the SRIO approach and −7.4 million t-CO_2 by the MRIO approach). The rise in emissions in China caused by Japan has slowed. On the other hand, according to the results of this chapter, China has not been causing the emission rises in Vietnam, India, or Indonesia.

Emissions embodied per unit of export from China decreased from 2005 to 2015 with all the selected countries, as shown in Table 11.3. This indicates that more low-emission technologies have been adopted in the production activities in China over ten years. In 2005, in all selected bilateral trade partners, the emissions embodied per unit of exports from China were larger than the emissions embodied per unit of imports from Vietnam (1.8 vs. 1.3

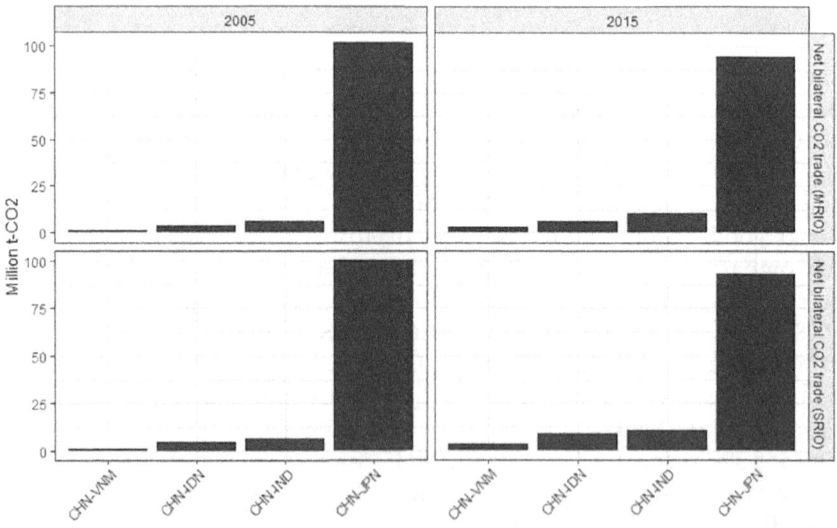

Figure 11.4 Total net bilateral emissions trade of China with selected Asian countries using the single-region input–output (SRIO) and multi-region input–output (MRIO) approaches.

Source: The authors' calculations based on the EORA database.

Table 11.3 Emissions embodied per unit of bilateral trade

	Emissions embodied per unit of bilateral trade, Unit: million t-CO_2/US\$ billion, Unit: million t-CO_2/US\$ billion							
	2005				*2015*			
	VNM	*IDN*	*IND*	*JPN*	*VNM*	*IDN*	*IND*	*JPN*
CHN's export to	1.8	2.0	2.4	2.2	0.9	1.0	1.1	1.1
CHN's import from	1.3	1.0	1.6	0.3	1.4	0.5	1.4	0.2

Source: The authors' calculations based on the EORA database.

million t-CO_2/US\$ billion) and India (2.4 vs. 1.6 million t-CO_2/US\$ billion). However, in 2015, the balance has reversed. The emissions embodied per unit of exports from China became smaller than the emissions embodied per unit of imports from Vietnam (0.9 vs. 1.4 million t-CO_2/US\$ billion) and India (1.1 vs. 1.4 million t-CO_2/US\$ billion). The structure of bilateral export from China to these countries has been switched to a smaller weight of pollution-intensive goods and services. If the China–Vietnam or China–India trade balance keeps growing according to this trend, China will cause emissions to rise in these countries. Moreover, on the import side, in all selected bilateral trade partners, the emissions embodied per unit of China's imports increased in the case of Vietnam. Vietnam was exporting more pollution-intensive goods and services to China from 2005 to 2015.

3.3 Bilateral CO2 trade at the sector level

The changes from 2005 to 2015 in bilateral CO_2 emissions based on the single-region and multi-region approaches are decomposed into sectors in this section. Figures 11.5–11.7 show the changes in the net trade balance of total emissions in the China–Vietnam, China–Indonesia, China–India, and China–Japan trade, respectively. There are three representative cases that show the diversity in the change patterns of net CO_2-embodied emissions. Because the net CO_2 emissions transferred from China to other countries were all positive, it can be interpreted that bilateral trade partners have caused the increase of CO_2 emissions in China. However, the trends—namely, the changes in net bilateral emissions from 2005 to 2015—follow different patterns.

Under both approaches, Figure 11.5 shows that China's net bilateral CO_2 export with Vietnam has largely grown from 2005 to 2015, especially in electricity supply, petrochemical products, and machinery sectors. The SRIO approach cannot cover the indirect emissions embodied in the domestic production activities induced by international trade, and therefore, such growth was underestimated compared with that under the MRIO approach.

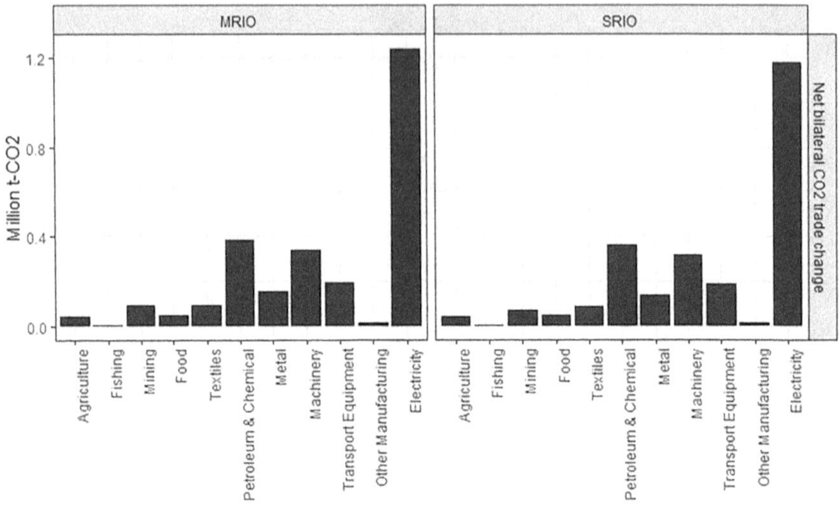

Figure 11.5 Changes from 2005 to 2015 in China's net bilateral CO_2 export with Vietnam at the sector level using the single-region input–output (SRIO) and multi-region input–output (MRIO) approaches.

Source: The authors' calculations based on the EORA database.

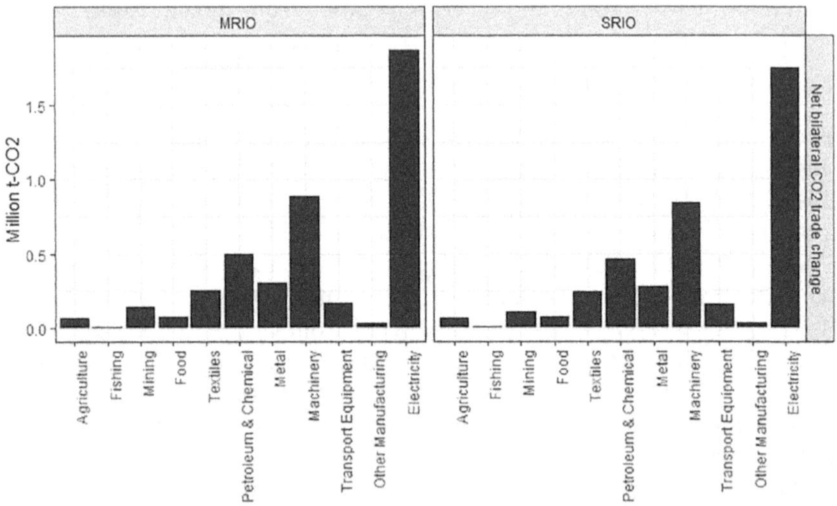

Figure 11.6 Changes from 2005 to 2015 in China's net bilateral CO_2 export with Indonesia at the sector level using the single-region input–output (SRIO) and multi-region input–output (MRIO) approaches.

Source: The authors' calculations based on the EORA database.

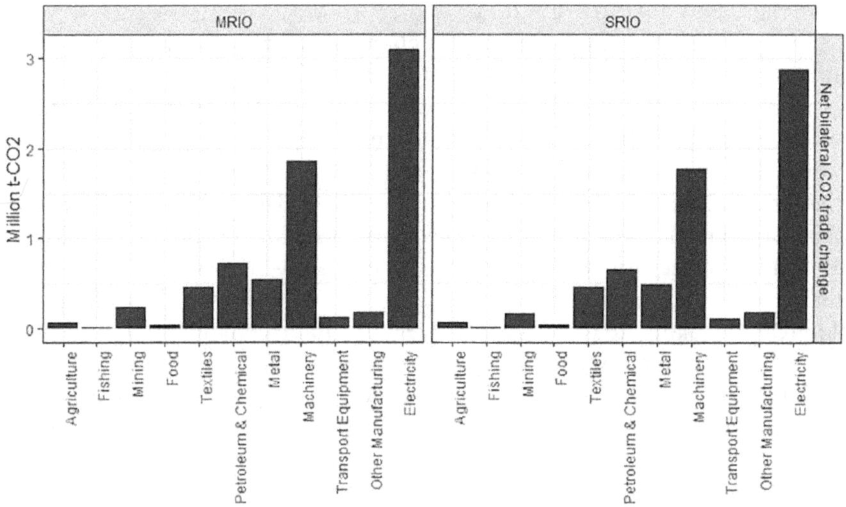

Figure 11.7 Changes from 2005 to 2015 in China's net bilateral CO_2 export with India at the sector level using the single-region input–output (SRIO) and multi-region input–output (MRIO) approaches.

Source: The authors' calculations are based on the EORA database.

In Figure 11.6 (China–Indonesia) and Figure 11.7 (China–India), similar to the China–Vietnam case, China's net bilateral CO_2 export has largely grown from 2005 to 2015. The top three sectors were the electricity supply sector, the machinery sector, and petrochemical products sector under both approaches.

In contrast to the cases for Vietnam, Indonesia, and India, China's net bilateral CO_2 export with Japan shrank in most sectors from 2005 to 2015, especially in the electricity supply, petrochemical products, and transportation equipment sectors. The net bilateral CO_2 trade increased in the textiles and other manufacturing sectors.

4 Discussion

In the bilateral CO_2 trade, China has been net exporting CO_2 through final demand exports (Figure 11.5, 11.6, and 11.7). Emissions embodied per unit of export from China decreased from 2005 to 2015 with all selected countries, indicating an improvement at the low-emission technology level in domestic production in China. However, the emissions embodied per unit of China's imports increased in the case of Vietnam. This implies that emission-intensive goods and services exported from Vietnam to China have increased during 2005–2015.

Such an increase can be related to changes in both the amount of bilateral trade (scale factor) and emission intensity (intensity factor). First, the exports of intermediate and final goods have significantly increased in many sectors, while the structure of bilateral export, especially the top five sectors were relatively stable from 2005 to 2015 (Table 11.4). In particular, mining, the largest export sector, increased from 1.71 to 3.82 US$ billion. Second, the change in the emission intensity varies by sector. While the agriculture and the food sector actually became less emission-intensive 2005–2015, the textile sector largely increased from 1.38 to 1.75 million t-CO_2/US$ billion. This can be related to the large increase in the intermediate input of electricity in the textile sector (third largest sector in 2015 with an input coefficient of 0.0326, shown in Table 11.4). The electricity supply sector was exactly the most emission-intensive sector in Vietnam, and the most emission-intensive sector in all countries discussed in this chapter. According to Chapter 2 in this book, the energy mix in power generation in Vietnam from 2005 to

Table 11.4 2005–2015 changes in Vietnam: input coefficients from the electricity supply sector and exports from Vietnam to China

2005		*2015*	
Direct-emission intensity of the electricity supply sector in Vietnam (million t-CO_2/US$ billion)			
32.12		34.54	
Input coefficients from the electricity supply sector (top 5 of all sectors) in Vietnam			
Top 5 sectors	Value	Top 5 sectors	Value
Mining	0.0457	Petroleum & Chemical	0.0367
Metal	0.0398	Wood and Paper	0.0360
Wood and Paper	0.0276	Textiles	0.0326
Other Manufacturing	0.0249	Metal	0.0315
Petroleum & Chemical	0.0246	Other Manufacturing	0.0258
Export as intermediate and final goods from Vietnam to China (top 5 of all sectors, unit: US$ billion)			
Top 5 sectors	Value	Top 5 sectors	Value
Mining	1.71	Mining	3.82
Agriculture	0.40	Agriculture	0.77
Machinery	0.21	Food	0.35
Textiles	0.18	Textiles	0.32
Petroleum & Chemical	0.10	Machinery	0.30

Source: The authors' calculations based on the EORA database.
Note: The input coefficient from the electricity supply sector refers to the monetary unit of electricity intermediate input to produce one unit of final product in each sector.

2015 has changed from hydropower to natural gas and then to coal. The ratio of coal power in installed capacity rose from 20% to around 35% in the 2005–2015 period. Driven by both bilateral trade amount (scale factor) and emission intensity (intensity factor), emission-intensive goods and services exported from Vietnam to China increased during 2005–2015.

China's net CO_2 export largely increased in its trade with Vietnam and Indonesia in 2015 (especially in the electricity supply, petrochemical products, and machinery sectors) compared with 2005. On the other hand, it shrank in the trade with Japan (especially in petrochemical products and transportation equipment). Considering China's growing net export of final goods and services during 2005–2015 in these three countries, the shrink of net CO_2 export to Japan can be more related to the decrease in domestic emission intensity in China (intensity factor) than changes in export scale (scale factor). As shown in Table 11.5, the direct-emission intensity of the electricity supply sector in China has dropped from 17.01 to 6.28 million t-CO_2/US$ billion. In fact, during 2005–2015, the standard coal consumption for power supply in large thermal power plants (above 6000 kW capacity) in China decreased from 370 to 313 g/kWh (China Electricity Council, 2017). Benefiting from the green power generation mix, the emission intensity of the petroleum and

Table 11.5 2005–2015 changes in China: input coefficients from the electricity supply sector and exports from China to Japan

2005		*2015*	
Direct-emission intensity of the electricity supply sector in China (million t-CO_2/US$ billion)			
17.01		6.28	
Input coefficients from the electricity supply sector (top 5 of all sectors) in China			
Top 5 sectors	Value	Top 5 sectors	Value
Mining	0.0669	Mining	0.0367
Metal	0.0588	Petroleum & Chemical	0.0360
Petroleum & Chemical	0.0566	Metal	0.0326
Post & Tele	0.0357	Wood and Paper	0.0315
Wood and Paper	0.0329	Education & Health	0.0258
Export as intermediate and final goods from China to Japan (top 5 of all sectors, unit: US$ billion)			
Top 5 sectors	Value	Top 5 sectors	Value
Textiles	24.77	Textiles	46.83
Machinery	17.86	Machinery	39.86
Mining	11.79	Petroleum & Chemical	22.17
Petroleum & Chemical	9.75	Food	16.36
Food	8.98	Transport	12.41

Source: The authors' calculations based on the EORA database.
Note: The input coefficient from the electricity supply sector refers to the monetary unit of electricity intermediate input to produce one unit of final product in each sector.

chemical sector in China also largely decreased, leading to a shrink of its net CO_2 export to Japan. It is also worth noting that, the share of mining goods exports from China to Japan dropped in 2015 compared to 2005 (11.2%–5.8%) as shown in Table 11.5, indicating the contribution of changes in trade structure to the reduction in China's CO_2 exports.

These results provide two implications. First, the result of domestic sector-level emission intensity can reveal which sectors generate higher emissions and pollutants. Second, an increasingly low-carbon power generation mix not only contributes to the national-level emission reduction directly but also helps other sectors reduce emissions (e.g., the petrochemical industry in China, the textile industry in Vietnam in a reverse way). Replacing domestic production with imports of emission-intensive goods does not help reduce global emission. Third, the change in export structure from China to Japan can reduce global emissions as long as it does not cause carbon leakage and relocation of non-power sectors from China to other countries.

Our analysis also shows that the results of the carbon leakage estimation can vary due to the applied approaches to some extent. The differences can be caused by the different approaches, the different definition of non-domestic emissions (e.g., emissions induced by the export of final goods and services in this paper, emissions induced by value added, Meng et al., 2013), and different effort-sharing principles (Höhne et al., 2014; van den Berg et al., 2020). In our analysis, MRIO estimates larger carbon leakages than SRIO. Seven methodologies (i.e., the IPCC, G8, UNDP, OECD, Garnaut, CCCPST, Srensen approach; Ding et al., 2010) have been proposed to establish an international standard, but no consensus has been achieved so far.

This chapter also has some limitations regarding the raw data of the IO tables and emission data. Although the tables from 2005 and 2015 were used in this chapter, they were all compiled using those years' purchase prices. The accuracy of the results could be improved if a table using comparable prices was used. In terms of the raw data on emissions, the results of emissions embodied in trade can be distinguished by sector but cannot be distinguished by energy carrier sources (e.g., by coal and oil) when the current data source is used. In other words, the current results of emissions from the mining sector refer to the emissions generated when coal is produced. It does not represent the emissions caused by the use or consumption of coal. Thus, the results of this chapter are limited in their ability to explore the impacts of coal industry investments.

5 Conclusions

In this chapter, we examined whether China has been causing the rise of CO_2 emissions among its bilateral trade partners (carbon leakage through trade from China to its bilateral trade partners). We selected four Asian countries (Vietnam, Indonesia, India, and Japan) and conducted an examination using two approaches (SRIO and MRIO analyses) in two target years (2005 and 2015).

Among all bilateral trade partners discussed in this chapter, the results show that from 2005 to 2015, the carbon leakage from Japan to China decreased. On the other hand, China increased the domestic CO_2 emission and their exports to Vietnam, Indonesia, and India from 2005 to 2015.

Our estimation shows that China's emissions embodied per unit of bilateral trade (namely, how much CO_2 emissions are generated per unit of bilateral goods and service trade) has been decreasing from 2005 to 2015. This indicates that more low-emission technologies have been adopted in domestic production activities in China over those ten years. We further looked into input coefficients from the electricity supply sector in all sectors. The improvement in power generation technologies and energy mix not only contributes to the national-level emission reduction directly but also helps other sectors reduce emissions (e.g., the petrochemical industry in China, the textile industry in Vietnam in a reverse way).

Our analysis also suggests using the MRIO approach to incorporate the indirect emissions embodied in the domestic production activities induced by international trade. This can avoid underestimation that would be caused by using the SRIO approach.

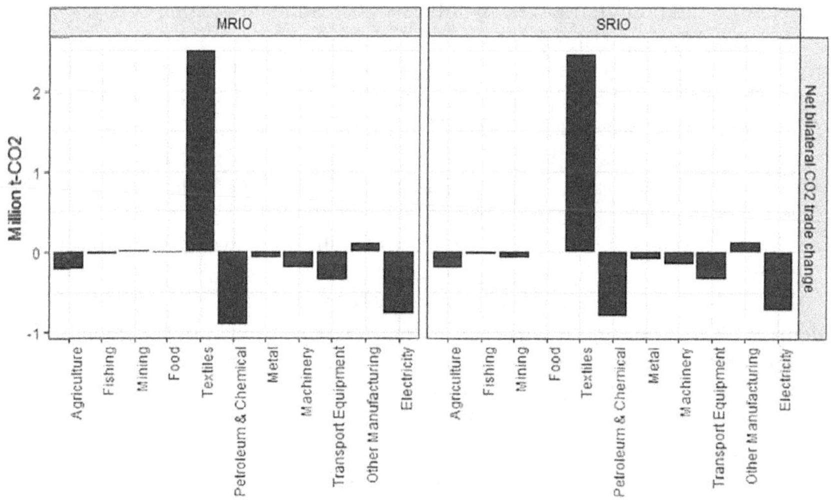

Figure 11.8 Changes from 2005 to 2015 in China's net bilateral CO_2 export with Japan at the sector level using the single-region input–output (SRIO) and multi-region input–output (MRIO) approaches.

Source: The authors' calculations based on the EORA database.

References

Chen, H., Zou, X., & Chen, Q. (2011). Export-oriented economy & environmental pollution in China: The empirical study by simultaneous equation model. *Energy Procedia*, 5, 884–889. https://doi.org/10.1016/j.egypro.2011.03.156

China Electricity Council. (2017). Annual Development Report on China's Electricity Industry, 2017. Beijing, China.

China Energy Group at Lawrence Berkeley National Laboratory. (2014). Key China Energy Statistics 2014. Lawrence Berkeley National Laboratory.

Cole, M. A. (2004). Trade, the pollution haven hypothesis and the environmental Kuznets curve: Examining the linkages. *Ecological Economics*, 48(1), 71–81. https://doi.org/10.1016/j.ecolecon.2003.09.007

Copeland, B., & Taylor, M. (1994). North-South trade and the environment. *The Quarterly Journal of Economics*, 109(3), 755–787. https://doi.org/10.2307/2118421

Dietzenbacher, E., & Mukhopadhyay, K. (2007). An empirical examination of the pollution haven hypothesis for India: Towards a green Leontief paradox? *Environmental and Resource Economics*, 36(4), 427–449. https://doi.org/10.1007/s10640-006-9036-9

Ding, Z. L., Duan, X. N., Ge, Q. S., & Zhang, Z. Q. (2010). On the major proposals for carbon emission reduction and some related issues. *Science China Earth Sciences*, *53*(2), 159–172. https://doi.org/10.1007/s11430-010-0012-4

Fan, X., Wu, S., & Li, S. (2019). Spatial-temporal analysis of carbon emissions embodied in interprovincial trade and optimization strategies: A case study of Hebei. *China. Energy*, 185, 1235–1249. https://doi.org/10.1016/j.energy.2019.06.168

Gill, F. L., Kuperan Viswanathan, K., Zaini, M., & Karim, A. (2018). The critical review of the pollution haven hypothesis. *International Journal of Energy Economics and Policy*, 8(1), 167–174.

Höhne, N., den Elzen & Escalante, D. (2014). Regional GHG reduction targets based on effort sharing: a comparison of studies. *Climate Policy*, 14:1, 122-147. https://doi.org/10.1080/14693062.2014.849452

Jayanthakumaran, K., & Liu, Y. (2016). Bi-lateral CO_2 emissions embodied in Australia–China trade. *Energy Policy*, 92, 205–213. https://doi.org/10.1016/j.enpol.2016.02.011

Mani, M., & Wheeler, D. (1998). In search of pollution havens? Dirty industry in the world economy, 1960 to 1995. *Journal of Environment and Development*, 7(3), 215–247. https://doi.org/10.1177/107049659800700302

Meng, B., Xue, J., Feng, K., Guan, D., & Fu, X. (2013). China's inter-regional spillover of carbon emissions and domestic supply chains. *Energy Policy*, 61, 1305–1321. https://doi.org/10.1016/j.enpol.2013.05.108

Shahbaz, M., Nasreen, S., Abbas, F., & Anis, O. (2015). Does foreign direct investment impede environmental quality in high-, middle-, and low-income countries? *Energy Economics*, 51, 275–287. https://doi.org/10.1016/j.eneco.2015.06.014

Taylor, B. R. C., & M. S. (2004). Trade, growth, and the environment. *Journal of Economic Literature*, XLII (March), 7–71

Temurshoev, U. (2011). Pollution haven hypothesis or factor endowment hypothesis: Theory and empirical examination for the US and China. *SSRN Electronic Journal*. https://doi.org/10.2139/ssrn.1147660

van den Berg, N.J., van Soest, H.L., Hof, A.F. et al. (2020). Implications of various effort-sharing approaches for national carbon budgets and emission pathways. *Climatic Change*, 162, 1805–1822. https://doi.org/10.1007/s10584-019-02368-y

Wiebe, K., & Yamano, N. (2016), Estimating CO_2 Emissions Embodied in Final Demand and Trade Using the OECD ICIO 2015: Methodology and Results, OECD Science, Technology and Industry Working Papers, No. 2016/05, OECD Publishing, Paris. https://doi.org/10.1787/5jlrcm216xkl-en

World Bank. (2011). GDP per capita (constant 2010 US$). https://data.worldbank.org/indicator/NY.GDP.PCAP.KD

Yang, H. Y. (2001). Trade liberalization and pollution: A general equilibrium analysis of carbon dioxide emissions in Taiwan. *Economic Modelling*, 18(3), 435–454. https://doi.org/10.1016/S0264-9993(00)00048-1

Table 11.A Sectors

No.	*Sector*	*Sector abbreviation*
1	Agriculture	Agriculture
2	Fishing	Fishing
3	Mining and Quarrying	Mining
4	Food & Beverages	Food
5	Textiles and Wearing Apparel	Textiles
6	Wood and Paper	Wood and Paper
7	Petroleum & Chemical	Petroleum & Chemical
8	Metal Products	Metal
9	Electrical and Machinery	Machinery
10	Transport Equipment	Transport Equipment
11	Other Manufacturing	Other Manufacturing
12	Recycling	Recycling
13	Electricity, Gas and Water	Electricity
14	Construction	Construction
15	Maintenance and Repair	Maintenance
16	Wholesale Trade	Wholesale Trade
17	Retail Trade	Retail Trade
18	Hotels and Restaurants	Hotels & Restaurants
19	Transport	Transport
20	Post and Telecommunications	Post & Tele
21	Financing	Financing
22	Public Administration	Public Administration
23	Education, Health and Other Services	Education & Health
24	Private Households	Private Households
25	Others	Others
26	Re-export & Re-import	Re-export & Re-import

Source: EORA database.

Part IV

Countermeasures and future challenges

12 Implications of East Asia electricity market integration on Southeast Asian economies and CO_2 emissions

Budy P. Resosudarmo and Yuventus Effendi

1 Introduction

In recent decades, there have been significant increases in electricity consumption around the world, including in the Southeast Asian region. In general, developing countries such as Vietnam and Indonesia had a remarkable increase in electricity consumption per capita from 2000 to 2015. Thus, trends indicate that in the next few years, electricity consumption would continue increasing in the Southeast Asian region. These increasing demands for electricity have been driven by the ongoing development of Southeast Asian economies, in particular, industrialization, access to electricity, and increasing household income (International Energy Agency, 2018).

Industrialization has been an important driver of electricity consumption as most industrial sectors are electricity intensive. In many countries, the industrial sector has been the largest electricity consumer of electricity. In 2010, for example, the global industrial sector accounted for approximately 74% of the total electricity consumption in that year (Wu et al., 2013). Increased access to electricity is another factor affecting the increasing electricity consumption. The number of people gaining access to electricity around the world has increased significantly since the mid-2000s, including in Southeast Asia. On average, approximately 50 million people every year had access to electricity for the first time between 2010 and 2017 (International Energy Agency, 2018). The third important factor is that as household incomes increase, their electricity demands increase as well. This is because of owning more household electric appliances, such as air conditioning and water heater appliances (Wolfram et al., 2012). Therefore, since the early 2000s, energy/electricity security has been an important issue in Southeast Asian countries (Nurdianto and Resosudarmo, 2016).

At the same time, CO_2 emissions have also become a concern among Southeast Asian countries. Figure 12.1 shows that Southeast Asia has been among the top CO_2 emitters globally. CO_2 emissions from Southeast Asian countries are still among the largest, even if only emissions from fuel combustion activities are taken into consideration. The electricity sector is among the largest contributors to CO_2 emissions from fuel combustion

DOI: 10.4324/9781003190905-16

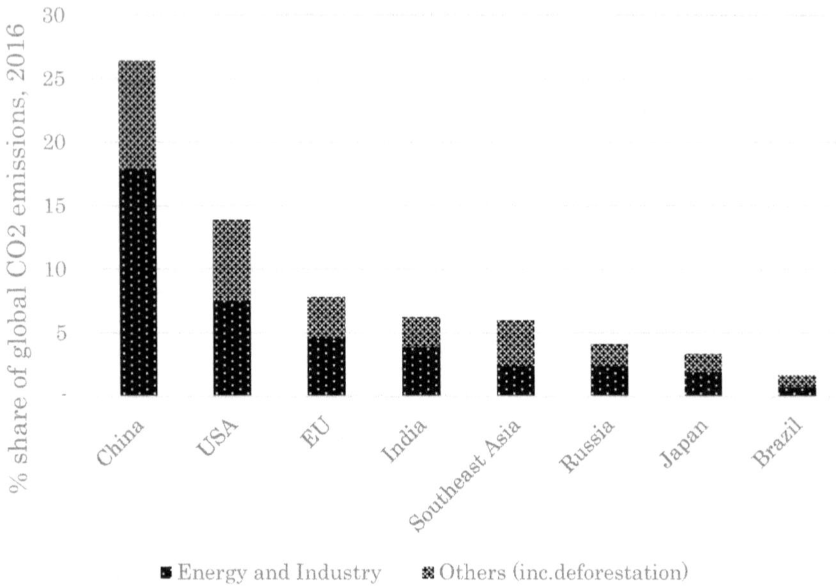

Figure 12.1 Top global CO_2 emitters.
Note: USA = United States of America; EU = European Union.
Source: World Resources Institute (2020).

activities. To improve electricity security as well as manage CO_2 emissions in the near future has been the topic of discussion in the region (Resosudarmo et al., 2021).

In order to improve electricity security and reduce CO_2 emissions in Southeast Asia, two broad ideas can be considered. First, more investments in renewable electric power plants would certainly mitigate CO_2 emissions. However, it is not yet clear whether it will significantly improve electricity security, efficient use of electricity, and economic development in the region. Second, regional electricity market integration is expected to improve electricity security. Countries either with surplus or capable of producing cheaper electricity would be able to supply neighboring countries in need. New investments on power plants in one country should, in theory, benefit other countries in the region as long as these countries are inter-connected. Hence, investments in the electricity sector would be more efficient. However, whether regional electricity market integration would lower the region's CO_2 emissions and economic development is an empirical question. In other words, what would the overall impact of economic activities and CO_2 emission leakage and relocation due to this regional electricity market integration on the region's CO_2 emissions and economic development.

Although studies on the impact of investments on renewable electric power plants on the economy have been available (Denholm et al., 2012;

Barbosa et al., 2017; Lilliestam et al., 2018), there is much less literature on the impacts of regional electricity market integration on the economy and the environment. Dahlke (2020) assesses the impacts of integrating energy market on energy prices and emissions in the Western US, and Newbery et al. (2016) analyze the impact of electricity market integration on the efficiency of the electricity trading system in European.

This chapter is different from the aforementioned studies, as it analyzes the impact of regional electricity market integration on both the economy and CO_2 emissions. This chapter uses the concept of East Asia electricity market integration and the regional electricity market integration and examines the impact of this integration on macroeconomic indicators, such as gross domestic product (GDP), sectoral outputs, and factor incomes; socioeconomic indicators, such as poverty incidence and income distribution; and CO_2 emissions in each Southeast Asia country.

To achieve the objective, this chapter develops an inter-regional social accounting matrix for East Asia (IRSAM-East Asia). It then derives an inter-regional constrained fixed price multiplier method to be able to analyze the impact of electricity market integration on the economy (Resosudarmo and Thorbecke, 1996; Hartono and Resosudarmo, 2008). To simulate the impact of economic changes on household incomes, household income microsimulation models for each Southeast Asian country are then constructed and utilized. Finally, sectoral CO_2 emission models are used to simulate impact of these economic changes on the level of emissions from Southeast Asian countries.

2 Regional electricity market integration

Regional electricity (or energy) market integrations, although not many, have been available throughout the world. An example is the Nord Pool, a trading electricity power market institution—initially—among the Nordic countries (Norway, Sweden, Finland, and Denmark)[1] and the Trilateral Market Coupling, a trading electricity power market institution—initially—among several Western Europe countries (France, Belgium, the Netherlands, Germany, and Luxemburg; Glachant, 2010). Since the establishment of these two electricity market integration institutions, members have been increasing.

The discussion on the possibilities to integrate electricity markets in East Asia region has been ongoing for a while. The first step toward this integration was an energy agreement between Thailand and the Lao PDR in the early 1970s. In 1981, Southeast Asian countries, which are members of the Association of Southeast Asian Nations (ASEAN),[2] agreed to establish an ASEAN Power Utility Authority, followed by having an ASEAN Energy Cooperation Agreement in 1986 (Shi and Kimura, 2010). Additionally, the progress in establishing East Asia electricity market integration has been relatively slow (Wu et al., 2013). Nevertheless, in 2005, during the East Asia

Summit, East Asian countries and Australia and New Zealand signed an initiative for Energy Market Integration (EMI). At almost the same time, ASEAN member countries attempted to establish a single market community within ASEAN members, similar to the European Union, including energy market (Wu et al., 2013; Nurdianto and Resosudarmo, 2016). Although there is no clear progress on the integrated energy market including the electricity market in East Asia until the writing of this chapter, several researchers are still optimistic that this integration would be happening in the next several decades (ERIA, 2014); their perspective is supported by incremental electricity integrations that keep taking place. For example, in 2019, Vietnam integrated its electricity system with those of Laos and Thailand. Discussions are underway on the possibility that Australia could export its green electricity in the near future (Garnaut, 2019). Therefore, this chapter focuses on the electricity market integration issue in the East Asian region as defined during the 2005 East Asia Summit, which covers not only Southeast Asian countries, China, Japan, and South Korea but also Australia and India.

3 Simulation scenarios

There are three main simulations in this chapter. The first simulation (SIM1) assumes that there is an increase in the output of the electricity sector in China by 10%.[3] The second simulation (SIM2) assumes an increase in the electricity output occurred in Indonesia by 10%. The last main simulation (SIM3) is assuming a 10% increase in the output of Vietnamese electricity sector.[4]

For each of these main simulations, this chapter considers three distinct situations. The first situation is the Business as Usual (BAU) situation in which there is no electricity market integration in East Asia (SIT1). This first situation mimics the current condition of the electricity market in East Asia, in which there is almost no connectivity between countries in East Asia. Thus, any increase in the electricity demand is fully fulfilled by the country itself.

The second situation (SIT2) is one where there is a fully integrated electricity market in East Asia that covers ASEAN member countries, Australia, China, Japan, India, and South Korea (also called as the East Asia electricity market integration). In this situation, it is assumed that any increase in electricity demand in a particular country is supplied by the country's domestic electricity production as well as electricity from other countries in East Asia. The electricity supplies from other countries would be through the inter-connected electricity transmission network across countries in East Asia. The contribution of each country as an electricity supplier is proportional to the electricity output of a particular country to total electricity output in the East Asia region. This second situation represents the aim of East Asia Energy Market Integration, which allows a fully integrated energy market among Southeast Asian countries, China, India, Japan, South Korea, and Australia.

The third situation (SIT3) is one where a fully integrated electricity market is only among Southeast Asian countries (i.e., the Southeast Asia electricity market integration). In this situation, any increase in a particular country is assumed to be supplied by the country's domestic electricity production and six Southeast Asian countries, namely, Indonesia, Malaysia, Thailand, the Philippines, Singapore, and Vietnam, and other ASEAN countries (as a group). This situation aims to capture the fact that Southeast Asian countries have been pushing to establish the ASEAN Economic Community, where an integrated energy market among ASEAN countries is one of their main targets (Nurdianto and Resosudarmo, 2016).[5]

Simulation results are presented in terms of relative to the outcomes under the SIT1. Any change in an indicator implies whether an integration in the electricity market in East Asia (SIT2), or only in Southeast Asia (SIT3), leads to better or worse off results compared to without any electricity market integration. In other words, the results presented in this chapter can be seen as the impacts of an integrated electricity market in East Asia (SIT2), or only in Southeast Asia region (SIT3).

4 Methodology

The first methodology utilized in this chapter is the inter-regional constrained fixed price multiplier method (Resosudarmo and Thorbecke, 1996, 1998).[6] This method can simulate a situation such that an increase in output (an electricity sector in this chapter) is supplied by domestic production or import. The method is as follows.

Figure 12.2 describes two regions (Region 1 and Region 2) inter-regional Social Accounting Matrix (IRSAM). Each region consists of production activities, factor inputs, and institutions such as households. Outputs of some

	Region 1		**Region 2**	**ROW**	**TOTAL**
Region 1	A_C^{11}	R^{11}	R^{12}	X_C^1	Y_C^1
	Q^{11}	A_{NC}^{11}	A_{NC}^{12}	X_{NC}^1	Y_{NC}^1
Region 2	Q^{21}	A_{NC}^{21}	A_{NC}^{22}	X_{NC}^2	Y_{NC}^2
ROW	l^1		l^2	t	Y_E
TOTAL	$(Y_C^1{}'$	$Y_{NC}^1{}'$	$Y_{NC}^2{}'$	$Y_E{}'$	

Figure 12.2 Structure of IRSAM with constrained sector.

productions in Region 1 are constrained $\left(Y_C^1\right)$ and others are unconstrained $\left(Y_{NC}^1 \; and \, Y_{NC}^2\right)$. The constrained sector in this chapter is the electricity sector, whereas other sectors are defined as unconstrained sectors. Also, there are exogenous accounts such as government, savings, and taxes, which are included in the rest of the world (ROW) column and row accordingly.[7]

Terms A_C^{11}, A_{NC}^{11}, R^{11}, and Q^{11} are matrices of expenditures among sectors within Region 1; A_C^{11} is among constrained sectors (electricity sectors in this chapter), A_{NC}^{11} is among non-constrained sectors, R^{11} is from non-constrained sectors to constrained sectors, and Q^{11} is from constrained sectors to non-constrained sectors. The term A_{NC}^{22} is a matrix of expenditures among sectors within Region 2. The terms A_{NC}^{12} and R^{12} are matrices of expenditures from sectors in Region 2 to sectors in Region 1. However, Q^{21} and A_{NC}^{21} are matrices of expenditures from Region 1 to those in Region 2. The terms l^1 and l^2 are leakages to the ROW, while X_C^1, X_{NC}^1, and X_{NC}^2 are vectors of injection from the ROW. Finally, t is a vector of exogenous not related to Region 1 nor to Region 2.

Figure 12.2 can be expressed mathematically as in equation (12-1).

$$d\begin{bmatrix} Y_C^1 \\ Y_{NC}^1 \\ Y_{NC}^2 \end{bmatrix} = \begin{bmatrix} A_C^{11} & R^{11} & R^{12} \\ Q^{11} & A_{NC}^{11} & A_{NC}^{12} \\ Q^{21} & A_{NC}^{21} & A_{NC}^{22} \end{bmatrix} d\begin{bmatrix} Y_C^1 \\ Y_{NC}^1 \\ Y_{NC}^2 \end{bmatrix} + d\begin{bmatrix} X_C^1 \\ X_{NC}^1 \\ X_{NC}^2 \end{bmatrix} \tag{12-1}$$

The matrices in equation (12-1) can be rearranged, following Hartono and Resosudarmo (2008) and Resosudarmo and Thorbecke (1996), and elaborated to depict the relationship in equation (12-2). This equation shows the impact of changes in outputs of the constrained sectors in Region 1 $\left(Y_C^1\right)$ as well as the changes of injections from the ROW to the non-constrained sectors in both Regions 1 and 2 to the outputs of the non-constrained sectors in both Regions 1 and 2 $\left(Y_{NC}^1 \text{ and } Y_{NC}^2\right)$ as well as the injection to Region 1.

$$d\begin{bmatrix} Y_{NC}^1 \\ X_C^1 \\ Y_{NC}^2 \end{bmatrix} = \begin{bmatrix} -R^{11} & I & -R^{12} \\ \left(I - A_{NC}^{11}\right) & 0 & -A_{NC}^{12} \\ -A_{NC}^{21} & 0 & (I - A_{NC}^{22}) \end{bmatrix}^{-1} \begin{bmatrix} -(I - A_C^{11}) & 0 & 0 \\ Q^{11} & I & 0 \\ Q^{21} & 0 & I \end{bmatrix} d\begin{bmatrix} Y_C^1 \\ X_{NC}^1 \\ X_{NC}^2 \end{bmatrix} \tag{12-2}$$

where $\begin{bmatrix} -R^{11} & I & -R^{12} \\ \left(I - A_{NC}^{11}\right) & 0 & -A_{NC}^{12} \\ -A_{NC}^{21} & 0 & \left(I - A_{NC}^{22}\right) \end{bmatrix}^{-1} \begin{bmatrix} -\left(I - A_{C}^{11}\right) & 0 & 0 \\ Q^{11} & I & 0 \\ Q^{21} & 0 & I \end{bmatrix}$ is called inter-regional constrained fixed price multiplier (IR-CFPM). Analyzing the impact of a change in constrained outputs on the non-constrained outputs using this multiplier is called the IR-CFPM method.

This IR-CFPM method is utilized to simulate the impact of an increase in electricity demand in a country in East Asia with and without an electricity market integration for the region or only for Southeast Asia on socioeconomic and environmental conditions among Southeast Asian countries. Important to note is the assumptions adopted under this method. First, it is assumed that prices are fixed and therefore do not change in any simulation. Second, integrating the electricity market does not incur any technical or administrative costs to any country. Third, how much electricity that a country would supply to other country's electricity demand under electricity market integration is exogenously determined.

The second methodology is the household income microsimulation method linking macroeconomic indicators in the IRSAM to the incomes of several different household groups, such that several household microeconomic indicators, such as poverty incidence, can be estimated. In the computable general equilibrium (CGE) model literature, the household microsimulation method usually has been utilized to construct the top-down CGE approach, that is, linking results from a CGE model to household micro indicators (Bourguignon and Bussolo, 2013; Yusuf and Resosudarmo, 2015; Nurdianto and Resosudarmo, 2016). This chapter offers a novel household income microsimulation approach on how to link an IRSAM to household incomes for different category groups. The two principles adopted are as follows. First, the total payment of production activities to production factors should be equal to the total income of all institutions such as household, government, and firm. Second, it is assumed that the average propensities to consume are unchanged. Therefore, the value of any element in IRSAM at row i and column j can be obtained by multiplying a particular element of average propensity to consume matrix with a total value of the corresponding column. Therefore, given new total values of outputs after a simulation, this assumption allows us to compute new total income values for different types of production factors (labor and non-labor incomes) related to urban and rural households available in the IRSAM. After computing new values of labor and non-labor income and utilizing equation (12-3), we can define total incomes for different household percentile c in urban or rural (ur) areas.

$$H_c^{ur} = \sigma_c^{ur} sl^{ur} \sum_v \sum_q \frac{N_c^{q,v}}{\sum_c N_c^{q,v}} lb^{q,v} + \varsigma_c^{ur} sh^{ur} \; inc\_sh_c^{ur} \sum_w \sum_q nlb^{q,w} \quad (12\text{-}3)$$

Equation (12-3) can be explained as follows. In each Southeast Asian country, households are grouped into 100 household groups, based on percentile of their incomes from the poorest to the richest, in urban areas and another 100 household groups in rural areas (Nurdianto and Resosudarmo, 2016). The index *ur* identifies whether a household group is in an urban or rural area. H_c^{ur} donates the total income of households in percentile c in the urban/rural areas.

Superscripts q and v denote production sectors in a region and labor types (skilled and unskilled labor). Term $N_c^{q,v}$ denotes the number of labor type v by sector q in household c. Therefore, term $\frac{N_c^{q,v}}{\sum_c N_c^{q,v}}$ is a sectoral labor share of household percentile c in sector q.

Furthermore, $lb^{q,v}$ is the total labor income type v in sector q and sl^{ur} is the share of total labor income of urban or rural households. Therefore, $\sigma_c^{ur} sl^{ur} \sum_v \sum_q \frac{N_c^{v,q}}{\sum_c N_c^{v,q}} lb^{v,q}$ is the total labor income of household group c in *ur* areas. Note that σ_c^{ur} is a constant scaling factors to adjust the value of total labor income from the household survey data, where all parameters in equation (12-3) are estimated from, into IRSAM value.

Superscript w denotes non-labor income types (land, natural resources, and capital). The term $nlb^{q,w}$ is non-labor income type w in sector q, and sh^{ur} is the share of total non-labor factor incomes for urban and rural households. Hence, $\varsigma_c^{ur} sh^{ur}\ inc\_sh_c^{ur} \sum_w \sum_q nlb^{q,w}$ is the total non-labor income of household group c in *ur* areas. Note that ς_c^{ur} a constant scaling factors to adjust the value of total non-labor income from the household survey data into IRSAM value.

After household income for all percentiles is computed in each Southeast Asian country, poverty incidence is estimated for both urban and rural areas following the method developed by Yusuf and Resosudarmo (2015). The third methodology is CO_2 emission models for all Southeast Asian countries enabling calculation of sectoral emissions from these countries. Coefficients of sectoral emission per unit output are estimated for these models.

The general procedure in analyzing the impact of an electricity market integration of East Asia on Southeast Asian economies is as follows. First, using the IR-CFPM method, as stated in equation (12-2), we observe the macroeconomic impacts of any changes in the electricity sectors in a country to other sectors in that country and in other Southeast Asian countries—particularly on production sector (industrial) outputs and labor and non-labor incomes.

Information on changes in labor and non-labor incomes is then inserted into the household income microsimulation models for Southeast Asian countries, as given in equation (12-3). Also, the changes of production sectoral outputs are inserted into the CO_2 emission models for Southeast Asian countries to predict the changes of total emission from the region.

5 Data

This chapter uses three datasets, namely, macro, micro, and CO_2 emission datasets. The macro dataset is the GTAP 9 Data Base, which is a global database describing bilateral trade patterns, productions, consumptions, as well as intermediate use of commodities and services among and within countries in the world. The main source of GTAP 9 Data Base is input–output tables for countries around the world, which is then combined with trade and other required data to form a global inter-country input–output table. Hussein and Aguiar (2012) claim that GTAP Data Base covers approximately 120 countries, which constitute approximately 98% of global GDP. The dataset is for the year 2011 and in million USD.

To construct the East Asia IRSAM, this chapter extracts and converts the input–output tables in the GTAP 9 Data Base based on McDonald and Thierfelder (2004) to become an IRSAM covering six Southeast Asian countries (Indonesia, Malaysia, Singapore, Thailand, Vietnam, and the Philippines) and the rest of Southeast Asian countries (i.e., Brunei, Cambodia, East Timor, Laos, and Myanmar as a group) as well as Australia, China, India, Japan, and South Korea. This chapter then restructures the IRSAM, so that the new structure is closely following those of Round (1985) and Resosudarmo et al. (2009).

The main distinct features of the East Asia IRSAM compared to GTAP Data Base is as follows. The East Asia IRSAM disaggregates the regional household account in the original GTAP into rural and urban households as well as firm and government accounts. In the original GTAP, the regional household account receives all income in a country and allocates the income into private expenditure, government expenditure, and savings–investment (McDonald and Thierfelder, 2004; Delpiazzo and Standardi, 2014). The main disadvantage of the regional household account concept is that there is no explicit connection among household, government, and saving–investment account. Thus, it cannot be seen that household is saving as well as paying income tax (McDonald and Thierfelder, 2004). The disaggregation of regional household account following Nurdianto (2011) and Delpiazzo and Standardi (2014) allows for richer specifications, in particular, inter-institutional transfers in each region (McDonald and Sonmez, 2004).

In the East Asia IRSAM, inter-institutional transfers from the government to households are in the form of social expenditures by the government by taking a percentage of social expenditure to GDP of each country. Government revenue is set up as a certain percentage of GDP for each country implying that the government could have a surplus or deficit budget. This feature does not exist in the original GTAP Data Base.

Table 12.1 Selected indicators of East Asian countries in IRSAM

	AUS	*CHN*	*JPN*	*IND*	*KOR*	*IDN*	*MYS*	*PHL*	*SGP*	*THA*	*VNM*	**XSE**
GDP (in million USD)	1,387,013	7,321,875	5,905,634	1,880,101	1,202,463	845,925	289,260	224,095	274,065	345,670	135,540	87,306
Production Factor (in million USD)												
Unskilled Labor	283,114	2,634,605	1,196,213	501,709	288,667	262,496	62,916	39,962	25,684	69,465	34,774	22,597
Skilled Labor	424,063	1,075,537	1,336,719	377,653	222,977	79,387	56,173	42,103	87,989	46,382	16,256	8,706
Non-Labor	506,111	2,966,695	2,296,768	856,281	535,534	465,919	157,040	132,219	140,201	194,592	60,964	56,003
Primary Energy Sectors (in million USD)												
Coal	51,189	150,156	108	11,050	225	33,580	160	401	0	717	3,995	25
Oil	17,797	122,491	540	23,892	3,426	33,680	17,625	591	117	7,314	11,054	5,875
Gas	13,693	834	2	3,085	367	15,927	8,580	4	0	2,970	96	6,152
Secondary Energy Sectors (in million USD)												
Electricity	41,336	291,461	237,714	116,028	51,118	16,631	10,190	7,435	8,002	12,834	16,933	1,896
PCP	45,939	599,692	365,381	281,925	193,142	54,084	35,568	14,440	73,102	70,207	8,399	1,732
GMD	3,194	6,755	2,442	8,925	388	7,377	5,393	857	12	8,298	2,190	905
CO_2 Emission												
Total Emission (in Mega tonne)	307	6,243	334	1,314	125	259	95	35	24	149	77	14
Emission Intensity (in kg per USD)	0.22	0.85	0.06	0.70	0.10	0.31	0.33	0.16	0.09	0.43	0.57	0.16
Intensity of Electricity (in kg per USD)	4.67	12.87	3.20	0.46	0.25	7.49	4.19	2.22	0.43	3.90	2.09	2.09

Note: Electricity = electricity sector, PCP = petroleum and coal products sector, GMD = gas manufactured distribution sector, Coal = coal mining sector, Oil = oil mining sector, Gas = natural gas mining sector.

AUS = Australia, CHN = China, JPN = Japan, IND = India, KOR = Korea, IDN = Indonesia, MYS = Malaysia, PHL = the Philippines, SGP = Singapore, THA = Thailand, VNM = Vietnam and XSE = Rest of Southeast Asian countries, i.e., Brunei, Cambodia, East Timor, Laos, and Myanmar.

To develop household income microsimulation models, that is, to estimate coefficients in equation (12-3), this chapter utilizes several household survey data across ASEAN countries. For Indonesia, this chapter uses the 2011 National Socio-Economic Survey (SUSENAS); the 2014 Household Living Standards Survey (VHLSS) is used for Vietnam; a combination of the 2012 Family Income and Expenditure Survey (FIES) as well as the 2012 Labor Force Survey (LFS) is used for the Philippines; and, finally, for Thailand, this chapter extracts the dataset from the 2011 National Socio-Economic Survey (SES). Due to data limitations, the sectoral labor share, as well as the income share of Malaysia, is assumed to be similar to those in Thailand. This chapter does not conduct any analysis on poverty incidence in Singapore and the rest of Southeast Asian countries. Furthermore, for Singapore, it is expected that there is no poverty in the country.

Finally, for CO_2 emission models, this chapter extracted CO_2 emission data, in the million tonne CO_2, by sector and by country available from the GTAP Data Base. For each sector, output-CO_2 emission intensity coefficients are calculated. These coefficients are then used to calculate the new CO_2 emission levels when there is a shock to the economy. Table 12.1 describes the selected macro and micro indicators of East Asian countries extracted from East Asia IRSAM and constructed from various survey data.

6 Results

In presenting the results, this chapter starts with describing macroeconomic impacts of an electricity market integration, in particular, changes in electricity and energy sectors, factor incomes, and GDP, on each Southeast Asian country (Tables 12.2 and 12.3). Then, it proceeds to show microeconomic impacts of an integrated electricity market on income distribution by percentile households and poverty incidence in each Southeast Asian country (Figures 12.3a–12.3d, 12.4a–12.4d, as well as Table 12.4). Finally, the consequences of an integrated electricity market on CO_2 emissions by Southeast Asian countries are presented (Table 12.5).

6.1 Macroeconomic impacts

Table 12.2 shows the sectoral and factor income impacts of an integrated electricity market in East Asia. The first panel denotes simulation results for SIM1 under SIT2, where an increase in electricity demand in China is supplied by all East Asian countries because of the East Asia electricity market integration. The results indicate that the electricity market integration magnifies the leakage of electricity demand growth in China to all Southeast Asian countries' electricity sectors. For example, electricity sector outputs of Indonesia and Vietnam are higher by approximately 4.24% and 3.87%, respectively, compared to the situation without any electricity

Table 12.2 Sectoral and factor income impacts on Southeast Asian countries (in %)

(%)	*SIT2*								*SIT3*							
	IDN	*MYS*	*PHL*	*SGP*	*THA*	*VNM*	*XSE*	*TOTAL*	*IDN*	*MYS*	*PHL*	*SGP*	*THA*	*VNM*	*XSE*	*TOTAL*
SIM1																
Secondary energy sources																
Electricity	4.238	3.863	3.880	3.860	3.863	3.869	3.863	3.950								
PCP	0.026	0.009	0.012	0.003	0.001	0.023	0.016	0.010								
GMD	0.082	0.170	0.267	0.038	0.187	0.235	0.041	0.154								
Primary energy sources																
Coal	-0.375	0.219	-0.214	-0.013	0.196	-0.311	0.030	-0.353								
Oil	0.019	0.004	0.009	0.003	0.000	0.004	-0.005	0.010								
Gas	0.113	0.112	0.039	0.016	0.106	0.027	0.157	0.120								
Factor incomes																
Land	−0.010	−0.007	0.003	0.000	−0.003	0.006	0.011	−0.003								
Unskilled Labor	−0.009	0.000	0.004	−0.002	0.003	0.019	0.011	−0.002								
Skilled Labor	−0.007	0.005	0.006	−0.002	0.005	0.039	0.010	0.002								
Man-made Capital	−0.020	0.006	0.010	−0.001	0.006	0.029	0.023	−0.002								
SIM2																
Secondary energy sources																
Electricity	−8.905	0.203	0.205	0.202	0.204	0.203	0.200	−2.398	−7.882	2.333	2.341	2.332	2.334	2.337	2.331	−0.107
PCP	−1.264	−0.041	−0.004	−0.139	−0.010	−0.005	−0.007	−0.316	−0.843	−0.023	0.002	−0.090	−0.004	0.007	0.001	−0.208
GMD	−3.110	−0.002	0.000	−0.005	−0.001	−0.002	−0.005	−0.939	−2.072	0.053	0.084	0.010	0.059	0.075	0.010	−0.585
Primary energy sources																
Coal	−0.769	−0.003	0.000	−0.186	−0.002	−0.007	−0.006	−0.665	−0.505	0.076	0.050	−0.120	0.061	0.014	0.016	−0.433
Oil	−0.858	−0.047	−0.008	−0.134	−0.010	−0.034	−0.082	−0.404	−0.572	−0.028	−0.001	−0.087	−0.004	−0.018	−0.054	−0.267
Gas	−0.308	−0.010	−0.003	−0.010	−0.005	−0.004	−0.004	−0.149	−0.205	−0.006	0.011	0.000	0.032	0.008	0.022	−0.092
Factor incomes																
Land	−0.082	−0.004	−0.001	−0.008	−0.004	−0.004	−0.006	−0.040	−0.056	−0.002	0.002	−0.004	−0.001	0.003	−0.001	−0.026
Unskilled Labor	−0.083	−0.003	0.000	−0.004	−0.002	−0.003	−0.005	−0.044	−0.057	−0.001	0.003	−0.002	0.001	0.008	0.000	−0.028

Skilled Labor	−0.084	−0.005	0.000	−0.003	−0.001	−0.003	−0.003	−0.022	−0.057	−0.002	0.003	−0.002	0.002	0.014	0.001	−0.013
Man-made Capital	−0.198	−0.006	0.000	−0.005	−0.002	−0.004	−0.012	−0.076	−0.138	−0.001	0.005	−0.002	0.002	0.011	−0.002	−0.051
Nat. Resource	−0.579	−0.030	−0.001	−0.071	−0.006	−0.017	−0.029	−0.314	−0.384	−0.017	0.004	−0.046	0.006	−0.003	−0.012	−0.205
SIM3																
Secondary energy sources																
Electricity	0.205	0.202	0.205	0.203	0.200	−8.901	0.191	−2.355	2.360	2.374	2.383	2.374	2.373	−7.860	2.366	−0.046
PCP	−0.003	−0.009	−0.003	−0.059	−0.033	−1.011	−0.013	−0.061	0.010	−0.001	0.003	−0.035	−0.019	−0.667	−0.003	−0.035
GMD	−0.003	−0.007	−0.003	−0.008	−0.010	−7.815	−0.042	−0.746	0.027	0.052	0.086	0.009	0.056	−5.174	−0.012	−0.449
Primary energy sources																
Coal	−0.008	−0.007	−0.004	−0.002	−0.010	−1.948	−0.018	−0.211	0.008	0.077	0.050	0.004	0.058	−1.288	0.014	−0.126
Oil	−0.005	−0.014	−0.004	−0.057	−0.032	−0.458	−0.010	−0.076	0.005	−0.005	0.001	−0.034	−0.019	−0.301	−0.005	−0.045
Gas	−0.004	−0.004	−0.003	−0.011	−0.018	−1.140	−0.015	−0.010	0.000	−0.002	0.012	0.000	0.024	−0.753	0.017	0.003
Factor incomes																
Land	−0.006	−0.018	−0.005	−0.100	−0.014	−0.552	−0.015	−0.061	−0.003	−0.011	−0.001	−0.066	−0.008	−0.364	−0.007	−0.039
Unskilled Labor	−0.004	−0.008	−0.004	−0.005	−0.009	−1.032	−0.013	−0.075	−0.001	−0.004	0.000	−0.003	−0.004	−0.682	−0.005	−0.048
Skilled Labor	−0.002	−0.006	−0.003	−0.005	−0.007	−1.671	−0.006	−0.086	−0.001	−0.003	0.001	−0.003	−0.002	−1.104	−0.001	−0.056
Man-made Capital	−0.004	−0.008	−0.004	−0.007	−0.010	−1.486	−0.012	−0.073	0.000	−0.003	0.003	−0.003	−0.003	−0.978	−0.002	−0.045
Nat. Resource	−0.006	−0.010	−0.004	−0.034	−0.021	−0.836	−0.013	−0.084	0.004	−0.004	0.002	−0.020	−0.003	−0.552	0.000	−0.049

Note:

Electricity = electricity sector, Coal = coal mining sector, Oil = oil mining sector, Gas = natural gas mining sector, PCP = petroleum and coal products sector and GMD = gas manufactured distribution sector.

Nat. Resource = natural resource capital.

IDN = Indonesia, MYS = Malaysia, PHL = the Philippines, SGP = Singapore, THA = Thailand, VNM = Vietnam, XSE = Rest of Southeast Asian countries (Brunei, Cambodia, East Timor, Laos, and Myanmar) and TOTAL = all Southeast Asian countries.

Table 12.3 Changes in Southeast Asian countries' gross domestic product changes (in %)

(%)	*IDN*	*MYS*	*PHL*	*SGP*	*THA*	*VNM*	*XSE*	*TOTAL*
SIM1								
SIT2	−0.017	0.005	0.008	−0.002	0.005	0.022	0.018	−0.003
SIM2								
SIT2	−0.157	−0.006	0.000	−0.004	−0.002	−0.004	−0.009	−0.064
SIT3	−0.109	−0.002	0.004	−0.002	0.002	0.009	−0.002	−0.042
SIM3								
SIT2	−0.004	−0.008	−0.004	−0.006	−0.010	−1.253	−0.012	−0.099
SIT3	−0.001	−0.003	0.002	−0.003	−0.003	−0.826	−0.003	−0.063

Note: IDN = Indonesia, MYS = Malaysia, PHL = the Philippines, SGP = Singapore, THA = Thailand, VNM = Vietnam, XSE = Rest of Southeast Asian countries (Brunei, Cambodia, East Timor, Laos, and Myanmar) and TOTAL = total Southeast Asia.

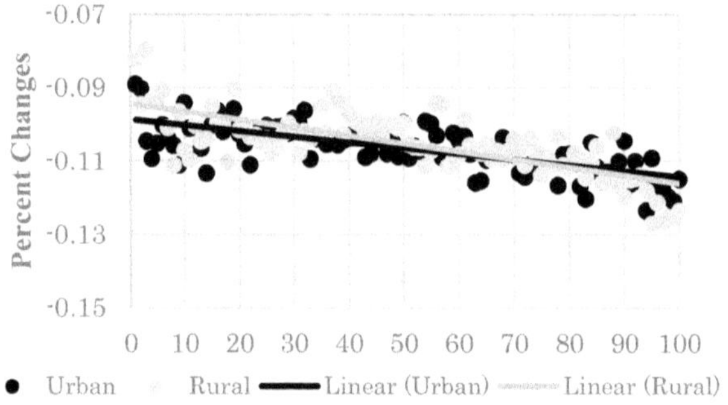

Figure 12.3a Percentage income changes of income percentile household groups in Indonesia under SIM2-SIT2.

Note: Horizontal axis lists income percentile household groups from the poorest to the richest.

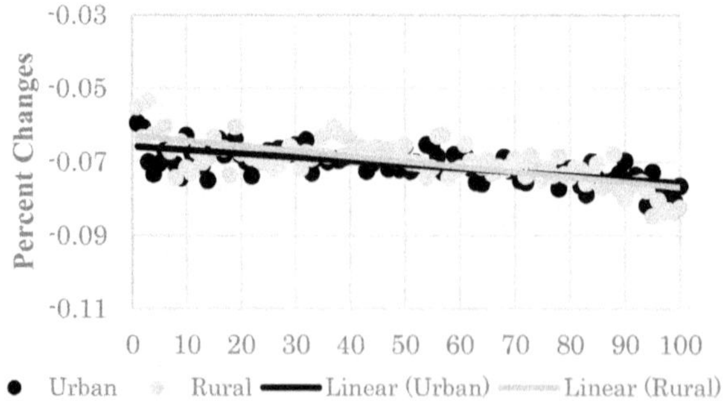

Figure 12.3b Percentage income changes of income percentile household groups in Indonesia under SIM2-SIT3.

Note: Horizontal axis lists income percentile household groups from the poorest to the richest.

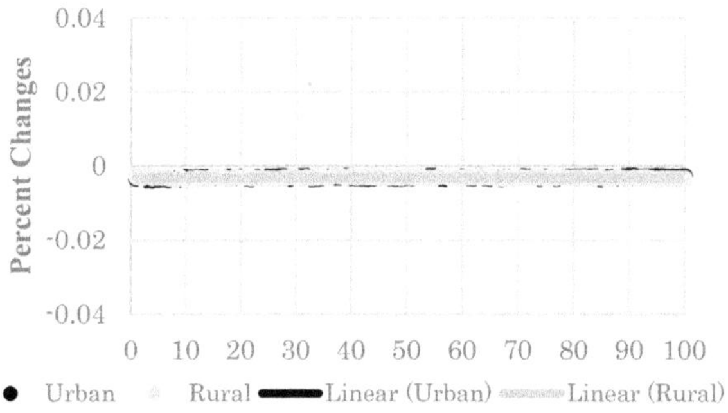

Figure 12.3c Percentage income changes of income percentile household groups in Indonesia under SIM3-SIT2.

Note: Horizontal axis lists income percentile household groups from the poorest to the richest.

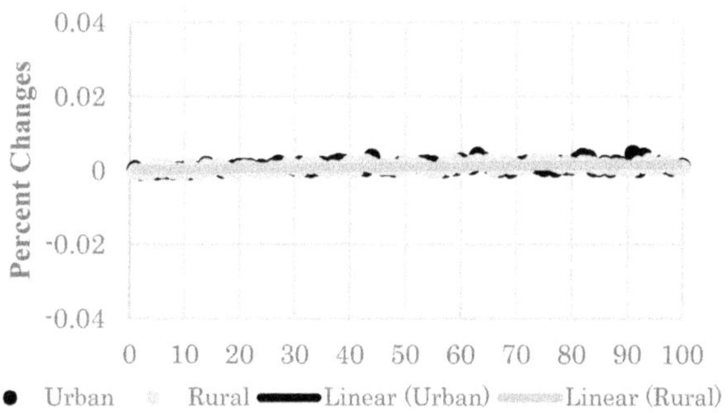

Figure 12.3d Percentage income changes of income percentile household groups in Indonesia under SIM3-SIT3.

Note: Horizontal axis lists income percentile household groups from the poorest to the richest.

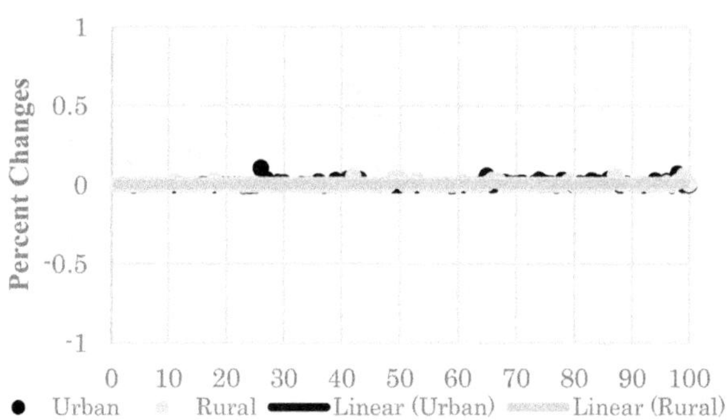

Figure 12.4a Percentage income changes of income percentile household groups in Vietnam under SIM2-SIT2.

Note: Horizontal axis lists income percentile household groups from the poorest to the richest.

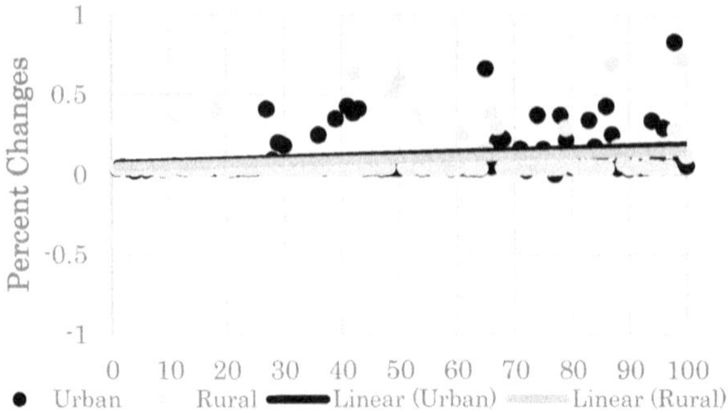

Figure 12.4b Percentage income changes of income percentile household groups in Vietnam under SIM2-SIT3.

Note: Horizontal axis lists income percentile household groups from the poorest to the richest.

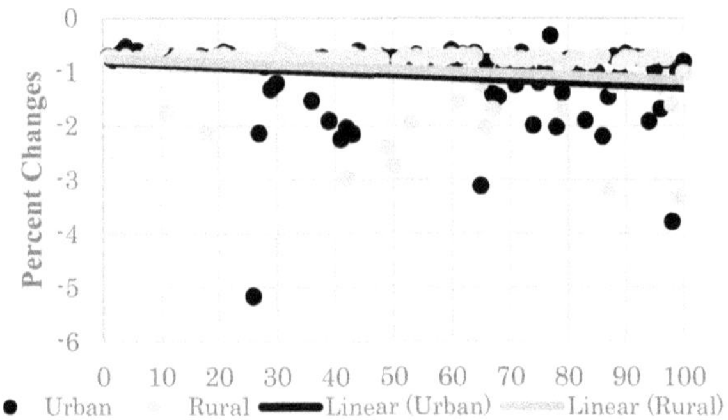

Figure 12.4c Percentage income changes of income percentile household groups in Vietnam under SIM3-SIT2.

Note: Horizontal axis lists income percentile household groups from the poorest to the richest.

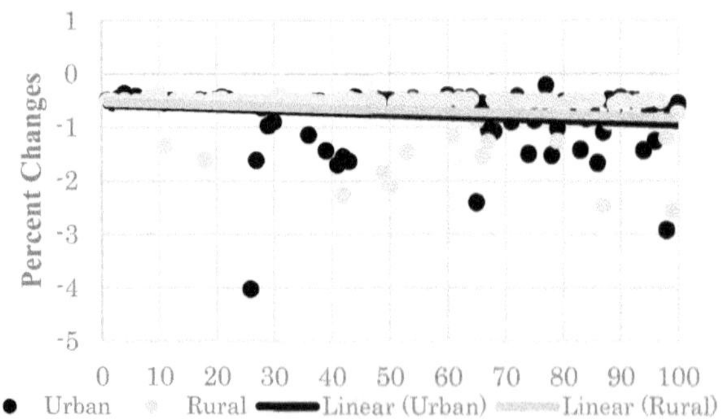

Figure 12.4d Percentage income changes of income percentile household groups in Vietnam under SIM3-SIT3.

Note: Horizontal axis lists income percentile household groups from the poorest to the richest.

Table 12.4 Changes in percentage of poverty incidence

		SIT2					*SIT3*				
(%)		*IDN*	*MYS*	*PHL*	*THA*	*VNM*	*IDN*	*MYS*	*PHL*	*THA*	*VNM*
SIM1	Urban	0.001	0.000	0.000	−0.001	−0.004					
	Rural	0.001	0.000	0.000	−0.009	−0.426					
SIM2	Urban	0.008	0.000	0.000	0.000	0.000	0.005	0.000	0.000	0.000	−0.002
	Rural	0.008	0.000	0.000	0.002	−0.010	0.005	0.000	0.000	−0.005	−0.181
SIM3	Urban	0.000	0.000	0.000	0.001	0.037	0.000	0.000	0.000	0.000	0.025
	Rural	0.000	0.001	0.000	0.008	1.587	0.000	0.000	0.000	−0.001	1.403

Note: IDN = Indonesia, MYS = Malaysia, PHL = the Philippines, SGP = Singapore, THA = Thailand, VNM = Vietnam and XSE = Rest of Southeast Asian countries (Brunei, Cambodia, East Timor, Laos, and Myanmar).

Table 12.5 Changes in CO_2 emissions (in percentage change)

(%)	*IDN*	*MYS*	*PHL*	*SGP*	*THA*	*VNM*	*XSE*	*TOTAL*
SIM1								
SIT2	2.042	1.747	1.835	0.561	1.315	1.788	1.350	1.724
SIM2								
SIT2	−4.734	0.084	0.097	0.026	0.067	0.093	0.064	−1.892
SIT3	−4.136	1.050	1.107	0.338	0.790	1.080	0.807	−1.155
SIM3								
SIT2	0.097	0.088	0.095	0.025	0.061	−4.456	0.053	−0.476
SIT3	1.143	1.072	1.126	0.344	0.800	−3.904	0.815	0.397

Note: IDN = Indonesia, MYS = Malaysia, PHL = the Philippines, SGP = Singapore, THA = Thailand, VNM = Vietnam, XSE = Rest of Southeast Asian countries (Brunei, Cambodia, East Timor, Laos, and Myanmar) and TOTAL = total Southeast Asia.

market integration in East Asia when the electricity demand in China increases by 10%.

An important result is lower outputs of coal and oil sectors in several Southeast Asian countries, such as in Indonesia, the Philippines, and Vietnam. This means that the opportunity to supply China with electricity could lower the countries' increase in exports of coal and oil to China in response to an increase in electricity demand in China. This situation, nevertheless, could potentially induce a higher level of CO_2 emissions from Southeast Asia, that is, CO_2 emission leakages from China to Southeast Asia.

Changes in electricity and energy outputs are then transmitted to changes in overall sectoral outputs and, finally to, factor incomes. Table 12.2 shows that in SIM1, the East Asia electricity market integration is mostly beneficial for skilled labor in Southeast Asia, except for those in Indonesia and Singapore. For unskilled labor and non-labor, the East Asia electricity market integration, in general, has lower benefits of an increasing electricity demand in China. Indonesia deserves particular attention because all factor incomes under an electricity market integration are lower than those without this integration. This indicates that it is more beneficial for Indonesia to export coal than electricity in responding to an increase in Chinese electricity demand. In general, in Indonesia, primary energy sectors create higher value-added (mostly rents to natural resource, land, and man-made capital) than the secondary energy sectors.

The next two panels in Table 12.2 show results of SIM2 and SIM3. These two simulations assume increasing electricity sector output values in Indonesia and Vietnam. Both countries have a relatively similar value of electricity outputs as indicated in Table 12.1. Therefore, the shocks are relatively comparable in terms of magnitude.

In the absence of electricity market integration, an increase in electricity demand in a country would be beneficial, in terms of having higher outputs of its electricity/energy sectors and higher factor incomes. An integrated electricity market in East Asia, or in Southeast Asia only, shares (or leaks) this benefit with other members where their electricity sectors are integrated. Therefore, electricity/energy outputs and factor incomes of the country where the increase in electricity occurs would not increase as high as when there is no electricity market integration.

As shown in Table 12.2 under SIM 2, the changes of electricity/energy outputs and factor incomes in Indonesia under electricity market integration situations (SIT2 or SIT3) are lower than those without electricity market integration (SIT1). A similar situation occurs in Vietnam under SIM3. It is therefore expected that the energy sectors and hence factor incomes of the country where the increase in electricity demand occurs would have a lower increase under an electricity market integration than under no electricity market integration.

For other countries receiving the spillover, it is difficult to determine what happens to them, that is, the sectoral and factor income dynamics are not straightforward to be described. For example, under SIM2, except for the Philippines, it seems more beneficial for Malaysia, Singapore, Thailand, Vietnam, and the rest of Southeast Asian countries to respond to the increase in electricity demand in Indonesia by supplying Indonesia with other goods and services than electricity. Almost all factor incomes in those countries have a lower growth under electricity market integration compared to without electricity market integration. A relatively similar situation occurs under SIM3.

Further examination of SIM2 and SIM3 shows that their impacts on energy sectors in Indonesia and Vietnam are different. Indonesia's electricity imports restrict growth of the country's crude oil (Oil) and coal outputs, while Vietnam's electricity imports restrict growth of the country's coal and natural gas. This difference in Indonesia and Vietnam is mainly because of the different energy sources for the countries' electricity sectors. Indonesia mostly uses oil and coal, while Vietnam mostly uses coal and natural gas.

Changes in factor incomes caused by the shocks in SIM1, SIM2, and SIM3 translate into changes in GDP for each country in the model (Table 12.3). These results highlight some possible answers to the following issue. Electricity market integration in East Asia is meant to increase electricity security in the region, because an increase in electricity demand in one country would also be supplied by other countries in the region. However, whether it could also serve as a potential channel leaking a positive shock in a country to others within the electricity market integration is less understood.

Table 12.3 shows that China's electricity growth under the East Asia electricity market integration is more likely to reduce the growth of total GDP of Southeast Asia compared to a situation without an electricity market integration (SIM1). Indonesia and Singapore would experience lower GDP, despite higher GDP in other Southeast Asian countries. In other words, an increase in electricity demand in China does leak to Southeast Asia inducing higher GDP growth for most Southeast Asian countries, because they now have an opportunity to supply China with their electricity, except Indonesia and Singapore.

When the increase in electricity demand is within Southeast Asian countries (SIM2 and SIM3), the GDP of almost all Southeast Asian countries' is higher without the existence of an electricity market integration. The existing trade structure within East Asia seems to be already in an optimal situation for most Southeast Asian countries. Shifting trade patterns within East Asia toward more electricity trades does not likely produce higher GDP among Southeast Asian countries.

When electricity market integration occurs only in Southeast Asia (SIT3), or the Southeast Asia electricity market integration, some countries could actually have higher GDP. The Philippines, for example, seems to be better off (i.e., having higher GDP) with the Southeast Asia electricity market integration when there is an increase in electricity demand either in Indonesia or in Vietnam. Thailand and Vietnam, as another example, seem to be better off when there is an increase in electricity demand in Indonesia under the Southeast Asia electricity market integration.

6.2 Distributional impacts

Table 12.4 presents how changes in rates of poverty incidence would be different between a situation with an electricity market integration and one without. In general, changes in rates of poverty incidence in Southeast Asian countries would be similar in both situations. When there is an increase in electricity demand in China (SIM1), rates of poverty incidence tend to be higher in Indonesia, Malaysia, and the Philippines under the existence of the East Asia electricity market integration than those when there is no electricity market integration. The opposite situation exists for Thailand and Vietnam.

When there is an increase in electricity demand in the Southeast Asian region, levels of poverty in the region in general are higher under an electricity market integration than those under no electricity market integration. Only a few cases under electricity market integration produce a lower poverty level. For example, the Southeast Asia electricity market integration would only lower poverty levels in Vietnam when there is an increase in electricity demand in Indonesia.

In terms of income distributional impacts of electricity market integration among household (in percentile) groups, the general pattern is as follows. The distributional impact of an electricity market integration tends be progressive; that is, the incomes of the rich would be more affected under an electricity market integration than those of the poor, in the country where electricity demand increases, in comparison to a situation where there is no electricity market integration. When the increase in electricity demand is in another member of the integration, the distributional impact of having an electricity market integration tends to be relatively flat among household groups. For example, in the case of Indonesia, progressive impacts seem to occur under an electricity market integration, when there is an increase in electricity demand in the country (Figures 12.3a and 12.3b). When the increase in electricity demand is in another country of the integration, the distributional income impact is relatively flat or slightly regressive (Figures 12.3c and 12.3d). A similar situation occurs in Vietnam: It is progressive in SIM3 (Figures 12.4c and 12.4d) and it is slightly regressive in SIM2 (Figures 12.4a and 12.4b).

The main reason for this could be because energy sectors tend to be man-made capital, land, and natural resource-intensive industries, and therefore most factor incomes go to owners of this capital, that is, richer household groups. Hence, energy sectors under electricity market integration could grow in response to an increase in electricity demand in the country in comparison to when there is no electricity market integration, and this situation affects richer household groups more than poorer household ones.

6.3 Environmental impacts

The impact of electricity market integration on CO_2 emissions in Southeast Asia is shown in Table 12.5. A growing electricity demand in China (SIM1) under the East Asia electricity market integration (SIT2) induces higher total CO_2 emissions from Southeast Asia; that is, creating CO_2 emission leakage from China to Southeast Asia. CO_2 emission leakage to the Southeast Asia region is because of the increase in electricity productions by Southeast Asian countries.[8]

Conversely, a growing electricity demand in Indonesia (SIM2) lowers the total CO_2 emissions from Southeast Asia under an electricity integrated market. This is because electricity market integration switches electricity supplies from CO_2-intensive Indonesia's electricity to other East Asian countries with less CO_2-intensive electricity sectors (Table 12.1).

A growth in electricity demand in Vietnam (SIM3) induces a lower total CO_2 emission from Southeast Asia under the East Asia electricity market integration (SIT2). This electricity growth induces a shift in electricity supply from Vietnam to East Asian countries whose electricity sector is less CO_2 intensive than Vietnam's. However, a growth in electricity demand in Vietnam under the Southeast Asia electricity market integration (SIT3) produces a higher total CO_2 emission from Southeast Asia. In Southeast Asia, many countries have more CO_2-intensive electricity sectors compared with Vietnam.

It can be concluded that the Southeast Asia electricity market integration would not reduce CO_2 emissions in Southeast Asia if the countries where electricity demands increase are having a cleaner electricity sector.

7 Conclusions

This chapter has aimed to analyze the inter-regional socioeconomic and environmental impacts of an integrated electricity market on Southeast Asian countries. An integrated electricity market has been considered an important measure to improve energy security in the region. However, the socioeconomic and environmental consequences have been less understood. To achieve this goal, this chapter utilizes an East Asia IRSAM. First, an inter-regional CFPM method is implemented at the East Asia IRSAM to simulate the macroeconomic impacts of an integrated electricity market integration in East Asia. Second, this chapter uses a household income microsimulation method to translate the macroeconomic impacts of an integrated electricity market into changes in incomes of various household groups (by income percentiles). These income changes allow us to observe the impact of an electricity market integration in East Asia on rates of poverty incidence in Southeast Asian countries. Third, a CO_2 emission model is developed to predict CO_2 emissions from Southeast Asian countries' production sectors.

This chapter analyzes the impact of an increase in electricity demand in a country in East Asia with and without an electricity market integration for the region (i.e., the East Asia electricity market integration) or only for Southeast Asia (i.e., the Southeast Asia electricity market integration) on socioeconomic and environmental conditions among Southeast Asian countries. Comparing simulation results with and without an electricity market integration shows the impacts of this integration on Southeast Asian countries.

Based on the analysis of this chapter, we draw the following conclusions. First, an electricity market integration, in general, does not obviously provide economic benefits, that is, positive economic leakages, for Southeast Asian countries. When there is an increase in electricity demand in a country outside Southeast Asia, all Southeast Asian countries, except Indonesia and Singapore, benefit from an electricity market integration in East Asia region. Their GDP under an electricity market integration would be higher than those under no electricity market integration. An increase in electricity demand in Indonesia and Vietnam (i.e., a country within Southeast Asia) reduces GDP growth in most Southeast Asian countries under an electricity market integration. In this case, only the Philippines might have a higher GDP under an electricity market integration.

Second, in most cases, an electricity market integration in East Asia, or in Southeast Asia only, produces higher rates of poverty incidence in most Southeast Asian countries than no electricity market integration does. The main reason for this is that electricity market integration restructures the economy of each country such that most factor incomes would be lower than those under no electricity market integration.

Third, in most cases, distributional household income impact of an electricity market integration in East Asia would most likely be progressive. Energy sectors, which are mostly affected by electricity market integration, are capital intensive and mostly owned by richer households.

Finally, electricity market integration in East Asia tends to increase CO_2 emissions from Southeast Asia, creating CO_2 emission leakage and relocation. Any increase in electricity demand from outside Southeast Asia increases electricity productions in Southeast Asia, inducing CO_2 emission leakage and relocation from outside Southeast Asia (mainly China) to Southeast Asia. Only when the increase in electricity demand comes from a Southeast Asian country with a high CO_2 intensity electricity sector, such as Indonesia, CO_2 emissions from Southeast Asia would be lower under an electricity market integration.

It is important to understand the drawbacks of the assumptions adopted in this chapter. First, it is assumed that prices are fixed and therefore do not change in any simulation. Electricity prices would most likely be lower under electricity market integration. The results in this chapter, hence, underestimate the impact of electricity market integration on the economy and CO_2 emission leakages and relocation.

Second, integrating the electricity market does not incur any technical or administrative costs to any country. Electricity market integration would most likely induce some technical or administrative costs. The results in this chapter, hence, could overestimate the impact of electricity market integration on the economy and CO_2 emission leakages and relocation. Finally, under electricity market integration, any increasing demand will be supplied by all country members of the integration, proportionate to their total electricity output. This situation may not be true.

This chapter certainly could enrich debates on whether an electricity market integration, besides improving energy security, would induce economic and environmental benefits in the region. However, further research overcoming the shortcomings in the chapter is warranted to provide more definite solutions to this issue.

Notes

1 See also: https://www.nordpoolgroup.com

2 The Association of Southeast Asian Nations (ASEAN) is a regional intergovernmental organization comprising ten countries in Southeast Asia, which promotes intergovernmental cooperation and facilitates economic, political, security, military, educational, and sociocultural integration among its members and other countries in Asia. Members of ASEAN are Singapore, Brunei, Malaysia, Thailand, the Philippines, Indonesia, Vietnam, Laos, Myanmar, and Cambodia.

3 China is chosen to represent a case in which the increase in electricity demand is in a country within East Asia but outside Southeast Asia. The impact on Southeast Asia of this case would most likely be similar than if the increase is in other East Asia outside Southeast Asia. The 10% is to represent a marginal change case.

4 Indonesia and Vietnam are the two countries in Southeast Asia where electricity demands have been fast increasing in the past three decades. Furthermore, their energy sector compositions are very different.

5 For SIM1, SIT3 will be the same as SIT1.

6 The inter-regional CFPM approach is relatively different from standard IRSAM multiplier. The explanation and derivation of standard IRSAM multiplier, for example, can be found in Resosudarmo et al. (2009).

7 The details of constructing East Asia IRSAM are available upon request to the author.

8 Even though China's electricity sector is more CO_2-intensive than those in other East Asian countries (Table 12.1), note that total emissions in East Asia are actually lower under East Asia electricity market integration (not presented in this chapter).

References

Barbosa, L.de S.N.S., Bogdanov, D., Vainikka, P. and Breyer, C. (2017). Hydro, wind and solar power as a base for a 100% renewable energy supply for South and Central America, *PLoS One* 12(3), 1–28, https://doi.org/10.1371/journal. pone.0173820.

Bourguignon, F. and Bussolo, M. (2013). Income distribution in computable general equilibrium modeling, in P.B. Dixon and D.W. Jorgenson (eds.), *Handbook of Computable General Equilibrium Modeling Vol. 1*, Oxford: Elsevier, 1383—1437.

Dahlke, S. (2020). Integrating electricity markets: Impacts of increasing trade on prices and emissions in the western United States, *International Journal of Sustainable Energy Planning and Management* 25, 45–60.

Delpiazzo, E. and Standardi, G. (2014). Introducing an explicit government institution in ICES model, Climate Impacts and Policy Division Research Papers Issue RP0243, Centro Euro-Medirerraneo sui Cambiamenti Climatici.

Denholm, P., King, J.C., Kutcher, C.F., and Wilson, P.P.H. (2012). Decarbonizing the electric sector: Combining renewable and nuclear energy using thermal storage, *Energy Policy* 44, 301–311.

ERIA, (2014). Investing in power grid interconnection in East Asia, ERIA Research Project Report 2013, No. 26, Economic Research Institute for ASEAN and East Asia.

Garnaut, R. (2019). *Super-Power: Australia's Low-Carbon Opportunit*y, Melbourne: La Trobe University Press.

Glachant, J.M. (2010). The achievement of the EU electricity internal market through market coupling, EUI Working Papers RSCAS 2010/87, Robert Schuman Centre for Advanced Studies, Florence School of Regulation.

Hartono, D. and Resosudarmo, B.P. (2008). The economy-wide impact of controlling energy consumption in Indonesia: An analysis using a Social Accounting Matrix framework, *Energy Policy* 36(4), 1404–1419.

Hussein, Z. and Aguiar, A.H. (2012). Macroeconomic data, in B. Narayanan G., A. Aquiar and R. McDougall (eds.), *Global Trade, Assistance, and Production: The GTAP 8 Data Base*, Indiana: Center for Global Trade Analysis, Purdue University, 47–58.

International Energy Agency. (2018). *World Energy Outlook 2018*, International Energy Agency, https://doi.org/10.1787/weo-2018-en.

Lilliestama, J., Barradi, T, Caldés, N., Gomez, M., Hanger, S., Kern, J., Komendantova, N., Mehos, M., Hong, W.M., Wang, Z., and Patt, A. (2018). Policies to keep and expand the option of concentrating solar power for dispatchable renewable electricity, *Energy Policy* 116, 193–197.

McDonald, S. and Sonmez, Y. (2004). Augmenting the GTAP Database with Data on Inter-Regional Transactions, Sheffield Economic Research Paper Series 2004009, Department of Economics, University of Sheffield.

McDonald, S., and Thierfelder, K. (2004). Deriving a global social accounting matrix from GTAP versions 5 and 6 data, GTAP Technical Paper No. 22, Purdue University.

Newbery, D., Strbac, G. and Viehoff, I. (2016). The benefits of integrating European electricity markets, *Energy Policy* 94, 253–263.

Nurdianto, D.A. and Resosudarmo, B.P. (2016). Economy-wide impact of a carbon tax in ASEAN, *Journal of Southeast Asian Economics* 33(1), 1–15.

Resosudarmo, B.P., Nurdianto, D.A. and Hartono, D. (2009). The Indonesian Inter-Regional Social Accounting Matrix for fiscal decentralisation analysis, *Journal of Indonesian Economy and Business* 24(2), 145–162.

Resosudarmo, B.P., Nurdianto, D.A. and Effendi, Y. (2021), Energy insecurity in the ASEAN region: The Implications of energy policy reform, *Singapore Economic Review* 68(2), 345–368, https://doi.org/10.1142/S0217590820430079.

Resosudarmo, B.P. and Thorbecke, E. (1996). The impact of environmental policies on household incomes for different socio-economic classes: The case of air pollutants in Indonesia, *Ecological Economics* 17(2), 83–94.

Resosudarmo, B.P. and Thorbecke, E. (1998). Reducing the number of pesticide related illnesses: The impact on household in Indonesia, *Bulletin of Indonesian Economic Studies* 34(2), 143–157.

Round, J.I. (1985). Decomposing multipliers for economic systems involving regional and world trade, *The Economic Journal* 95: 378, 383–399.

Shi, X. and Kimura, F. (2010). *Energy market integration in the East Asia summit region: Review of initiatives and estimation of benefits,* ERIA Research Project Report 2009, No. 13, Economic Research Institute for ASEAN and East Asia.

Wolfram, C., Shelef, O. and Gertler, P. (2012). How will energy demand develop in the developing world? *Journal of Economic Perspectives* 26(1), 119–138.

Wu, Y., Kimura, F. and Shi, X. (2013). Energy market integration in East Asia: Deepening understanding and moving forward, in Y. Wu, F. Kimura and X. Shi (eds.), *Energy Market Integration in East Asia: Deepening Understanding and Moving Forward*, Oxon: Routledge, 1–201.

Yusuf, A.A. and Resosudarmo, B.P. (2015). On the distributional impact of a carbon tax in developing countries: The case of Indonesia, *Environmental Economics and Policy Studies* 17(1), 131–156.

13 China's carbon-energy policy and Asia's energy transition from carbon leakage, relocation, and halo perspectives

Conclusions and the future

Akihisa Mori

1 Research questions of this book revisited

The Paris Agreement spurs system transformation toward carbon neutral and climate resilient development around the world. Green recovery from the COVID-19 pandemic coupled with digital transformation intensifies global competition over green technologies, infrastructure, systems, and platforms, prompting governments to renovate policies and institutions, and to redirect expenditure for developing infrastructure.

China emerges as a top runner in the global competition amid the COVID-19 pandemic. Strict city-wide lockdown, large-scale surveillance supported by digital monitoring systems, and preparation of made-in-China medical facilities, supplies, and vaccines to reduce the epidemic enable the country to accelerate digital transformation and to revitalize production of conventional goods and services. The 14th Five Year Plan (FYP, 2021–2025), the first FYP after the commitment to carbon neutrality by 2060 at the United Nations General Assembly, raises the ratio of non-fossil fuel sources in China's energy mix from 15% in the 13th FYP to around 20%. The plan also sets targets to build 1200 GW of wind and solar capacity by 2025—higher than that of coal power capacity in 2016 (Braun, 2021).

The ambitious targets and industrial fostering policies for wind and solar power have boosted Chinese manufacturers. They have capitalized on domestic and foreign markets to enjoy economies of scale, lowering leveraged cost and upgrading technologies. As a result, wind and solar power become competitive with coal power (IRENA, 2020). An increasing number of companies around the world import wind and solar power technologies from China to increase installed capacity, which is expected to generate carbon halos effect in the end.

However, a large-scale integration of renewable-energy-sourced electricity (RES-E) into the grid goes beyond a change in energy mix to demand a whole system change from fossil fuel-intensive, vertically integrated, and

DOI: 10.4324/9781003190905-17

hierarchical and centrally controlled electricity supply system toward a capital-intensive, distributed, and smart grid-based electricity system. As pointed out in Chapter 2, the system change poses three challenges: taming the incumbent influential regime actors; reconciling the compelling narratives of "energy for development," "energy for industrial development," and "energy for all"; and reducing uncertainty and unpredictability of the new system and the transition process.

In addition, an industrial transformation from a polluted "factory of the world" to a clean, green producer of homegrown high-tech and digitalized goods and services reduces domestic pollution-production, accelerates consolidation, and generates massive unemployment in pollution-intensive sectors such as coal and coal-intensive industries. A perception of an unpromising future can incentivize these industries to geographically diversify their investments in countries with loose regulations, increasing the probability of causing carbon relocation.

Against these conflicting perspectives, this book raises three research questions.

a How has China's carbon-energy policy incentivized outward FDI in coal power and renewable-energy-sourced electricity (RES-E) projects and exports of these technologies?
b How have Chinese outward FDI in and exports of coal power and RES-E generated energy transitions in host countries and caused carbon leakage, relocation, and halos?
c Can regional connectivity be a countermeasure to minimize carbon relocation and enhance the carbon halo effect in the context of China–Asia energy relations?

2 China's carbon-energy policy and firms' responses

A scenario input–output analysis in Chapter 3 finds that a large-scale integration of RES-E reduces CO_2 emissions without significantly affecting GDP and employment at the national level. However, coal power and its related industries such as mining, coal products, and transportation will have negative impacts on output and employment. Although larger job creation effects of the solar power industry can mitigate the negative impacts of an energy switch as opposed to wind power, it does not mean that employees working at coal power or mining will get jobs at solar power manufacturing. Improper regulation of transaction cost associated with the energy transition can be a driving force for incumbent coal power generation companies to geographically diversify their business portfolio into foreign countries, joining in foreign coal power projects. The Chinese government may push their outward FDI to mitigate the transaction costs of the transition, at the cost of an increase in CO_2 emissions in foreign countries.

A retrospective analysis of Chinese solar photovoltaic (PV) manufacturers in Chapter 4 shows that successful commercialization of the passivated emitter and rear cell (PERC), as well as investments in PV module manufacturing equipment, has enhanced technological capabilities and the competitive edge of emerging Chinese manufacturers, eliminating incumbent manufacturers from the domestic market. The enhanced competitive edge, coupled with the phase-out of feed-in tariff (FiT) for solar power in China, drives Chinese manufacturers toward exports, supplying trade partners more efficient solar PV at a lower price.

Despite the stronger competitive edge, Chinese power companies, manufacturers, and developers have made much less investments in foreign RES-E projects than coal power, as shown in Chapter 5. Although this result can be biased against RES-E projects, most of which are small-scale and out of coverage of the database on which the analysis is based, the chapter finds that Chinese power project developers have proactively responded to the stringent regulations and the Belt and Road Initiative (BRI) to increase investments and contracts in foreign power projects.

Given the continuous increase in installed coal power generation capacity in China, this result implies that China's carbon-energy policy and BRI have incentivized Chinese power generators, manufacturers, and developers to make outward FDI in power projects, but have not relocated their plants to foreign countries.

3 Impacts on energy transitions, carbon relocation, and halos in Asia in action

A computable general equilibrium (CGE) model analysis in Chapter 6 shows that China's outward FDI in coal power projects is likely to increase global CO_2 emissions, but the extent varies by energy mix in power generation and non-electricity sectors. China's outward FDI in power projects in coal-rich countries, especially those rich in low-quality coal such as India and to a lesser extent Indonesia, will increase CO_2 and sulfur dioxide (SO_2) emissions in host countries that significantly outweighs a decrease in emissions in China. Furthermore, a declining demand for coal in China's electricity sector may reduce the global coal price, which may stimulate coal consumption in non-electricity sectors in both China and coal-dependent countries. In contrast, FDI in coal-poor countries or those using high-quality coal may not increase emissions so much as to outweigh a decrease in China.

Matching econometrics in Chapter 7 elucidates that renewable energy policies, such as renewable portfolio standard and a FiT, significantly increase imports of wind and solar power components from Asia—dominated by China to satisfy the renewable energy target in host countries. However, host countries experienced difficulties in increasing imports when Chinese manufacturers directed production capacity to fill out domestic demand stimulated by the same policies in Asian countries, typically in China. Coupled with the recent investments in production capacity for PERC PV by Chinese manufacturers, renewable energy policies are more likely to increase imports of PERC PV.

The impacts on energy transitions and carbon relocation and halos effects are more or less similar in India, Indonesia, and Vietnam. As shown in Chapter 5, they were largest host countries of China's outward FDI in coal power projects when the Chinese government began stringent carbon-energy-environmental policies and the BRI. To invite Chinese investors, financiers, and developers, they have changed the elements of complementarities along the value chain of the electricity supply system. They reallocated domestic coal to new coal power plants that were built by Chinese investments, financial supports, or under the engineering, procurement, and construction contracts with Chinese companies. The Indonesian government was forced to provide full guarantee to the credit risk of the state-owned utility to ensure loan repayment to Chinese financial institutions (Mori, 2020). The consensus of interest between China and host countries resulted in the large Chinese investments in and developments of coal power plants, enhancing generation capacity and enabling electricity supply to wider areas at an affordable cost, but at the cost of increase in air pollution and CO_2 emissions. In other words, China's carbon-energy policy and BRI caused carbon relocation effect by stimulating outward FDI in coal power projects in an unintentional and indirect manner.

China's presence as a technology supplier remains unchanged or even larger in the transition toward an RES-E-based electricity system. Chinese manufacturers compete to supply a range of solar PV modules from low- to high-end consistent with the needs of host countries, whereas manufacturers in these host countries tend to have insufficient capability to supply components and insufficient product branding or quality, trust, or loyalty. However, the Chinese government restricts exports of solar PV *cells*, not to mention foreign investments in manufacturing plants, to prevent manufacturers in host countries from enhancing technological capabilities through reverse engineering (Chapter 8). A number of domestic and international developers and independent power producers (IPPs) invest in solar power projects under a FiT or join reverse auctions to win concessions of solar power projects, bringing in imported solar PV modules from China. As a result, the most of the host countries have not succeeded in developing domestic solar PV manufacturers and national technological capabilities for developing solar PV. In other words, they have not gained carbon halos effects through Chinese exports of solar PV.

Coupled with the excess installed capacity of coal power in the Java-Bali Grid and the lock-in into a coal-based electricity supply system, the lack of carbon halos effects prompts the Indonesian government to narrow the scope of favorable RES-E policies for electrification in off-grid areas. In India, coupled with divergences in political, economic, and strategic interests, it triggers repercussions from overdependence on Chinese manufacturers, leading to an anti-dumping duty on solar cell (Chapter 9).

Japan also goes through the negative feedback effect without having the carbon halo effects. Chinese solar PV manufacturers emerged as competitors to Japan's once-world-leading manufacturers. The Japanese government has placed energy security as the top priority in energy policy, strengthening lock-in and coalition of nuclear power in the narrative of optimal energy mix (Mori, 2019). Japanese solar PV manufacturers and solar power developers are required to contest the nuclear power-based, vertically integrated electricity supply system to scale them up and gain economies of scale to compete with Chinese ones. The coalition is so powerful that Japanese solar PV manufacturers and solar power developers fail to do so, resulting in large market deployment by Chinese solar PVs. Chapter 10 finds that Japanese manufacturers' loss of a competitive edge redirects the principle of Japanese energy policy toward technology self-sufficiency through research and development (R&D) of advanced RES-E technologies, and diversification of energy sources to ensure energy security, rather than anti-dumping measures.

The carbon relocation and a lack of carbon halo effect in the electricity sector do not imply that China is generating carbon leakage. Chapter 11 shows that China *reduced* exports of CO_2 emissions to Japan during 2005–2015, implying *shrinking* carbon leakage *from* Japan. This reduction accrues to the decrease in carbon intensity in electricity, chemical, and transport equipment sectors, as well as the shift of exports toward less carbon-intensive sectors. In contrast, the country increased exports to Indonesia and Vietnam in the same period, implying increasing carbon leakage *from* them. This comes from the rise in carbon intensity in electricity generation in both countries that rapidly shifted toward coal-based power generation, as well as increase in the trade volume. These findings suggest that China may increase CO_2 emissions globally by increasing imports of carbon-intensive goods from countries with higher carbon intensity even if the country reduces the emissions domestically.

To summarize the results, China's outward FDI in coal power projects has pushed transitions to and strengthened lock-in into a coal-based electricity system, thus increasing CO_2 emissions. In contrast, China's outward FDI and exports of solar PV technologies have generated carbon halo effect marginally at best, and discouraged host country governments from implementing favorable RES-E policies in the extreme. These outward FDI and exports might have caused partial carbon leakage in the electricity sector, because Chinese power companies continue to operate most of the efficient coal power plants within China. Nonetheless, they can add on global increase in CO_2 emissions because they have increased coal power and carbon intensity in industries in host countries and China's shift to less carbon-intensive industries increases imports of carbon-intensive goods from these host countries.

4 Regional market integration as a countermeasure?

The integrated assessment of regional electricity market integration in Chapter 12 shows that it is regionally efficient location of electricity generation rather than optimization of the energy mix through the reduction of new power plants that will generate newly installed capacity for fossil fuel power and reduce CO_2 emission in the region by regional market integration. Countries with low levelized cost of electricity (LCOE) in coal power—due to easier access to cheap coal, coal power technology, or lax environmental regulations—are more likely to increase coal power generation and CO_2 emissions, whereas those with low LCOE in RES-E, typically China, will reduce coal power generation and CO_2 emissions.

This finding implies that regional electricity market integration and connectivity is more likely to cause carbon relocation effect than carbon halo effect unless host countries develop domestic high-tech RES-E technologies and capitalize on the integrated regional market to enjoy the economies of scale for RES-E technologies. This implication is in line with Khosla et al. (2020), who argued the essential role of public sector enterprises (PSEs) in leveraging economies of scale, reinforcing complementarities between global value chains and related domestic technology policy choices, and strengthening domestic academia-industry R&D linkages as an integral part of the energy policy mix.

However, findings from the analysis of Chinese solar PV manufacturers in Chapter 4 suggest that the chances may become less and less likely. Chinese manufacturers have already commercialized the PERC and enhanced competitive edge against solar PV manufacturers around the world, and against coal power. As pointed out in Chapter 5, they have invested in few solar PV manufacturing plants in foreign countries, and thus spillover effect can hardly be expected.

To summarize, regional market integration and connectivity cannot be expected as a panacea.

5 The future

This paper has two main contributions to the arguments over international trade, FDI, and the environment. First, it expands the concept of pollution haven and halos and carbon leakage to define carbon relocation and halos that explain impacts of both outward FDI in power projects and international trade of RES-E technologies on CO_2 emissions in host countries.

Second, it adds empirical novelty to the underlying mechanisms that generate carbon relocation and halos, the extent carbon relocation and halos in the electricity sector can contribute to carbon leakage in a country, and effectiveness of regional electricity market integration and connectivity as countermeasures to carbon relocation.

Novelty invites the next research agenda. We point out three of them as future research directions.

First is to explore the effectiveness of emerging innovative green finance instruments. The global divestment movement gives additional driving force by pressuring multilateral development banks, public export credit agencies, financial institutions, institutional investors, and businesses in OECD member countries to move out of fossil fuel industries, including coal power plants. Local protests against coal power become fierce around the world. In response, some developing countries such as Vietnam, Bangladesh, and Kenya give up advancing China-backed coal power projects under preparation.

The movement itself does not provide any alternatives that can reconcile the divestment with other objectives of energy policy such as energy security and energy justice. As illustrated in Figures 2.1 and 2.2, the transition from fossil fuel-intensive toward a capital-intensive RES-E-based electricity system is accompanied by changes in the elements of complementarities in the electricity system, which requires investments in and rearrangements of the elements of technologies, organizations, institutions, and infrastructure. Traditional formal financial institutions are generally less willing to make loans for these new capital-intensive power generation plants (Haskel and Westlake, 2018).

Green finance such as green bonds, green banks, and community-based green funds can potentially overcome financial bottlenecks (Sachs et al., 2019). Pension funds are providing financial capital for these new innovative financial instruments (Rifkin, 2019). Environmental, social, and governance (ESG) investments have gained momentum. If green finance provides financial capital that enables host countries to reconcile divestment and other energy purposes, they will be attracted to use it to change the elements of complementarities toward RES-E-based electricity system instead of relying on Chinese outward FDI and development finance.

Second is to investigate tipping points and decisive factors that affect incumbent influential firms' responses. Firms are not homogeneous. They have different perceptions on damages caused by policy and institutional changes, and are diverse in knowledge, prior experience, assets positions, and organizational culture on sustainable practices (Teece et al., 1997; Hartmann et al., 2020). As responses to policy and institutional changes prompt them to take heterogeneous responses, resulting in changes to their competitive edge and market share, they perceive conflicts of interest among them and they may become reluctant to take collective actions or lobbying to the government. Such dynamics will generate policy feedback effects, co-evolving policy and institutions, and firms' strategies (Mori, 2021). Given that complete or partial relocation of industrial plants, industry, *and* production processes can be categorized as a geographical diversification strategy, carbon leakage, relocation, and halo effects should be investigated in the context of sustainability transitions in China.

Third is to explore how to connect Chinese outward FDI with local as well as global value chain. Chinese outward development finance and FDI are often criticized for allocating infrastructure projects that would bring political gain and satisfy leaders' selfish interests rather than local benefits (Dreher et al., 2014), and creating an unfavorable degree of dependency on China in terms of value chain as well as finance (Collier, 2018). They are also criticized for demanding fair treatment to host countries despite unfair treatment to foreign companies in the domestic market including forced joint companies with Chinese counterparts; insufficient protection of intellectual property rights; preferential treatment of state enterprises; and subsides from central and local governments (Chapter 8). These criticisms suggest China's outward FDI and exports narrow spaces for industries and business in host countries to gain economic benefits in the transitions to RES-E-based system.

Even if domestic manufacturers can hardly compete with Chinese ones and have to reply on Chinese solar PV cells and modules, distributed renewable energy access systems—stand-alone, off-grid renewable-based systems that can generate and distribute energy independently of a centralized electricity grid—still have a potential for job creation in many countries (REN21, 2020). Local community power enterprises may support the local economy by involving local companies in installation, racking and mounting, cabling, and wiring. However, it has to be balanced with LCOE (IRENA, 2020).

Given that a large-scale integration of RES-E into the grid requires the transformation to a capital-intensive, distributed, and smart grid-based electricity system, grid companies with smart grid will be platformers in the electricity system and generate the highest value added in the whole value chain. In reference to ongoing platform business, grid governance will be a decisive role in just transitions to the RES-E-based system, and RES-E technologies will fall into a low value-added segment. In fact, Chinese state grid companies acquire grid companies in the Philippines (Lema, 2007), Brazil (China Daily, 2017), Portugal, Italy, Greece (Xinhua, 2017), and Laos (RFA's Lao Service, 2021). It is a promising but challenging research agenda to be tackled in the future.

References

Braun, S. 2021. Is China's five year plan a decarbonization blueprint? *DW* (5 March 2021), https://p.dw.com/p/3pfo9/, [accessed 21 March 2021].

China Daily, 2017. State Grid to buy remaining stake in Brazil's CPFL, (1 September 2017), https://www.chinadaily.com.cn/business/2017-09/01/content_31409824.htm/, [accessed 2 August 2020].

Collier, A. 2018. *China Buys the World: Analyzing China's Overseas Investments*, Palgrave MacMillan: Singapore.

Dreher, A., A. Fuchs, R. Hodler, B. Parks, P.A., Raschky, M.J. Tierney, 2014. Aid on demand: African leaders and the geography of China's foreign assistance. AidData Working Paper No. 3, AidData, https://ncgg.princeton.edu/new_ipes/2014/papers/F915_rm1.pdf/, [accessed on 18 October 2019].

Hartmann, J., A.C. Inkpen, K. Ramaswamy, 2020. Different shades of green: Global oil and gas companies and renewable energy, *J Int. Bus. Stud.*, https://doi.org/10.1057/s41267-020-00326-w.

Haskel, J., S. Westlake, 2018. *Capitalism without Capital: The Rise of the Intangible Economy*, Princeton University Press, Princeton.

IRENA, 2020. *Renewable Power Generation Costs in 2019*, International Renewable Energy Agency, Abu Dhabi, https://www.irena.org/-/media/Files/IRENA/Agency/Publication/2020/Jun/IRENA_Power_Generation_Costs_2019.pdf/, [accessed 14 January 2021].

Khosla, R., A.S. Kamat, V. Narayanamurti, 2020. Successful transitions clean energy technology in emerging economies: Learning from India, China, and Brazil, *Progress in Energy* 2, 043002, https://doi.org/10.1088/2516-1083/abb52b.

Lema, K., 2007. China State Grid group wins Philippine power auction, *Reuters* (12 December 2007), https://uk.reuters.com/article/philippines-privatisation/update-4-china-state-grid-group-wins-philippine-power-auction-idUKMAN22547220071212/, [accessed 2 August 2020].

Mori, A., 2019. Temporal dynamics of infrasystem transition: The case of electricity system transition in Japan, *Technol. Forecast. Soc. Change* 145, 186–194, https://doi.org/10.1016/j.techfore.2017.05.00.

Mori, A., 2020. Foreign actors, faster transitions? Co-evolution of complementarities, perspectives and sociotechnical systems in the case of Indonesia's electricity supply system, *Energy Res. Soc. Sci.* 69, 101594, https://doi.org/10.1016/j.erss.2020.101594.

Mori, A., 2021. How do incumbent companies' heterogeneous responses affect sustainability transitions? Insights from China's major incumbent power generators, *Environ. Innov. Soc. Tr.* 39, 55–72, https://doi.org/10.1016/j.eist.2021.02.003.

REN21, 2020. *Renewables 2020: Global Status Report*, https://www.ren21.net/wp-content/uploads/2019/05/gsr_2020_full_report_en.pdf/ [accessed 24 March 2021].

RFA's Lao Service, 2021. Laos Grants 25-Year Concession to Chinese Company to Manage Power Grid: Critics worry about increasing Chinese control over Laos' infrastructure, (16 March 2021), https://www.rfa.org/english/news/laos/grid-03162021152622.html/, [accessed 19 March 2021].

Rifkin, J. 2019. *The Green New Deal: Why the Fossil Fuel Civilization Will Collapse by 2028, and the Bold Economic Plan to Save Life on Earth*, St. Martins Press, London.

Sachs, J.D., W.T. Woo, N. Yoshino, F. Taghizadeh-Hesary, 2019. Importance of green finance for achieving sustainable development goals and energy security, In: Sachs, J.D. et al. (eds.), *Handbook of Green Finance: Energy Security and Sustainable Development*, Springer Reference, 3–12, https://doi.org/10.1007/978-981-13-0227-5_13.

Teece, D, G. Pisano, A. Shuen, 1997. Dynamic capabilities and strategic management, *Strateg. Manag. J.* 18, 509–533, https://www.jstor.org/stable/3088148.

Xinhua, 2017. China's State Grid completes purchase of Greek power grid operator stake, *China Daily* (21 June 2017), https://www.chinadaily.com.cn/business/2017-06/21/content_29833439.htm/, [accessed 2 August 2020].

Index

Note: Bold page numbers refer to tables; *italic* page numbers refer to figures and page numbers followed by "n" denote endnotes.

For Product Safety Concerns and Information please contact our EU representative GPSR@taylorandfrancis.com
Taylor & Francis Verlag GmbH, Kaufingerstraße 24, 80331 München, Germany

www.ingramcontent.com/pod-product-compliance
Lightning Source LLC
LaVergne TN
LVHW021120300926
849160LV00010B/788

* 9 7 8 1 0 3 2 0 4 1 8 9 6 *